D1234266

WILD LIFE

Irus Braverman

WILD LIFE

THE INSTITUTION OF NATURE

STANFORD UNIVERSITY PRESS

STANFORD, CALIFORNIA

Stanford University Press
Stanford, California

©2015 by the Board of Trustees of the Leland Stanford Junior University.
All rights reserved.

Portions of this book are informed by previously published articles and
chapters: "Conservation without Nature: The Trouble with *In Situ* versus
Ex Situ Conservation," *Geoforum* 51 (2014): 47–57; "Governing the Wild:
Databases, Algorithms, and Population Models as Biopolitics," *Surveillance
& Society* 12, no. 1 (2014): 15–37, and "Captive for Life: Conserving Extinct
Species through *Ex Situ* Breeding," in *The Ethics of Captivity*, ed. Lori Gruen,
193–212 (Oxford University Press, 2014).

No part of this book may be reproduced or transmitted in any form or by any
means, electronic or mechanical, including photocopying and recording, or in
any information storage or retrieval system without the prior written permission of Stanford University Press.

Printed in the United States of America on acid-free, archival-quality paper

Library of Congress Cataloging-in-Publication Data

Braverman, Irus, 1970- author.
  Wild life : the institution of nature / Irus Braverman.
     pages cm
  Includes bibliographical references and index.
  ISBN 978-0-8047-9322-3 (cloth : alk. paper)
  ISBN 978-0-8047-9568-5 (pbk : alk. paper)
  1. Wildlife conservation. 2. Endangered species. 3. Captive wild animals.
  4. Naturalness (Environmental sciences) I. Title.
  QL82.B75 2015
  333.95'416--dc23

                              2014035422

ISBN 978-0-8047-9476-3 (electronic)

Typeset in 10/14 Janson

For Tamar

Contents

Acknowledgments

This was supposed to be a short article. It started as my previous book, *Zooland*, which documents the shift of zoos from entertainment into conservation institutions, was winding down. On a miserable winter Saturday, when it felt as though one would never see the sun again, I arrived at the Buffalo Zoo, wet and cold, to attend a conference, "The Future of Zoos." There, I witnessed a debate between animal rights activists and zoo professionals regarding the ethics of keeping elephants in captivity. "The only ethical place for elephants is in the wild," said one speaker. "There is no such thing as wild," responded a zoo expert. "Everything is managed." I decided to follow up on this debate with just a few short interviews. Once I started, however, it was difficult to stop. More than 120 interviews later, this project still continues to expand in multiple directions.

Wild Life is about divides, and about how a seemingly marginal scientific divide between two technical terms, *in situ* and *ex situ*, has come to represent deeply held beliefs by conservationists about the definition of wilderness and about the nature of captivity. It was not easy to bridge this divide, even as a researcher. Because so many of my previous book's contacts were based in the zoo world, it was hard to gain access to the world of wildlife managers and field conservationists, who typically inhabit a very different professional sphere, as I will discuss in this book. Fortunately, some sympathetic zoo experts who had already experienced the difficulty of crossing this divide in their own work provided invaluable advice. Their willingness to share their personal connections and their professional knowledge with me was instrumental to this project. For example, one former zoo administrator generously offered to put me in touch with the director of the U.S. Fish and Wildlife Service. With the director's blessing, it became significantly easier to gain access to many field biologists throughout the United States.

I have many people to thank. I am especially indebted to those interviewees who saw the importance of what I was doing and went out of their way to assist me, despite not always agreeing with me about the details. These include Dan Ashe, Onnie Byers, Miguel Canals, Bill Conway, Jim Dietz, Bob Johnson, Katherine Meyer, Mike Oetker, Stuart Pimm, Jeff Powell, David Rabon, Terri Roth, Alex Travis, Will Waddell, Tom White, and Dave Wildt. I am especially indebted to Kierán Suckling for devoting long hours to explaining the stakes of this subject to me, and to Bob Lacy for patiently walking me through the complex algorithmic world of population management. Special thanks also to Phil Miller for adding such delightful humor to it all. Each and every one of the conservationists interviewed for this project has taught me a great deal about the power of hope and how it can bring about change, against all odds—as well as how to keep on going when it doesn't.

The book has also greatly benefited from the insights of many colleagues. I am particularly grateful to David Delaney, Carrie Friese, Jim Igoe, Jamie Lorimer, Jack Schlegel, and Mick Smith for their detailed comments on the entire manuscript and to Wendy Brown, Lori Gruen, Kevin Hilgarten, Errol Meidinger, Harvey Neo, Jessica Owley, Peter Steeves, and Mariana Valverde, as well as my co-fellows at Cornell's Society for the Humanities, for their reading of particular chapters at different stages. I would also like to deeply thank my research assistants Eleanor Gold and Adam Dunstan for their extraordinary work of transcribing, researching, editing, and indexing and, most importantly, for never tiring of debating the issues that kept flaring up. Michelle Lipinski from Stanford University Press provided much-appreciated editorial assistance. Research for this project was funded by the American Council of Learned Societies' Charles A. Ryskamp Research Fellowship and by the Baldy Center for Law & Social Policy.

Finally, I would like to express my heartfelt gratitude to my family, who supported me through the myriad trials of this project and who accompanied me to many of its remote sites—both *in situ* and *ex situ*—releasing hellbenders into streams, feeding sick Puerto Rican parrots, and driving long distances to rainforests, deserts, and cities while tolerating my constant ranting about the meaning of it all. My life partner, Gregor Harvey, has invested his heart and mind in this project, providing me with emotional and editorial support as well as with a healthy dose of pragmatism. My now seven-year-old daughter, Ariel, was also an enthusiastic supporter. She was especially fond of the "snot otter," her favorite name for the eastern hellbenders, the huge salamanders whom she helped carefully place under selected boulders in Allegheny streams as part of their reintroduction.

Wild Life is dedicated to Tamar, our now four-year-old daughter and sister. Tamar has accompanied me on many adventures over the course of my fieldwork, and has shown herself to be a true princess—especially that one time when she received a wet kiss on her nose from a leaping coquí. Although she does not quite understand why it has taken me so long to write this book ("Are you done yet? And how about now?"), she has endured my many absences bravely. Tamar: may you linger in your magical kingdom, in which humans and nonhumans, living and nonliving entities play together across and beyond the divides.

Abbreviations

AMLD	Assoçiacão Mico-Leão-Dourado (Golden Lion Tamarin Association)
ARKS	Animal Records Keeping System
AZA	Association of Zoos and Aquariums
BIAZA	British and Irish Association of Zoos and Aquariums
C2S2	Conservation Centers for Species Survival
CBSG	Conservation Breeding Specialist Group
CBW	Captive-Bred Wildlife
CITES	Convention on International Trade in Endangered Species of Wild Fauna and Flora
COSEWIC	Committee on the Status of Endangered Wildlife in Canada
DEC	Department of Environmental Conservation (New York State)
DFTD	Devil Facial Tumor Disease
DPS	Distinct Population Segment
EAZA	European Association of Zoos and Aquaria
ESA	Endangered Species Act
ESU	Evolutionary Significant Unit
GRB	Genome Resource Bank
IMP	Intensively Managed Population
ISIS	International Species Information System
IUCN	International Union for Conservation of Nature
MedARKS	Medical Animal Records Keeping System

MEE   Managed Environmental Enclosures

MMPA   Marine Mammal Protection Act

NMFS   National Marine Fisheries Service

PHVA   Population and Habitat Viability Assessment

PIT   Passive Integrated Transponder

PVA   Population Viability Assessment

RFID   Radio Frequency Identification

SARA   Species at Risk Act

SPARKS   Single Population Analysis and Records Keeping System

SSC   Species Survival Commission

SSP   Species Survival Plan

TAG   Taxon Advisory Group

USFWS   United States Fish and Wildlife Service

WAZA   World Association of Zoos and Aquariums

WCS   Wildlife Conservation Society

WWF   World Wildlife Fund

ZAA   Zoo and Aquarium Association

ZIMS   Zoological Information Management System

WILD LIFE

Natural Life

[We must] abandon the dualism that sees the tree in the garden as artificial—
completely fallen and unnatural—and the tree in the wilderness as natural—
completely pristine and wild. Both trees in some ultimate sense are wild; both in
a practical sense now depend on our management and care. We are responsible for
both, even though we can claim credit for neither.
—William Cronon, "The Trouble with Wilderness"[1]

Did you know about the plight of the Polynesian tree snails? Until recently,
these tiny arboreal land snails slid plentifully across the Pacific Rim. Much
of what is known about this genus—referred to by scientists as *Partula*
snails—is the result of five decades of work by evolutionary biologist Henry
Crampton in the early twentieth century.[2] Over the last few decades, a tragic
chain of events has caused the snails' decline. The tragedy began with an
accident: humans inadvertently introduced the giant African land snail (*Lissachatina fulica*) to the Society Islands of French Polynesia, inflicting severe
agricultural damage on the landscape. In 1977, the carnivorous rosy wolf
snails (*Euglandina rosea*) were intentionally introduced from Florida into the
islands as a form of biocontrol over the African snail. But the wolf snails
had a slightly different menu in mind: they preferred to prey on the islands'
endemic *Partula* snails.

By the mid-1990s, fifty-six of the seventy-two *Partula* species in French
Polynesia were extinct, and the rest were on the brink of extinction.[3] In the
late 1980s, several species were taken into captivity. These snails survive

in controlled containers of various sizes in a few small rooms tucked away in the back of zoos—such as the room depicted in Figure 1 at the London Zoo.[4] The International Partula Conservation Programme facilitates the captive breeding of fifteen *Partula* species and two additional subspecies in sixteen collaborating zoos worldwide.[5]

A tiny room in a tucked-away corner of a zoo—this is not exactly what most of us imagine when we think about nature conservation. More likely, we imagine snowcapped mountains, vast forests with chirping birds, or hot deserts with cacti and snakes. Most of us also do not imagine a twenty-square-meter fenced-in *Partula* reserve in French Polynesia—likely the smallest in the world, smaller even than the *Partula* room at the zoo[6]—as part of wild nature. This reserve was actively cleared of predators so that the zoo-bred snails could be reintroduced into their historic range.[7]

Is the recovery of the *Partula* snails through captive breeding and re-introduction into fenced areas an attempt at conservation, or something

Figure 1: *Partula* snails are kept alive in aquariums inside a small room at the London Zoo. According to the IUCN Red List of Threatened Species, many of these snails are Extinct in the Wild. Photo by author, March 14, 2013.

altogether different? Whereas some argue that today's skyrocketing extinction rates call for a more intense conservation of species in captivity (also known as *ex situ*), proponents of exclusive on-site conservation (also known as *in situ*) question the validity of saving species away from their "natural" habitat. In the words of an assistant director of the United States Fish and Wildlife Service (USFWS): "There are people who think that *ex situ* should not happen [and] there are people who believe that *in situ* is wasted cost."[8]

Wild Life explores the impact of the *in situ–ex situ* divide on contemporary conservation practices and the recent attempts to bridge and even collapse it. I also examine the emerging understanding that all forms of wild nature—both *in situ* and *ex situ*—may need to be managed in perpetuity. What challenges does such an understanding pose to our definitions of nature and to the role of management in conservation? To better grasp the complexities of these issues, I conducted in-depth interviews with more than 120 prominent conservationists from across the globe.

In Situ–Ex Situ

Conservation scholars have suggested that "anyone who has taken a course in conservation biology, or even read a book on the subject, knows that there are fundamentally two kinds of conservation: *in situ* and *ex situ*,"[9] which are the Latin terms for "in place" and "out of place." Although understudied by academics and mostly unheard of by the general public, the *in situ–ex situ* dichotomy has shaped—and still continues to shape—the development of nature conservation and its institutional alliances over the past few decades. Lurking beneath the surface of the *in situ* and *ex situ* dichotomy are its older and seemingly less scientific cousins: wilderness versus captivity and nature versus culture.

The *in situ–ex situ* divide is a divide between the professional and scientific disciplines of zoo and lab experts, on the one hand, and field biologists and wildlife managers, on the other hand. It is also a physical divide, both between captive and wild animal bodies and between captive and wild geographies. The two conservation regimes are further separated by different funding sources, distinct biological goals, databases that do not talk to each other, and discrete population models.

Because the *in situ–ex situ* divide has become embedded in separate academic disciplines, professional networks, administrative systems, funding mechanisms, and spatial configurations, challenging it is not an easy task. Despite this, integrative models that attempt to link *in situ* and *ex situ* management are becoming increasingly popular, especially in the emerging science of small population management. The recent One Plan approach is one example of this integration: its goal is to bring to one table, physically and by representation, all the relevant human and nonhuman parties—both *in situ* and *ex situ*—for an effective management of the imperiled species. Such an integrated administration of wild life is carried out through detailed micro-management, minute calculations of viability, and scrupulous devotion to endangered life. The stories I tell in this book about the dramatic efforts to save species on the brink of extinction illuminate the complexities of these practices, the questions that they raise about the relationship between conservation and nature, and the high stakes involved in the preservation of life—human and nonhuman—on this planet.

In addition to these remarkable narratives of species conservation, *Wild Life* explores the codependency between, and the co-production[10] of, *in situ* and *ex situ* conservation. Without a wild, free, and pristine nature, conservation in captivity is meaningless; and without the notion of captivity, wilderness as the very opposite of captivity cannot exist. However, neither the idea of Nature with a capital "N" nor that of captivity as its other can account for the multiple and dynamic natures that in fact proliferate in a variety of sites around the world.

In Situ *and* Ex Situ: *A Few Stories, Many Questions*

The Puerto Rican crested toad (*Peltophryne lemur*) is listed as Critically Endangered by the International Union for Conservation of Nature (IUCN)—a global environmental network that includes more than 1,000 government and nonprofit member organizations, as well as 11,000 volunteer scientists, in 160 countries. Until very recently, the toads' only known breeding site was a parking lot in Guánica that floods during the hurricane season. In a controversial decision, some of the toads were transferred to North American zoos for captive breeding. Simultaneously, a multi-agency effort resulted in the construction of secondary breeding ponds to provide a much-needed habitat for reintroducing the toads into Puerto Rico. Between 1983 and 2014, 290,000 tadpoles from zoos across North America made the journey over the ocean into Puerto Rico and were then carefully transported by jeep to their breeding ponds.[11] Although the ponds are human-constructed, when the toads disperse from them they resume their role in the ecological community and voluntarily return to the ponds to breed.[12]

Are these actions elements of *in situ* (on-site) conservation, or are they part of *ex situ* (off-site) conservation? What are the boundaries between the managed, the artificial, and the constructed, on the one hand, and the wild, original, and untouched by humans, on the other hand? And what if a species' "natural" place of origin has changed so much—through global warming, for instance—that her most viable habitat is now situated far from that "original" nature? What is the meaning of *in situ* conservation when the existence of a natural ecosystem, in its historical sense at least, is increasingly unrealistic, and can be obtained only through intensive human management? How do we conceive of a nature that is highly dependent on human manipulation?

Consider next the Rio Grande silvery minnow (*Hybognathus amarus*), once common and now one of the most endangered fish in North America. The minnow's sole remaining habitat dries out every year due to drought and irrigation. "Every year, from April through June, our staff is out in the 150-mile stretch [of the Middle Rio Grande] . . . chasing larger volumes of water than normal down the river because we know those spikes will trigger the fish to spawn," explains Kimberly Ward, an aquarist at Albuquerque's BioPark. "We use a device called the Moore egg collector to catch the eggs on a screen . . . and to carefully remove them using a spoon," she tells me.[13] In the spring of 2013, 64,000 eggs were scooped with spoons and thus saved (Figure 2).[14] The eggs were then transferred to hatcheries for propagation and, once the dry season ended, the newly hatched fish were released back into the river. Ward tells me that in addition to the scooping efforts, "in the late summer and fall—after the fish have spawned in the river and egg collection efforts have finished [and] when the river dries in certain places—[the] USFWS staff goes out to salvage any Rio Grande silvery minnows detected in drying pools and transports them in live wells using SUVs to non-drying areas of the river."[15] In 2013, 83 percent of all extant Rio Grande silvery minnows were reintroduced from hatcheries.[16] "Now we're supplementing the wild population, as opposed to the wild population supplementing the hatchery," a prominent USFWS fish expert tells me.[17]

Figure 2: Officials from the USFWS, ABQ BioPark, Santa Ana Pueblo, and SWCA Environmental Consultants scoop up Rio Grande silvery minnow eggs into Moore egg collectors, May 2013. Courtesy of Kimberly Ward, ABQ BioPark.

The Pahrump poolfish (*Empetrichthys latos*) provides yet another example of the co-production and codependency of *in situ* and *ex situ* conservation and their codependency. In 1967, this fish was listed as endangered under the U.S. Endangered Species Act (ESA). Depletion of groundwater by commercial agriculture had limited the poolfish's range to a single spring in Pahrump Valley, near Las Vegas. Instead of saving all the fish in one basket, in the early 1970s the USFWS decided to transfer the remaining poolfish into two sites: a set of artificial ponds in eastern Nevada and a game refuge in Las Vegas, where the fish were eventually housed in an aquarium. The spring dried out in 1975, but the Pahrump poolfish survives and is self-sustaining in both the aquarium and the artificial ponds.

Although the Rio Grande silvery minnow still exist *in situ*, their existence is highly dependent on conservation efforts (namely, on biologists routinely chasing after them with spoons and transporting them in SUVs). The Pahrump poolfish, on the other hand, exist *ex situ*—in an aquarium located outside their historic range—but are self-sustaining: no spoons or SUVs required.[18] Should these differences matter? How can they be evaluated and compared? And, more practically perhaps, how should these two populations be counted when assessing the threat status of their species?

Will either count when discussing whether the species is "conserved" for recovery plans? And do the painstaking efforts to keep these species alive against all odds make sense?

Partula snails, Puerto Rican crested toads, silvery minnows, and Pahrump poolfish—all are considered successful integrations of *in situ* and *ex situ* conservation. But such collaborative efforts are not always—or even usually—this successful. One ill-fated example is the case of the greenback cutthroat trout (*Oncorhynchus clarki stomias*). This fish was listed as endangered by the USFWS in 1967. A decade of hatchery breeding and reintroductions brought the species back to the brink of recovery, or so it was believed. As a result, in 1978 the fish's risk status was downgraded to threatened.

However, a DNA study conducted in 2012 revealed that many of the populations previously identified as greenback cutthroat were actually the similar Colorado River and Rio Grande cutthroat species who,[19] as "non-native" competitors for habitat and food sources, in fact threaten the target species. Currently, the only remaining population of "pure" greenback cutthroat trout lives in a small tributary of the Arkansas River. As it turns out, recovery actions planted the "wrong" fish throughout the species' range, rendering more than a hundred stream reaches uninhabitable for the "right" fish. The greenback cutthroat trout was once again listed as endangered.[20] This story exemplifies not only the priorities that conservation management establishes in the name of genetic purity, but also the challenges of captive breeding and the limits of scientific knowledge.

The dusky seaside sparrow (*Ammodramus maritimus nigrescens*) provides another important example of the relationship between captive and wild management, and demonstrates the significance of management decisions about captive breeding for the very survival of species.[21] The dusky sparrows' decline began in 1940, when pesticides were first sprayed to control mosquitoes on the marshes of Merritt Island and along the St. Johns River in Florida. Then, man-made floods devastated the sparrows' nests. Finally, in the 1960s the marshes surrounding the river were drained to facilitate the construction of a highway to nearby Disney World. By 1979, only six dusky seaside sparrows were known to exist, and the USFWS ordered their capture.[22]

Unfortunately, the few remaining duskies were male. After considerable debate, the USFWS hybridized them with a close subspecies to save them from extinction. This was the first deliberate hybridization to take place under the ESA. The plan was to "backbreed" the hybrids (namely, cross them with an organism that is genetically similar to one of the parents) so as to ultimately produce a bird as genetically close to the dusky as possible. The recovery program proceeded swimmingly until a change in administration at the USFWS resulted in the reinterpretation of the hybrid policy in a manner that terminated the program altogether. The last remaining dusky seaside sparrow died at Disney World on June 17, 1987.[23]

Conservationists around the globe contend with such excruciating circumstances on a routine basis. In the 1960s, Brazilian biologists estimated that only 200 golden lion tamarins (*Leontopithecus rosalia*)—a primate species endemic to the coastal forests of the Brazilian state of Rio de Janeiro—still survived in the wild. They started an international captive breeding program involving more than a hundred agencies and facilities, including zoos from around the world. Alongside the captive breeding efforts, captive-bred tamarins were reintroduced into the Brazilian forests, and forest corridors were planted by local communities to connect the fragmented tamarin territories. After three and a half decades of intense conservation management, in 2013 there were 2,100 golden lion tamarins in seventeen fragmented populations in Brazil, one third of which were descendants of the captive breeding program.[24] According to the coordinator of the international captive breeding effort, "the golden lion tamarin program has been a model for how to integrate *in situ* and *ex situ* efforts. What has made the program [so successful] is that [it is] an integration and a cooperation—a collaboration—between all these different stakeholders and parties."[25]

Then there are the remarkable efforts to save the Tasmanian devils (*Sarcophilus harrisii*). Once prevalent on the Australian island of Tasmania and famous for their depiction in Warner Bros. cartoons, in the mid-1990s large numbers of devils in the wild started contracting fatal carcinogenic tumors. Under these urgent conditions, the Australian government—in collaboration with universities, scientists, conservation organizations, and zoos—devised an ambitious recovery plan. As one IUCN partner told me, "We needed to plan for the possibility that at some point the captive population would be all that was left of the species."[26] By 2013, the program had 660 cancer-free Tasmanian devils in zoos and sanctuaries, 15 of which were recently released onto Maria Island off the shores of Tasmania, where they had never lived before.

*   *   *

I will further expand on all these stories over the course of this book. As the stories show, government agencies, field experts, zoo administrators, and population managers are only a fraction of the massive behind-the-scenes international network of knowledge, genetic material, and human and nonhuman animals that constitute global species conservation today—all entangled in messy efforts to save life. The stories also present in vivid detail the attempts to integrate, and the challenges of integrating, the traditionally insular and bifurcated systems of *in situ* and *ex situ* conservation.

But while they all focus on life and survival, these stories are also about death and extinction. Indeed, not all species are as "lucky" as the devils, the silvery minnow, and the golden lion tamarins of this world, and even among such lucky species, not all individuals are deemed worth saving, or in fact survive such saving. In the shadows of the heroic efforts to save wild life, one inevitably finds sacrifice and catastrophe. Such life-and-death stories illustrate the high stakes involved in figuring out what conservation should look like at a time when the long-established definitions of nature have collapsed.

Inter Situ *Hybrids*

Within the current paradigm, *in situ* conservation and *ex situ* conservation—namely, conservation inside and outside of "wild nature"—are conjoined in a system of meanings and symbols. *Wild Life* traces the dynamics of *in situ* and *ex situ* conservation, as these apparatuses shift and transform into various configurations of experts, agencies, ideas, sites, bodies, and networks. Such *inter situ* dynamics are compatible with emerging critiques of wilderness that speak in the language of "naturecultures"[27] and wildness[28] and that question the simplistic division between nature and culture in a way that illuminates their interdependence and irrevocable fusion.

My aim, I should clarify, is not merely to replace the bifurcation between wilderness and captivity with a continuum between the two, but is far more radical: to acknowledge that there is not one nature but many, and to assert that our definition of nature urgently needs rethinking. Global warming, disease, drought, and deforestation are only a few of the reasons why the existing habitats of a growing number of species are becoming less viable.

In many cases, what conservationists refer to as a natural habitat must be actively managed alongside the construction of an alternative one. Captive settings are increasingly functioning as such alternative habitats, and are thus gaining greater importance for species conservation. More and more examples emerge in which the last handfuls of animals from a species on the brink of extinction are transferred into intensely managed sites to ensure their survival. In such cases, a livable nature is constructed in captivity for the conservation of threatened life.

Conceptualizing Nature

In *Ecology without Nature*, Timothy Morton argues that "the very idea of 'nature' which so many hold dear will have to wither away in an 'ecological' state of human society."[29] "Putting something called Nature on a pedestal and admiring it from afar," he says, "does for the environment what patriarchy does for the figure of Woman. It is a paradoxical act of sadistic admiration."[30] He concludes: "Strange as it may sound, the idea of nature is getting in the way of properly ecological forms of culture, philosophy, politics, and art."[31] Morton especially takes issue with the romantic aestheticization of nature, arguing that nature "must be addressed critically, precisely because we care about [it] and we care about the earth, and indeed, the future of lifeforms on this planet."[32]

Morton's critique of Nature is closely aligned with William Cronon's critique of wilderness in his 1995 essay "The Trouble with Wilderness." There, Cronon defines wilderness as a particular cultural and historical phenomenon that is unique to the United States and that idealizes nature as pristine and untouched. According to Cronon: "Wilderness is the natural, unfallen antithesis of an unnatural civilization that has lost its soul."[33] Yet, he adds, "wilderness gets us into trouble only if we imagine that this experience of wonder and otherness is limited to the remote corners of the planet, or that it somehow depends on pristine landscapes we ourselves do not inhabit." Instead, Cronon argues that we must "abandon the dualism that sees the tree in the garden as artificial—completely fallen and unnatural—and the tree in the wilderness as natural—completely pristine and wild. Both trees in some ultimate sense are wild; both in a practical sense now depend on our management and care."[34]

In recent years, a growing number of scholars have been rethinking the alienation between nature and culture.[35] The critical question, as framed by British science and technology scholar Carrie Friese, is this: "If nature can no longer be understood as a ground for culture, do nature and culture collapse into one another and therein dissolve? Or is a new kind of relationship between nature and culture taking form?"[36] Whereas the response of science studies scholar Bruno Latour is that political ecologists should abandon the idea of nature altogether,[37] scholars such as Sarah Franklin, Celia Lury, and Jackie Stacey explore how nature-culture relations are reworked in ways that denaturalize and renaturalize a nature that is no longer assumed to be unitary, fixed, and singular.[38]

Unlike much of this scholarship, *Wild Life* does not propose a new definition of nature, nor does it suggest abandoning nature altogether. Instead, it explores how prominent conservation experts understand the conceptual and real changes in nature, and how these changes in turn inform their everyday conservation practices. *Wild Life* is an ethnographic account of the administrative structures and networks of the emerging institution of natures.

In the process of researching and writing *Wild Life* I observed a curious phenomenon: a deep discrepancy between the fidelity of many of my interviewees toward the ideals of nature and wilderness, and the ways in which their actual management practices reflect the messiness and pluralities of these constructs. In light of the recent mass proliferation of scholarly literature pointing to the urgent need to rethink nature, the nature-bound rhetoric of many of the conservation experts interviewed for this project merits some attention. I shall trace such tensions between rhetoric and practice throughout the book.[39] Although *Wild Life* focuses more on describing and documenting this phenomenon and less on explaining it, I would offer at the outset that behind the attachment of many of my interviewees to traditional articulations of nature lie the practical implications of letting go of this nature. Their concern, specifically, is that "without a Nature to protect and a Science to unequivocally define its properties and mark its boundaries, real world experiments risk becoming aligned with the interests of the powerful,"[40] and with corporate interests in particular. Along these lines, certain scholars have argued that any shift in ecological ideas and practices must remain acutely aware of the neoliberal mind-set, which circumscribes any experiment and frames its outcomes.[41]

The rhetoric-practice discrepancy has recently been stoked by the passionate debate that is unfolding in conservation biology between Michael Soulé (widely considered the cofounder of this discipline) and Peter Kareiva (chief scientist for The Nature Conservancy), and their respective camps, regarding the renaming of the current geological epoch as the Anthropocene: the Age of Man. While this debate has seeped into a vast range of disciplines, from geology to philosophy and geography, and plays out slightly differently in each, my book examines how it has been unfolding in the context of conservation. The debate over the Anthropocene may help explain the wariness on the part of conservationists toward any rhetorical challenges to the nature-human divide.

The Biopolitics of Wild Life

If the reframing of nature and wilderness provides the first theoretical foundation for this book, French historian and philosopher Michel Foucault's concept of "biopolitics" serves as its second. According to Foucault, in the premodern period sovereign power was characterized by "the right to decide life and death"—that is, the right to *take* life or *let* live.[42] Foucault argues that with the development of bourgeois society and capitalism in the eighteenth century, this ancient right has been replaced by what he calls "biopower": a "power to *foster* life or *disallow* it to the point of death."[43] Biopower takes two main forms.[44] One centers on the individual body, "its disciplining, the optimization of its capabilities, the extortion of its forces, the parallel increase of its usefulness and its docility, its integration into systems of efficient and economic control," what Foucault characterizes as "an *anatomo-politics of the human body*." The other centers on the body of the species, "the body imbued with the mechanics of life and serving as the basis of the biological processes: propagation, births and mortality, the level of health, life expectancy and longevity," what Foucault defines as *"regulatory controls: a biopolitics of the population."*[45] Foucault argues that the power to kill, formerly the highest function of sovereign power, was supplanted by "the power to invest life through and through," to administer bodies and manage life.[46]

Foucault establishes strong connections between notions of biopower, discipline, and governmentality, promoting the idea that beyond the threat of force by the sovereign, humans are governed through modes of disciplinary subjectification. Accordingly, Nikolas Rose, alone and with Paul Rabinow,[47] has argued for the inapplicability of biopower in the nonhuman context. Animals cannot be subjectified through such means, so the argument goes, hence they cannot be subjects of biopower.[48] This book seeks to refute that argument. Although Foucault admittedly uses the term "biopolitics" only to describe the project of governing *human* bodies, populations, and life, *Wild Life* joins a growing scholarship that extends the scope of biopolitics to the realm of governing nonhuman animals.[49] Doing so, I claim, not only appreciates the entanglements of human and nonhuman, but also recognizes their co-production.[50]

Foucault also speaks of a new relationship between history and life, which places humans both outside history, in their biological environment, and "inside human historicity, penetrated by . . . techniques of knowledge and power."[51] The tense interrelations between *in situ* and *ex situ* conservation unearth the inherent instability between the human *experience of life* as part of biological, or natural, existence, and the human *management of life* as outsiders to this nature and as part of history. By expanding Foucault's biopolitics into the realm of species conservation, this book offers a remaking of the relatively wild, rather than of wilderness in its ideal state; it is a remaking by layers, through multiple shadings, rather than polar extremes.[52] One of my interviewees has referred to this as "as wild as possible" conservation.[53] Bolstered by enhanced population management regimes, such aspirations toward the wild*er* rather than the wild*est* are a mark of the transition of contemporary conservation discourses from sovereign power to biopower.

My use of the term "wild life" in this book—in its two word variation— signals my extensive drawing on both the critical literature on wildness and Foucault's notion of governing life.[54] In the increasing fluidity between *in situ* and *ex situ* management, the question of "make live" is becoming extremely complex and involves overlapping and contested typologies. Husbandry practices, database tools, and population management models increasingly drift from *ex situ* conservation in zoos to *in situ* conservation in the wild and vice versa, as the interactions between these sites become more and more frequent. Within all these practices and models, "the life of bodies and populations is ratio-ized in finer and finer ways, with increasing possibilities for inter-comparison."[55] Ultimately, the aim of species conservation is to determine how best to classify, calculate, rank, manage, and thus save (certain) nonhuman life.

How I Came to Write This Book

This project began after five years of research on North American zoos that culminated in the publication of *Zooland: The Institution of Captivity*.[56] At that point, I was ready to research a different topic altogether. However, many open questions from my work on zoos still demanded my attention. One such question was how zoos—in their newly established role as conservation institutions—compare with other sites of species conservation: might the difference between conservation in zoos and in the wild be depicted as one of degree? My interviewees for the zoo project, who were interested in situating zoos as part of the global conservation effort, consistently used the terms "*in situ*" and "*ex situ*" when addressing my questions. As an academic with no formal training in conservation, I was unfamiliar with the meaning of these terms. This book is my attempt to unpack them.

Wild Life draws on more than 120 interviews, mainly with conservation biologists and wildlife managers, many of whom combine *in situ* and *ex situ* work in their respective institutions—government agencies, zoos, and other conservation organizations. I began my exploration of *in situ* and *ex situ* by connecting with some of the zoo professionals I had interviewed previously. These interviews with prominent zoo experts snowballed into others, and soon I left the familiar compounds of the zoo community to explore the world of field conservationists, mostly scientists at the USFWS and the IUCN. Relying on engaged ethnographic research, *Wild Life* sketches the various approaches to the wild-captive divide expressed by these conservation experts, documenting both the tenacity of this divide and how it is increasingly being challenged in conservation circles.

As a work of collaborative ethnography, *Wild Life* builds on the relationships I have cultivated with many of my interlocutors.[57] The conservationists I interviewed for this project all had fascinating perspectives to share. I was especially intrigued to learn how my interviewees have come to dedicate their own lives to the life of another species and to witness the unique interspecies connections that have emerged through this lifelong commitment.

While my interviewees belong to diverse conservation organizations and communities, their work often oscillates between the bifurcated worlds of *in situ* and *ex situ* conservation. They themselves, in effect, are *inter situ* hybrids, carving out their unique interpretations of the dichotomy and identifying their own paths for moving beyond it. As one conservation biologist told me: "I'm sort of on a mission, if you will, of bridging the gap between *in situ* and *ex situ*."[58] In this sense, my interviewees are neither typical nor representative of the conservation community, and thus, by definition, this work is not based on a statistical sample of conservation experts. On the contrary, I deliberately sought out conservation practitioners who were open to questioning prominent assumptions about what counts as conservation. I then prompted them to engage with me in exploring the meaning and significance of the divide between *in situ* and *ex situ*—to contemplate, together, how conservation may exist without a unitary and fixed form of nature, and to craft a more nuanced understanding of wildness, conservation, and life.

In addition to its intense reliance on in-depth interviews, *Wild Life* also draws on a range of participatory observations. A Conservation Breeding Specialist Group (CBSG) workshop that I attended in Arizona in March 2013 that focused on the recovery of the Sonoran pronghorn antelope triggered my interest in programs established by the USFWS in accordance with the Endangered Species Act. In August 2013, I participated in a reintroduction of the eastern hellbender into one of the Allegheny River drainages, an experience that contributed to my understanding of the increasing cooperation between zoos and governmental agencies in the management of wildlife. In October 2013, I participated in CBSG's annual meeting at Walt Disney World Resort, Florida, and in April 2014 I attended a meeting of the Committee on the Status of Endangered Wildlife in Canada (COSEWIC) in Halifax, Canada. In January 2014, I visited the Iguaca and Río Abajo aviaries for the management of the Puerto Rican parrot, as well as a number of reintroduction sites for the Puerto Rican crested toad—all in Puerto Rico. Finally, I visited and observed a number of zoos, including the London Zoo, the National Zoo, the Smithsonian Conservation Biology Institute at Front Royal, Virginia, Disney's Animal Kingdom, and the Buffalo Zoo.

A Few Words about Structure

Wild Life contains six chapters, each depicting a different facet of the interface between *in situ* and *ex situ* conservation, as conservation management proceeds, roughly, from bifurcation to amalgamation. Whereas the chapters focus on what conservationists *say* about various aspects of the complex relationship between wild and captive, each is prefaced by a story about a particular species on the brink of extinction that documents what conservationists actually *do* in these contexts. Together, the rhetoric and the practices of conservationists illuminate the interplay between captive and wild management, the importance of this interplay for the lives of relevant species, and the immense challenges to overcoming the foundational divide between these species' *in situ* and *ex situ* management. To move beyond the *in situ–ex situ* divide, or even to understand its limitations, we need to consider more thoroughly the ways in which it is entrenched in historical processes, administrative practices, and personal convictions. We need to understand that neither wilderness nor captivity is easily defined or easy to see, that neither is hell or paradise, and that contemporary challenges call for a serious rethinking of both.

The first story highlights the plight of the Puerto Rican crested toad and the local battles for protecting this species' habitat. Next, the northern white and Sumatran rhinos' stories depict the dangers of fragmented management and how a lack of cooperation can result (and, indeed, has resulted) in the survival or extinction of a particular species. By contrast, the golden lion tamarin of coastal Brazil and the black-footed ferret of the North American prairies are viewed by many conservationists as exemplars of the fruitful integrations between *in situ* and *ex situ* management. Yet such success stories, too, offer a glimpse into the challenges faced, and the many sacrifices made, in the process. My next story returns to Puerto Rico to depict the range of innovative captive breeding strategies deployed to save the thirteen surviving endemic Puerto Rican parrots. The story of the red wolf follows, paving the way for the final chapter's in-depth discussion of metapopulation management. Finally, the Tasmanian devil's conservation management program in Australia demonstrates the cutting-edge implementation of metapopulation management through four *inter situ* models, managed together under one plan.

Although the species highlighted in the inter-chapter stories are by no means the only ones managed through integrative programs, many of my interviewees perceive the programs described in those stories as the quintessential examples of integrative management from around the world.[59] Still, some asked that I tell the conservation stories of other species, too. Soon, the chapters themselves came to be riddled with stories. The dusky seaside sparrow, Gila trout, eastern hellbender, Schaus swallowtail, ring-tailed lemur, and American burying beetle, as well as numerous other species stories, add flavor to the chapters' more conceptual and analytical fare and also soften the initial essay/chapter, practice/rhetoric structure of the book.

Each species-focused essay is loosely related to the chapters that both follow and precede it. Chapter 1, "Bifurcated Life," discusses the institution of the divide between *in situ* and *ex situ* and traces the administrative, disciplinary, regulatory, and historical aspects of this divide. A collage of narratives by numerous conservationists demonstrates how the *in situ* and *ex situ* terminology has shaped their thinking and everyday practices. The chapter also dedicates considerable attention to the meaning of nature, both in its manifestation as wilderness and in the context of the recent debate over the Anthropocene. Throughout, I show how conservationists oscillate between eroding the *in situ–ex situ* dichotomy and fortifying it, in turn highlighting their deep commitment and simultaneous ambivalence toward the idea of wild nature.

Chapter 2, "Captive Life," opens with the story of Marius, the giraffe killed by the Copenhagen Zoo for being "surplus" to the genetically managed *ex situ* population of his subspecies. The chapter then traces the evolution of zoos from entertainment institutions into the quintessential sites of *ex situ* conservation, a capacity that is most pronounced in the depiction of zoos as Noah's arks or as repositories of "insurance" populations. This chapter highlights the ethical dilemmas that conservationists must confront upon deciding if and when to transfer the surviving members of imperiled species into captivity, documenting how these decisions are affected by the divergence between the focus on individual animals by animal rights activists and the species-oriented focus by conservationists. Finally, I discuss individual members of species who are captive-for-life—namely, for whom the captive facilities are the only foreseeable viable habitat. Such situations question not only the traditional *in situ–ex situ* distinction but also the nature of *ex situ* itself, as they highlight the value we assign to life—"in" or "out" of site.

If the first two chapters focus on the institutionalization of, and the juxtaposition between, *in situ* (Chapter 1) and *ex situ* (Chapter 2)—Chapter 3, "Continuous Life," documents how conservation is currently understood as morphing into a continuum between the two poles. From the endless combinations of *in situ* and *ex situ* that spring up almost daily, I briefly describe seven *inter situ* nodes: genebanks, zoo breeding centers, conservation farms, conservation hatcheries, protected areas, wildlife refuges, and national parks. I start with the node perceived by many of my interviewees as closest to the *ex situ*—or captive—pole, and gradually move along the continuum toward what is generally perceived as closest to the *in situ*—or wilderness—pole. But while documenting the continuum approach in species conservation, I simultaneously challenge its linearity and fixity, pointing to the inherent fluidity among and within the sites. I observe that while the practitioners who perform this work on the ground are fully aware of this fluidity, their conceptual framework often lags far behind.

Because of the complex interrelations between *in situ* and *ex situ*, the movement between the two has become its own site of management. Chapter 4, "Dynamic Life," focuses on reintroductions—the primary mode of movement from captivity into the wild—and on the "soft law" that regulates this movement. My discussions of the reintroductions of the Schaus swallowtail butterfly and the eastern hellbender, as well as the translocations of the ring-tailed lemur, serve to demonstrate some of the difficulties that ensue when animals are transferred between captive and wild settings, and the strategies taken up by conservationists to deal with such difficulties.

Chapter 5, "Regulatory Life," centers on the U.S. Endangered Species Act (ESA) of 1973. This focus serves the book's broader goal of exploring both the powers and the limitations of legal devices for regulating the *in situ–ex situ* divide. I illustrate the critical importance of categorizing animal bodies as existing either *in situ* or *ex situ* for assigning them with legal protections, and how these categories both collapse and reemerge. Finally, the chapter shows how this divide still matters for administrators who assess, count, or discount animal bodies for listing and recovery.

Chapter 6, "Integrated Life," looks at the *in situ–ex situ* divide from the point of view of database systems, population management models, and algorithmic properties. Specifically, the chapter demonstrates how *in situ* and *ex situ* have emerged as two separate administrative systems and how they are increasingly bleeding into each other and becoming integrated. CBSG's One Plan approach in particular aims at translating the geographic and genetic fragmentation of populations and the alienation between their managers into integrative networks. Although the rhetorical distinction between *in situ* and *ex situ* conservation is far from dead, models such as the One Plan are increasingly enhancing the interconnections between these two conservation poles.

Wild Life concludes with the story of Rotoroa Island in New Zealand, demonstrating the emerging understanding among certain conservationists that nature may need to be managed in perpetuity. This understanding raises urgent questions about nature's definition, the definition of conservation, and the role that managing both nonhumans and humans should play in the conservation of natures.

Puerto Rican Crested Toad

The Natural Resource Secretary called me to his office to fire me. "Miguel, why do you worry so much? Why do you get in trouble, Miguel? Why do you bring so many problems, Miguel? Please, Miguel, why [do] you care?" And I tell him, "Look, when my granddaughter [will] ask me 'What's a crested toad?' and I'm going to tell her that they don't exist anymore, and I was the Biologist of Guánica In charge of that animal and I let them be killed—what [will] I say? . . . And so I tell him: "We are all Puerto Rican, but most Puerto Ricans haven't been born yet. So we have to leave this for our grandchildren and grandchildren and grandchildren." And the guy started, he was like this, he said: "You make me cry," he told me.

—Miguel Canals, Forest Ranger, Guánica State Park, Puerto Rico[1]

The Puerto Rican crested toads (*Peltophryne lemur*)—the only "native" toads of Puerto Rico and the Virgin Islands—are small, nocturnal amphibians with a unique upturned nose (crest—hence the name) that gives their head the look of a foreshortened baby caiman (Figure 3).[2] The toads' life cycle depends on the presence of karst topography, a formation of porous limestone bedrock that, among other things, causes water to drain very quickly through the stone, providing a small window of time for the toads

---

Figure 3: Puerto Rican crested toads mating in a tub at the Buffalo Zoo, November 2005. Buffalo Zoo herpetologist Penny Felski explains that the captive toads are conditioned for breeding by fasting, undergoing a brief cooling period, being fed and treated with an anti-fungal bath and, finally, being introduced to each other in tubs set up to simulate breeding ponds. Felski tells me: "Here, the male [on top] grasps the female in amplexus—an amphibian mating position—while waiting to fertilize the eggs that she will lay" (interview). Courtesy of John W. Kast.

who use the pools to breed. This habitat has been steadily disappearing for decades, especially in the highly developed northern part of the island. By the 1950s, the Puerto Rican crested toad was considered extirpated from the wild.

In 1966, reports of toad sightings surfaced in northern Puerto Rico, "but no one knew how much stock to put in those stories."[3] In 1974, Professor Ernesto Estremera played some recordings of crested toads for his high school students, telling them that "these toads no longer exist in Puerto Rico."[4] A student from Quebradillas raised his hand and told Estremera that he had heard those calls before, on his father's land.[5] This property had "a cow on it, and a few horses, and a cattle trough that was constructed from concrete for the cows to have a water source. . . . And, lo and behold, that turned out to be the case."[6] Estremera was delighted; so too were numerous herpetologists, who descended on Quebradillas to conserve what were perhaps the last few members of this species in existence. Juan Rivero, then a herpetologist at the Mayaguez Zoo in Puerto Rico, took some specimens back to the zoo and when those bred, Mike Evans, a biology student working at the zoo, contacted his friend Rick Payne, the reptile curator at the Buffalo Zoo, to see if Buffalo wanted any of the offspring.[7] They did, and this serendipitous chain of events is how the collaboration with North American zoos began.

Many people were upset over the transfer of the toads into captivity, and over their transfer away from the island in particular. "It was controversial," says Bob Johnson, curator of reptiles and amphibians at the Toronto Zoo, which got involved shortly after Buffalo. Johnson later became the first coordinator of the toad's Species Survival Plan (SSP)—the program established by the North American Association of Zoos and Aquariums (AZA) to facilitate captive breeding between accredited zoos.[8] Initiated in 1984, the Puerto Rican Crested Toad SSP was the first amphibian captive breeding program in a zoo. The toad was designated as endangered by Puerto Rican law in 1984, as threatened by the U.S. federal Endangered Species Act in 1987, and as Critically Endangered on the IUCN Red List of Threatened Species in 2004.[9]

"Some people thought they shouldn't have collected them from the wild," Johnson reiterates. "But if this were the case they likely would have disappeared entirely," as all water sources in northern Puerto Rico have been drained for human use.[10] He further explains that human water management prevents the formation of natural pools that provide breeding sites for the toads—meaning that the toads' already small populations, limited to habitats with karst formation, are curtailed even further. "We're building ponds now," Johnson continues. Initially, the architectural model for the ponds was "the cow model, of course. Because we knew it worked," he says, referring to the cow troughs on the high school student's land in Quebradillas that provided breeding ground for the toads.[11] We figured that "if we build these ponds, [the toads] are going to find their way to them, so that's what we're doing."

In addition to helping construct artificial ponds for the toads to breed in, zoos have been providing a steady supply of toadlets and tadpoles for re-introductions to Puerto Rico. The toadlets are flown in from North America and released during the hurricane season. "We do timed breeding in November, hoping there's a hurricane," Johnson tells me. "If there isn't one, we have no water to put the toads in,"[12] In such instances, the biologists involved in the recovery program have needed to come up with innovative strategies, such as trucking in water to fill the reproduction ponds.[13]

In early 2014, approximately 600 toads were managed in captivity among thirty-one zoos.[14] According to Diane Barber of the Fort Worth Zoo, who replaced Johnson as the SSP program's coordinator when he retired, "we currently only have fifteen institutions that participate in captive breeding efforts for reintroduction. Their toads are kept in permanent isolation rooms, separate from all other zoo animals, to reduce the risk of introducing novel pathogens to wild populations."[15] A manufactured seasonal change—whereby the temperatures in the room are dropped abruptly for four weeks, rainfalls are simulated by using sprinklers,[16] and recorded breeding calls are played—re-creates the toad's ideal mating conditions. "When everything works, a female can lay up to 4,000 eggs that typically hatch within 24 hours," the Toronto Zoo website indicates.[17]

Alongside the genetically valuable toads, toads who are over-represented within the program's breeding population are considered "surplus" and used by zoos as "exhibit toads." The genetically valuable tadpoles hatched in North American zoos are released in Puerto Rico every year to sustain and rebuild the wild population (Figure 4). As I have mentioned in the introduction, between 1983 and 2014, 290,000 tadpoles were released into man-made ponds in Puerto Rico.[18]

Even so, one of the more difficult challenges of the program has been the acquisition of land for breeding sites. "We had a few release ponds

Figure 4: A joint *in situ–ex situ* team collects weight, length, and DNA samples from each toad (seen here in plastic bags) and tests them for chytrid fungus before releasing them in northwestern Puerto Rico in November 2013. Earlier that day, the toads were flown into Puerto Rico from North American zoos. Courtesy of Carlos Pacheco, USFWS.

in the north," Johnson says, but "we didn't have 'protected areas' in the north like we did in the south. The development in the north is tremendous. It's all homes, and holiday homes, and hotels—so most of those cattle troughs were being destroyed. As a cattle pasture, [the land] was worth nothing—but as a hotel site it was worth a fortune."[19] In fact, the Toronto Zoo tried to buy a small tract of land with a pond that would have been a perfect release site for the toad, but the $18,000 price tag proved prohibitively expensive. Although he raised almost the entire sum, Johnson came up short by $5,000. "So we never did it," he tells me. "We were so close, and this site had some endangered plants on it, and some lizards. It would've been a dream site. But it never happened."[20]

The toad's story in the south has been no less dramatic. Guánica State Forest in southwest Puerto Rico is a dry forest that lies in a rain shadow—the side of a mountain that normally receives very little rainfall—and gets heavy rain only during hurricanes.[21] In 1984, Hurricane Klaus caused a beachside parking lot in Tamarindo, near the state forest, to flood. Miguel

Canals, the forest ranger at Guánica, arrived at the site that day. He re-counts the day's events in detail:

> One day, on the 4th of July, 1984, I was driving this road that we're driv-ing on now at about 6 a.m., [estimating] damage to the forest because twenty inches of rain had [just] fallen in forty-eight hours. It was a mess. While I was driving right here, I reached an area where I could not pass. All this was serendipity. And I stopped . . . and suddenly I heard some-thing: *Aklukluklukluklu, Aklukluklukluklu.* "What the hell is that sound?" I asked. So I started looking around, and I looked in the man-grove and I saw a little toad, and I looked at it and I said, "Well, that's not a bufo, that's not any toad I know!" . . . I got into the water and I captured one, and then I noticed the crest. I had never seen one in my life. But just like the crested toad, it had this crest here. . . . So, I called San Juan in the morning, 7:30 a.m., and I said: "Look, *mira,* This is Miguel. I found these toads. I am very sure it is a crested toad." I remember when the guy I talked with started laughing and said to the herpetologist that was near him, "*Mira!* He is crazy! Miguel says that he has a crested toad at the beach, in the salt flat!" And I heard that and I said, "*Mira!* I no crazy! I no crazy! I'm sure that he is a crested toad!" They came that same night. And I took them driving at night and suddenly three crested toads were crossing the road, so we stopped—and then they went crazy. "Oh, I can't believe it! Oh my God! Oh!"[22]

Meanwhile, Guánica's mayor had sent workmen to drain the parking lot so that fishermen and tourists could visit the beach.[23] Only at the last moment did Canals manage to stop the workers from doing so. "This area has been the crested toads' for the past half million years," Canals tells me. "The arti-ficial thing is the parking lot."[24] More intervention was needed, however, for the toads' breeding to be successful. To this end, a secondary breeding pond was built out of concrete in nearby Manglillo Grande and has been populated annually. Since 1992, seventeen zoos have released more than 144,653 tad-poles at Manglillo, one of six current release sites for the toads.[25] Tamarindo remains the primary wild habitat of the Puerto Rican crested toad, and Canals insists that "his" wild population not be mixed with any captive ones.

In the late 1980s, population biologist Bob Lacy—then chairperson of IUCN's Conservation Breeding Specialist Group (CBSG), a group of scien-tists who facilitate workshops to advance the integration of wild and captive management—was invited to apply a Population Habitat Viability Assessment (PHVA) model for the crested toad program.[26] Lacy recalls his initial, not very hopeful, perspective on the program's potential success: "The crested toad is a really difficult species to protect and recover," he tells me. "There was one small, highly artificial breeding site left in the wild at the time, and not much more than that. You had a small number of animals, and major threats ahead of it that would be really difficult to address. . . . So from the first analyses I did, I was skeptical that this was even worth trying. There were just a lot of challenges."[27]

Nonetheless, the PHVA meeting proceeded, bringing together "the zoo people, the wildlife managers, the field people, and the biologists to say: 'What do we have to do? Let's get together and put together a plan for how we're going to protect this species.'"[28] Not everyone participated in this meeting, however. Lacy tells me that there were tensions "that oscillated between skepticism and hostility towards the U.S. federal government's involvement in Puerto Rican conservation, as well as other typical battles." Specifically, he recounts:

> Puerto Rican herpetologists and conservation groups were never happy
> with the program because they had some solid evidence that, separate from
> the main population that the governments and the zoos were all working
> with, there were still some scattered, individual Puerto Rican toads in the
> habitat and that the government was so focused on pursuing their plan that
> they were ignoring the fact that there were possibly other toads out there
> and other habitats that could be protected. So there was a faction that had
> important thoughts about important conservation actions that were outside
> of the process.[29]

Despite the aim of inclusivity, there ended up being quite a few fissures between the relevant conservationists over how to best manage the toad. These fissures were still evident when I visited Puerto Rico in 2014.

Even after the core group of conservation experts drew up a recovery plan based on the PHVA modeling, considerable challenges remained. What has played in the toads' favor, paradoxically, has been their non-charismatic nature. "This species is so low-key," Lacy tells me. "They're basically little ugly toads. It is almost impossible to ever see them; they're underground for 360 days out of the year. So they're not going to ever be the high-profile golden lion tamarin, Tasmanian devil, black-footed ferret kind of things, or even the Puerto Rican parrot."[30] This, according to Lacy, has actually enabled the collaboration to take off with relatively low conflict levels, limited to squabbles with local conservationists. Nowadays, the USFWS describes the toad's recovery program as one of the two most important conservation programs that it facilitates on the island, the other being the Puerto Rican parrot program (which I will discuss later).[31]

Despite their lack of charisma, the toads—with some help from Miguel Canals and local residents—were able to defeat Club Med's aspirations to turn Guánica into a beach resort. Canals recalls the 1989 events:

> Club Med was very important in helping us develop a conscience for the toads. "I am going to take those toads and put a hundred [of them] in one sack and throw them into the sea!" the mayor told me. And that's when we started to fight them. And then we marched through the streets of San Juan, and we invaded [the contested area], and we stayed there three weeks. [Eventually,] the Supreme Court voted in our favor. The historians say that it was in Guánica that everything changed. Because before, the environmental fight was for the health of the communities because of contamination [and] pollution. In Guánica, the environmental groups got involved in diversity and in protecting our fauna and flora.[32]

Another threat the toad has faced, in addition to habitat loss and Club Med, has been competition from the marine toad (*Bufo marinus*), which is much larger in size and more abundant in numbers. The marine toad was introduced to Puerto Rico (and Australia) from Jamaica to serve as a biological form of pest control of the sugarcane beetle. Because of competition for limited resources, such as breeding sites, shelter, and food, the "invasive" toad quickly became a threat to the "native" one.[33] The efforts to strengthen crested toad populations have therefore proceeded alongside the "elimination" of thousands of marine toads. Canals proudly showed me a photo he took of some 1,000 marine toads in the back of his truck. "We kill them, you know," he explained.[34]

In 2013, the USFWS, in partnership with the Puerto Rico Department of Natural and Environmental Resources and the AZA, released more than 71,000 tadpoles and 520 toadlets to Puerto Rico's northern and southern karst areas—"a record-breaking number of tadpoles released within a single year."[35] The current goal of the recovery program is to create new ponds that support six self-sustaining populations—managed together as a metapopulation[36]—three in the north and three in the south.[37] In the 1990s, scientists from Guánica State Forest and the Toronto Zoo tracked the toads by fitting them with specially tailored tiny backpacks, each equipped with a radio transmitter.[38] As the SSP coordinator of this program, Diane Barber keeps a record of the participating toads, which includes their breeding history as well as data on their reintroduction and monitoring. Barber also recommends which captive individuals to mate for optimal genetic diversity in the population.[39] As for the extent of the program's success, it is—as are many other issues in species conservation—debatable. Canals tells me: "We should be aware that after twenty years of releasing tadpoles, we have only observed three reproductive events in only one area, Manglillo, and a few adult toads in the other areas."[40]

Hybridization has been another contested issue in this program. For most of the program's existence, the northern and southern toad populations were managed separately: they lived in different zoos and were subject to distinct population management plans. Since 2013, however, these two populations have been crossbred. Barber explains that "the northern population of toads had a best-case scenario of less than 32 percent genetic diversity, which was an unsustainable population [in the] long term." After years of deliberation, the recovery team decided that "rather than letting them die out entirely due to the results of inbreeding depression, which we were starting to observe," the northerns would be crossbred with the southerns.

"Hybrids are the future of the toad," Bob Johnson tells me.[41] "But we're only putting the hybrids outside of the toads' current range," he clarifies. Johnson is quick to admit the dangers of this hybridization: "If you're adapted to the northern environment, or you're adapted to the southern environment, and you hybridize, then you get animals adapted to neither environment."[42] At the same time, he also believes that with this "new evolutionary material," the toads should be able to survive in both environments because "they've got all the templates from which to adapt to the environments we're putting them into."[43] Bob Lacy concurs: "I was not impressed by the differences people are seeing between the north and the south. It didn't look to me like enough of a difference that I would worry about mixing them. So there are genetic differences, but there are genetic differences between populations of all kinds of species."[44] For this reason, Lacy prefers not to refer to the toad's interbreeding as hybridization.

Canals disagrees. He believes that the distinctions between the northern and southern crested toads are both substantial and significant: "That's why I don't allow *anybody*—any zoo, anything—that pulls in here, the natural area, to mix the natural population with that from the zoo. I don't want this species,

I don't want those genes—the population at Tamarindo is healthy."[45] Barber does not understand what all the fuss is about. "We would never consider placing introduced toads into a natural, wild population of this species for many reasons—genetic, disease, et cetera," she tells me. "There are cases where translocations (wild to wild) would be considered, but not captive to wild."[46]

Hybridization (or crossbreeding) is a contentious topic in general, not only in the context of the toad. "If you're a purist," Johnson explains, "you want every evolutionary significant unit maintained in its integrity." But biologists are increasingly witnessing the drawbacks of this position. When you hybridize, Johnson tells me, this "really allows you to set the animals off on a new evolutionary trajectory."[47] When a species like the Puerto Rican crested toad is reintroduced into areas where there have not been toad populations for many years, this new abundance of genetic material can provide a massive advantage to their survival. Either way, Barber clarifies, "we no longer have a pure northern toad in captivity, nor at our release sites in Puerto Rico."[48] She explains that "we simply don't have the space in zoos across the [world] to manage small genetic units of individual species, and sometimes if *ex situ* management is an essential component of recovery efforts, program leaders must make tough decisions when it comes time to manage dwindling, fragmented populations on extremely limited budgets and space."[49]

But the most important take-home message from this program, according to Johnson, is that the toads' conservation would have been impossible without community support. "It's not me, it's the sacrifices people have made," he tells me.[50] "People looked after us, so it's just that sense that we're all these little tendrils, that we're connected," he explains. This connectedness that Johnson refers to occurs not only between people. "I have a sense that I'm so connected organically to everything—trees, plants, bugs—that the loss of any of those things is a personal loss," Johnson says. "It's a loss in my body, in my life—so I take that personally. And that's why I'm driven."[51] Barber agrees. "I'm confident that we will be able to recover this species in the near future," she says. "Why? Because we have a lot of partners involved that feel the same way and care about the natural wonders of Puerto Rico— small or large. We may not be related by blood, but we are family when it comes to this little toad, and will stick together to be successful."[52]

CHAPTER I

Bifurcated Life

What is it that we want? Much of what conservation biology must do is confused by notions of animal "wildness," and "freedom," and even by the belief of a few that when a species' historical home is altered, that species is no longer worthy of interest.

—William Conway, President, WCS (1992–99), and Audubon Medal Winner, 1999[1]

According to conservation biologist Kent Redford and his two colleagues, the version of ecology taught in the 1960s and 1970s presented a world in which ecosystems returned to a stable equilibrium after perturbation, or disturbance.[2] In this view of the world, all conservationists had to do was remove outside stressors such as human influences, and success would be accomplished. "We have come to understand," these prominent conservation biologists counter, that "the natural world is not organized this way. . . . The world does not consist of species found only in the wild or only in zoos. They are instead found in a bewildering array of combinations of reliance on human action [or inaction] for conservation. . . . So why then does the conservation community in general, and the zoo community in particular, insist on dichotomizing conservation as either *in situ* or *ex situ*?"[3]

Redford's question, posed to the conservation community in 2013, is central to this book. I ask accordingly: How did we arrive at this dichotomy in conservation? Who is involved in its construction and contestation? And what do they think about it? This chapter will sketch the history of the schism between *in situ* and *ex situ* in conservation and will describe its institutionalization. Traditionally, *in situ* has been synonymous with field conservation, while *ex situ* has been associated with zoos and captive breeding. I will recount responses from numerous conservationists about how the *in situ–ex situ* relationship has shaped their thinking and informed their everyday practices. To understand the meaning and importance of the terms "*in situ*" and "*ex situ*" in conservation, I will start by briefly discussing their use in other disciplinary contexts.

In Situ–Ex Situ: *An Interdisciplinary Perspective*

The terms "*in situ*" and "*ex situ*" are used in a wide variety of disciplinary contexts. In art, "*in situ*" refers to a work made specifically for a host site, or one that takes into account the site in which it is installed or exhibited, also referred to as "site-specific" art. In computer science, an *in situ* operation is one that occurs without interrupting the normal state of a system. For example, an *in situ* upgrade would allow an operating system, firmware, or application to be upgraded while the system is still running. Within public international law, "*in situ*" refers to a government with effective control over a certain territory, in contrast to an exiled government. And in architecture, "*in situ*" refers to construction that is carried out at a building site using raw materials, as opposed to prefabricated construction, whereby building components are made elsewhere and then transported to the building site for assembly.[4]

Closest by far to nature conservation, in archaeology, "*in situ*" refers to an artifact that has not been removed from its original place of deposition. By contrast, an artifact that was not discovered *in situ* is considered out of context and therefore usually meaningless to archaeologists.[5] For example, "*in situ*" often refers to ancient sculptures that were carved in place, such as the Sphinx or Petra, which are distinguished from statues that were carved and moved, such as the Colossi of Memnon.[6] *In situ* in this case is the place where an item was first excavated. "If talking from an archaeological perspective, the *country of origin* is where the thing has been dug from, not where it came from," says George Abungu, a cultural heritage professional and the former director general of the National Museums of Kenya. "That discovery moment—that is the place of origin. So if it is in Kenya and you dig it there, it belongs to that particular place . . . that is where it belongs."[7]

The various definitions of "*in situ*"—although quite different from one another—all assert the importance of the place of origin. Similarly, the terms "*in situ*" and "*ex situ*" are used in conservation to establish a scientific place-based hierarchy. But the use of this terminology by conservationists is also unique in relation to other disciplines. The prevalence of nature in this discourse reifies the schism between the two poles, creating what is often an adversarial relationship: *in situ* versus *ex situ*.

In Situ versus Ex Situ in Nature Conservation

The terms "*in situ*" and "*ex situ*" are foundational to contemporary discourses of conservation.[8] Before it was taken up by conservation biology in the 1980s, *ex situ* conservation was associated with the agricultural history of domestication and migration, and with the development of seed banks in particular. The term "*in situ*" appears in many texts as a reference to a plant's original habitat. Its earliest use in the context of conservation appears to have been made during a 1967 Technical Conference on the Exploration, Utilization and Conservation of Plant Genetic Resources.[9]

In the 1980s, the terms "*in situ*" and "*ex situ*" gained traction as stand-ins for "natural" and "captive." This was especially true in zoo circles, where the legitimacy of holding animals in captivity has been increasingly contested by animal rights and welfare advocacy, and hence the very use of the term "captivity" has become problematic.[10] Instead, "*ex situ*" was meant to highlight the scientific properties of such initiatives. In the words of Evan Blumer, conservation biologist and former director of The Wilds, a captive breeding center for zoos: "The terminology began with this binary of captive versus wild, and then got broadened and softened by bringing the Latin into it with *in situ* and *ex situ*."[11] Today, *ex situ* conservation is performed by an array of organizations that hold wild plants, animals, or genetic material, including seed banks, arboreta, botanical gardens, aquariums, and zoos.[12]

Institutionalizing the Divide: Regulatory Regimes

A range of administrative processes and regulatory regimes institutionalize the *in situ–ex situ* schism and, along with it, the split between wild and captive management and that between nature and society. Legal texts both rely upon and reinforce the understanding of *in situ* and *ex situ* conservation as the foundational spatial division in nature conservation, and have regulated it in a variety of ways. In particular, the *in situ–ex situ* divide figures in one of the most important legal texts in conservation to date, the 2002 Convention on Biological Diversity (CBD), an international treaty signed by 193 countries.

The CBD defines "in-situ conservation" as "the conservation of ecosystems and *natural* habitats and the maintenance and recovery of viable populations of species *in their natural surroundings*."[13] The term "ex-situ conservation" is defined in the same text as "the conservation of components of biological diversity *outside their natural habitats*."[14] Whereas *in situ* is conservation's ultimate goal, *ex situ* is dependent upon it, and limited in that it must be executed "predominantly for the purpose of complementing in-situ measures."[15] CBD's Article 9 establishes along these lines that "each Contracting Party shall, as far as possible and as appropriate, and predominantly for the purpose of complementing in-situ measures: . . . (d) Regulate and manage collection of biological resources from natural habitats for ex-situ conservation purposes so as not to threaten ecosystems and in-situ populations of species, except where special temporary ex-situ measures are required."[16] Such legal definitions invoke the terms "natural surroundings" and "natural habitats" as if they were self-explanatory, constructing a place-based hierarchy.[17] According to John Fa and his colleagues, "since the 1992 Earth Summit in Rio de Janeiro, Brazil, *in situ* conservation has been designated, expressly, as the legal and institutional priority. [The Convention for Biological Diversity] and other global instruments and funding strategies . . . relegate *ex situ* approaches to a subordinated supply role."[18]

The International Union for Conservation of Nature (IUCN)—the leading international conservation network in the world—similarly establishes the *in situ–ex situ* divide as a central pillar of conservation. According to the IUCN definitions, "*Ex situ* collections include whole plant or animal collections, zoological parks and botanic gardens, wildlife research facilities, and germplasm collections of wild and domesticated taxa."[19] The following IUCN statement illustrates the centrality of *in situ* to the organization's mission:

> IUCN affirms that a goal of conservation is the maintenance of existing genetic diversity and viable populations of all taxa *in the wild* in order to maintain biological interactions, ecological processes and function. . . . The threats to biodiversity in situ continue to expand, and taxa have to survive in increasingly human-modified environments. . . . The reality of the current situation is that it will not be possible to ensure the survival of an increasing number of threatened taxa without effectively using a diverse range of complementary conservation approaches and techniques including, for some taxa, increasing the role and practical use of ex situ techniques.[20]

Texts produced by zoo organizations also show a prioritization of *in* over *ex situ* conservation and the justification of *ex situ* only as a supportive measure to *in situ*. For example, the World Association of Zoos and Aquariums (WAZA)—a global organization with more than three hundred members, including zoos, aquariums, wildlife associations, and corporate partners—defines conservation as "the securing of long-term populations of species *in natural ecosystems and habitats wherever possible.*"[21]

The *in situ–ex situ* paradigm also appears in other regulatory contexts. For example, according to the policies of the IUCN Red List of Threatened Species—widely viewed as the most comprehensive and objective global standard for evaluating the threat status of plant and animal species—a species that is Extinct in the Wild is defined as "non-conserved," even if it still exists in captivity.[22] In the words of an IUCN member: "Real conservation is [defined as] self-sustaining populations *in nature*. If a species in total is only in captivity [we] call that 'not conserved.'"[23] Regulatory norms thus prioritize the conservation of species depending on their location either "in" or "out" of nature.

Institutionalizing the Divide: Networks and Funding

Conservation's regulatory regimes provide both a reason for and an expression of the bifurcated relationship between *in situ* and *ex situ* in conservation. Another reason for and expression of this bifurcated relationship has been the often-rocky dynamics between accredited zoos and the IUCN. Although members of the zoo community helped to found IUCN in 1948, it was not long before the two communities experienced a breakdown in trust. Christoph Schwitzer works both at Bristol Zoo Gardens and with IUCN's primate specialist group. He tells me that "the IUCN is made up of volunteers, thousands of them. And it's only as good as its people, really."[24] More often than not, he explains, field biologists distrust zoos, and as a result, the IUCN has veered toward non-cooperation with zoo institutions.

Funding sources, too, both rely on and reinforce the *in situ–ex situ* divide. In a 2013 *WAZA Magazine* issue dedicated in its entirety to the integration of species conservation across the *in situ–ex situ* divide, zoo expert John Fa and his colleagues point out that the largest source of international biodiversity funding—the Global Environmental Facility, which is a funding mechanism of the CBD—has no focal area for *ex situ* activities.[25] Research scientist Pierre Comizzoli at the Smithsonian Institution similarly reflects that "organizations such as the World Wildlife Fund, or Conservation International, or The Nature Conservancy, are never going to give me one dollar for the research I'm doing here in the lab because, first of all, they have other priority projects, and [also]—they don't necessarily recognize the importance of this."[26]

Alex Travis is an associate professor of reproductive biology and faculty director of the environment at Cornell University. Travis strongly believes that the separate funding sources for *in situ* and *ex situ* conservation perpetuate this problematic divide. Speaking as a research scientist at a conservation-oriented lab, he notes that "funding was one of the big causes of the divide in the first place."[27] Many field conservationists are wary of losing their money for what they perceive to be the high costs of assistive reproductive technologies in captive management, he explains. "There is this idea that if you just took that money and used it for habitat preservation—working with communities, anti-poaching patrols, whatever the *in situ* project of choice was going to be—you could get so much more bang for the buck because you'd be saving many species in that habitat."[28] For this reason, Travis continues, "the funding agencies that would support those different types of work kind of split."

To receive funding for conservation projects, conservation organizations must typically demonstrate that they are doing *in situ* work. As a result, conservation labs have a harder time obtaining funding from conservation sources and are impelled to seek funding from other sources, such as the

National Institutes of Health. In many cases, financial necessities result in the reorientation of the labs' research projects into ones that contribute to human health.[29] Travis also explains that many conservationists believe that *in situ* and *ex situ* institutions compete for the same funding, which feeds into the alienation between the respective communities. Travis vehemently disagrees. "The world is not one pot," he tells me. Different sources of funding do not necessarily compete, and so the threat felt by many within the *in situ* community toward the *ex situ* world is unfounded, in his opinion.

Finally, according to Travis the *in situ–ex situ* divide in funding makes initiatives that integrate the two quite difficult to execute. "I think a lot of us see the obvious connections between *in situ* and *ex situ* conservation," he says. "But there are very few funding mechanisms that do both."[30] It should be the role of academics to bridge the underlying professional and disciplinary divides, Travis believes.

Field versus Zoo: Notes from the Trenches

The hierarchical relationship between *in situ* and *ex situ* conservation is not only the result of regulatory regimes or of administrative, organizational, and funding processes, but is also the way many conservationists have come to define and experience their work, as I have discovered in many of the interviews conducted for this project. Such a preferential treatment of *situ* is therefore far from being semantic or academic; instead, it manifests in the everyday relationships between conservation professionals, organizations, and projects around the world.

The *in situ–ex situ* schism is particularly apparent in the tense professional relationship between conservationists who work in the "field," and those who work in captive settings, mostly zoos but also laboratories. Despite the disagreements between these two groups, they do typically share a belief both in the importance of the *in situ–ex situ* divide and in the priority of *in situ* over *ex situ* conservation. Whereas a few of my interviewees—who, again, are not typical conservationists in that most of them work in both worlds— have insisted that the tensions between field and zoo conservationists are merely memories from a distant past,[31] the vast majority commented on the ongoing and at times devastating implications of these tensions. Christoph Schwitzer says, for example, "We still work in two parallel worlds. On the one hand, you have the IUCN that is comprised of all the field people, many of which are skeptical of the value of *ex situ* conservation and of zoos in general. And on the other hand, you have the zoo community. Both communities have their own conservation planning meetings and processes, but there's no link."[32] Schwitzer continues: "The *ex situ* zoo community and the *in situ* conservation community have two completely separate processes of species conservation planning [that] are being carried out totally separately. There is no cross-pollination by default."[33] Kathy Traylor-Holzer of the IUCN explains, similarly, that "generally speaking, both in the United States and around the world, the wildlife authorities do their own thing and use their own science and their own planning for wild populations, and zoos . . . do their own planning toward sustaining their species. And a lot of it has always gone on separately."[34]

I ask my interviewees about the reasons for this separation. Schwitzer offers: "The biggest problem in conservation is conservationists. Field people accuse zoo people of just wanting to make money on exhibiting animals" and of holding animals in improper conditions for this purpose, he tells me, while "zoo people accuse field people of all sorts of things, [such as] sitting there in the field doing their research and not making any difference to the conservation of the population. So you have this mutual mistrust."[35] Tara Stoinski is both director of primate research at Zoo Atlanta and chair of research and conservation at the Dian Fossey Gorilla Fund International, which is dedicated to the conservation and protection of gorillas in their African habitats. Stoinski's work thus already bridges the *in situ* and *ex situ* divide. She points out that "traditionally, [zoos] have been disliked by many of the field people because they don't like to see those animals in a captive setting and they don't necessarily feel like zoos are contributing all that much to their conservation. . . . I personally love being involved in both."[36]

The U.S. Fish and Wildlife Service (USFWS) is probably the organization with the largest number of *in situ* biologists in the United States; situated within the U.S. Department of the Interior, this federal agency is dedicated to the management of fish, wildlife, and natural habitats. Its responsibilities include the enforcement of U.S. federal wildlife laws (and the ESA in particular), the protection of endangered species, the management of migratory birds, the restoration of nationally significant fisheries, and the conservation of wildlife habitat. Alongside its Endangered Species program, the USFWS manages the National Wildlife Refuge System and the National Fish Hatchery System—both of which I will discuss later.

USFWS Assistant Director Bryan Arroyo tells me about the *in situ–ex situ* divide. In his words, "*ex situ* is the one that people early on in conservation didn't really support."[37] But Arroyo observes that currently, "there is less reluctance than in the past to bring species on the brink of extinction into captivity" and that, in fact, "it's now seen as another tool." "Whereas before, [*ex situ*] was a last resort," he explains, "in modern times, *ex situ* is on the table from day one. . . . We will reach out to the AZA and say: 'Hey, is anyone interested in this salamander?' And lo and behold, from time to time, someone will raise their hand and say, 'Hey, I've got a guy that knows that kind of stuff.'"[38] Even though he is open to this form of conservation, Arroyo nonetheless depicts *ex situ* as a secondary tool that should be used only when species are critically imperiled. He explains in the context of USFWS's Gila trout recovery program: "The reason we have them in hatcheries is not that we're trying to breed them as a solution, but that we're saving them from wildfires! . . . So we will go out there—in vehicles, in helicopters—and get 'em out of there, away from the fires. We will breed them, of course, because we had them in captivity, but as soon as there's habitat to go out to, we put them all out."

The Center for Biological Diversity is a conservation organization with headquarters in the southwestern United States that advocates for the protection of species diversity and works to "secure a future for all species, great and small, hovering on the brink of extinction."[39] Since its founding in 1989, the Center for Biological Diversity has been using biological data to petition governmental agencies (mainly the USFWS) to better enforce the ESA. Kierán Suckling, the organization's director, reflects on the *in situ–ex situ* divide: "The wildlife managers—the last place they want to go is *ex situ*, it's hell. . . . Consequently, we don't even use the term—the term itself is suppressed."[40] He further explains that

> in addition to the problem of substituting captive breeding for habitat protection—which is a very real problem—captive breeding is also hell because it is so expensive and disaster prone. It is an extremely cost-intensive, risky system. It is not a coincidence that the emergency room is the most expensive place in the hospital and where the most deaths occur. So when wildlife managers express a preference for in-situation conservation—it is not only about ideology, it's about the reality of management cost, capability, and success.[41]

The central concern that many field conservationists have about *ex situ* conservation has been that investment in this type of conservation might end up compromising investments in existing natural ecosystems. Because of this concern and others, some field experts have been reluctant to explore the *ex situ* avenue until only a handful of animals from an imperiled species are left in the wild, although they realize that by that point it might be too late.

In 2010, the Conservation Breeding Specialist Group (CBSG)—a scientific specialist group working under the auspices of the IUCN that advances the global integration of *in situ* and *ex situ* conservation—convened a workshop on intensively managed populations (IMPs). This workshop, held in San Diego, attempted to move beyond the dichotomized *in situ–ex situ* paradigm to identify the central barriers to improving the success rates of conservation programs. The participants suggested what they saw as an alternative to the *in situ–ex situ* system: a focus on varying degrees of management. I will describe this workshop in detail in Chapter 3. Here, however, I would like to highlight the explanation offered by the workshop participants for why the implementation of the IMP approach has been so difficult:

> Population management plans by the *ex situ* community are often developed in isolation from the development of species field conservation plans (and vice versa). Historically there has been poor integration of the efforts of these two communities, although there are notable exceptions. Zoos have evolved quickly, and unevenly, in their conservation roles and commitments, and there is some level of mistrust of their conservation intentions. In some cases, funds and other efforts contributed by zoos to field conservation projects have not been used or accounted for sufficiently, or have not produced the anticipated or desired results.[42]

The participants concluded that these factors, while not the only ones, "have led to misunderstanding, miscommunication and mistrust on both sides."[43] To productively implement the IMP approach, they believe, the current divisions between these two communities will have to be acknowledged and bridged.

Nature versus Society

John Robinson is senior vice president and director of international conservation at the Wildlife Conservation Society (WCS), a large nonprofit conservation organization that encompasses five zoological parks in New York and more than five hundred conservation projects around the globe.

His is a slightly different perspective on the *in situ–ex situ* divide. In Robinson's words,

> *Ex situ* really comes from a tradition of small population management in zoos. The overall thrust is how do you take the tools and the perspectives of demography and of genetic management to manage small populations—and that really comes out of the traditional zoo approach. On the other extreme, a lot of *in situ* conservation activities are less about population management, less species-focused, and more site-based, more looking at the social and economic context—looking at how conservation fits into things like national priorities.[44]

From Robinson's perspective, while *ex situ* projects are mostly managed by conservation biologists who focus on small population management, a large number of *in situ* programs "are not even run by biologists; the biological perspective is not part of the conservation plan."[45] Whereas *ex situ* conservationists focus on nonhuman animal populations, Robinson says, *in situ* conservationists work on transforming the socioeconomic and political context of the relevant site. Take the elephant as an example, he suggests. "There is a whole tradition of biologists working with elephant populations, worrying about their demography, et cetera"—these are the *ex situ* folks. "But we [*in situ* folks] deal with the political questions of how do we put into place a moratorium around ivory trade, how do we deal with consumer demand issues in China, how do we deal with the illegal trafficking. This is what *in situ* conservationists are worrying about, not so much what's happening with the biology of the animals."[46]

Robinson's perspective casts the *in situ–ex situ* divide in a particular light: he argues that while *ex situ* is about managing nonhuman animals, *in situ* is about governing humans. This perspective runs contrary to the more common alignment of field conservationists with animals and wilderness, and of zoo people with humans and the city. Although Robinson's depiction of the *in situ–ex situ* divide is different from that of many of my other interviewees, I would propose that it similarly reiterates this divide.

Theorizing the Divide

To use the terms "*in situ*" and "*ex situ*" in the context of nature conservation assumes that there can, in fact, be a place that is "inside" nature, which may then be contrasted with a place that is "outside" of this nature.[47] Indeed, traditional notions of nature conservation rest upon this dichotomy. Furthermore, at the core of the division between *in situ* and *ex situ* conservation lies the idea shared by most, if not all, conservation practitioners that what they call natural ecosystems are the species' optimal habitats. But how to define such natural ecosystems? Some refer to the concept of wilderness for this purpose, pointing back to the time and place before humans entered the picture as the critical historical moment for defining a natural ecosystem.[48] William Conway, former president of WCS and one of the world's leading zoo experts, differs. "Original habitat depends on how original you want to be," he tells me. "We usually apply the same sort of meaning as we do to history: history [starts from] when we were here, and 'original' is the way it was when we remember it. But it doesn't necessarily mean it was here the day of the dinosaurs. So these terms have to be taken with a great deal of flexibility."[49]

The ideal of a nature untouched by humans has come under scrutiny in the last two decades, especially through the many critiques of wilderness. "Wilderness," William Cronon wrote in 1995, "tends to privilege some parts of nature at the expense of others."[50] The ideal of wilderness under critique is the unexplored wilderness—an impossible, as well as a colonial, ideal, Mark David Spence notes in *Dispossessing the Wilderness*. "Native peoples shaped these environments for millennia," he writes. Such "romantic visions of primordial North America have contributed to a sort of widespread cultural myopia that allows late-twentieth-century Americans to ignore the fact that national parks enshrine recently dispossessed landscapes."[51] Since *in situ* landscapes have always felt the effects of human habitation, the division between "nature" and "culture," if not entirely false, is certainly misleading. Spence also points out that this perceived division between nature and culture has had a great impact upon the practice of conservation in the United States and elsewhere.[52]

In addition to his critique of wilderness, Cronon also cautions against this term's recent displacement by the term "biological diversity." "Defenders of biological diversity," he says, "often point to 'untouched' systems as the best and richest repositories of the undiscovered species we must certainly try to protect. Although at first blush an apparently more 'scientific' concept than wilderness, biological diversity in fact invokes many of the same sacred values."[53] This is an important point to bear in mind, as many of the conservation biologists interviewed here relate to biodiversity as the *sine qua non* of their profession. In Caroline Fraser's words, "Biodiversity loss is now lining up to be the greatest man-made crisis the world has ever known."[54]

Alongside the particular critiques of wilderness, many poststructuralist scholars criticize nature more broadly as providing an ideological cover for the workings of power.[55] According to Ursula Heise, the skepticism toward nature is why, for these scholars, "engagements with the state of the natural world outside its uses for social politics had been extremely difficult to undertake."[56] Jean-François Lyotard, Jean Baudrillard, and Fredric Jameson have separately, and in different ways, deemed the disappearance of nature the most distinctive mark of late twentieth-century society in their respective theories of the postmodern. Heise explains this stance: "Along with historicity and authenticity, nature has disappeared behind or beneath layers of representation and simulation too thick to allow for any direct grasp of the real."[57] For these theorists, the postmodern moment is when the concept of nature as existing outside human society became hard to maintain. For this reason, Heise sees the trope of "the end of nature" as one of the hallmarks both of the transition from modernity to postmodernity and of "the emergence of a global human presence that leaves no particle of nature unaltered."[58]

In line with the poststructuralist critique, science and technology studies (STS) criticizes the ideal of nature as working hand in hand with the misleading premise that science is an arbiter of truth.[59] In his *Politics of Nature*, French sociologist of science Bruno Latour argues, accordingly, that "nature is the chief obstacle that has always hampered the development of public discourse."[60] Latour refers to this type of nature approach as "mononaturalism,"[61] suggesting that the modern condition, predicated on a split between nature and history (or nature and society), has produced instead an endless series of natureculture hybrids.[62] He further stipulates that political ecology "does not speak about nature and has never sought to do so. It has to do with associations of beings that take complicated forms."[63] In this view, nature as separate from society has always been a cultural construction.

Human geography has also seen a recent proliferation of scholarship on naturecultures and wildness. Sarah Whatmore, Jamie Lorimer, and Steve Hinchliffe promote a distinction between the anti-modern "wilderness" and a co-productive, multispecies "wildness."[64] In the words of Whatmore and Thorne: "Reconfiguring the 'wild' on the 'inside' connects such strategic places to the myriad everyday interweavings of human and animal lives—in cities and gardens as well as forests and deserts." This reminds us, they write, "that the 'wild' is not confined to the creatures and (always unpeopled) spaces of television wildlife programmes, and that even here, perhaps most of all here, the 'expert' re-orderings of these already-inhabited ecologies in the networks of science, commerce and governance are a deeply political, and rightly contested, business."[65] Steve Hinchliffe's appeal for a "careful political ecology" similarly advocates a mode of field science that remains open to the emergence or "likely presence" of nonhuman "wild things."[66] He points out that "there is no timeless Nature, rendered as an eternal present or absent, to sit mutely outside an evolving society."[67]

Jamie Lorimer and Clemens Driessen situate these contemplations in the context of conservation. They ask: "Where and how is science to be done when laboratories have taken over the world and all are affected by the consequences? Who should environmentalists trust and what should they value if Nature has come to an end?" In response, they explore the epistemic contrast between laboratories and field sites from three angles: found-made, order-surprise, and secluded-wild. Their discussion of the found-made angle is of particular interest to me here. Lorimer and Driessen suggest that whereas the field is conceived as found rather than made, the lab is perceived as made and thus as free from the distractions and contaminations of the wild. The idea is that within the four walls of the lab, scientists may gain full control over the subjects of their study.[68] Another difference between field and lab, according to Lorimer and Driessen, is their visibility: field sites are considered more publicly visible than labs, and interventions in their domain are seen as having "real world" consequences.[69]

Lorimer and Driessen question these common conventions, arguing that "the ubiquity of modern science . . . has erased the boundary between the lab and field."[70] Drawing on Michel Callon, they offer the concept "wild experiments" to denote "intense, open, high quality public debates" among "emergent collectives of experts," which provide a bridge between what were previously separate constructions of wild and experimental.[71] In their view, environmentalism is "a series of *wild experiments* that cannot make recourse to Nature."[72] This view recognizes a range of sites as hybrids that are neither found nor made. Both the found-made and the field-lab binaries correspond in many ways to the *in situ* and *ex situ* divide in conservation, and the "wild experiments" correspond with the proliferation of *inter situ* hybrids.

The Anthropocene in Conservation

The nature-culture divide has recently reasserted itself in the conservation context through the new debates over the Anthropocene, a concept offered by certain geologists to indicate a new epoch in geologic time that differs from the current epoch (the Holocene) in its anthropogenic, or human-created, environmental changes. The Anthropocene concept has triggered highly emotional responses among conservationists, from enthusiastic endorsement by some to vehement opposition by others.[73]

The pro-Anthropocene camp in conservation—which refers to itself as the New Conservation Science (NCS)—criticizes "traditional" conservation biologists for clinging to anachronistic definitions of wilderness and presents itself as endorsing postmodern human-nature entanglements that call for more sophisticated understandings of nature and conservation. In the words of Peter Kareiva, Michelle Marvier, and Robert Lalasz, the central proponents of this new scheme, "conservation's continuing focus upon preserving islands of Holocene ecosystems in the age of the Anthropocene is both anachronistic and counterproductive."[74]

These claims have been challenged by many conservation biologists—Michael Soulé, Kierán Suckling, Stuart Pimm, and Daniel Doak, to name a few—who claim that the wilderness argument is merely a straw-man exercise by the NCS camp to obscure its own anthropocentric mission and to legitimize anthropogenic change. According to Kierán Suckling, "it is not environmentalists who are naïve about wilderness; it is Kareiva et al. who are naïve about environmentalists." "Environmental groups have little interest in the 'wilderness ideal,'" Suckling continues, "because it has no legal, political or biological relevance when it comes to creating or managing wilderness areas. They simply want to bring the greatest protections possible to the lands which have been the least degraded."[75]

But while they disagree on the definition of nature, the two camps share a dualistic understanding of the relationship between humans and nature. Kareiva and Marvier state, for example, "*Conservation* as Soulé framed it was all about protecting biodiversity because species have inherent value. . . . We argue that nature also merits conservation for very practical and more self-centered reasons concerning what nature and healthy ecosystems provide to humanity."[76] In other words, "instead of pursuing the protection of biodiversity for biodiversity's sake, a new conservation should seek to enhance those natural systems that benefit the widest number of people, especially the poor."[77]

If the Kareiva camp positions itself on the side of nature for the sake of humans, the Soulé camp provides a mirror image in its insistence that conservation must be performed only for nature's sake. The anti-Anthropocene camp asks, accordingly, "If the mission of conservation becomes first and foremost the promotion of human welfare, who will work for the protection and restoration of the rest of nature[?]"[78] Michael Soulé reflects in our interview: "If you see human beings as the major instrument in destroying most of the world's biodiversity—which they are—then it's easy to say that we're not part of nature."[79] Within the rhetoric of both camps, then, there is little recognition of the co-production of nature and human.

Although they remain committed to the nature-human dualism, the two camps differ substantially on the role of capitalism in this dualism. "Instead of scolding capitalism," Kareiva and his colleagues write, "conservationists should partner with corporations in a science-based effort to integrate the value of nature's benefits into their operations and cultures."[80] By contrast, the Soulé camp cautions that such collaborations would amount to "selling nature down the river."[81] According to Soulé, the NCS promises a shining neoliberal future of economic growth, not conservation, in partnership with "institutional allies and supporters of the new environmentalism."[82]

Indeed, much of the criticism directed toward Kareiva's "green neoliberalism" has focused on its economic underpinnings and its reliance on a definition of nature as resource, which in turn reiterates the very alienation between nature and society (and between nonhumans and humans) that many neoliberal frameworks are founded upon.[83] Specifically, opponents of green neoliberalism argue that while this viewpoint insists on pristine nature as one of its prime imaginings and "selling points," its simultaneous debunking of such nature in fact enables the globalization, commodification, and abstraction of its projects. Kierán Suckling further criticizes green neoliberalism's capitalist underpinnings: "We [now] approach an Anthropocene endgame where there is no more extra nature. The frontier is closed. Henceforth every acre preserved or taken back for wildlife is an acre out of Capital's hide. Thus Capital must destroy the very concept of nature and the independence of plants and animals. These will live only where and to the extent [that] those in power (for now) let them." At the same time, Suckling opposes the use of the term "Anthropocene" because, in his words, "the depoliticized discourse of the Anthropocene buries all these issues."[84]

In his 2014 article "The Capitalocene," sociologist Jason Moore similarly criticizes the current state of environmental thought.[85] Instead of the term "Anthropocene," which, in his words, "does not challenge the naturalized inequalities, alienation, and violence inscribed in modernity's strategic relations of power, production, and nature," Moore argues that the term "Capitalocene" better emphasizes the effects of industrial capitalism. Environmental thought, he argues, pays lip service to the idea that humans are part of an ecological web, while simultaneously treating human thought and culture as something separate, unique, and self-contained. "Holism in philosophy, dualism in practice," Moore observes.

What I have found, by contrast, is that conservation biologists are often dualistic in their philosophy and holistic in their practice. Suckling explains this phenomenon:

> Because they lack a language to describe it and, frankly, an interest in describing it, endangered species managers are often accused of having a naive dualist understanding of nature/culture. Their praxis, however, indicates a sophisticated bricolage approach to the world, where whatever can best save species now is adopted, whether that means a very hands-off approach for wilderness-spectrum creatures like the wolverine, restoring evolved habitat condition on a landscape level for rural-spectrum species like the Mexican spotted owl, creating cement-lined outdoor ponds for a deeply human dependent species like the tui chub, or maintaining tree snails in university laboratories because there is no safe habitat (now) to put them into, for the most human dependent species.[86]

Yet alongside his recognition of both the complexity and the diversity of conservation practices, Suckling himself slips back into dualism when talking about *in situ* and *ex situ* conservation. "The captive breeding facility is the hyper image of the Anthropocene," he tells me succinctly,[87] equating *ex situ* conservation with the Anthropocene camp and thus rendering it dangerous.

Despite their recognition that wilderness in its pure (namely, human-free) form does not exist, Suckling and many other conservationists I have interviewed are still unwilling to let go of the term "nature" as a placeholder for a stable principle upon which conservation decisions can be based. But while they cling to the ideal of the wild as the ultimate other, these same conservationists operate in a way that recognizes that nature is increasingly dependent on human management and that, for a growing number of cases, self-sustainability is not realistic in the foreseeable future.

Conclusion

The dividing line within postmodernism between those who emphasize "the end of man" and those who emphasize the "end of nature" is drawn with an animal claw.

—Kierán Suckling, Director, Center for Biological Diversity[88]

Birds on the Edge is a captive breeding project of the Durrell Wildlife Conservation Trust in the United Kingdom. Its mission is to restore the native bird species of Jersey and the Channel Islands that are listed by the IUCN as Extinct in the Wild. The Jersey red-billed chough (*Pyrrhocorax pyrrhocorax*) is one such species. A large black bird with a bright red curved beak, the Jersey chough survived alongside humans on the isle of Jersey, eating insect larvae that she could reach through the short, cropped grass at the cliffs. "We used to have sheep farming right up to the edge of [the] cliffs," says Elizabeth Corry, senior birdkeeper at Durrell.[89] "And with the sheep around, [the cliffs] would be grazed." When Jersey's agricultural focus shifted to potatoes and cows, Corry continues, the *lack* of human management of the landscape caused the chough's habitat to deteriorate. The last wild Jersey chough was sighted in Jersey in 1929 by an egg collector, who later took the last chough eggs from Jersey.

The goal of Birds on the Edge has been to reintroduce the chough and other species to Jersey through intense landscape management. The choughs who are currently at Durrell were transferred from Cornwall's Paradise Park in the United Kingdom.[90] They are temporarily held in an *ex situ* breeding program until their *in situ* habitat is restored and they can be reintroduced into their re-managed habitat, Elizabeth Corry says. This story is but one example of the many stories that illustrate the trouble with the nature-culture divide and the unpredictable codependencies between *in situ* and *ex situ* conservation.

I began this chapter with the question raised by Kent Redford and his colleagues: why does the conservation community insist on dichotomizing conservation as either *in situ* or *ex situ*? Drawing on numerous interviews that reflect on the relationship between *in situ* and *ex situ* conservation, the chapter has then explored *how* the conservation community has been reproducing this divide on the regulatory, institutional, financial, professional, and personal scales. What has emerged from this mosaic of perspectives is that the *in situ–ex situ* divide is still very much alive, and that to understand its limitations and possibly move beyond it, we must recognize and understand the ways in which personal, professional, financial, and administrative convictions perpetuate it.

Northern White and Sumatran Rhinos

All the money we spent on protecting the northern white rhino, millions and millions of dollars,[1] and at the end of the day, twenty years from now, you could put southern white rhinos in there and you would never notice the difference.
—John Lukas, President, International Rhino Foundation[2]

They look completely different: their horns look different, their heads look very different.
—Susie Ellis, Executive Director, International Rhino Foundation[3]

Initially, it was difficult to find conservationists who would tell me the story of the northern white rhinoceros.[4] Those who ended up sharing this and the Sumatran rhinoceros stories with me did so because they believed that there were important lessons to be learned from their tragic outcomes. I will start with the story of the northern white rhino and then move to discuss the Sumatran rhino.

In 1997, the fate of the northern white rhinoceros (*Ceratotherium simum cottoni*) was decided behind closed doors. In a conference room in San Diego, California, the IUCN African Rhino Specialist Group convened an emergency workshop for rhino specialists and zoo professionals from around the world to plan a last-ditch effort to save the rhino. At that time, there were only thirty animals of this subspecies left in the wild.

Figure 5: Kes Smith, Pete Morkel, and team immobilizing a northern white rhino and inserting a transmitter into his horn to "improve the rhino's security" (Smith, e-mail communication). Garamba National Park, the Democratic Republic of the Congo, 1995. Courtesy of Kes Smith.

John Lukas, president of the International Rhino Foundation, was then also director of White Oak Conservation Center, a large breeding facility for zoo animals. Having worked with rhinos for decades, he knew just how precarious their situation was, and how little time remained to save them from extinction.

For Lukas and others who have dedicated their careers to the conservation of rhinos, these animals have a rare appeal. "Rhinos have an ancient, eternal beauty," write rhino conservationists Lawrence Anthony and Graham Spence.[5] "With their massive bodies, clad in thick folds of prehistoric body armour topped by a magnificent scimitar horn, they fascinate like few other creatures." Once found across large parts of Africa, populations of northern white rhinos have been decimated for their horns, which are used for traditional medicines in Vietnam and China. "On the streets of China or Vietnam," Anthony and Spence explain, "the horn is more valuable than gold." "Do what a poacher does and look at a rhino and see a three-foot-long horn made of pure gold. Game rangers are in the unenviable and extremely hazardous position of trying to protect solid gold."[6] Despite the numerous guards assigned to protect the rhinos, poaching continued. When the experts convened in 1997, the surviving wild northern white rhinos resided in the Democratic Republic of Congo, a country with a track record of instability and the real possibility of, as Lukas puts it, "imploding multiple times."[7]

At the San Diego workshop, the experts agreed that it was imperative to establish a solid "insurance population" of captive-bred animals in case the wild population should go extinct. "The wild ones were the flagship of a much broader conservation effort for a valuable National Park and World Heritage Site and many other species," rhino expert Kes Smith tells me.[8] "However," she continues, "it was recognized that while wild conservation was [the] first priority, in a potentially unstable region it was important as a second priority to develop a backup population elsewhere, from both captive and wild."[9]

At the time, there were nine captive rhinos, divided between the San Diego Zoo Safari Park and the Dvůr Králové Zoo in the Czech Republic.[10] Neither of the captive groups was breeding within itself, but together, the rhino specialists hoped, they could become the core of a captive breeding program. Toward the end of the workshop, representatives from the two zoos and wildlife managers from Kenya met privately to discuss the details of this consolidation. When they finally emerged, they announced that the plan had fallen through. Lukas recounts: "I don't know what the issue was, and I never did find out. But they were against moving their animals for whatever reason, and . . . without everybody doing it, it wasn't going to happen."[11] Kes Smith explains that "[some] wanted the backup group to be in Africa, [but] the zoo people felt [that] their rhinos were too old and too used to captivity to go to a backup group in Africa. That was the impasse."[12]

This was only one in a series of unfortunate human decisions that have led to the near extinction of the northern white rhino. In 2005, almost ten years after the failed attempt to consolidate all captive rhinos into one space, rhino experts negotiated a controversial plan to take most of the wild rhinos from their war-torn region into a safe reserve in Kenya.[13] Lukas describes this reserve, Ol Pejeta, as "a rhino sanctuary and one of the largest managed ranches in Kenya. In the center is a fenced rhino sanctuary where some work had been done with black rhinos and it was very heavily protected. They have a chimp sanctuary there, there's lots of tourism, so it's a very safe ranch and we felt that it could be protected there."[14] The rhinos in the sanctuary each had a personal armed guard to prevent poaching.[15]

Still, the decision to move the rhinos to Ol Pejeta was not easy, mostly because conservationists viewed this sanctuary as a captive facility. *Ex situ* is not the first choice for wild animals, Lukas tells me. "The real depth of conservation is the animals which you're trying to conserve living in nature, . . . which means you need a functioning ecosystem. . . . Really, the conservation of a species only happens in the wild."[16] Yet with an unstable and declining wild population, the decision was finally made to take all the wild animals into captivity in order to preserve their future possibilities for reintroduction. In Lukas's words,

> The main thing we do in this business is try to preserve options for the future. . . . If the [purpose] of the captive population is to restore the population in the wild, eventually—that's a good purpose. So we worked hard on that. We got approval, everything was a 'go.' But all of a sudden, it got very political. It reached the media. . . . It was implied that everybody was going to make lots of money off these animals. African countries always feel, and with good reason, that people are taking their resources and making money off of them and they get nothing.[17]

As a result, the Congolese government backed out of the deal, and the last wild rhinos remained in Congo, declining to four animals in Garamba National Park in 2007. These animals have not been sighted since, save one uncon-

firmed sighting in 2012.[18] Hence, although the northern white rhinos are classified by the IUCN as Critically Endangered, they are, in the opinion of many
rhino specialists, actually Extinct in the Wild.[19] Smith says in response, "I do
not agree with classifying northern whites [as] Extinct in the Wild, though I
agree they are certainly very close to it. . . . There are reports of them in the
wooded reserves around Garamba and still reports from Sudan."[20]

The northern white rhinos have not fared well in captivity, either. In San
Diego, Nola and Angalifu are both too old to reproduce,[21] and the Dvůr
Králové Zoo holds only one remaining rhino, after transferring its other
rhinos to Kenya's Ol Pejeta Conservancy. In 2013, there were four northern
white rhinos in Kenya. "Its extinction is at this point considered inevitable,"
writes Elizabeth Kolbert in *National Geographic*.[22] "It was left too long," laments Susie Ellis of the International Rhino Foundation. "But they're living out a very nice existence, and most of us can live with that," she says.[23]
Ellis's statement conveys the tensions between life on the individual scale,
which is lived "nicely," and life on the scale of the species, which is rapidly
proceeding toward extinction, or is being "lived out," in her words. On the
brink of extinction, the death of the individual becomes synonymous with
the death of the species and gains immense significance as such. For this
reason, the IUCN Red List of Threatened Species has been circumspect in
its pronouncement of the "living out" phase: "Based on Vortex modeling,
in the absence of finding any additional rhino in the wild, this subspecies is
highly unlikely to be viable in the longer term."[24]

Still, two last-ditch survival efforts are being explored: hybridization and
cryogenics. According to the IUCN, "it appears that the best that can currently be hoped for is to conserve as many adaptive Northern White Rhino
genes as possible for eventual reintroduction back to the wild, but this will
require inter-crossing with [the] Southern White Rhino."[25] The two are
closely related, having split from each other only some 20,000 years ago,
which is considered quite recent in evolutionary terms. Scientists have thus
been debating whether the two rhino taxa should be classified as distinct
species or as two subspecies. This seemingly nitpicky classification debate
between "lumpers" and "splitters" is of crucial importance to the survival of
the northern white rhino: if classified as a subspecies, the hybridization
of this taxon would be justified in the eyes of many scientists.[26]

Cryogenics is the rhino's second "last hope, suspended in a frozen cloud,"
Kolbert writes.[27] "When they're gone, all we will have left is their cell lines,

which hopefully we have collected," Ellis tells me.[28] According to Ellis, although the Dvůr Králové Zoo has not been "too keen" on artificial reproduction, "some reproductive materials and cell lines have nonetheless been collected for future work."[29] "We messed this up with the northern white rhino and it can never happen again," Ellis concludes passionately. "We have to take the lessons, as painful as they are, forward, as we deal with other critically endangered species like the Javan rhino, where there are only forty-four animals left—maybe—and the Sumatran rhino, where there are only about one hundred animals left. We just can't let this happen again."[30]

Yet history has a tendency to repeat itself, and this is no less true in the human-rhino context. On the other side of the world from their African kin, the Sumatran rhinos (*Dicerorhinus sumatrensis*) face a situation that is just as precarious. The precise number of Sumatran rhinos who exist in the wild is contested, partly because each conservation organization has its own method for estimating their population numbers.[31] In 2013, the organizations reached a fragile consensus that one hundred Sumatran rhinos remain in the wild.[32] "The general policy is that we have to save whatever we have," says Widodo Ramono, executive director of Yayasan Badak Indonesia (YABI), the Rhino Foundation of Indonesia, which has been overseeing the protection of rhinos in Indonesia for three decades.[33] In 1984, a plan was made to capture some of the remaining wild Sumatran rhinos for a captive breeding program.

Malaysia initially agreed to send a number of its rhinos to the United States for this purpose, but pulled back at the last moment. "It became an issue of national pride," says Terri Roth, director of the Center for Conservation and Research of Endangered Wildlife at the Cincinnati Zoo & Botanical Garden. "Malaysia basically decided it was not going to send any rhinos out of the country, that they were going to do it all themselves in their own country."[34] In 2003, a disease struck the sole captive breeding facility in Peninsular Malaysia, resulting in the death of all the rhinos in that facility within three weeks. "The worst-case scenario happened and all the rhinos were lost," Roth recounts. "Meanwhile," she tells me, "we also realized that their wild population was gone. They'd all been poached. It was really, really devastating."[35] At the time, Malaysia still claimed a small population of about thirty wild rhinos, but by 2013 most scientists believed that fewer than five remained. As a result, the only viable wild Sumatran rhino populations are in Indonesia.[36]

In 1985, a Rhino Trust Agreement was signed between several American zoos and the Wildlife Department of Indonesia. On the basis of this agreement, Indonesia sent approximately forty wild rhinos to zoos for captive breeding. Ramono explains, "It was a good move, because we understood that the situation of the rhino is really grim."[37] Seven of the rhinos were transferred to three zoos in the United States, while others were sent to management facilities in the United Kingdom, Indonesia, and Malaysia. In Indonesia, the remaining captive rhinos are held in a rhino sanctuary. "I know people like to call them something else, . . . they don't want to call them zoos," says Roth about rhino sanctuaries. "[But] really, the main difference is just that the rhinos are not on exhibit. Otherwise, they're maintained very similarly to how they're maintained in zoos."[38]

Ramono recalls just how difficult the decision to transfer the wild rhinos into captivity was for the Indonesian government. "It was difficult to make people understand that *ex situ* is also very important in support of *in situ* conservation," he says.[39] With a 90 percent decline in the wild population, however, wildlife managers were willing to consider *ex situ* management. Nonetheless, there was much resistance, Ramono says. Terri Roth tells a similar story. "The word was, basically, that the Sumatran rhino would never reproduce in zoos, that if you didn't get them out of zoos and back into the natural forested habitat they would never reproduce," she says.[40]

Shortly after the rhinos' transfer into captivity, the three American zoos decided to consolidate them with Roth at the Cincinnati Zoo. For the two preceding decades, Roth had been dedicated to finding a way to breed Sumatran rhinos in captivity. Previously, all of her attempts had failed. But with all the rhinos in one place, she was able to discover that female rhinos have a very narrow estrus window and that if this window is missed, the female will not be receptive. In 2001, Andalas—the first Sumatran rhino ever to be born in captivity—was born in Cincinnati.[41] Andalas was sent to Indonesia, where he sired another calf, Andatu. Andalas' mother, Emi, also gave birth to two additional calves—Suci, who remained in Cincinnati, and Harapan (seen in Figure 6), who resides at the Los Angeles Zoo. Emi died in 2009. Terri Roth mourns her death: "No animal at the Zoo was more beloved than this amazing rhino who contributed more to saving her species than any other Sumatran rhino in the world."[42]

"The animals are not yet saved," Roth says, "but we now know how to breed them."[43] This partial success, according to Roth, is an example of

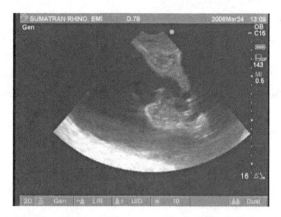

Figure 6: Ultrasound of female rhino Emi at seventy-eight days of gestation, Cincinnati Zoo & Botanical Garden. Terri Roth monitored Emi to ensure that her pregnancy was progressing properly. Roth says: "The [rhino] fetus is very small but you can see his entire outline as he is [lying] on his back in the amniotic fluid. By this stage, one can see limb movement (they are very active) and the heart beating, which assure us that all is well" (e-mail communication). The calf, Harapan, was born at the zoo in 2007. Courtesy of Terri Roth, Cincinnati Zoo & Botanical Garden.

"why these collaborations are so important." Nonetheless, she laments, "it just hasn't really swayed what people are going to do from here forward."[44] For the time being, Roth tells me, most of the efforts are focused on keeping the wild animals in their range and protecting them in the field.

With human encroachment continuing to occur on the edges of Indonesia's national parks, however, the government has been considering designating some of these areas as "intensive management zones."[45] "It's a portion of the forest where you really draw a hard line in the sand and you say, 'This is the pristine area, we're going to really patrol this area, we're going to really maintain this area, there will be no encroachment, there will be no roads. And maybe what we will end up with is a small but viable population of rhinos that are actually safe,'" Roth explains.[46] Debates about this form of semi-wild management are still ongoing, demonstrating just how fraught, and also how important, the negotiations of *in situ* and *ex situ* conservation are in the everyday management of species on the brink of extinction.

Reflections on what went wrong with rhino conservation are also still ongoing. "There are several reasons why Sumatran rhino conservation hasn't been successful," Karen Dixon of SOS Rhino tells me. "One of them is that for thirty years, Western groups came in and said, 'Here's a plan!' [But] the Malaysians weren't in the room. . . . So nothing happened."[47] Bob Lacy, CBSG chairperson at the time, reflects back on the northern white rhino experience. This is a perfect example, he tells me, of how the failure of *in situ* and *ex situ* agencies to collaborate can lead to the extinction of species or subspecies. "It was an absolute stalemate among the different organizations," he says in the context of the northern white rhino. "And that led to the extinction of the subspecies."[48]

CHAPTER 2

Captive Life

I think it was William Douglas who said, "I don't know what the definition of pornography is, but I know it when I see it." And captivity is pretty easy to see.
—Dan Ashe, Director, USFWS[1]

In February 2014, two-year-old giraffe "Marius" was culled at the Copenhagen Zoo. The act of culling Marius, his subsequent public dissection, and the feeding of his flesh to the zoo's lions—all triggered dramatic responses around the world. "Rather than Marius being a tragic exception, the killing of animals considered to be surplus to requirements by zoos is something which is common in the industry," Liz Tyson, director of the Captive Animals' Protection Society—a United Kingdom–based animal rights organization—was recorded saying.[2] Tyson continued: "It has long been recognized that conservation success is achieved not in city centre zoos or safari parks, but in natural habitats. We would urge anyone with a passion for conservation to support effective in situ efforts which are truly making a positive impact on species conservation."[3]

Needless to say, European zoo officials saw things rather differently. According to the European Association of Zoos and Aquariums (EAZA), in 2008 the regional Antelope and Giraffe Taxon Advisory Group (TAG) held 754 giraffes, managed in seven separate breeding groups called

European Endangered species Programmes, or EEPs—one for each of the six subspecies and one for hybrids and unknowns.[4] Bengt Holst, scientific director at the Copenhagen Zoo, explained that the giraffe EEPs aim at "ensuring a healthy giraffe population in European zoos." "As [Marius's] genes are well represented in the breeding programme," he told the press, "and as there is no place for the giraffe in the Zoo's giraffe herd[,] the European Breeding Programme for Giraffes has agreed that Copenhagen Zoo euthanize the giraffe."[5] Although it triggered a host of death threats toward Holst and his family, Holst's statement expresses a view widely accepted by zoo professionals: that zoos must constantly balance between the welfare of individual animals and the future sustainability of their populations. While perceived as cruel by animal rights proponents, such a focus on populations is in fact the underlying assumption of all conservation plans, in zoos and elsewhere.

Marius's death sheds light on other issues, too: the debate between controlled breeding through contraception, as is the common practice in North American zoos, and "breed and cull" practices (whereby zoo animals are allowed to reproduce as part of their welfare, and the surplus animals are later culled), which are becoming increasingly common in northern Europe; the deeply divergent perspectives on captivity held by zoos and animal welfare and rights activists; and varying assumptions about nature in different cultures. I discussed many of these issues in *Zooland*,[6] and others have been covered by the press following the culling at the Copenhagen Zoo.[7] This chapter will propose a slightly different perspective on the Marius affair: I will try to craft a nuanced understanding of the complex and changing role of zoos as *ex situ* conservation institutions, offering a perspective from the conservation world that challenges Tyson's assertion that there cannot and should not be an *ex situ* side to conservation.

In *Zooland*, I argued that the zoo is the quintessential institution of nonhuman captivity.[8] *Wild Life* expands on the dual role of zoos as both institutions of captivity and institutions of conservation. In this chapter, I will examine the zoo as the primary *ex situ* conservation institution, situating it within the evolving landscape of contemporary conservation. I will highlight, in particular, the dilemmas that conservationists confront when deciding if and when to transfer animals into captivity, and the different approaches to this issue among conservationists, animal rights activists, and animal welfare proponents. Finally, I will discuss those cases in which the only remaining members of a species are captive-for-life. In these cases, the captive facility becomes the only viable habitat for that species. Such situations not only question the traditional *in situ–ex situ* distinction and the priority of *in situ* over *ex situ* conservation, but also reveal the changing nature of *ex situ* itself, highlighting the unstable values we assign to life, "in" or "out" of context.

On Naturalia *and* Artificialia

Zoos have been around for centuries. The earliest zoos date back to the dynastic kingdoms of Nebuchadnezzar of Babylon and Wen Wang of China. In the seventeenth century, these menageries of exotica were beginning to emerge alongside museums as scientific institutions that focused on ordering nature.[9] The history of zoos is thus deeply entangled with that of museums and other early natural history collections. The control of nature and the religiously motivated quest to understand God's creation were the goals of early collection practices and the driving force behind the ordering and cataloguing of artifacts and living things.[10] Collectors of the sixteenth and seventeenth centuries in particular devised strategies for systematically categorizing the objects in their possession.

But although the collected objects were recorded and displayed in an organized manner, the criteria for their organization were usually subjective. One collector, John Tradescant, employed "an organizational principle based on a classificatory system which differentiated between the wonders of nature, or *naturalia*, on the one hand, and the works of man, or *artificialia*, on the other."[11] This type of division was common in the seventeenth century's collections of curiosities. However, Tradescant's collection was unique in that "objects placed into the first category, that of *naturalia*, were further classified into subcategories consisting of the three primary orders of nature (animal, plant, and mineral), as then defined."[12] Objects placed into the category of *artificialia* were also placed into subcategories. As curator David Berry notes, "Within the encyclopedic context, all forms of data held equal weight when considered as parts of the whole of knowledge."[13] Little priority was attached to one form of evidence over another, whether natural or artificial.

In *Possessing Nature*, history of science scholar Paula Findlen argues that collecting in the sixteenth and seventeenth centuries was a way of "maintaining some degree of control over the natural world and taking its measure."[14] According to Findlen, these two activities, collecting and interpreting nature, met in the museum. "Possessing nature was part of a more widespread delight in collecting objects of scientific worth. . . . Along with art, antiquities, and exotica, nature was deemed a desirable object to own."[15] The museum collection thus "enhanced the Aristotelian definition of knowledge as a product of sensory engagement with nature."[16]

In *Zooland*, I pointed to the strong connections between zoos and natural history museums and suggested that these institutions share not only major goals and missions but also an administrative culture.[17] Both zoos and museums manage what they both refer to as "collections" and "exhibits" through regimes of classification, routinely administered by keepers, curators, and registrars.[18] In menageries, the predecessors of modern zoological gardens, living animals replaced the dead *naturalia* of early museum displays. Museums didn't have to feed their paintings, but animals in zoos required intense maintenance that involved husbandry practices. Later on, this extra attention to the zoo's *naturalia* evolved into breeding plans and care manuals, which are typically unnecessary in museum contexts. Judith Block, registrar emeritus of the Smithsonian's National Zoo and one of the first registrars in the United States,[19] shares her historical perspective on the zoo-museum link:

> You can compare [living collections] to a museum collection in that a painting needs the right humidity, security, and protection from light, stuff like that. The same with a live animal: you have to make sure that it's . . . safe and has the right temperature and humidity. . . . A wildebeest [is not] so unique that it's irreplaceable in the same way that a Rembrandt [painting] would be. This wildebeest is one of a species and has characteristics that will be useful for the population, but it's one of many [and thus] not so special.[20]

Zoo expert William Conway makes a similar comparison, but ends up elsewhere. In his words: "Why, for heaven's sake, should we preserve fifteenth-century Dutch paintings? Who cares?" His response: "They are pretty to look at; well, so are animals. [But the animals] are very much more than that. You are going to preserve [them] because people have a sense of wanting to preserve something outside of themselves; [because] ultimately, wild animals are the most exciting, the most diverse, the most fascinating, the most beautiful expression of life."[21] Although relevant here for its comparison between zoo and museum collections, Conway's statement is rooted in a later stage of zoo evolution, which I will discuss in the next section. In the earlier menagerie stage of zoo development, the animal's domination by humans was not only visible; it was essential.[22] The design of this exhibit thus included visibly human artifacts and, most prominently, bars and cages.[23]

Zoos as Ex Situ *Conservation Institutions*

The involvement of zoos in conservation is a fairly new phenomenon that began post–World War II, with the inception of the World Association of Zoos and Aquariums (WAZA) and alongside the establishment of the IUCN.[24] More pronounced links between zoos and conservation began in the 1970s and accelerated with the establishment of the EEPs in Europe and the parallel North American Species Survival Plan (SSP) programs of the AZA toward the end of the 1970s.[25]

Under the zoo's new mission of nature conservation, the living animal has become an important component in a broader and more sophisticated exhibit of nature. To facilitate this outlook, immersion design has become the most advanced exhibit style: designed to immerse the zoogoer in what is presented as the natural habitat of the displayed animal, immersion includes an array of sounds and sights from the perceived wild and an obscuration of any human elements that might taint the view of the natural.[26] At the zoo exhibit, nature is made visible, while culture is erased. The *in situ–ex situ* divide, as well as the preference of conservationists toward *in situ*, is thus already embedded within *ex situ*'s desire to become *in situ*.

More than ever before, then, the existence of the modern zoo has come to depend on an idealization of nature.[27] In its self-proclaimed role as a conservation institution, the zoo's survival has come to rely on the continued identity of the animal as wild, exotic, and other.[28] Without such a wild, free, and timeless nature, the very notion of captivity is shattered. If every *situ* (including nature) was but another form of captivity, why would zoos bother exhibiting nature in the first place? And why would 700 million people from around the world flock to visit zoos each year? As I discussed at length in *Zooland*, the perception of nature advanced by the zoo is one of an Edenic, untouched (by humans), and most importantly, *wild* nature— the ultimate other of the zoo's captivity.[29] Similarly, without the city and its mode of captivity, pristine nature or wilderness, as the very opposite of captivity, could not exist.

The modern institution of nonhuman captivity (the zoo) has thus evolved hand in hand with the modern institution of nature (wilderness) and alongside conservation administrations that effectively manage this productive schism. The wild animals at the zoo are thus no longer objects of *naturalia* by themselves; rather, they require the construction of a nature "out there," and the existence of body doubles in that nature—the zoo animals' duplicates in the wild, for which they serve as ambassadors—to be considered worth exhibiting and conserving in captivity.

In the 1970s, several legal codes came into effect that limited the power of zoos to take certain wild animals from their habitats. To survive, zoos needed to find a way to produce their own animals. Fortunately, animals reproduce themselves. Nonetheless, the task of orchestrating such reproductions from a genetic standpoint and the scientific and ethical dilemmas involved have proven to be quite challenging.[30]

The zoo's institutional shift to conservation has been more than an imposition of outside legal norms, however. Increasingly, zoo personnel include scientists who have recently completed their doctorates in various *in situ* settings and who are quite passionate about conservation. These applied scientists have been looking for ways to address what they perceive to be the most urgent challenge of conservation: the rapid disappearance of existing ecosystems and wildlife.[31] Many of them have, by now, become well positioned in various zoo administrations to push their institutions toward a stronger focus on conservation. Western zoos have responded to the challenge, producing complex conservation agendas that include education, participation in and management of independent *in situ* projects, fundraising for *in situ* projects, and captive breeding for zoo animal reintroductions. From WAZA's Code of Ethics and Animal Welfare: "Assisting in achieving the conservation and survival of species must be the aim of all members of the [zoo] profession."[32]

Zoos as Educators

Many accredited zoos raise funds for *in situ* projects or send researchers into "the field," but chief among the ways in which zoos claim to contribute to *in situ* conservation is public education. An estimated one in ten of the world's population visits a zoo each year,[33] amounting to 700 million people worldwide.[34] In Europe, it is estimated that "more than 140 million people visit [zoos] each year, equivalent to approximately one in five European citizens."[35] Zoos are thus "well placed to make more people aware of the importance of biodiversity."[36] Accredited zoos argue that once visitors learn to care about the wild animals they encounter in zoos, they will also be inclined to contribute to the conservation of their conspecifics (namely, members of the same species) in the wild.

In the preamble to its 2010 "5-Year Strategic Plan," the AZA, which represents all accredited zoos in North America, states: "Accredited zoos and aquariums are gateways through which millions of people learn about and value the rich diversity of life that is humankind's wildlife heritage."[37] According to EAZA, European zoos empower "European citizens to learn about and contribute to global biodiversity conservation goals."[38] Similarly, the Japanese Association of Zoos and Aquariums (JAZA) notes that "the social objectives of modern zoos and aquariums is [*sic*] to . . . foster the sense of values and environment for feeling, thinking about, and acting on our connection with the life that exists on this earth."[39] Like the AZA, EAZA, and JAZA, the Asociación Latinoamericana de Parques Zoológicos y Acuarios has as one of its main goals to develop "the ability to induce a significant and verifiable impact in [*sic*] the Latin-American environmental issues within its members."[40] Many other zoo associations, such as the African Association of Zoos and Aquariums and Australasia's Zoo and Aquarium Association (ZAA), make similar statements about their goals.[41]

Clearly, contemporary zoos perceive themselves as a "gateway" through which they may educate broad and diverse audiences about the value of nature. To do this, zoos have designed exhibits that enable visitors to intimately encounter the wonders of nature, which the zoos believe will in turn convince their visitors of the importance of nature's conservation. This encounter relies heavily on the visual spectacle of wild animals and their display as body doubles of their conspecifics in the wild. "Unlike other international conservation NGOs, zoos have a physical site that can be visited," write EAZA Executive Director Lesley Dickie and her colleagues. "People don't tend to weep for the process of desertification but they are often inspired to act by the plight of charismatic species."[42]

They also argue that such emotional responses can be harnessed for conservation purposes.

Curiously, the arguments about the importance of conservation education in zoos have rarely been tested through comprehensive studies. However, a 2014 survey of 6,000 visitors to thirty zoos and aquariums in nineteen countries indicated that visitors indeed showed an improved understanding of biodiversity and could identify an individual action that would bolster biodiversity after their visit.[43] Despite this, the study ends with the following conclusion: "Regrettably, increased awareness does not necessarily change behavior. The world's zoo and aquarium communities must also help to drive important behavioral and social changes to assist conservation."[44] Clearly, the educational significance of zoos for conservation is a topic that warrants further attention.

Ex Situ *Breeding*

Although zoos use education to increase support for *in situ* conservation, education by itself is not considered *ex situ* conservation. By contrast, captive breeding is undoubtedly a defining strategy of *ex situ* conservation, and is in fact the quintessential *ex situ* strategy. Because of its capacity to establish a reserve for endangered and even for extinct wild animals, captive breeding creates what is often referred to in the conservation literature as "insurance"[45] or "assurance"[46] populations. The idea is that once the natural ecosystem is back on its feet, or once the population strengthens, members of the insurance population can be reintroduced "back" into the wild. In this context, too, comprehensive statistics were hard to come by.[47]

Again, because modern environmental laws have prohibited the taking of certain animals from the wild (although notably, there remains significant trade in wild invertebrates, fish, certain birds, and a few other taxa), the zoo's *naturalia* must be (re)produced "outside" of nature. To make this possible, a science of small population management that evolved in the context of *in situ* conservation now flourishes in zoos. This science relies on sophisticated algorithms that assess the viability of small animal populations.[48] Such models supplant natural selection with complex calculations of life.[49]

In 1973, Gerald Durrell, founder of what is now the Durrell Wildlife Conservation Trust and the Durrell Wildlife Park, wrote: "In many cases the population of a certain creature has dropped so low that it can no longer hope to survive unaided. . . . If breeding colonies of these can be set up in ideal surroundings, with unlimited food supply, freedom from predators, and their offspring guarded from the moment they are born, then these species can survive."[50] Although captive breeding has evolved considerably since Durrell wrote these words, the principle remains similar. More recently, Christoph Schwitzer has also argued for the increasing relevance of captive breeding, stating that "it is a very important tool, and will become much more important in the future for species conservation planning and species conservation action."[51] Paul Pearce-Kelly of the London Zoo adds: "If [many species] are going to survive—not be conserved, but survive—they're going to need *ex situ* support."[52]

Outside the zoo world, prominent conservationists have similarly expressed their support of captive breeding for conservation. For example, Joshua Ginsberg, senior vice president of the Global Conservation Program in the WCS, believes that "there is a great place in society for good zoos,"[53] offering that *ex situ* breeding allows for the development of "assurance" colonies.[54] Bob Lacy similarly suggests that "*ex situ* populations need to be viewed as an insurance policy. [I] would rather see some of the animals be intensively managed until [things can be fixed] in the wild."[55]

Simon Stuart is chair of IUCN's Species Survival Commission (SSC), a science-based network of more than 8,500 volunteer experts from almost every country of the world.[56] Stuart shares his perspective on the history of the relationship between *in situ* and *ex situ*: "The *in situ* and *ex situ* sides of the world are much closer now than they were twenty years ago. [Whereas] *in situ* is what we want to achieve . . . a lot of the time we have to use *ex situ* in order to get there."[57] The recognition of *ex situ* as a form of conservation is particularly significant when expressed by this prominent officer at the IUCN, an organization with a strong *in situ* focus and a history of ambivalence toward zoos (Chapter 1). In the 1970s, the IUCN established the Conservation Breeding Specialist Group (CBSG), the largest of more than 130 science groups under the purview of the SSC. The explicit aim of CBSG has been to integrate *ex situ* and *in situ* management. I will further discuss CBSG's work in Chapter 6.

Species Survival Plans (SSPs)

In the late 1970s, the North American AZA set up a comprehensive network of animal programs—especially Species Survival Plans (SSPs) and Taxon Advisory Groups (TAGs)—to collectively manage breeding in zoo facilities across the region. It was understood that without frequent, carefully planned contraception and inter-zoo transfers for breeding, managed animal populations would quickly succumb to inbreeding. The initial purpose of these programs was to create a sustainable population of selected species—in and for zoos. For this purpose, zoos established an insular "ecosystem" comprising islands of accredited zoos. I have called this amalgamation of fragmented zoo territories "zooland."[58] In zooland, animal programs serve as control towers for the movement of zoo animals among accredited zoos. In January 2015, the AZA managed 478 such animal programs.[59] Parallel to the North American administration, regional zoo animal programs also came into existence in Europe and Australasia, and in 2013 WAZA managed eleven taxa on a global scale through Global Species Management Plans.[60]

The first SSP program, the Tiger SSP, was developed at the Minnesota Zoo by Ulysses Seal, who was also responsible for initiating a scientific approach to the management of endangered species in captivity, using the tiger as a model.[61] As the first chairperson of CBSG, a position he held from 1979 to 2003, Seal facilitated more than two hundred workshops in over sixty countries, implementing integrative population management approaches to species conservation. In 1974, Seal and Dale Makey established the International Species Information System (ISIS), "an international database to help zoos and aquariums accomplish long-term conservation management goals."[62] Thirty years later, ISIS maintained records for more than two million captive animals from almost 15,000 taxa and 10,000 species.[63] Chapter 6 further discusses the importance of databases such as ISIS for both institutionalizing and bridging the *in situ–ex situ* divide.

Whereas the initial goal of many zoo animal programs was to create sustainable populations within zoos in isolation from animal populations outside the zoo, they were soon reconceived as a modern Noah's ark: sustaining threatened species until they could be reintroduced "back" into nature.[64] Indeed, in the 1980s many zoo officials believed that breeding animals in captivity for eventual reintroduction to the wild would become the central goal of their work in zoos.[65]

Around the same time, conservation biology emerged as a scientific discipline. According to Kent Redford and his colleagues, "conservation biology marked a shift in the management of living collections away from displays only and toward population management designed to sustain genetically diverse, demographically stable, and viable captive populations . . . that were to serve as assurance colonies should wild populations go extinct."[66] Captive breeding by zoos has thus served both as a strategy for creating a sustainable pool of rare animals for exhibit and as a way of producing captive reserves for endangered animals *in situ*. To produce such reserves, the zoo has been managing its animals with an eye toward their conspecifics in the wild, albeit with minimal actual genetic exchange with *in situ* populations.

Increasingly, however, scientists have been questioning the effectiveness of isolated *ex situ* breeding—namely, breeding that is limited to captive populations—for conservation. Some have argued accordingly that "there are far too many endangered species and not nearly enough space to breed them all in captivity and, in many cases, far too little habitat remaining in which to reintroduce them. In addition, reintroduction programs are difficult and expensive, and have been criticized for treating the symptoms of species loss rather than the causes."[67] In light of these criticisms and others, scientists and zoo experts have largely abandoned the ark metaphor,[68] focusing, as they did initially, only on the sustainability of animal populations within zoos.

The reorientation of zoos toward the exclusive sustainability of zoo animal populations is also the explicit goal of AZA's 2010 action plan. This plan, which came into effect in 2012, classifies animal programs into three categories according to their sustainability within North American zoos: green programs, which are demographically sustainable for at least one hundred years; yellow programs, which are potentially sustainable within the same time frame; and red programs, which have fewer than fifty individuals and are categorized as unsustainable. The AZA prioritizes green and yellow programs for collective management and recommends that red programs be phased out or, in the language of certain zoo experts, "bred for extinction."[69] In 2011, accredited North American zoos contained 30 green, 278 yellow, and 240 red programs.[70]

Soon after AZA's action plan was announced, various zoo experts have come to realize that "many of the red coded species are not only underrepresented in zoos (*ex situ*) but are also endangered in the wild (*in situ*)."[71] As a result, some zoo professionals have been criticizing AZA's new priorities for *ex situ* breeding as conflicting with the priorities of *in situ* species conservation, where the most threatened species are typically assigned a higher conservation priority. To what extent AZA's plan will ultimately redefine the breeding focus of zoo animal programs remains to be seen.

As I have shown, animal program models have oscillated between the management of zoo animals in isolation from, and in connection with, the wild. In the most recent turn of events, the re-focus of zoos on the exclusive sustainability of their own animal populations is being questioned. As part of this turn, some voices are now calling for a new era in zoo conservation, one that follows but is distinct from the previous "Noah's ark" and "zooland" phases. In "Achieving True Sustainability of Zoo Populations," population biologist Robert Lacy argues, accordingly, that "zoos were once reliant on harvest from the wild to populate their exhibits; in the past few decades zoos proudly and appropriately shifted away from reliance on continued wild collection to breeding of closed populations; perhaps we need now to move to a third era of thinking about the best way to care for species assurance populations."[72] The era that Lacy proposes involves integrated metapopulation management across the *in situ–ex situ* divide (Chapter 6). But to get there, he acknowledges, one must first bridge the still-polarized views on *in situ* and *ex situ* conservation.

Ex Situ *as Last Resort*

Many conservationists see *ex situ* conservation as a third-best solution—after the preferred no-management-at-all approach and the second-best *in situ* management. Alongside the practical problems with *ex situ* conservation, this hierarchy is also rooted in the commonly held perception by field conservationists that zoos engage in captive breeding for their own institutional interests rather than for the survival of species. As a result, certain field scientists have been wary of including zoos, and *ex situ* breeding practices more generally, in recovery plans.[73] Some have even refused to define *ex situ* practices as conservation, either because they believe that zoo animals cannot perform their ecological functions in *ex situ* settings or because they hold that these animals cannot behave naturally in captive settings. Trevor Sandwith, director of IUCN's Global Protected Areas Programme, expresses such wariness toward *ex situ* when he tells me in an interview:

> The [zoo] animal still looks like a waterbuck but it's no longer one that knows what to do when the lions come around. . . . If you speak to a conservationist and you ask: "What does it take to conserve a species?" . . . their first answer would be: "Well, we've got to understand how that species interacts in a natural ecosystem, what it requires, and how it contributes to the conservation of other species." So the best thing to do would be to manage the environment in which the species occurs rather than [managing] the individual species.[74]

Still, for some species there may be little choice beside *ex situ* conservation. Established in 2007, the Amphibian Ark is a joint effort by three principal partners—WAZA, CBSG, and the Amphibian Ark Alliance—to address the current extinction crisis in amphibian species, whose numbers have already declined globally by one third. Exposed to new diseases such as the chytrid fungus (*Batrachochytrium dendrobatidis*), amphibian species are now crashing in very short order.[75] "Without immediate captive management as a stopgap component of an integrated conservation effort, hundreds of amphibian species could become extinct," reads the Amphibian Ark's website.

The Amphibian Ark's relationship to the *in situ–ex situ* divide is expressed in the following statement from the organization: "Our vision is the world's amphibians safe in nature, and our mission is ensuring the global survival of amphibians, focusing on those that cannot currently be safeguarded in nature."[76] According to the Amphibian Ark's program director, Kevin Zippel, his organization manages species that "are Extinct in the Wild and exist on the planet only for the very fact that they exist in captivity."[77] The idea, in other words, is that select species from the wild that would otherwise go extinct are to be maintained in captivity until their survival can be secured in the wild.[78] Under this approach, conservation in captivity is justified only when conservation in the wild is no longer a valid option—namely, as a measure of last resort.

Alternatively, a small number of interviewees have implied that captive populations are legitimate and even necessary in and of themselves, and not only for supplementing the wild. While working on *Zooland*, I sometimes encountered a claim by zoo experts that captivity can in fact benefit wild animals by saving them from the stress of surviving in the wild. Although such views have not been popular among my zoo interviewees for this project, they nonetheless afford yet another glimpse into the traditional ideological differences between field and zoo experts.

Somewhat more typical among zoo conservationists is the position that while the animals are not better off in captivity, there is no problem keeping them there, from the animal's viewpoint at least. This position can be traced back to the influential work of Heini Hediger, widely considered the father of zoo biology, in the 1950s. Peter Dollinger, director emeritus of WAZA, is clearly influenced by Hediger's approach when he tells me that "the idea of freedom is a human idea. Animals have their needs, and they must [be satisfied] both *in situ* and at the zoo. So if a zoo enclosure provides all [of the] elements they need, that is okay for them."[79] This approach is very much in line with Hediger's statement that "the goal of conserving threatened wildlife populations could be pursued by a benevolent regime of scientific management within their curiously well-ordered microcosms of nature."[80]

Similarly, WAZA Director Gerald Dick believes that animals don't care if they are managed under *in situ* or *ex situ* conditions. What matters to them, he suggests, is "that they can perform their natural behavior, that they are in a habitat with food, and that they can survive."[81] Zoo designer Monika Fiby speaks, additionally, about human responsibility toward animals that depends not on the naturalness of their habitat but on the degree of freedom they are afforded whenever humans manage their care. "Sometimes in the wild, animals have less and less choices," she says, and hence humans have a higher degree of responsibility. The difference between zoos and the wild, in Fiby's words, is "the degree of our responsibility—how much we are responsible for their welfare. If we need to manage them then we are, to a certain degree, responsible."[82]

If some zoo experts feel that wild animals do not long for the wild when in captivity, others have wondered if *in situ* animals can know that they are being managed although they live in the wild. Norwegian philosopher Morten Tønnessen writes along these lines: "One might be tempted to state that the wolves of Scandinavia are actually no longer wild, but that this, alas, is kept secret from the wolf. For all the wolf knows, it is still a wild animal—and it still behaves like one. But are we justified in claiming that a (more or less) free-ranging wolf is truly wild, simply because it does not know that it is being thoroughly managed?"[83] Underlying these queries are myriad assumptions about the point of view of the animals. But should the definitions of *in situ* and *ex situ* depend on the particular animals' life-world, on their perspective? Surely, snails and toads experience captivity differently than, say, rhinos or wolves. Should we incorporate this perspective into our definition and treatment of *in situ* and *ex situ*, and if so, how?

Extinct in the Wild

According to Kent Redford and his colleagues, "Conservation biology was founded with a focus on the plight of species by a group of scientists that included representatives of the zoo and botanical garden communities."[84] This depiction defines both the goal of species conservation as preventing extinction and the orientation of conservation biology toward crisis management.

The IUCN's Red List of Threatened Species (in short, the Red List) is the epitome of conservation biology's focus on extinction.[85] From the Red List's website: "The introduction in 1994 of a scientifically rigorous approach to determine risks of extinction that is applicable to all species, has become a world standard."[86] The Red List classifies all taxa into nine categories: Extinct, Extinct in the Wild, Critically Endangered, Endangered, Vulnerable, Near Threatened, Least Concern, Data Deficient, and Not Evaluated.[87] Quantitative calculations are increasingly replacing expert knowledge in IUCN's evaluations of the threats to species and their risk of extinction.[88]

The Red List category Extinct in the Wild is especially informative for understanding the relationship between *in situ* and *ex situ* conservation. The Red List defines a taxon as Extinct in the Wild "when it is known only to survive in cultivation, in captivity or as a naturalised population (or populations) well outside the past range."[89] Schwitzer explains that "there is a distinction between Extinct, which is basically gone . . . and Extinct in the Wild, which simply means that all the animals left are in captivity somewhere—whether in a zoo or in a reserve—but not in the wild."[90] In 2014, the Red List assessed thirty-two animal species as Extinct in the Wild.[91] Of these, eleven were *Partula* snails—whom I discussed in the opening paragraphs of this book.

Many species of the *Partula* genus are currently maintained in captivity (Figure 1). "It's not a zoo saving them, not a museum, but it's all of us working together," says Paul Pearce-Kelly, coordinator for the Partulid Global Species Management Programme. "There's no question that if we didn't intervene to the degree we are, there'll be a lot of species lost, even beyond what there already is."[92] Père David's deer is another example from this category. According to the IUCN: "The species became Extinct in the Wild due to habitat loss and hunting. The size of the reintroduced population was only 120 in 1993, although it has increased to over two thousand since that time. . . . The present re-introduced populations are contained within enclosures and are essentially still subject to captive management."[93]

As a result of the amphibian crisis, new species are added to the Extinct in the Wild category by the day. Kevin Zippel tells me that "when the amphibian extinction crisis came to light and we realized how many species were in such dire need, and how relatively few resources they needed to be saved, suddenly the ark metaphor became useful once again."[94] "In cases with truly no alternative to extinction in the wild," writes ecologist Robert Loftin along these lines, "taking the remnant into captivity for the purpose of augmenting the population through captive breeding is justified. The difficulty," he adds, "is to discern when this is and is not the case."[95] In the context of amphibians, conservationists have noted that "the maintenance of assurance populations in captivity may be the only route to survival for hundreds of species of amphibian, until a future point where chytrid [fungus] is, if ever, eradicated from, or controlled in, the environment."[96]

Nevertheless, the decision to take the last specimens of a species on the brink of extinction into captive facilities is controversial and exposes the still prevalent tensions between *in situ* and *ex situ* conservation. Zippel has come up with the following model to deal with some of these tensions, which have also surfaced in his organization:

> The Amphibian Ark [has created] an objective process to evaluate which species needs what kind of help, and uses the expertise of the *in situ* people to determine that. We don't even involve the *ex situ* people in species selection. [We] just have the *in situ* people develop the list: these species need to have assurance populations in captivity, these species need to have head-starting programs, but these ones need to be protected in the field, these ones need research in the field, these ones need mass breeding to counter over-collection. So we've got seven or ten different categories of conservation intervention . . . and then [we] hand them to the *ex situ* folks.[97]

Although the Amphibian Ark is considered a collaboration between *in situ* and *ex situ* scientists, the organizational process that Zippel describes nonetheless grants *in situ* scientists the upper hand in deciding whether and when it is time to move certain species into captivity and how much to intervene in their management. This upper hand, Zippel explains, enables a fragile balance that is intended to recover the trust between *in situ* and *ex situ* amphibian experts.

Bred or Dead? Individuals versus Species

Conservation experts may disagree on *when* the situation has become dire enough to justify the transfer of individual animals from *in situ* to *ex situ* settings, but there is an increasing agreement that captivity can and should serve as the last resort for a species on the brink of extinction. By contrast, animal rights proponents question the validity of privileging the interests of species or populations over what they claim are the rights of individual animals.

The case of the California condor (*Gymnogyps californianus*) demonstrates the difference between the individual- and the species-oriented approaches of rights advocates and conservationists, respectively, and how these differences manifest in decisions about captive breeding. Here is how the condor episode unfolded, from William Conway's perspective:

> I was on the special committee put together by the American Ornithologists' Union and the National Audubon Society some years ago to decide whether it made sense to take condors into captivity. There was a very large and vocal group of critics saying, "No, no, no! *Better dead than bred!!*" Well, we met at length in California and I wrote much of the program, and we said, "We have no choice: if we leave them out there, they will be dead." They said, "Fine." [But] we didn't agree with that [and] when we finally got down to twenty-two birds we took them into captivity.[98]

Initially, the National Audubon Society opposed transferring the condors into captivity. One of its members, ornithologist Rich Stallcup, was recorded saying: "Must we still try to conceal the guilt of condor spoilage? Must we burden and demean the doomed skymasters with electronic trinkets, then imprison them in boxes and demand that they reproduce? Or can we just say, 'Yes, el condor, we blew it long ago, we're sorry. Fly, stay as long as you can, and then die with the dignity that has always been yours.'"[99]

Figure 7: A California condor flies over California's Bitter Creek National Wildlife Refuge, 2003. Every condor is fitted with a radio transmitter and a solar-powered GPS device that sends more than one thousand daily locator points per day, helping monitor and gather scientific data about the bird. Photo by USFWS, Creative Commons-2.0-Generic license.

Stallcup's approach echoes the argument of prominent animal rights theorist Tom Regan that "the general policy regarding wilderness would be precisely what the preservationists want—namely, let it be! . . . Were we to show proper respect for the rights of the individuals who make up the biotic community, would not the community be preserved? And is not that what the more holistic, systems-minded environmentalists want?"[100] Just how deeply alienated the species conservation and animal rights paradigms are from each other can be gleaned from Regan's following statement: "The rights view is a view about the moral rights of individuals. Species are not individuals, and the rights view does not recognize the moral rights of species to anything, including survival."[101] Regan defines the requirement that individual organisms be sacrificed for the whole as "environmental fascism."[102] Underlying this approach is the view that "breeding animals in captivity is in some sense breeding the wild out of the animal,"[103] or that a California condor "is only five percent bone and feathers. Ninety-five percent of condor is place."[104]

In 1986, the National Audubon Society filed a lawsuit against USFWS's decision to transfer the last remaining condors into captivity, claiming that it violated the Endangered Species Act (ESA), the Administrative Procedure Act, and the National Environmental Policy Act. Audubon's preliminary request for an injunction barring the capture of the wild condor was granted, but reversed on appeal. The U.S. Court of Appeals in the District of Columbia held: "We believe that the Wildlife Service's decision to capture the remaining wild condors was manifestly defensible."[105] Over the years, the captive California condor has been reintroduced into the wild, and more than three hundred condors now inhabit large areas of Arizona and California (Figure 7).[106]

Dan Ashe is the director of USFWS, the federal agency responsible for enforcing the ESA in the United States. For Ashe, the condor is the prime example of a successful collaboration between *in situ* and *ex situ*. In his words: "There was a time when there was no ecological context for condors. There were some twenty-two birds remaining in the wild, and we captured them all, and put them all into the captive propagation program. If we had left them in the wild, they would have gone extinct."[107] Instead, he tells me, "with the help of zoos, we learned how to breed them in captivity. And when we began to regain the ecological context for them, then we released them into the wild, and they are, as we speak, expanding their range and number."[108] From Ashe's perspective, the act of *ex situ* conservation is, more than anything else, an act of "preserving the potential."[109]

Kierán Suckling, director of the Center for Biological Diversity, situates the USFWS decision on condors in its broader historical context. "The initial focus of the USFWS on habitat protection to the exclusion of captive breeding was irrational," he tells me.[110] "Indeed, if you want to pursue a historic trajectory from the 1960s to the present, I'd say the [dusky seaside] sparrow and the condor are critically important. The sparrow was the first and only species that went extinct after [an] ESA listing that could have been saved. . . . That experience has dramatically influenced all species management since, and was a major point of discussion regarding the condor. The condor was a very near miss—as close to extinction as you can imagine. That was also a shock with lasting reverberations."[111]

The whooping crane (*Grus americana*) presents a similarly dramatic success story. This American bird plummeted to only sixteen living specimens in 1941, and was listed as threatened in the first version of the ESA in 1967 and as endangered in 1970.[112] Since then, captive breeding programs and successful reintroduction efforts have increased the number of wild birds to more than four hundred, with an additional two hundred or so in six captive facilities.[113] Whooping crane chicks hatched in a facility either remain in captivity to maintain the health and genetic diversity of the captive flock or are reared in experimental reintroduction programs for release into the wild.

The whooping cranes, many of whom were captive-bred, are now flying migratory routes they have not flown for decades.[114] The birds are taught their migration route by first being conditioned to follow costumed pilots in ultralight aircraft. Initial migration experiments using sandhill cranes, completed in fall of 2000, successfully led eleven cranes 1,250 miles from Wisconsin to Florida. The birds wintered in Florida and then migrated back to Wisconsin on their own in the spring. Following this success, the first attempt to lead whooping cranes in their historic migration route was made in 2001. Seven birds made it to Florida and the five that survived returned to central Wisconsin on their own the following spring. An additional sixteen birds were successfully reintroduced into the flyway in 2002.[115]

The debates over the condors' and cranes' transfer into captivity highlight the tensions between the focus of animal rights advocates on the individual animal and the focus of conservationists on populations and species.[116] "How to balance the welfare and rights of individual animals against the value of captive breeding to reintroduction programs and our obligations to sustain populations, species, and ecological communities and processes?"[117] asks environmental scholar Bryan Norton in his edited volume *Ethics on the Ark*. "Do we have any responsibility to try to prevent extinction . . . even if doing so in some way mentally or physically 'harms' individual animals?"[118]

This discussion circles back to the story of Marius at the outset of this chapter, placing Liz Tyson's sweeping comments in the press against *ex situ* conservation in a broader context. In our interview, Tyson, a leading animal rights proponent in the United Kingdom, presents a slightly more nuanced position. She shares that her strategy for deciding on difficult ethical questions pertaining to animals is to ask herself what would be the just solution if humans were in the same situation.[119] Applying this strategy, Tyson draws an analogy between insurance populations for nonhuman species, on the one hand, and human war refugees, on the other:

> You look at a war-torn country, and rather than actually trying to do something to help the people there, you collect a group of people of the same nationality, put them in a safe house, and say, "We've dealt with that problem, [and] once that war has run its course, then we'll put these nice, safe people back." But you haven't saved anything, because you haven't protected the people whose lives are actually in danger.[120]

Although clearly distrusting of captivity, Tyson's statement still regards as ethical the option of taking individual animals into captivity when their lives "are actually in danger."

Whereas animal rights advocates and conservationists often hold polarized views on the extinction-versus-captivity (or dead-versus-bred) debate, animal welfare advocates typically attempt to identify a middle ground between these philosophies. Marc Bekoff, emeritus professor of ecology and evolutionary biology at the University of Colorado, coined the term "compassionate conservation" to describe an international movement that advocates incorporating animal welfare concerns into the work of conservation "for the betterment of both."[121] He argues that "combining considerations of animal welfare and conservation" will lead to "a reduction in harm in the suffering of individual wild animals, and will improve conservation outcomes."[122] "We must be motivated by the universal moral imperative, namely, 'first do no harm,'" he offers.[123]

Drawing on Bekoff's approach, Chris Draper, senior scientific researcher for the Born Free Foundation in the United Kingdom, presents his position on the merits of *ex situ* breeding. While he agrees that individual animals may be taken into captivity, Draper offers a few stipulations, including that these animals are members of species who are on the brink of extinction, that the individual animals are properly cared for, and that they are promptly returned to their places of origin. In his words: "If there is a justification to do something like that, to really take the last individuals in, it should be with the view of getting them the hell out of there as quickly as possible. There's no point catching the last individuals [and putting them] into captivity without doing something to restore their habitat in the wild."[124] Draper explains his position through the polar bear example:

> Let's take a hopefully hypothetical situation where there is no polar ice cap on the planet. What do we do with the polar bears that are in captivity at that point? . . . I will be probably ruthlessly honest here and say that it doesn't matter, because under current management they're not going to breed to sustainable numbers, and they're going to be extinct in captivity anyway. . . . Let's not be distracted by the glitz and glamour of the snazzy captive stuff. For the long run, it's going to be little more than a costly diversion.[125]

Animal welfarist Koen Margodt inserts a slightly different tone into this conversation. "Is it better to vanish in the wild than to lead a rich life in captivity?" she asks. "Would it be more desirable to die free rather than to live in captivity?" "Fortunately, the actual picture is not such a black-and-white one," she concludes.[126] Like Margodt, many conservationists are now thinking beyond the dead-or-bred polarity of the *in situ* versus *ex situ* approaches.

But even when thinking beyond the traditional polarities, the path is still replete with difficult decisions. Conservation biologist Stuart Pimm shares with me one of his concerns with regard to captive-for-life species: "If they only exist in zoos they only exist in zoos, but at least you've kept hope alive. They're still there, you still have the pieces. The question is whether the golden lion tamarin that spent a generation or two in captivity, is it really a golden lion tamarin when you put it back?"[127] In a growing number of cases, this question is becoming theoretical, as the idea of ever "putting back" certain captive species is increasingly unrealistic.

Captive—For Life?

If the remaining members of a species held in captivity no longer have a wild nature to return to, are humans still ethically obliged to save them, or should they refrain from doing so? What happens when animals are "all dressed up but [with] no place to go?"[128] Should humans save species that can exist only in captivity?

The response from the conservation experts I interviewed for this project was uniform: save them first—you never know what the future holds. In the words of Christoph Schwitzer: "There is an inherent value in saving every single species; I just don't want my children to grow up without blue-eyed black lemurs, or even some odd frog species, or a mosquito."[129] Ecologist Robert Loftin writes, similarly, that "it is better to have the species in captivity than not to have it at all."[130] He continues: "Conditions could conceivably change, more habitat might become available, public attitudes might shift, or environmental contamination might decrease. Unlikely as these scenarios are for some animals, at the very least keeping the biological species in existence in some form, even in a cage, keeps some future alternatives open to some extent."[131]

These questions are becoming a matter of concern not only for zoos, but for every conservation organization that engages in captive breeding across the globe. Such organizations are confronted with the problem of what to do when there is little or no hope for reintroducing captive endangered animals into the wild. The captive-for-life animals are not only on the brink of extinction in terms of their low numbers, but are also situated outside of their ecological context in terms of habitat. Both species-less and site-less, captive wild animals who live solely outside of their ecological context are thus reduced to a biological existence as mere life, to a status of living dead.

USFWS Director Dan Ashe reflects on the limited capacities of his agency with regard to captive-for-life species:

> We certainly don't have the resources to keep everything that is being threatened with extinction in captivity. And we're facing that critical issue with the masked bobwhite, with the Atwater's prairie chicken, with native Hawaiian birds like the 'Alalā—where we have been keeping them in captivity for many, many years, and we don't seem to be able to figure out

how to reintroduce them back into the wild with success. At some point in time, we will have to address the reality, and we may have to let go of these species and just say "we've done the best we can do." And if we do, they're either likely to be maintained by a zoo or some other institution, or they'll go extinct.[132]

How will conservation agencies deal with such precarious life,[133] which is becoming a reality for a growing number of species? Ashe responds in a sobering tone: "You let them out, and you hope for the best. And if they can't gain a toehold in the wild and survive, then they go extinct."[134] The only other option, Ashe says, is to euthanize these animals. "I think we're increasingly facing the need to build the capacity to do that. We need the biological capacity, the ethical capacity, and the risk management capacity."[135]

USFWS Assistant Director Bryan Arroyo disagrees. Referring to this as "the God question," Arroyo responds: "As a species, I don't think we have the right to terminate anything. And frankly, this is where the moral character of our country [the United States] comes through. I mean, this country has had a historically continual commitment to ensuring that life is protected."[136] According to Arroyo, then, the protection of life above everything else is not only the proper ethical and religious stance, but also the proper patriotic stance.

Mike Oetker, deputy regional director of USFWS's southeastern region, also takes issue with Ashe's statement, although from a different perspective than Arroyo's. While he agrees with Ashe that the USFWS will need to tackle the "captive-for-life" dilemma very soon, Oetker disagrees with Ashe's proposed solution. "We have spent our careers saving and managing species," he tells me, "and then just to say we're going to let these go? That's a very hard thing for a biologist; it's not a natural thing."[137] Oetker also points out that the ethical debate is broader than one of animals perishing in captivity: "The number of species that we can handle is getting less and less every day," he explains. "And at the same time, some of the fish and wildlife are going in the opposite direction. If you take a fish that we don't already have in the hatchery system, and we don't have the money or the ability . . . to take that fish on—then we have made a de facto decision to let the species go on its own." Oetker clarifies: "By not taking action, we're also deciding." The decision to keep certain species alive ("making live") is therefore inevitably also a decision to not save others—the "letting die" component of conservation's biopolitics.

Is the passive decision not to "take on" a species different from the active decision to send a species that is already "on," "out on a lifeboat," as Ashe suggests? Although they may appear abstract, these questions are very real for many biologists, especially those who manage endangered fish. Oetker tells me that the bonytail chub, along with the Colorado pikeminnow, the razorback sucker, and the humpback chub, used to swim thousands of miles up the Colorado River to spawn. "When the big reservoirs went up, they blocked the fish's migration pattern and the water flows no longer trigger the cues for the fish to spawn," he explains. All four species were listed under the ESA as endangered. "The bonytail chub is functionally extinct in the wild," Oetker says. The only adult fish that are capable of spawning are located at Dexter, a USFWS hatchery in New Mexico dedicated to propagating endangered species. Whereas the bonytail chub proliferates in captive settings and artificial pools, these fish cannot survive in their natural habitat. "They reproduce on their own in our ponds," Oetker tells me. "They proliferate wherever we put them—*except* when we put them in the Colorado River. We don't know why. Why can they do so well in the hatchery system, but not in the wild?"

Still, Oetker has not given up, not even on the bonytail chub. He believes that in order to let go of a species, scientists must first figure out whether the species is so genetically compromised that they can never exist on their own; then scientists must decide whether human action is what has caused the species' current failure to survive in the wild. "Once we can determine that, then we can answer the question of whether or not we may walk away," Oetker says.[138] According to Oetker, then, the management decision whether to let die or make live, in Foucault's terms, hinges on human causation.

As these stories demonstrate, conservation management is an extraordinarily engaged process of keeping species from going extinct. This serves to highlight the affirmative properties of conservation's biopolitical regime. At the same time, as Oetker's narrative so strikingly reveals, walking away from a species is also an affirmative management action. The passive-active binary that lies at the heart of Foucault's "*make* live–*let* die" paradigm is thus, at best, too simple to attest to the complexities of decision-making in the contemporary conservation world. A more subtle way of thinking about agency and action is called for that lends itself more accurately to the nuanced gradations between letting and making and between living and dying.

Conclusion

As traditional zoos become larger and more naturalistic, sanctuaries in the wild are becoming smaller and more artificial.

—Ballou, Gilpin, and Foose, *Population Management for Survival and Recovery*[139]

A satirical article published in *The Onion* in 2014 wittily captures the codependency of nature and zoos and their co-productive entanglements. Posing as a news piece, the article described a progressive zoo in California—the Redding Wildlife Park—that has decided to take the naturalistic exhibit principles, and the importance of maintaining a connection with the *in situ* environment, seriously. "It's not ideal for [wild animals] to be taken out of their natural environments," says the director of this imaginary zoo, "so the least we can do is make them feel as threatened and encroached-upon as possible. Then it'll feel like home."[140] The said director was also quoted saying: "When you see the sallow, hopeless look in their eyes as they spend another fruitless day hunting for food, you know you've done your job. . . . Ensuring each animal is as miserable as it would be in the wild is our ultimate goal." And the satire goes on:

> "When I go to Redding, I'm always motivated to help out by making a donation of a plastic shopping bag or some old batteries that the staff can dump into the animals' food and drinking water," patron Joanna Mills told reporters, saying that she's considered volunteering certain weekends to pitch in with the zoo's simulated oil spills. "And whenever I'm near an outdoor enclosure, I always toss an empty water bottle right at the rhinos or the families of orangutans."[141]

Like every satire, this satire, too, is based on a sad truth. When I forwarded it to a few zoo people, a prominent zoo designer took it seriously and contacted the AZA to protest. Of course, the AZA told him that Redding Wildlife Park was not on their list of accredited zoos. Upon hearing this, the designer got back to me, all worked up. Finding out that the article was a satire, he was relieved: "I've had clients who [asked me to design] zoo exhibits showing habitat destruction . . . and actually had such a client in a zoo senior management team yesterday. So the subject was too close to see the dark humor. I will say the 'satire' was well done."[142]

The satire was indeed well done—not only because it highlights the degrading state of "nature" that can no longer provide for many species, and thus the zoo's intensifying role as their "more natural" home, but also because the zoo's simulacrum of nature sometimes ends up being less natural than the fictional zoo's toxic exhibits. The satire thus shines a powerful light on what Jean Baudrillard has referred to as hyperreality:[143] zoo exhibits are monuments for a nature that is no longer, and perhaps never was, and natural ecosystems are romanticized, perhaps even as a simulacrum of the zoo.[144] "Redding Wildlife Park" thus foregrounds the questions: What is natural, and why should we conserve it?

Golden Lion Tamarin

> This is one of the most successful reintroductions ever. From almost being extinct to being removed from the critical list.
> —Stuart Pimm, Conservation Biologist[1]

In the early 1960s, Brazilian biologist Adelmar Coimbra-Filho discovered a living population of the golden lion tamarin (*Leontopithecus rosalia*), a primate species thought to be nearly extinct in the wild.[2] At that time, Coimbra-Filho estimated Brazil's newly discovered wild population at 600 individuals.[3] But in a cruel twist of fate, it soon seemed that this rediscovery had occurred just in time for conservationists to watch the tamarins die out. By 1972, it was estimated that there were fewer than 200 golden lion tamarins in the wild and fewer than 75 in captivity. Coimbra-Filho issued an urgent call for help. If something was not done, and fast, the golden lion tamarin would become truly extinct.[4]

Having only recently arrived at the National Zoo in Washington, D.C.,

---

Figure 8: An adult male golden lion tamarin carrying triplets born in his group in Silva Jardim, Rio de Janeiro, Brazil. Although twins are the norm for golden lion tamarins, triplets are seen occasionally. The dye mark and radio collar on the adult tamarin indicate that he lives in one of the groups monitored by the Associação Mico-Leão-Dourado (AMLD). Courtesy of Andreia F. Martins.

Devra Kleiman "had a way of getting people to do things that they weren't always sure they were going to do."[5] Together, Kleiman and Coimbra-Filho initiated the push for the captive breeding of golden lion tamarins. In a radical move, they persuaded zoos not only to loan their golden lion tamarins to one another for conservation breeding and to manage all the animals in collaboration, but also to transfer their institutional ownership of the tamarins to the Brazilian government, so that one agency would own all the golden lion tamarins in the world. All the zoos in the Cooperative Research and Management Agreement set up by Kleiman complied, except Monkey Jungle, Inc., a Miami zoo that insisted on private ownership.[6] The single-ownership issue was critical, notes Bengt Holst, director of research and conservation at the Copenhagen Zoo, one of more than a hundred zoos currently participating in the program. "Most animals in zoo animal programs all over the world are owned by zoos," Holst clarifies.[7]

Golden lion tamarins are reddish-gold monkeys, with little gray faces and bodies no longer than an adult human's forearm. The reasons that they have been nearly driven to extinction are their desirability in the exotic pet trade and the destruction and fragmentation of their habitat to less than 2 percent of its original area.[8] When Coimbra-Filho noticed the dramatic decline in the tamarin population, he decided to work the three captive populations—in Brazil, Europe, and North America—into one conservation program. Jennifer Mickelberg of Zoo Atlanta is the current coordinator of the Golden Lion Tamarin Captive Breeding Program—the program that manages the international captive population of golden lion tamarins among zoos. She explains that Coimbra-Filho "started to work in Brazil, and then connected with Devra [Kleiman] and started to work with North America, and they reached out to Europe and started to form collaborations there. And so the regional populations were managed collectively very early in the program, promoting collaborations so [that] the population could increase."[9]

The captive program was housed primarily in North America and in Europe, where "zoos worked together to improve breeding and increase the [tamarin] populations so that animals could eventually be available for reintroduction," Mickelberg says. Until that point, zoos were unsuccessful in breeding tamarins, for unknown reasons. "It was Devra at the National Zoo who figured out the trick to breeding tamarins and changed the direction of the captive program: tamarins needed to be housed in monogamous pairs for breeding and needed protein in their diet."[10]

Recognizing the critical decline in the species' natural habitat, the collaboration also founded the Poço das Antas Biological Reserve, the first biological reserve in Brazil, located in the state of Rio de Janeiro, in 1974.[11] In 1992, the collaboration became the Assoçiacão Mico-Leão-Dourado (AMLD), a Brazilian nonprofit dedicated to the conservation of golden lion tamarins and their habitat. The AMLD has since spearheaded the international collaboration among local landowners, community leaders, various levels of government, Brazilian universities and professional societies, 150 zoos worldwide, and conservation organizations.[12] Conservation efforts, especially reintroductions, have been successful in large part due to the local expertise and presence of the AMLD, says James Dietz, founding director of Save the Golden Lion Tamarin, a U.S.–based organization that provides financial and technical support for AMLD's efforts.[13]

The first thirteen captive tamarins were reintroduced into the Poço das Antas Biological Reserve in 1984,[14] and there were several subsequent reintroductions over the next decade. The initial reintroductions were extremely challenging. First, the captive-bred tamarins had difficulty adjusting to their wild habitat. In a 2002 study of the reintroduced tamarins, Tara Stoinski and her colleagues noted that captive-bred tamarins forage more, use lower substrates when foraging, and fall more frequently than do their wild-bred counterparts.[15] Benjamin Beck's team documented that some of these falls and errors in foraging resulted in the animals' premature death.[16] Unfortunately, there was not much to be done that could have saved those individuals who weren't well equipped to deal with the wild, Mickelberg tells me. "The thing about reintroducing golden lion tamarins," she says, is that "there's this notion that they needed a lot of pre-release training. But it turns out [that] the most important thing for golden lion tamarins is post-release monitoring—really intense monitoring."[17]

Beck and Castro state similarly that although the first tamarins were intensely trained prior to their release—with puzzle boxes to teach them how to forage for food, and a constantly changing built environment to teach them how to survive in their new arboreal habitat—post-release monitoring was what contributed most to the tamarins' continued survival.[18] "If they got lost, they were picked up and brought back to the nest box," explains Mickelberg. "If they had a medical issue, a vet was brought to them. At least initially, they were [provided with] food and a nest box, and slowly weaned off of these things as they started to find their own food and find their own nest sites."[19] She continues: "As reintroduced golden lion tamarins began to eat natural foods and to move through their territories, the feeding/observation visits by the field researchers were progressively reduced from daily to three days a week, then to once a week, and finally to once a month. Provisioning was eventually discontinued except when bait was used to trap animals to replace radio collars and dye marks."[20] By 2014, only three wild tamarin groups were fed by humans, mostly so they could be observed by tourists.[21] The post-release monitoring was especially vital due to the imminent threat of poaching. Indeed, one of the first reintroduced tamarins was killed by a wealthy citizen of Rio in what Beck refers to as a "callous act of vanity" that almost jeopardized the entire tamarin conservation program.[22]

The reintroductions of the captive-bred tamarins into the wild were not only difficult but also incredibly expensive. Each reintroduced golden lion tamarin cost the project an estimated $22,000 for the first six years.[23] Translocation is another, less expensive, conservation strategy that was used extensively in the management of the golden lion tamarins. According to this program's definitions, reintroduced animals are animals moved from captivity into the wild, while translocated animals are those captured from their wild habitat and then transferred to a location from which the species had been extirpated.[24] In 2000, 120 translocated tamarins were dispersed among sixteen groups.[25]

Each of the two transfer strategies—reintroduction and translocation—has its own rationale and emphasis: whereas the reintroductions were carefully planned to provide new genetic stock from the captive population, translocations have been an emergency measure for maintaining genetic variability between isolated wild populations.[26] Differences in growth rates between translocated and reintroduced populations have resulted in differences in post-release monitoring. Except in occasional and rare instances, the reintroductions of captive tamarins have stopped.

Identification and tracking are an essential part of the management of both captive and wild tamarin populations, and data on both populations is collected in studbooks and coordinated by studbook keepers. This is unique, as captive animals in other programs are not usually monitored closely upon their reintroduction into the wild.[27] Female golden lion tamarins typically give birth to twins, who cling to their mothers for a brief period before the male tamarins become their primary caregivers (as shown in Figure 8).[28] Because golden lion tamarins live in monogamous family groups, the studbook keepers "know who the parents are, and those are monitored frequently enough that we can even get birth dates," says Mickelberg. "That has allowed us to construct a pedigree for the reintroduced population, and the same was true for a pretty large component of the wild, the *true* wild population."[29]

Jonathan (Jon) Ballou, a population biologist and the previous studbook keeper for the golden lion tamarin, integrated population modeling into this program. Using Population and Habitat Viability Assessment (PHVA) to simulate the effects of various threats over a certain number of years, Ballou helped the AMLD collaboration establish its main priorities for saving this species from extinction. The first PHVA, facilitated by IUCN's CBSG in 1990, concluded that to save the tamarins from extinction, the population must grow by the year 2025 to 2,000 individuals living on at least 25,000 hectares of protected forests.[30] Since there were seventeen isolated tamarin populations in the wild, "we needed to come up with a strategy for moving animals around so that small populations don't get too inbred, or die out," Ballou says.[31] Ballou also tells me that many of the tools used for the population management of golden tamarins in the fragmented forests, especially Vortex and ZIMS (Chapter 6), were adapted from software used in zoos.[32] The AMLD 2013 Annual Report further describes the similarities between the wild- and captive-based management of tamarins:

> AMLD manages GLTs [golden lion tamarins] in forest fragments in the same way that 150 zoos worldwide manage the 500 GLTs living in captivity. We move GLTs from one fragment to another (translocation) to solve demographic problems and to minimize inbreeding and the loss of genetic diversity. In 2013 AMLD documented the birth of twins to a "native" female and an adult male translocated into Poço das Antas Reserve in 2011. The translocated male was a descendent of zoo-born GLTs reintroduced into empty forest fragments in the 1990's and had never seen a "native" GLT. Planning and documenting these births is evidence of AMLD's ability to manage and monitor small and isolated GLT populations to achieve science-based conservation goals.[33]

Managing multiple distinct populations is not easy, especially when those populations include both captive tamarins reintroduced to the wild and wild tamarins translocated between different areas. This is why, Ballou says, an approach that brings together all the human parties involved in the species' conservation and manages the various animal populations through a meta-population analysis—promoted by CBSG as the One Plan approach—has been so vital to the success of the golden lion tamarin program.[34] "There's one common set of goals, and the role of the *ex situ* population is carefully defined, [and] there's one committee that oversees both the management of the wild and the captive populations," Ballou tells me.[35]

The challenges facing the tamarin program were not limited to breeding tamarins in captivity and training them to survive in the wild; they also included combating the prejudices of fellow conservationists. "Somewhere in the concept of wild populations [is] the idea that these populations are what they were a thousand or two thousand years ago," Ballou tells me. "And part of that [was] the idea that they're undergoing natural selection and they're evolving in this wild environment." Ballou sees things differently, however. From his perspective, "we think about these wild populations [as] kind of becoming mega-zoos. We fence the reserve, and start providing supplemental food, and when that happens, we've clearly stepped over some boundary. But my thoughts are that we've already stepped over a boundary, [and] the boundary is that the populations are too small to be experiencing natural selection anymore." The idea of a wild habitat, he finally remarks, "is kind of a fuzzy thing to define."[36]

Despite the numerous challenges to this program, the golden lion tamarin populations have been so successful that the small Brazilian team of field conservationists has not been able to keep up with their growing numbers and stopped inserting detailed studbook entries for the wild tamarins.[37] "We've had to really step back from a lot of the detailed data we were collecting, and just have a few focus groups that we're looking at and do general censuses every so often," Mickelberg tells me.[38] To meet these challenges, recent collaborations between the AMLD and the Universidade Estadual do Norte Fluminense have devised new census techniques using playbacks of recorded tamarin vocalizations.

In 2003, the golden lion tamarin was downlisted to Endangered on the IUCN Red List of Threatened Species, an improvement from this species' 1996 Critically Endangered status.[39] In 2013, there were an estimated 3,316 golden lion tamarins in the wild: 3,210 in the São João River Basin and 106 in Cabo Frio[40]—a considerable increase from Coimbra-Filho's count of fewer than 200 in 1970. Nearly 40 percent of these tamarins were from reintroduced captive populations and their descendants.[41] "The goal was to get these captive populations to live long enough in the wild to breed," Mickelberg tells me. "And I think that's a good lesson for a lot of reintroduction programs," she says. "There has been so much emphasis on getting those captive-born individuals to survive. But in reality, if they reproduce they've done a good

job and that's, I think, a great expectation for them." Once tamarins reproduce, Mickelberg and others have explained to me, their wild-born offspring
do not experience the same limitations as the captive-born populations.[42]

Currently, the main challenge of the program is to establish corridors
between existing forest fragments through reforestation.[43] These corridors
allow the tamarins to "make the population management decisions on their
own," Bengt Holst from Copenhagen Zoo tells me. The process involves
taking seeds from local forest trees and placing them in small pots "just like
in a nursery." "One by one they nurse them," Holst says, "until they're at a
certain size, and then they find out where exactly to establish this corridor.
Then they go out planting these things [Figure 9], and then of course the
[trees] have to grow, until they've reached a certain size and [are] hopefully
able to give fruit, because that's what actually attracts the tamarins to follow
that route."[44] Finally, the corridors are ready for the tamarins. "The exciting thing," Holst tells me, is to discover "how far they will go, and will they
only go into the mid-part and establish their territory there? This is a very

Figure 9: Local groups planting tree corridors that link golden lion tamarin populations
between fragmented biological reserves. Courtesy of Luis Paulo Ferraz and the AMLD.

long process, and the unique thing is that the tamarins do not need to be trained—they just follow the tree path planted for them. They have to go by themselves, and that's why it takes time."[45]

The golden lion tamarin program is probably the most famous example of integration between *in situ* and *ex situ* conservation management.[46] The program's achievements against all odds, I am told, are mainly the result of the unusual early collaboration between Devra Kleiman from the zoo community and the Brazilian biologist Adelmar Coimbra-Filho.[47] Other invaluable participants have included Benjamin Beck and James Dietz from Save the Golden Lion Tamarin,[48] Jon Ballou and Jennifer Mickelberg, who have provided the population management perspective, and the local Brazilians who have been planting forest corridors, assisting landowners, training local teachers, and monitoring the tamarin populations and their habitats on the ground.[49] "All these people are so dedicated to these animals that they would go out in the mornings to protect them and come home at night just to go to sleep with their own families, over and over again," Holst tells me. "They dedicated their lives to these animals."[50]

CHAPTER 3

Continuous Life

We think of captive breeding facilities as human spaces: we build, manage, and control them; we choose which animals to bring into them, which to mate together, which to transfer to other facilities, and which to euthanize. As the future unfolds, who can deny that the continuum of captive-managed-wild will inexorably shift leftward?
—Kierán Suckling, Center for Biological Diversity[1]

While some conservationists still use the terms *in situ* and *ex situ* as place-holders for the wilderness-captive poles, many others are increasingly viewing that relationship as a gradation rather than as a simple polarity. This chapter will document the view expressed by many of my interviewees that *in situ* and *ex situ* indicate a continuum of management intensity rather than mutually exclusive opposites. From the countless existing combinations of *in situ* and *ex situ* between zoo and wilderness, I will briefly describe seven *inter situ*[2] nodes: genebanks, zoo breeding centers, conservation farms, conservation hatcheries, protected areas, wildlife refuges, and national parks (Figure 10). I will start with the genebank, which is the node that is perceived by many of my interviewees as closest to the *ex situ*—or captive—pole, and will gradually move toward the national park, which is generally perceived as closest to the *in situ*—or wilderness—pole. These examples are by no means exhaustive.[3]

Although this chapter traces the predominant linear logic presented by many of my interviewees, I do not endorse it. Instead, I will show the inherent messiness and fluidity between and within the sites. I will also highlight the

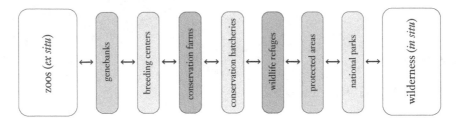

Figure 10: Many conservationists imagine *in situ* and *ex situ* on a continuum, with zoos situated on the one end and wilderness on the other end. Created by author.

impossibility of stratifying these sites within rational and quantifiable configurations. While the practitioners who perform this work on the ground are fully aware of these subtleties, their conceptual framework for recognizing and describing them often lags far behind.

Nature-Captive Continuum

In "The Long Overdue Death of the *Ex Situ* and *In Situ* Dichotomy in Species Conservation" (2013), Kent Redford, Deborah Jensen, and James Breheny offer a clear articulation of the continuum idea.[4] According to these biologists, conservation sites can be divided into five levels: captive managed species, intensively managed species, lightly managed species, conservation dependent species, and self-sustaining species. Self-sustaining, or successfully conserved, species are those who are demographically and genetically robust. Self-sustaining species also have representative populations distributed across the historical range in ecologically representative settings, have replicate populations within each ecological setting, and are resilient across the range.[5] The continuum thus progresses in a linear fashion, from the most intense to the least intense degree of human manipulation.

Many of my interviewees similarly used the term "continuum," or some version thereof, to describe the relationship between *in situ* and *ex situ*. Lee Ehmke is director of the Minnesota Zoo and president of WAZA. In our interview, Ehmke emphasizes what he sees as the increasingly gray areas between the two conservation poles: "There are very few places of wildlife habitat left unmanaged on earth—there is always some level of control or manipulation that has to happen. In zoos, that level of control and manipulation is very high. And so the expertise of managing small populations in zoos has been practiced but not perfected. [But] zoos are way [more] ahead of the game than what is happening in a national park."[6] Kierán Suckling of the Center for Biological Diversity agrees that the relationship between *in situ* and *ex situ* is more of a continuum than a divide. In his words, "If you wanted to, it wouldn't be hard to make a list of ten scaled steps between fully captive and fully wild. . . . Virtually, there's an infinite number."[7] "It's a continuum, [rather] than two distinct things," Tara Stoinski of Zoo Atlanta tells me along these lines. "For some species that continuum is much more blurred, and for others it is a little bit more distinctive."[8]

Michael Soulé, one of the founders of conservation biology in the mid-1980s, is also a proponent of the continuum model. He tells me that while in certain zoos "all the animals are kept in cages or in fenced areas under human control and domination, . . . there are [zoos] where some creatures are in semi-wild and more natural enclosures. So it's a matter of degree."[9] Some of my interviewees have pointed to The Wilds as an example of a natural zoo enclosure. The Wilds comprises nearly 10,000 acres of reclaimed mine lands in southeastern Ohio, which makes it one of the largest zoological facilities in the world. Evan Blumer, director emeritus of The Wilds, identifies myriad configurations "that are beginning to pop up as points on the continuum between *in situ* and *ex situ*, whether they are conservation centers like The Wilds, protection zones for rhinos in Zimbabwe, or sanctuaries for confiscated wildlife in Cameroon—all the way down the line."[10] "The fact is," Blumer argues, "that virtually nothing is left that doesn't have some level of management."[11] For Blumer, as well as for Ehmke, Stoinski, and Soulé, the critical factor in determining a site's position on the continuum is the degree of human manipulation.

The idea of a continuum determined by the intensity of human management was also promoted at a 2010 CBSG workshop that brought together field conservationists and select zoo participants (discussed briefly in Chapter 1). The workshop's participants coined the term "intensively managed populations," or IMPs, to highlight that conservation sites are better characterized by the *degrees* of human management of nonhuman populations and habitat than through a bifurcated *in situ–ex situ* approach. The participants came up with the following definition for an IMP:

> [The IMP is] dependent on human care at the individual and population level for its persistence. *Ex situ* populations that depend on managers for food,

medical treatment, living space, protection from predation, and access to mates are clearly intensively managed. Some wild populations are reliant on at least some of these kinds of individual care and would also fall within the scope of IMPs. Populations living without regular intervention for individuals but requiring management at the population level (e.g. protection from poaching) or habitats will often be "light managed" or "conservation dependent."[12]

In this account, as in the accounts presented by many of my interviewees, the distinguishing factor between the various sites is the intensity of human management. Yet one could imagine other possible factors, maybe even ones that are not human-focused. Such possible factors include the charisma of the relevant humans and nonhumans in each site, the threats to and risks faced by the species, the relevant legal regimes, and the particular animal's perspective.

How should conservationists decide when to manage a species more intensively, and how much human intervention is acceptable to keep the species alive? How should they decide when to move the species into captivity—and from captivity back into the wild? And what is the price of such intensive forms of management? While most of my interviewees decry the need for such intensive management, some do not. For instance, David Wildt of the Smithsonian Institution tells me in the context of rhinos that he "relish[es]" the challenge of managing sustainable populations under adverse conditions.[13] Whatever their personal preference, the conservationists I interviewed have all agreed that nature will require human management in perpetuity[14]—or in human perpetuity, at least.

Alongside the promotion of a continuum alternative to the *in situ–ex situ* dichotomy, a growing number of voices challenge this dichotomy on broader grounds. Some point out that it is outmoded in the face of today's ecological challenges. William Conway says, accordingly: "Really, the *ex situ* and *in situ* thing is irrelevant now. . . . [Climate] change is becoming so dramatic that . . . *in situ* and *ex situ* are artificial concepts as we look into the future. Habitats are moving and changing, climate is changing, animal populations in the past have been able to move to adapt to them; sometimes, lots of times, they couldn't and became extinct before humans came around."[15] Rather than fretting over the now-meaningless dichotomy between *in situ* and *ex situ*, Conway argues, we should decide how to deal with the entire world becoming a megazoo.

Within this megazoo, management intensity depends on a range of factors. And just as wild spaces encompass varying degrees of management intensity, so do zoos. According to CBSG senior officer Kathy Traylor-Holzer, who facilitated the IMP workshop, of the 4,733 threatened vertebrate taxa that existed in the world in 2011—as assessed by the Red List—14.7 percent were held in zoos. But although zoos are typically classified as intensive management sites, their management intensity varies: approximately 9 percent of endangered taxa are lightly managed through studbooks, 8 percent are managed more intensively through loose plans, and 5 percent are managed most intensively through SSP programs and their equivalents around the globe.[16] Even in zoos, then, only a relatively small percentage of species experience the highest management level.

Genebanks

Although most of my interviewees see the zoo as the quintessential site of *ex situ* conservation, there are myriad other constellations of *ex situ* conservation that are neither zoos nor other typical captive facilities. Cryopreservation is one example. Genome Resource Banks (GRBs) contain frozen repositories of biological material, including sperm and embryos, tissue, blood products, and DNA. According to Traylor-Holzer, genebanks are *ex situ* institutions. Freezing life is, literally, the ideal type of preservation, except that it requires life's temporary annihilation: it is about preserving life in its cellular form by wrapping it in a cloud of nitrogen. At the same time, genebanks are also different from traditional conservation in that they focus on a scale other than that of the individual, population, or species: "they're just animal parts, not entire animals," says Traylor-Holzer.[17] Valued for its genetic distinctiveness and singularity, this cellular form of life becomes mere life, in the biopolitical sense: insular, monadic, and radically devoid of context.[18]

The National Zoo's GRB contains more than two thousand samples of frozen sperm, oocytes, embryos, or gonadal tissues from one hundred species, which account for almost 2 percent of all mammalian species worldwide.[19] The zoo takes pride in its artificial insemination of captive cheetahs with frozen sperm imported from Africa as well as in its augmentation of black-footed ferret populations by producing multiple offspring with cryopreserved sperm.[20] The zoo also highlights its collaborations with the Chinese government to develop a sperm GRB for the giant panda "as a hedge against extinction and to support breeding programs."[21]

Despite these remarkable achievements, Traylor-Holzer remains skeptical about the actual importance of cryopreservation for conservation. "Twenty years ago," she says, "[GRB] was the dream of the future that was going to save everything. [But] then some reality set in." Still, she acknowledges the technology's many benefits: "You can use something like artificial insemination to bring those genes back to what you took from the wild. You can counteract all the loss of genetic variation that happened over the last decade. . . . It's a way of freezing in time the genetic variations."[22]

Tellingly referred to as frozen zoos, genebanks are viewed by many conservationists as a problematic form of conservation, if at all. For most species, this technology has proven to be too complicated, too expensive, or both, they claim. Additionally, some have suggested that the animals produced through cryopreservation will not know "how to live in the world as a wild animal" because they will depend on humans to teach them how to behave in the environment they were created for.[23] The underlying message, then, is that wildness is not something to be taught by humans and, in fact, it is precisely that which cannot be taught. But as we shall see, this is not strictly true.

In summer 2013, I visited the genebank at the Smithsonian Institution, one of only a few that operate within a zoo facility. Reproductive biologist Pierre Comizzoli took me for a tour of the bank: a small room, with tanks scattered about it (Figure 11). I found it hard to comprehend the vast diversity of life captured in such an unimpressive site. For Comizzoli, this is both his lab and his field.

> You have lab people who are developing fantastic tools, but they are concentrating their efforts and their intellect on the lab, and they don't really see the rest. And then in the field, you have the people who are dedicating their whole life to saving the last population of a super-rare species, and they're not necessarily going to understand why you have so much money spent in the lab when [it] could be spent in the field. The problem is that you have two worlds that rarely meet.[24]

This statement highlights the continued centrality of the lab/field dyad for understanding the *in situ/ex situ*, natural/artificial, and zoo/wild divides.

Nonetheless, Comizzoli remarks that "the wild populations [rather than the zoo animals] are really the ones telling you the truth on what's good in terms of genes." He then reflects on just how limited human knowledge about cellular life is, and questions the idea that humans can fully control life—"they

Figure 11: Cryopreservation tanks at the Smithsonian Conservation Biology Institute, Washington, DC. Photo by author, May 11, 2013.

can manage it, repeat certain successes, but never fully understand it."[25] Even in the highly controlled environment of the nitrogen zoo, where life is frozen under strict conditions, life processes never fail to surprise the scientist.

Zoo Breeding Centers

William Conway once calculated that all North American zoos would fit into the space of one of New York City's boroughs.[26] This spatial restriction has various ramifications, one of which is the impact on the breeding success of certain species who require more room to breed. To overcome this problem, a few zoos have decided to collaborate in designing large breeding centers. A breeding center consortium called the Conservation Centers for Species Survival (C2S2) demonstrates this management strategy. Established in 2005, C2S2 comprises five centers in the United States: Fossil Rim Wildlife Center in Texas, Omaha's Henry Doorly Zoo and Aquarium, San Diego Zoo Global, the Smithsonian Conservation Biology Institute, and The Wilds. Collectively, C2S2 manages more than 25,000 acres, all devoted to endangered species study, management, and recovery.[27] For example, 120 of the 160 cheetahs in accredited North American zoos reside at C2S2.[28]

In addition to mitigating the spatial restrictions of its individual institutions, C2S2 developed in response to what some felt was AZA's unsustainable animal programs model, and the weak status of AZA's recommendations in particular.[29] My interviewees clarify that the goal of breeding centers is to increase the sustainability of zoo collections and that this does not necessarily translate into an increase in species viability in the wild. The breeding centers usually engage in intensive management; the animals who reside there are fed, monitored, bred for sustainability within the zoo population, and finally displayed in the zoos' exhibits. At the same time, these centers are different from zoos in their large, park-like enclosures that are especially suited for large herds. In addition to the sheer size of its centers, C2S2's advanced reproductive strategies that provide animals with mating choices have also enhanced breeding successes.[30]

In 2013, I visited the Smithsonian Institution's Front Royal facility in Virginia, one of C2S2's five participating institutions. Paul Marinari, senior curator at the facility, showed me around. I expected to see cheetahs and wolves roaming the rolling hills, with black-footed ferrets tagging along closely behind. Instead, I saw many cages, some not as natural looking as the immersion exhibits I have documented in zoos. The cheetahs were not viewable that day, as they were having a veterinary checkup, and the black-footed ferrets resided inside a large building that resembled many holding areas I had visited in accredited zoos.[31] When I voiced my expectations to Marinari, he responded: "Whereas many of the breeding centers in Texas are more like safari parks because they are open to visitors, Front Royal is closed to the public, except one weekend a year." This, he explains, is for a reason: "We are more science-based. Our facilities have to be designed to function . . . so that our animal care staff can work with the animals."[32]

Even among the five C2S2 partners, then, there are variations in management style and intensity. The Front Royal facility resembles a lab more than a safari park. In fact, the animals there are in many ways managed more intensively than those residing at the zoo. Nonetheless, in terms of their size and invisibility to human spectatorship, most breeding centers are closer to what one perceives as *in situ*.[33]

Conservation Farms

Like other sites explored in this chapter, farms are also of different natures. There are conservation farms and farms for meat production, as well as commercial farms that reproduce endangered species for hunting and for the exotic pet trade. Certain conservationists criticize such farms for their commodification of the animals and thus refuse to see them as conservation sites. However, some of these farms deliberately contribute to the protection of habitats and manage a growing number of endangered species. In Canada, a recent legal debate has ensued over the status of bison ranches, charging officials with the interpretation of the statutory term "wild by nature." I will start this section by exploring the complexities of this question in the Canadian context and then move to discuss farms in other geographical contexts.

The Committee on the Status of Endangered Wildlife in Canada (COSEWIC) is a group of experts that assesses imperiled wildlife species in Canada, a task they have been assigned by the Species at Risk Act (SARA)—the Canadian equivalent of the U.S. ESA.[34] "The assessment stage is important," explains COSEWIC chair Marty Leonard, as it "identifies species, does assessment and recommends status, but [leaves the] ultimate decision with [the] government."[35] In 2010, COSEWIC approved its Guidelines on Manipulated Populations.[36] These guidelines instruct species assessors not to consider "any manipulated populations established for purposes other than species conservation (for example, those established for commercial purposes)" as part of the wildlife species being assessed by COSEWIC, "provided the population is geographically or genetically distinct from the wildlife species under assessment, and there is no intention that the population contribute to the wild population."[37] Conversely, when "captive and cultivated" populations are held for conservation purposes, they "will be included as part of the wildlife species being assessed."[38] These populations will, however, be excluded from the application of quantitative criteria to establish status. This complicated apparatus can be summarized as follows: captive and cultivated populations that are bred for conservation purposes and that undergo processes of natural selection are assessed, but do not quantitatively count, when determining the threat status of a species or population.

SARA coined the concept "wild by nature" to determine the legal protection afforded to species.[39] Canadian government officials have interpreted this concept as referring to species with recent wild ancestors.[40] This interpretation has raised myriad complications: how to assess native wildlife species that include (re-)introduced, hybrid, supplemented or captive populations—all of which are defined by the guidelines as "manipulated" populations?[41] And what is the relation of "wild by nature" to "manipulated populations"?[42] These questions and others are becoming critical in a growing number of assessments. In my observations of the COSEWIC meeting in the spring of 2014,[43] for example, discussions on how to assess the risk rates of rainbow trout populations included considerations of whether or not the descendants of stocked or hatchery fish should count as part of the fish's "wild" population,[44] a question that I will further tackle in Chapter 5.

Recently, COSEWIC set up a special committee to handle the broader implications of the definition of "wild by nature."[45] One of the first issues the new committee has been charged with is how to assess the Plains bison (*Bison bison bison*) and the wood bison (*Bison bison athabascae*).[46] The distinction between the wild and commercial populations of both species could not be made on either geographical or genetic grounds.[47] Nonetheless, the decision was made that "commercial bison are not contributing to the wild." Leonard explains: "In my mind, if they are not being raised for conservation purposes (i.e., no intention that they contribute to the wild) *and* they are not subject to natural selective pressures (e.g., predation, mate competition)— then they [should] be omitted from consideration."[48] Interpreting SARA's "wild by nature" and the manipulation guidelines, COSEWIC decided not to include the Plains bison's commercial (or farm) populations in this species' assessment.[49] Indigenous groups have contested this decision, claiming that their bison are farmed for cultural rather than commercial purposes and are therefore "wild by nature" and should be considered in the assessment. Clearly, COSEWIC's decision whether or not to count bison on a ranch or hatchery fish as part of the "wild" population translates into distinct legal protections that have very real consequences for the lives of these and related populations.

South Africa provides myriad additional examples for the blurred lines between conservation and commercial farming of wild animals. Peter Dollinger, former WAZA director, explains that there is "a huge trade in antelopes and giraffes and rhinos in South Africa."[50] "These farms make a living off of [saving] wildlife," he tells me, emphasizing that some don't see those two enterprises as conflicting.[51]

In 2004, the World Wildlife Fund (WWF) issued a statement about the Convention on International Trade in Endangered Species of Wild Fauna and Flora (CITES)—the central treaty regulating the international trade in threatened animals. This statement highlights some of the problems emerging from the disconnect between the commercial management of endangered animals and their management for conservation. From the WWF statement: "commercial trade continues in Appendix I [i.e., most endangered] species with little or no attention focused on the *in situ* conservation of those species."[52] As an example, the WWF points to the "highly successful captive breeding programmes for *Crocodylus siamensis* (Siamese crocodile) . . . [which] breed and export tens of thousands of live crocodiles and products annually. . . . At the same time, the species continues in drastic decline [in the wild] . . . and is now virtually extinct in Thailand, where the last survey located only three animals remaining in the wild."[53]

That crocodiles are listed on the IUCN Red List as Extinct in the Wild despite their existence in captive commercial programs demonstrates that, categorically, commercially bred life is irrelevant for conservation. Marking commercial captive animals as un-wild, in other words, warrants their exclusion from conservation's domain. This illustrates that biological life is not categorically wild; instead, life must exist within a particular context and adhere to a certain set of conditions to become wild and thereby to count for conservation purposes.

Conservation Hatcheries

Hatcheries are an increasingly important *inter situ* node. The U.S. fisheries program includes seventy national fish hatcheries, three of which are dedicated solely to spawning endangered and threatened fish. USFWS Assistant Director Gary Frazer provides a historical context for the U.S. hatchery system, describing its transition from recreation to conservation:

> Our hatchery system evolved at a time when producing fish for recreational purposes was primary. It then moved its mission into mitigation for large federal water projects that might compromise certain stocks of fish.

[Finally,] the Endangered Species Act and other aspects of aquatic conservation became more focused upon the species at risk of blanking out, and they moved into a supplemental production mode. Freshwater mussels, plants, toads, you name it—if they're aquatic, and they're endangered, we have some hatchery or aquatic center involved in some capacity.[54]

Mike Oetker, deputy regional director of USFWS's southeast region, reiterates: "It used to be 'produce more, more, more,' but now we're more focused on genetics, and survival, and disease control. . . . And that's a huge shift in the mind-set of the hatchery system."[55]

Conservation hatcheries function differently from recreational ones. Oetker explains, for example, that "when your facility has the last remaining individuals of a species, the risk of a system failure—electrical outage, pump failure, introduction of a disease or a parasite—is far more consequential than if you're producing rainbow trout." Additionally, he tells me that unlike the recreational hatcheries, "we're always trying to put ourselves out of business." In other words, "if we bring a fish into the hatchery system, our goal is to get it in the wild to a point where it no longer needs [us]. You need to make sure that whatever you produce in your conservation hatcheries has a place to go. Otherwise, you're just stocking to maintain a species that never has any chance of going."[56]

Jeff Powell agrees. Powell is a project leader at Mora National Fish Hatchery in New Mexico—one of the three USFWS facilities dedicated to endangered fish. Powell tells me that the goal of the Gila trout program (*Oncorhynchus gilae*, pronounced "hee-la") is to recover the Gila trout so that they are no longer dependent on the hatchery's captive breeding program. "So we're trying to get them back into their native habitat to create a self-sustaining population—and until that point is reached, we want to back them up in the facility," he explains. Powell articulates the priorities: "We try to maximize fish staying in the wild, and when that's not feasible—that's when we bring them into our facility here at the fish hatchery."[57] Like so many others interviewed for this project, Oetker and Powell insist that the value of the hatchery fish is determined exclusively in relation to the value of the wild species, again expressing the dominant preference toward *in situ* conservation.

"A fish is not a fish. It's an art form," says Gary Frazer. "And there are some real masters of it."[58] Powell, who is one such "master" of fish recovery, explains the uniqueness of the Gila trout program in comparison to trout programs in commercial facilities. First, he says, "what we do here is we bring in wild broodstock to infuse the genes into our program. We do this to help prevent genetic drift by continually adding new genes to the captive population. Each individual fish is genetically tested prior to spawning."[59] The captive Gila trout recovery is also unique in its "naturalistic rearing" techniques. The hatchery's design imitates the Gila's natural habitat, including a series of interconnected pools, "so that these wild fish could choose which artificial habitat they occupy. We can't make it perfect, but we put artificial plants and they get fed a semi-live diet as well."[60] Even with a boost of live insects, however, the Gila trout tend to miss certain nutrients from the wild, which is where the "semi-live" pellet supplement comes in handy.[61]

The management of Gila trout is not restricted to the space of the hatchery; it also extends to the wild. "We never want to keep all our [fish] eggs in one basket, either *in situ* or *ex situ*, in case something catastrophic happens on either end," Powell tells me.[62] On average, the Mora hatchery stocks Gila streams with more than ten thousand Gila trout per year. "It's a careful process to determine which streams get stocked and where," he says. In preparation for this stocking, a team of biologists ensures that the designated streams are empty of resident fish. "We want the stream free from non-native fish species," Powell explains, "because we don't want [Gila trout] to hybridize with rainbow trout."[63] The streams are cleared by applying piscicides (a chemical substance poisonous to fish) or using electro-shock, although sometimes, Powell tells me, the streams are cleared naturally, for example by fire events.[64]

Even after the reintroduction is over, the crew continues to carefully monitor habitat conditions and will step in when there is trouble (Figure 12). In cases of fire outbreaks, for example, the biologists will ride on mules "deep inside the Gila wilderness," in Powell's words, and will use helicopters "to rescue the valuable wild Gila trout out of the stream and into the temporary safety of the hatchery."[65] Once the threats are mitigated and after the stream is again made "safe," the Gila trout are reintroduced back into the river—and so the process repeats itself.

Humans on mules, Gilas in helis, and electro-shocked "non-native" fish on neither—the biopolitical order is clearly established. Whereas the wild is constantly produced in the image of the hatchery—stocked by Gila and cleared of others—the captive habitat is naturalized through designs that include ideal spawning conditions and careful attention to genetic diversity rates.

Figure 12: Jeff Powell, project leader at the Mora National Fish Hatchery, USFWS, monitors Gila trout with a backpack electro-shock device in 2012. The USFWS uses the same backpack electro-shocker to remove "non-native" fish from the streams prior to Gila reintroductions. Courtesy of Jeff Powell, USFWS.

The pallid sturgeon (*Scaphirhynchus albus*) is a second fish on the brink of extinction that demonstrates the fluidity between wild and captive sites. For Oetker, the eighty-pound, six-foot sturgeon easily competes with the elephants and tigers of the terrestrial world. "They're a prehistoric fish," he tells me excitedly. "They saw the dinosaurs come and go and have evolved very little over 110 million years. It's a neat creature." Since the 1980s, however, the sturgeons have been in serious trouble: although their life span can reach one hundred years, they have not spawned in more than fifty. In 1990, the USFWS listed the pallid sturgeon as endangered under the ESA and issued a biological opinion that changed the usage and operation of the Missouri River to protect this fish's habitat. Oetker laughs when he tells me that "we had everybody, from Montana to Missouri, up in arms. Everybody had their own concerns. [But] at the end of the day, the law of the river was the Endangered Species Act."

The sturgeon is now managed intensively, including genetic testing and tracking through Passive Integrated Transponder (PIT) tags that provide a lifetime bar code for every individual fish. "We were pretty much down to a place where we could name them," Oetker recalls about the level of management at the time that he was involved in this program. Later, the USFWS developed a captive broodstock of pallid sturgeon for reintroduction into the wild. According to Montana Fish, Wildlife & Parks, the broodstock will serve as a source of genetically pure fertilized pallid sturgeon eggs after the existing wild adult populations become extinct. The Montana website states: "Female pallid sturgeon do not become sexually mature until they are approximately 15 years old, so it remains to be seen whether the hatchery program will successfully achieve its goal of restoring the pallid sturgeon in Montana."[66] Despite these immense efforts, Montana estimates that the sturgeon will become extinct by 2018.[67]

The captive-wild distinction is further muddled when scientists predict that a particular taxon is unlikely to ever be self-sustaining in its natural habitat. Take, for example, the Mohave tui chub (*Siphateles bicolor mohavensis*). This six-inch-long, brassy-brown fish has inhabited the Mojave River basin since the Pleistocene epoch (more than 11,700 years ago). The fish was saved from extinction by a group of visionary high school students, who rehabilitated two Mojave River drainages with help from Boy Scouts and community members.[68] In 2012, the Mohave tui chub population was estimated at 8,500 individuals in five populations—all in human-made habitats situated in the fish's historic range.[69] Suckling remarks: "So they basically try to be as wild as possible, and sometimes that's not very wild."[70]

Protected Areas

Another *inter situ* node is the globally protected area. According to the IUCN, "a protected area is a clearly defined geographical space, recognised, dedicated and managed, through legal or other effective means, to achieve the long term conservation of nature with associated ecosystem services and cultural values."[71] Such areas include wildlife refuges, national parks, wilderness areas, community conserved areas, and nature reserves. I will discuss the wildlife refuge and national parks in more detail in the following two sections.

There are approximately 210,000 protected areas in the world; they are designated by national governments and reported to IUCN's global dataset. Trevor Sandwith is director of IUCN's Global Protected Areas Programme. I ask him about the criteria for listing protected areas and whether zoos or other captive breeding facilities meet these criteria. His response:

> A protected area is an area that is deliberately designated to conserve bio-diversity and associated ecosystem services. You have to distinguish that from a zoo, where you may be looking at a largely modified environment in which components of another ecosystem have been brought there, perhaps for captive breeding purposes. But when we talk about protected areas we're essentially talking about a *natural* ecosystem—you know, *in situ*.[72]

In a 2010 study of management effectiveness, the IUCN assessed more than 8,000 sites from protected areas around the world. It found that half of the sites were not managed optimally. "That meant that on the bottom, half were [either] not managed at all or were actually subject to quite severe pressures." On the positive side, Sandwith explains that "some of them were managed, and in improving states of management."[73] As a result of this study, the IUCN decided to design a Green List, which would function parallel to its well-recognized Red List. Sandwith explains the need for this list: "Whenever something goes extinct everybody jumps on it and it's all over the press—everyone seems so excited by the fact that we're really in trouble."[74] Whereas the Red List symbolizes crisis, the Green List symbolizes hope—an opportunity to improve and move forward. "So we see it as a much more voluntary and open-ended place, where any aspirant protected area agency or manager could say, 'We're improving and enhancing our performance and we're going to achieve these outcomes.'"

In contrast to the Red List's exclusive focus on particular species, the Green List will be about the preservation of populations, communities, ecosystem functions, and societal needs—what Sandwith refers to as "equitable government."[75] He says: "The IUCN is saying that it really makes sense to have a universal standard around the world, which is not subject to whether you're a developing or a developed country, or whether you've got issues with your legal system or not. In the end, we're just asking the objective question: this area was established to conserve, . . . what's our objective measure for *that*?"[76] If the goal of the Red List has been to provide a uniform system by which to assess the threat level of all species across the globe, the Green List will soon map and rank the world's protected habitat in terms of management successes.[77]

One interesting debate is whether a conservation success must be the result of a conservation action. For example, if the species bounced back on its own, would that be considered a success in terms of the site's ranking in this program? Certain proponents of the Green List initiative for species have argued against including such improvements in the Green List assessments, while others would like to see the Green List as the mirror image of the Red List and thus as reflective of the species' condition rather than of management success.[78]

But what does successful management mean? And would success mean that managers would be putting themselves out of work? One way or the other, the days of hands-off management seem to be coming to an end; instead, nonhuman life is increasingly assessed, ranked, and managed to the finest degree through the use of risk, threat, and success calculators as well as through placement on a growing number of colorful lists.

Wildlife Refuges

Nature reserves are often viewed as one of the last wilderness frontiers, where animals can still engage in their natural behaviors. The nature reserve is a generic name for a range of site types, one of which is the American national wildlife refuge. In the United States, the earliest effort to set aside an area of federally owned land for wildlife was President Ulysses Grant's 1886 protection of the Pribilof Islands in Alaska as a reserve for the northern fur seal,[79] and the first federal land specifically set aside for a non-marketable form of wildlife was Pelican Island in 1903. By the end of his administration in 1909, President Theodore Roosevelt had issued fifty-one executive orders, establishing wildlife refuges in seventeen states and three territories. In 2013, this system consisted of more than 520 sites and encompassed over 93 million acres.[80]

The Cabeza Prieta and Kofa National Wildlife Refuges in Arizona serve to illustrate the difficulties with fixing sites on a linear management continuum. At these refuges, USFWS experts have attempted to increase the numbers of the Sonoran pronghorn antelope—which declined to just 21 animals in 2002 and rebounded to an estimated 160 animals in 2013[81]— with the aim of reintroducing them to their historic range. The prong-horns are fed and studied in large enclosed refuges. Just before their reintroduction, carefully selected pronghorns are herded into small hold-ing pens (Figure 13).

James Atkinson, Sonoran pronghorn recovery coordinator, describes the reintroduction process as follows: "We'll put them in what we call a holding pen, which is a five- or ten-acre pen, which will hold them for two to three weeks and get them reacclimated [as well as] fix the anesthe-sia. Then—once they're kind of gelled up as a unit—off they go!"[82] "Off they go" refers to the transfer of the pronghorn from the semi-captive conditions of the refuge into the semi-wild conditions in nature, often just outside the refuge's fence. There, too, the pronghorns are provided with supplementary feeding and water points. Atkinson estimates that for this near-extinct species to survive, human intervention will be required in perpetuity.[83]

Figure 13: Sonoran pronghorn antelopes in a corral trap (boma) at the Cabeza Prieta National Wildlife Refuge's captive breeding pen. After they are trapped, individuals are transported to the relevant release site. Photo by Tim Tibbitts, 2011. Courtesy of James Atkinson, USFWS.

National Parks

National parks are another type of protected areas. Many still imagine parks as places of pristine wilderness, especially when situated in exotic geographies such as Africa. Yet a closer look into some of them questions this image. Peter Dollinger points out that "in South Africa, . . . there is no single wild lion." He gives Kruger National Park as an example. In this 600-square-kilometer large park, he says, "the problem now is how to keep the lions 'under the pill' because otherwise, the population would become too big." "Everywhere, they have to cull," he exclaims.[84]

In 1987, Kenya's Lake Nakuru National Park was fenced.[85] From that point on, the park's animals have needed ecological, behavioral, genetic, and demographic management; additionally, they have been selectively culled and treated for disease. According to Conway, "only continual monitoring can determine how Nakuru's megazoo species are affecting each other and their habitat. . . . Only a constantly updated management plan will provide for responsive supervision."[86] For Conway, the difference between *ex situ* and *in situ* becomes that between a zoo and a megazoo.

British geographer Andrew Norton compares zoos and African safaris. He writes: "The nature on display is implicated in a hidden nexus of capital and power relations, including colonialism and capitalism; habitats and species populations are managed and animals become domesticated, through exposure to tourists rather than caging; and the experience is a constructed one which offers access to a 'wild,' primeval nature and attempts to hide its material and symbolic construction."[87] According to Norton, the cage that marks the boundaries of captivity at the zoo has merely been replaced by a more sophisticated form of confinement through capitalist performances of ecotourism at the African safari.

Tara Stoinski works at Zoo Atlanta and also as a field researcher at Dian Fossey Gorilla Fund International. Her work with the eastern mountain gorillas (*Gorilla beringei beringei*) in Rwanda has provided her with a slightly different perspective than Norton's on the role of ecotourism in conservation. In her words:

> The parks where the mountain gorillas live have twenty times the average number of rangers compared to the Third World average. To me, this is great because it's a success story that the [gorilla] numbers there are increasing. But in reality, this is a huge wake-up call for conservationists [that]

our traditional methods, our limited amounts of money, and the small level of protection we are able to provide to these areas are probably, in the long run, not working. We don't hear great stories coming out of the conservation world about species doing well.[88]

Stoinski believes that the success of the gorilla program in Rwanda is the direct result of heightened surveillance by scientists and tourists. "The oldest individual we have is thirty-four," she tells me. "He was born when Dian Fossey was alive and every single day of his life someone has been there, documenting what his group does, what he's done, et cetera."[89] Census numbers indicate that in 2013 there were 880 mountain gorillas in Rwanda and Uganda. Gorilla tourists are restricted to designated ecotourism sites, where a single hour of gorilla sighting costs $700.[90] Spaces are limited and booked far in advance. "The fact that someone is looking in on every single gorilla, basically every single day," says Kristen Lukas of Cleveland Metroparks Zoo, and that "they can literally be counted and be known—creates that connection that makes people want to protect them."[91]

Gorilla conservation is considered a success story not only *in situ* but also in zoos. The estimated 850 western lowland gorillas (*Gorilla gorilla gorilla*) living in zoos are categorized as a fully sustainable "green" population—not a frequent occurrence in zoo animal programs.[92] Lukas compares the life of gorillas in zoos and in parks:

> In zoos they are physically limited in their space, but the mountain gorillas [in the wild] are also physically limited in their space because of the pressures from the growing human populations around them. That has definitely influenced the way that they group, the way that they move, and even the types of groups that they form. . . . In both cases, the gorillas are habituated to the presence of humans. But I was struck [in Rwanda] by how they could care less that we were there. In fact, I've seen gorillas in zoos react more to visitors than the gorillas that I saw there.[93]

Lukas's narrative considers the gorillas' perspective when thinking about their wildness. It implies that different species and even different individuals will respond differently to captivity at different times and places. This recalls the question I posed in Chapter 2: should the animal's perspective be included when defining *in situ* and *ex situ* conservation—and if so, how?

While both the gorilla experts and gorilla spectators travel between *in situ* and *ex situ*, the respective gorilla populations do not, or rarely do.[94]

When I ask why, Stoinski mentions the tensions between zoo biologists and field biologists. Evidently, despite the increasing integration between *in situ* and *ex situ*, such tensions still exist, impacting the lives of the nonhuman populations involved.

A 2013 study on lions in African reserves by Craig Packer and more than fifty colleagues similarly challenges conventional perspectives on national parks and what sort of management works best for wild animals.[95] This study includes lion count data from more than forty sites across Africa and an analysis of the most effective management strategies for lion conservation. The study found that lion populations in fenced reserves are significantly closer to their estimated carrying capacities—the size of the population that can be supported by an area without that area suffering environmental degradation[96]—than unfenced populations, and much less expensive to conserve. It finally projects significant decline of the unfenced lion populations in the coming decades.

Hamish Currie is director of the South African organization Back to Africa. In his view, "there are very few places left that are really 'wild.' So whether you like it or not, you have to manage wildlife in an area the size of the Kruger National Park, which is hundreds of kilometers long. You have disease that has to be managed, you have species that are diminishing very rapidly." "We talk '*in situ*' and '*ex situ*,'" he tells me, while "in most scenarios, we are managing animals."[97] Currie also points to the alienation between local field people, on the one hand, and non-local zoo scientists and academics, on the other hand—especially when it comes to making hard decisions about wildlife management in Africa.

One of the central reasons for the differences between local and non-local conservation efforts, Currie believes, is the West's romanticization of Africa. In his words, "Too many academics [and] people working in zoos think about this vast continent of Africa—where animals are running around, moving vast distances, all the genetic exchange is taking place—and that's the wild. What they don't realize is that it's now being boiled down to smaller and smaller pockets and [that] within those pockets, animals might have to be managed."[98] Currie thus perceives the *in situ–ex situ* divide as a form of colonialism. The Europeans took wild African animals from their natural habitats for their zoos, he tells me, and now they are refusing to return them to Africa, basing this refusal on the rigid regulations of *in situ–ex situ* transfer by Western conservation organizations such as the IUCN.

According to Currie, then, the scientification of the *in situ–ex situ* divide and the regulations of this divide serve to naturalize and thereby obscure the colonial power relations performed in the region.

A parallel perspective has recently been on display in the context of museums, which have faced similar demands for returning "native cultural heritage" artifacts to their countries of origin.[99] In the words of a *New York Times* reporter: "The news has become astonishingly routine: a major American museum announces it is relinquishing extraordinary antiquities because a foreign government claims they were looted and has threatened legal action or other sanctions if it doesn't get them back."[100] Currie's critique thus reaffirms the historical commonalities discussed in Chapter 1 between live and dead matter, between *naturalia* and *artificialia*, and between "place of origin" models—as these are negotiated in both museums and zoos.

Conclusion

In a perfect world, we won't have to manage. . . . But to get there, there's going to have to be more management.

—Karin Schwartz, Population Biologist[101]

Many of my interviewees envision the changing relationship between *in situ* and *ex situ* conservation in terms of a continuum that regards management intensity as its exclusive criterion. This chapter has documented seven types of sites that have emerged between the two poles of zoos and wilderness, acknowledging that countless other *inter situ* nodes also constantly emerge in this in-between space. Despite the chapter's linear presentation of the seven nodes, I have attempted to show that these sites are in fact quite fluid and can be characterized by a variety of factors beyond management intensity. The various natureculture sites that pop up between *ex situ* and *in situ*, the chapter has demonstrated, are never static or independent: animal bodies and parts, as well as data and expertise, constantly shift and seep between them. The term "continuum" thus serves to legitimize the *in situ–ex situ* divide by granting it nuance.

The production of artificial currents in naturalized hatcheries, the electro-shocking of streams in wildlife reserves, and the culling of lions in South Africa's national parks—all are examples of interconnections that move beyond the continuum's linear stratification. The predetermined priorities and linear gradations that are the hallmarks of the continuum model thus simply do not reflect the complexities of modern conservation practices and their dynamic natures. Instead of "continuum," I would thus argue, a more apt term for such nodes and networks is "*inter situ* hybrids." Steve Hinchliffe writes along these lines that "it should not be assumed that the facts of conservation, the real issues, pre-exist action and are thereby invariably polluted by human values, politics, cultures, ways of seeing and so on."[102] For Hinchliffe, when put into practice, the facts are not always so obvious and should be understood as "in process rather than clear cut issues."[103] In practice, conservation work requires careful attention, creativity, and a flexibility that the rigid assumptions of real nature and linear continuums cannot provide.

Black-footed Ferret

In spring 2013, the Colorado Independent CattleGrowers Association issued a statement opposing the reintroduction of the black-footed ferrets (*Mustela nigripes*) to sites spanning their historic range. The association argued that prairie dogs (genus *Cynomys*), burrowing rodents native to the grasslands of North America and a necessary prey base for ferrets, "are responsible for massive amounts of destruction on grasslands used to support cattle operations."[1] Not all rancher groups were opposed to the reintroduction, however. The Colorado Cattlemen's Association partnered with USFWS officials, the state government, and tribal and other landowners to develop the Safe Harbor Agreement (SHA), granting financial compensation to ranchers who provide a habitat for black-footed ferrets (Figure 14).[2]

Many ranchers, such as those in Colorado, consider prairie dogs to be pests, especially because of the danger that their burrows can pose to cattle

Figure 14: This endangered black-footed ferret is part of a group of thirty ferrets released onto cattle rancher Gary Walker's (center) land in Colorado. Photo by Marla Trollan/ USFWS, October 2013. Creative Commons-2.0-Generic license.

and humans.[3] However, the endangered black-footed ferrets depend on them: prairie dogs make up about 90 percent of the ferrets' diet;[4] additionally, ferrets do not build their own burrows, but occupy or invade prairie dog burrows. The voluntary wildlife conservation program, which offers financial incentives to ranchers for allowing prairie dog towns on their land, has helped the black-footed ferret program become what many believe is the most successful integrated conservation program in North America.

Opposition from ranchers was not the first obstacle that the black-footed ferret recovery efforts have faced. The ferrets were considered extinct in the late 1970s, until a small population was discovered in Wyoming in 1981.[5] Conservationists focused their recovery efforts on that population—only to see these ferrets nearly die out due to sylvatic plague, a variation of the bubonic plague that devastated Europe in the fourteenth century. From 1985 to 1987, twenty-four black-footed ferrets were captured and transferred into captivity in southeast Wyoming for a breeding program. Unfortunately, the Wyoming Fish and Game Department failed to quarantine them during the transition and, as a result, six died shortly after from canine distemper.[6] The eighteen surviving wild-born ferrets became the founders of the entire ferret population that exists in the world today.

Certain scientists questioned whether it was worth the trouble to attempt a conservation project for a species with fewer than twenty living members. After all, they argued, the genetic diversity of the population would end up dooming it anyway.[7] Furthermore, many were skeptical about the ability of a federal program to successfully recover the ferret population, following the spectacular failure of a similar program for black-footed ferret conservation in the 1970s. "There was really a reluctance to repeat that over again," says Paul Marinari, senior curator of animal operations at the Smithsonian Conservation Biology Institute and studbook keeper for the black-footed ferret recovery program.[8] "There was this group of people that thought, 'Okay, let's just leave them in the wild and let nature take its course.' . . . [Even] Wyoming Game and Fish was at first against bringing them into captivity."[9]

By 2014, more than 8,100 black-footed ferret kits have been born into the program.[10] Of these, more than 3,500 were released into the wild.[11] Marinari tells me:

> [We] have gone from a wild population of zero to a wild population of between 500 and 800. Since 1996, we've consistently been producing enough kits to support reintroduction activities. Over 200 kits per year go out for

reintroduction, and that right now is sufficient. On the scale that it's been done, I'm convinced that the black-footed ferret is the most successful captive breeding and reintroduction program that has ever existed.[12]

The zoo program, Marinari clarifies, is "one small part of the whole recovery program." He further describes that "there's an executive committee, there's a captive breeding subcommittee, there's a field subcommittee, there's a plague vaccine subcommittee, there's a landowner incentive subcommittee, . . . all under the black-footed ferret recovery implementation team, which is basically a consortium of thirty-five different agencies."[13] In his capacity as the ferret's studbook keeper, Marinari routinely works with the USFWS to determine which captive black-footed ferrets will be reintroduced every year. "Only starting with eighteen individuals," he explains, "we had to make a lot of assumptions about the genetics of the ferret population. They're pretty much all related in the first place."

Marinari and many others attribute the extraordinary success of the ferret reintroductions to the One Plan approach applied by the recovery program. The One Plan, a conservation approach developed by IUCN's Conservation Breeding Specialist Group (CBSG), is an algorithmic population management analysis performed in an intensive workshop setting that "develops integrated species conservation plans across an interactive wild–*ex situ* spectrum"[14] (Chapter 6).

As the program's studbook keeper, Marinari coordinates the captive ferrets' mating.[15] In captivity, female ferrets go into estrus during the spring. The captive females are closely monitored in the early months of the year so that the keepers can introduce the selected mates at the correct time.[16] However, the ferrets do not always comply with Marinari's "dating service" recommendations. He tells me that captive ferrets are "going to choose for themselves whether they're going to like the animal that we just put in there, or not. And if they don't, they're going to fight and try to kill it. [So] you keep trying until you find one that eventually works."[17] Although the ferrets' choices are limited by genetic calculations, their individual responses nonetheless impact the course of the breeding program, demonstrating that recognizing the agency of nonhuman animals is important for successful conservation.

Whereas the mating of wild ferrets is not managed as closely as that of the captive ferrets, the differences are not as dramatic as one would expect. Marinari tells me that although ferrets in the wild seem to make their own mating choices, these choices, too, are restricted, this time by access. Nonetheless, the management of these populations differs in terms of tracking and monitoring. Generally, it is more difficult to track and monitor wild ferrets. "Right now, most of the animals are kissing cousins; everybody is basically a full cousin," says Marinari. "But although the wild ferrets are just as related to one another [as the captive ferrets], it is difficult to continue managing their population through studbooks like it's done with the captive population." Once kits are born in the wild, the male ferret leaves, Marinari explains. And because they are solitary, "we have no way of telling who the father is [as] moms are [also] very accepting of kits from other litters."[18]

Before captive ferrets are reintroduced into the wild, they undergo extensive preconditioning, including vaccination against the sylvatic plague. Reintroduction sites may receive "a minimum of twenty juveniles, and they may get one or two of the adults. So you may send a mom, who is four years of age, with her kits."[19] If that happens, the mother must be preconditioned to provide food not only for herself but also for her kits. Marinari tells me: "All the animals that go out for release, at this point in time, have to go through [a] preconditioning period, which means they have exposure to a live prey—prairie dogs—and they have spent a minimum of thirty days in an actual prairie dog burrow system."[20] Preconditioning, accompanied by extensive post-release monitoring, makes for much greater chance of success for the reintroduced ferrets (Figure 15).[21]

Figure 15: A black-footed ferret learns how to catch a live prairie dog as part of his or her pre-reintroduction training at the National Black-Footed Ferret Conservation Center in Colorado. Photo by USFWS, December 2013. Creative Commons-2.0-Generic license.

Population biologist Robert (Bob) Lacy has a slightly different story to tell than Marinari's about the same program: "At one point, the program was viewed more as a model of agencies *not* working together," he tells me. There were "major problems and battles between groups over who had control, . . . between state versus federal versus nonprofit groups, et cetera."[22] Lacy also questions the program's success narrative more generally. In his words:

> What is hidden in the numbers [is that] the population is not yet self-sustaining. [Instead,] it is being sustained by continual releases in most of the wild populations, which suggests that if they stopped releasing—the population would crash. Of six to eight release sites, only two are . . . thriving, but even those are highly vulnerable, still, and in fact some of them have recently had significant declines. So it's true that the program has been a great success in terms of getting the breeding going and having the animals released year after year after year, . . . but I would not yet be confident that the species is on the road to recovery. It's been pulled away from the brink, but it still has a long way to go. [For example,] they still have to vaccinate the animals to protect them from disease. If they stopped doing that, the ferrets would die.[23]

Lacy finally tells me that in addition to their disagreements over the success of the program, the experts have disagreed about the appropriate size of the ferret release sites. Lacy believes, for example, that the current size of the reintroduction sites is problematic, as there "are simply not big enough areas of prairie dogs to sustain long-term healthy populations of ferrets."[24] "What you really want to do," he tells me, "is release ferrets in a wide landscape with prairie dogs scattered across the landscape over a large area so [that] no one disease outbreak will decimate the prairie dogs and the ferrets." Underlying the resistance to larger-scale reintroduction sites, according to Lacy, are political interests: "A strong part of this is the battle with ranchers. Fish and Wildlife and state agencies have treaded lightly on the prospect of trying to increase prairie dog numbers," he explains.[25]

At the end of 2013, approximately 300 black-footed ferrets were housed across six North American facilities (*ex situ*) and 500 ferrets inhabited twenty reintroduction sites (*in situ*), spanning eight U.S. states as well as Mexico and Canada.[26]

CHAPTER 4

Dynamic Life

Because of the complex and sensitive interrelations between *in situ* and *ex situ*, and the growing mobility of nonhuman animals (and of human conservationists) between the two, such movement has become its own site of management. Roughly speaking, when the transfer of animals occurs from the direction of *ex situ* to that of *in situ*, it is called "reintroduction." Philip (Phil) Miller, senior program officer at CBSG, tells me along these lines that "*ex situ* breeding should be used [to create] reservoirs of animals that can be released back in the wild through the whole process of reintroduction."[1]

This chapter's focus is on reintroductions—conservationists' primary mode of moving nonhuman animals (as well as plants) from captivity into the wild—and on the "soft," or non-binding, legal guidelines enacted by the IUCN to regulate this movement.[2] My discussions of the Schaus swallowtail and the eastern hellbender reintroductions will detail some of the difficulties that ensue when animals are physically moved from captivity into the wild and vice versa, and how conservationists have been dealing with these difficulties. Afterward, I will briefly discuss IUCN's guidelines on the management of *ex situ* populations, which are an example of the regulation of animal movement in the "opposite" direction: from the wild into captivity. Along with the movement of animals between the traditional sites of "in" and "out," however, movements in other directions are increasingly taking place, and will be discussed through the story of the lemurs' translocation to Sir Richard Branson's Moskito Island.

The Schaus Swallowtail: Fluttering Between In Situ *and* Ex Situ

The Schaus swallowtail (*Heraclides aristodemus ponceanus*) is a large and colorful butterfly endemic to southern Florida. In 1973, this butterfly was listed as threatened under the ESA and in 1984 the butterfly's status was upgraded to endangered,[3] making it the only one of more than 573 swallowtail butterfly species to be listed as endangered.[4] So widespread in the early 1900s that they were described as bobbing along South Florida's breezes by the hundreds, the Schaus swallowtails succumbed to habitat destruction and anti-mosquito insecticides sprayed in the region.[5] In a serendipitous occurrence, just two months before Hurricane Andrew swept through in 1992, the USFWS granted the University of Florida permission to remove one hundred Schaus swallowtail eggs to serve as the starter nucleus of a large-scale captive propagation program. Following the destruction wrought by the hurricane, the USFWS committed major funding to continue the field surveys and the captive propagation program, as well as to implement experimental reintroductions of the species within protected habitat areas.[6]

Thomas Emmel, now a retired University of Florida professor, directed the captive breeding project for more than twenty years. Establishing the program cost $50,000 ("these butterflies are damn expensive," says Kierán Suckling[7]), obtained largely from federal sources. Despite the fact that the USFWS recognized the importance of captive propagation, the agency's preference toward *in situ* conservation was clearly emphasized throughout. Accordingly, the 1999 federal recovery plan stated: "All future efforts to captively breed Schaus swallowtail butterflies should be conducted in situ in as natural conditions as possible. Preferably, butterflies should be raised in enclosures in suitable habitat within the historic range. Captive propagation efforts closer to release sites are preferable for many species. This would limit transport time and possible difficulties in achieving a successful release."[8] Emmel describes USFWS's strong preference for *in situ*: "The Fish and Wildlife Service and the National Park Service were so hyper about the relatively small population [of these butterflies] that was there even before the hurricane that they didn't want females or even males handled much. [So] they didn't want us to bring them up to [the university facility in] Gainesville where we could have done a great deal of work for the full lifetime of the female in captivity."[9] Instead, Emmel and his staff had to keep the females in "big netting tents over the torchwood trees. And each butterfly had to be in a separate tent." Still, Emmel tells me, the researchers were able to track the eggs that the females had laid in the tent and to "keep a complete notebook of all the eggs and the closest subsequent larvae and to trace them back to the appropriate females. . . . Then, with the next generation in captivity, we out-crossed for maximum genetic diversity."[10] The breeding progressed well and reintroductions commenced in 1995; by 1997, thirteen new *in situ* populations were established.

The reintroductions were not by any means easy. In the early 1990s, the University of Florida had thousands of butterfly pupae ready for release. But when Emmel and his team began asking park managers for permission to release the butterflies on their land, they were met with a resounding refusal or, at best, resistance. Here, from Emmel's account:

> Nobody wanted them! The local land managers said: "No, we know that the Schaus swallowtail once included this area, but we don't want any release there because we have so much to handle now with paperwork and we don't want to deal with an endangered species being reintroduced and all that." And here we started with the naive viewpoint that everyone would welcome the revival of the endangered species, and provide a new point of interest for visitors to that area, et cetera. But probably the greatest shock in those years was that nobody wanted it, it was an orphan. An endangered species had become an orphan.[11]

"We could keep it in the orphanage up here in Gainesville, but we couldn't find any foster parents," Emmel continues. It was partly the amount of intense management the pupae needed that triggered the reluctance toward swallowtail reintroductions on the part of land managers. But even the adult butterflies, Emmel says, were rejected by them. "It took us until 1995 to finally get several land managers to agree to accept it," he tells me. At last, their persistence had paid off and "eventually, we got them released as far south as the southern middle Keys."[12]

The "trick" that helped persuade enough landowners to open their land to swallowtail reintroductions, according to Emmel, was the legal redesignation of the populations destined for release in sensitive areas as "non-essential experimental populations," a designation that I will discuss at length in Chapter 5. The reintroductions ended up progressing so well that the species' geographic range quadrupled from what it had been twenty years before Hurricane Andrew. Due to these successes, in 1999 the USFWS declared the Schaus population stable and stopped its funding of Emmel's captive breeding project.[13] Although Emmel managed to sustain the captive butterfly population at the university facility for a couple of years with private funding, this funding quickly dried up. In his words:

> In 2000 we ran out of money. We couldn't afford to pay even the poor students, [whom we had hired] year after year on a prayer and a promise. So we wrapped it up and just shut down the colony. That was what we were forced to do, believe it or not. If land managers don't want them released in their area, . . . or if the agency that controls the breeding permits won't give you permission [to breed], or if the state doesn't approve it for one reason or another—then you've got trouble. . . . It's astonishing. The inside story is just almost beyond belief.[14]

Shutting down the colony meant, in this context, letting the last of these endangered butterflies die out without producing offspring. How difficult this was for Emmel was evident from his tone of voice as he recounted this episode to me. "Working with endangered species is very much a roller coaster—emotionally, psychologically, and physically," he told me.

> You have periods of intense fieldwork under extremely arduous conditions: the temperature is 105 degrees, humidity near 100 percent, billions of salt marsh mosquitoes so bad that you're wearing ant nets and mosquito jackets to keep them off you, and you're working for weeks out there marking and releasing, trying to understand these butterflies. You're doing captive propagation back here year-round with a bunch of dedicated student helpers

who are doing much of the actual work. And then you go down there after a couple of years of no support and no releases and you see that the population has dwindled.[15]

Unfortunately, drought years followed, and the Schaus swallowtail population experienced a dramatic decline.[16] In 2011, Emmel documented that the population had diminished from forty-one butterflies to five, with only a single female.[17]

As a result, in June 2012 the USFWS issued an "emergency authorization" to collect and captively breed Schaus swallowtail butterflies.[18] However, no swallowtail butterflies were found that year. This led to a massive critique of the USFWS by the conservation community—both for its initial decision to stop captive breeding and for its belated decision to resume it. One butterfly expert was quoted saying: "The government owned this bug, and they dropped the ball."[19] "It's frustrating to have your hands tied . . . by bureaucratic indecision that lets things drift so far downward," Emmel remarked at the time.[20] Reflecting on the program a few years later, Emmel tells me: "with all endangered species projects the funding is always erratic. You can always expect them to be almost always late, or they'll skip a year or two or three thinking that you can just start it up again a couple of years later. . . . It's highly variable. What's needed is greater continuity in support, a commitment . . . that endangered species research should be continued or guaranteed in some way."[21]

A similar, albeit less well-documented, story is currently unfolding in the case of the Lange's metalmark butterfly (*Apodemia mormo langei*).[22] "It's ridiculous," Kierán Suckling comments. "The captive breeding programs in both cases should never have been canceled."[23] Such stories, and many others, demonstrate the fraught and codependent relationship between *in situ* and *ex situ* conservation and the dramatic impact of decisions to move animals—or not to move them—from *in situ* to *ex situ* and back.

As for the Schaus swallowtail, expanded late-season surveys in 2013 found thirty-one individuals.[24] One hundred eggs were collected from four females that year and propagated in captivity by Emmel and his team (Figure 16). By mid-2014, the butterflies who hatched from the original hundred eggs—known as "founders"—produced approximately one thousand larvae, and Emmel's team planned to reintroduce two to three hundred adults into the wild.[25]

Figure 16: Schaus swallowtail butterfly number 158, held by Thomas Emmel in 2013. Upon emergence from their sac, every captive adult is marked with a number on the underside of the wing. Schaus swallowtail 158 was marked on the day of her or his first capture, released, and then re-captured several days later. Courtesy of Thomas C. Emmel.

Reintroductions: From Ex Situ *to* In Situ

Reintroductions are but one of a wide variety of actions that involve the translocation of individual animals and populations for conservation purposes. Other actions include reinforcement, introduction, assisted colonization, and ecological replacement.[26] According to IUCN's reintroduction and translocation guidelines, within the variety of conservation translocations, the term "reintroduction" refers to "the intentional movement and release of an organism inside its indigenous range from which it has disappeared." "Reintroduction aims to reestablish a viable population of the focal species within its indigenous range," read the guidelines.[27] Case studies published in 2011 reported on 184 selected reintroductions from 24 different countries around the world in which captive-bred animals were released to reestablish or reinforce a wild population.[28] The only readily available overall reintroduction numbers are for the years 1990–1994, during which there were more than 13 million global captive-bred animal reintroductions, mostly of fish, toads, and salamanders.[29] Zoos provided animals for about half of these reintroductions.[30]

The success rates of reintroductions are debatable. While some scientists have asserted that only 10 percent of reintroductions have resulted in a self-sustaining wild population,[31] others estimate that 38 percent of projects reintroducing captive-bred animals were successful.[32] All agree, however, that reintroductions are a risky endeavor. Kierán Suckling of the Center for Biological Diversity reflects on some of the risks: "Many captive breeding, semi-captive breeding, and translocation programs fail, get revised, fail again, et cetera, for a decade or more, before they start to work," he says. "To succeed," he explains, "we have to discover and reproduce the critical aspects of nature necessary for the species to survive reintroduction and breed. We very often don't know how to do this when we start the captive breeding program. And even when the program succeeds, we often don't precisely know what factor made the difference after years of failure."[33]

Mark Stanley Price, chair of IUCN's Task Force of the Reintroduction and Invasive Species Specialist Groups, notes that reintroductions are particularly problematic when the reintroduced animals are transferred from *ex situ* conditions. He explains: "Zoos keep animals for release back into the wild, but protect them from predation and give them three square meals a day and water. Well, those are selective pressures. So after a few generations, these animals may well lose their adaptation to their real conditions, [and] when you put them back in the wild, they'll just die."[34] Research on the reintroduction of carnivores supports Stanley Price's claims, demonstrating higher success rates when using wild-caught, as opposed to captive-born, animals. Sociologist Carrie Friese argues more generally that "zoo animals become reliant upon humans in a way that delimits their ability to live in noncaptive settings."[35] Accordingly, individual black-footed ferrets who were reared in outdoor pens—where they had to predate on prairie dogs who established a burrow system within the pen—were more successful in comparison to cage-reared ones, where prairie dogs were provided rather than hunted.[36]

But reintroduction practices are evolving, and have changed rapidly over the last few decades. Stanley Price describes their historical trajectory:

> In the early days of reintroduction, [conservationists] were hopeless; people just let the animals out. And you [had to wonder], "Well, why did

you let out so many? Why did you let out ten and not twelve? Why did
you do it all at once? Why didn't you let out five this year and five next
year?" Every reintroduction is a risky exercise. Some are going to go under
[i.e., die]. But if you don't know why they die, then you don't know what to
do. And that's why we're saying: think about it, model it, optimize it, and
monitor it.[37]

Now, with more attention paid to the minute details and with the advances
in science and technology, "reintroductions have really taken off," according
to Stanley Price.

Conservationists refer to the fraught transitional phase between *ex situ*
and *in situ* as the "adaptation stage." For certain species, like the black-
footed ferret and the golden lion tamarin, this stage has been intensely re-
searched; for others, less so. And while the stories of ferret and tamarin
adaptations and their successful reintroductions are recited whenever one
mentions this term, many other reintroductions, such as those of the eastern
hellbender, occur far from the limelight.

Head-Starting the Eastern Hellbender

Growing more than two feet long, eastern hellbenders (*Cryptobranchus
alleganiensis alleganiensis*) easily win the title of North America's largest
amphibians. They are stout-bodied salamanders, also called by many colorful colloquial names, including "alligators of the mountains," "big water
lizards," "devil dogs," "mud devils," "walking catfish," "water dogs," and
the most accurate of all in my seven-year-old daughter's opinion, "snot
otters."[38] Eastern hellbenders can still be found in streams ranging from
New York to Mississippi, although their numbers are shrinking quickly. As
fully aquatic salamanders, hellbenders never leave the water. Water pol-
lution and the creation of reservoirs have therefore been major factors in
their decline.[39]

Nowadays, the hellbenders are protected by law and are the focus of considerable conservation efforts. Not too long ago, however, their extermination was the explicit goal of state operations. In the 1920s and 1930s,
hellbenders were subject to a massive eradication campaign. For example,
Pennsylvania offered bounties of 25 cents per hellbender with the explicit
goal of eliminating the salamanders from trout streams because they were

mistakenly believed to be poisonous and to feed on trout.[40] Such misconceptions are still rampant and result in the death of numerous protected hellbenders, especially at the hands of fishermen.[41]

The eastern hellbender is listed as endangered in Maryland, Ohio, Illinois, and Indiana and as threatened in Alabama. In New York State, this subspecies is found only in the Allegheny and Susquehanna River watersheds. As a result of their limited distribution and their dramatic decline, in 1983 the New York State Department of Environmental Conservation (DEC) listed hellbenders as a species of special concern and is currently taking action to prevent them from becoming threatened or endangered. In 2013, the Center for Biological Diversity filed a lawsuit against the USFWS for failing to list the eastern hellbender as a threatened subspecies under the federal ESA.[42]

Whether or not the hellbender is listed, and under which list(s), are questions of acute importance in a conservation regime that relies heavily on such lists to classify, measure, and generate priorities among species. These struggles over the hellbenders' threat status demonstrate what I have referred to elsewhere as the "technology of listing" in conservation: administrative listing decisions often have life-or-death consequences, rendering a listed species' life valuable and grievable and an unlisted life insignificant and killable.[43]

In 2009, New York State devised a plan that included both habitat restoration and a larvae "head-start" program for the hellbenders. The habitat restoration plan has focused on the re-creation of the hellbenders' critical habitat. Hellbenders use large flat stones for cover, and so Kenneth Roblee, a wildlife biologist at the DEC, worked with the New York State Department of Transportation (DOT) to purchase and place huge flat stones, similar to the ones that were previously removed from streams for construction, back into the streams to enhance breeding and nursery habitat. More than 33 tons (2,300 square feet) of such boulders were placed in selected sections of the Allegheny River watershed for this purpose.[44] "The DOT is committed to rebuilding and maintaining our transportation system to the benefit of all New Yorkers," DOT Commissioner Joan McDonald said in a press release, including the hellbenders among those New Yorkers on the receiving end of state benefits.[45]

Alongside habitat restoration, the hellbender recovery program also includes a head-start strategy, making it unique among the animal programs discussed in this book. Simply stated, the strategy utilized in this context consists of collecting hellbender eggs from the wild, hatching and propagating them in captivity, and then reintroducing them into the wild before they reach sexual maturity.[46] The hellbenders are thus removed when they are in the most vulnerable developmental stage and reintroduced once they are larger and better equipped to deal with the various threats in their habitat.

The head-start contract was awarded to the Buffalo Zoo. Since 2009, about 700 hellbender eggs have been collected from the Allegheny River watershed and transferred to the zoo, where herpetologist Penny Felski has been carefully attending to their needs with such success that surplus hellbenders have been transferred to other zoos, some to be reared for reintroduction and others for display.[47] At the zoo, all the hellbenders are measured, weighed, and implanted with a Passive Integrated Transponder (PIT) tag, which enables their identification both in captivity and in the wild.[48]

Born wild, reared in captivity, and then transferred back to the wild, hellbenders complicate the notion of a clean *in situ–ex situ* dichotomy, suggesting that not just sites of geographical habitat, but bodies, too, may be *inter situ* hybrids. Below, my personal observations of the hellbenders' reintroduction detail the complexities of the movement between captive and wild for both the human and the nonhuman animals involved.

It is August 2013, and more than 150 PIT-tagged juvenile hellbenders are being transported from the Buffalo Zoo back to the Allegheny River watershed as part of their annual reintroduction. My then six-year-old daughter and I have joined Felski for the trip. Felski is both sad and elated as she accompanies her hellbenders to their old-new home. Constructing a makeshift station in the stream that includes weighing equipment and a transponder reader, Felski documents every hellbender before sending them off to the crew situated deeper in the stream. "Those are their little toe pads—aren't they cute?" Felski shows my daughter. "And look how each one of them is so different: this one has those brown spots on its face, and this has pink all over its back!"[49]

Meanwhile, farther down the stream, Roblee and five men from the Seneca Nation lift flat boulders to determine the best spot for each hellbender's release. "It needs to be flat enough for the hellbender to be protected, but with a crevice that would let it catch crayfish when they swim by," Roblee explains. The boulder is also inspected for competition. "You don't want it to be occupied by another hellbender or anything else," Roblee tells me as he rules out all of my suggestions for placement. After lengthy negotiations over each particular boulder and its suitability as the animal's new habitat, the hellbender is gently placed in a net and carried to the location ("We don't want them to panic, because then they release this intense liquid and exhaust themselves," says Felski).[50]

The reintroduction I witnessed was what biologists call a "hard release." In this case, after four years of being reared in individual aquariums at the Buffalo Zoo (Figure 17), the hellbenders are released into the Allegheny stream. The exact location of the release, as well as the identity of each reintroduced hellbender, is finally documented by two graduate students with a GPS device and a notebook (Figure 18). A few days earlier, in preparation for the hellbenders' passage to wild adulthood in the Allegheny, "we threw some crayfish into their aquarium to train them to

Figure 17: The hellbenders' habitat at the Buffalo Zoo, where each individual inhabits a separate aquarium, on the morning of their reintroduction into the Allegheny River. Photo by author, August 1, 2013.

Figure 18: Re-identified and freshly weighed by Felski, the hellbenders are then transported by net to their release site down the stream, where Jolene and Rebecca of New York State's DEC, GPS and notebook in hand, document the precise release location. Photo by author, August 1, 2013.

detect crayfish smell and associate it with food."[51] This was the full extent of the hellbenders' pre-release training.

Soft releases are different, Roblee explains. The only soft release in this program, performed in 2012 by a graduate student, involved a cage within which the hellbenders were released into the stream so that they could remain protected while adapting to their new environment. Nearly all of that year's eighteen soft-released hellbenders escaped—and were likely consumed shortly afterward by raccoons.[52] The success of the hellbenders' hard releases has also been questionable. Of more than one hundred hellbenders reintroduced in 2012, the recovery team found only eight in the release site a few months later. "I want to believe that they just made their way to another part of the stream," Felski tells me. "It's more likely that they got eaten by raccoons," Roblee says in response.[53] Half of the eighty hellbenders planned for release in summer 2014 were to be reintroduced in individual cages, this time in a soft release managed by New York State.[54]

As this and many other reintroduction stories reveal, the physical transfer of animal bodies from captivity into the wild requires constant readjustment to accommodate the varying needs of different species at different times and locations. These movements raise numerous questions: how to decide when to take a species into captivity in the first place, and then how to determine whether, when, where, and how many members of this species should be reintroduced—and when to stop? Each reintroduction, like every species, presents its own unique story. The stakes, too, vary significantly from one case to the next: conservationists have been willing to take risks with hellbender reintroductions that they would not take with the northern white rhino, black-footed ferret, Tasmanian devil, or golden lion tamarin.

To create a common baseline for addressing these questions, in 1987 the IUCN drafted a policy statement that recommended the initiation of a captive propagation program for taxa with fewer than one thousand individuals,[55] and is currently considering decreasing this figure.[56] Under this standard, two thousand large vertebrate species would require captive propagation assistance to avoid extinction.[57] In 1995, zoos managed approximately 160 taxa through captive breeding programs—about 8 percent of IUCN's recommended figure for captive propagation.[58]

Despite the low success rate of reintroductions, many conservationists still see them as the primary purpose for maintaining animals in captivity and they are consequently becoming more frequent.[59] The increasing traffic between *ex situ* and *in situ* conservation sites has prompted intensified regulation, including "soft laws" such as standards and guidelines. Below, I outline the global guidelines articulated by the IUCN for regulating *inter situ* traffic. Although not binding in the formal legal sense, the IUCN guidelines are the foundation for many binding legal systems in a variety of national and international contexts.

Regulating Inter Situ *Traffic*

IUCN's 2013 Guidelines for Reintroductions and Other Conservation Translocations distinguish between different types of animal movement for conservation: "(i) reinforcement and reintroduction *within* a species' indigenous range, and (ii) conservation introductions, comprising assisted colonization and ecological replacement, *outside* indigenous range."[60] The guidelines define "indigenous range" as "the known or inferred distribution generated from historical (written or verbal) records, or physical evidence of the species' occurrence,"[61] explaining that "translocations of organisms outside of their indigenous range are considered to be especially high risk given the numerous examples of species released outside their indigenous ranges subsequently becoming invasive, often with massively adverse impact."[62] In the words of Stanley Price, who facilitated the regulatory efforts: "Indigenous means where [a species] used to be." "If you don't say something like that," he explains, "you'll have people releasing animals all over the place." This is far from merely a theoretical concern. "The record of people just releasing things irresponsibly has led to the whole problem of invasive species, which is costing us billions of pounds a year."[63]

IUCN's guidelines for reintroductions are concerned only with transfers from outside the indigenous range to inside it; they do not apply to the movement of free-ranging populations within the indigenous range, even when one of the sites is intensively managed.[64] Thus, while the guidelines formalize and facilitate certain forms of movement, their definitions simultaneously reinstate a certain binary. The precise relationship between the binary of inside and outside an indigenous range and that of the *in situ–ex situ* divide is complex. How is indigenous range different from *in situ*, and is everything outside a range *ex situ* by definition? While a species' occurrence at a zoo would likely not be considered within the species' indigenous range, it is much less clear whether semi-captive and semi-wild settings can be classified as such.

Stanley Price provides his perspective on some of these questions. Conservation should aim "to protect a viable number of species in their *natural* homes," he tells me. Nonetheless, he is the first to admit that "we don't have wilderness any longer; it's a lovely romantic notion, but everything is man-influenced now." Nature as an ideal type is "fraud," he states flatly. "We don't live in a stable system. It has changed historically and it's going to change in the future. . . . [So] all one can really do is to guide people."[65]

Alongside the movement of animals into their indigenous range, animals are also transferred "from the inside out"—namely, from their indigenous range into captivity. The IUCN Technical Guidelines on the Management of *Ex Situ* Populations for Conservation[66] regulate the movement of bodies from the wild into zoos. Starting with the laws against taking certain wildlife into captivity enacted in the 1970s, wild-to-captive traffic has been strictly prohibited for many species. However, ecological changes such as habitat loss, invasive species, and disease are increasingly requiring the transfer of wild animals into captivity for the survival or future recovery of their species (Chapter 2). For this reason, *ex situ* conservation is becoming widely acknowledged as a legitimate strategy. How to best regulate the movement from *in situ* to *ex situ* is thus becoming a question of increasing concern for experts from across the conservation world.

The 2013 draft of IUCN's new guidelines for *ex situ* conservation management articulates a five-step process for any decision to transfer a wild animal into captivity: (1) an evaluation, (2) an assessment of the potential role of *ex situ* management in the conservation of the particular species, (3) the precise characteristics of the *ex situ* population needed to fulfill the identified conservation role, (4) an appraisal of feasibility and risk and, finally, (5) the formation of an educated and transparent decision.[67] Kathy Traylor-Holzer of CBSG has been coordinating these regulatory efforts. Her aim in drafting the guidelines, she tells me, has been to help decision makers figure out whether it is "appropriate to use some kind of *ex situ* management to support a broader conservation goal for a species."[68]

Translocations: The Case of Lemurs on Moskito Island

The movement of species is not confined to the traditional transfer of animal bodies from "out" to "in" and vice versa; multiple other movements between various *inter situ* contexts exist that complicate this dichotomy. As I shall show here, characterizing such movement as merely moving animals from one type of *situ* to another would fail to account for the differences between different individuals, species, and settings. The various movements are referred to, broadly, as "translocations." IUCN's 2013 Guidelines for Reintroductions and Other Conservation Translocations discussed above define translocations as "the deliberate movement of organisms from one site for release in another . . . intended to yield a measurable conservation benefit at the levels of a population, species or ecosystem, and not only [to] provide benefit to translocated individuals."[69]

Although reintroductions are defined by the IUCN as a subset of translocations, when field conservationists refer to translocations they typically exclude reintroductions.

While translocations remain controversial, IUCN's reintroduction guidelines state that conservationists may be required to rely on them more and more in the future. According to these guidelines: "There are increasing and acute pressures on much of the world's biodiversity due to loss of habitats and reduction in their quality, biological invasions, and climate change. The latter is the main force behind the proposition to move organisms deliberately outside their indigenous ranges . . . an exercise of greater potential risks than a reinforcement or reintroduction."[70] The guidelines require a formal risk assessment prior to each translocation to evaluate both the potential risks to other species living in the area and the socioeconomic risks to human populations.[71]

A recent story exemplifies some of the challenges of conservation translocations. In 2011, billionaire Sir Richard Branson, owner of the Virgin Group, decided to dedicate Moskito Island, one of his two private islands in the Caribbean, to helping conserve lemurs—a taxon comprising 104 species listed as the most threatened primates in the world (Figure 19). The lemurs are threatened by deforestation in their native Madagascar— some 8,000 miles away from Branson's island—where political turmoil has accelerated illegal logging. "He wanted to give lemurs a different home, somewhere away from Madagascar, because he saw Madagascar going down the drain," says Christoph Schwitzer, coordinator of IUCN's SSC Primate Specialist Group and an expert on lemur conservation.[72] "Maybe [Sir Richard] has got some people to say it is all right—but what else lives on the island, and how might they be affected?" Simon Stuart, chair of IUCN's SSC, remarked on the BBC.[73] Stuart also told the BBC that this project could contravene IUCN's Guidelines for Reintroductions and Other Conservation Translocations, which, in his words, were "designed to prevent the repetition of disastrous events such as the introduction of rabbits and cane toads to Australia."[74] Despite outspoken resistance from many conservationists, the first consignment, consisting of several dozen ring-tailed lemurs, was transferred to Moskito Island from zoos in Sweden, South Africa, and Canada in 2011.[75] Apparently, Sir Richard believes that lemurs could ultimately be reintroduced from Moskito Island back to Madagascar.

Figure 19: A ring-tailed lemur at the Smithsonian's National Zoo interacts with an enrichment pumpkin on Halloween. The National Zoo's lemurs are part of the Ring-Tailed Lemur SSP, coordinated by the AZA with the goal of keeping the captive lemur population genetically viable. Photo by Meghan Murphy/Smithsonian, CC BY-NC-ND 2.0.

But Sir Richard's is not the only, or even the first, effort to save the lemurs. Captive breeding programs already exist for this purpose. Schwitzer tells me accordingly: "We did a Red List and conservation planning workshop for lemurs in July 2012. We obviously had lots of lemur experts there, from all over the world, many of whom were from Madagascar, but we also had people from the zoo community there." The proceedings of that workshop were integrated into a lemur conservation strategy for 2013–16, "which will be a site-based conservation strategy. So we have thirty priority sites for [*in situ*] lemur conservation in Madagascar, but we also have a big *ex situ* chapter, [with plans] to establish four different *ex situ* lemur breeding centers in Madagascar."[76] The priority of these breeding centers, Schwitzer explains, is to "build up local expertise [in Madagascar], using expertise from the zoo community."

Although the focus of the conservation strategy was limited to *ex situ* sites in Madagascar, Schwitzer does not rule out the option of translocating lemurs to other *ex situ* sites, even if they are situated halfway across the planet. However, he insists that in such cases the lemurs should be confined in enclosures. In his words:

> I told [Sir Richard] that he can have as many lemurs as he likes on his island, but he should build an enclosure for them [and that] even if that enclosure is several hundred hectares large, that is fine, as long as the animals are in a controlled environment and don't eat up all the endemic species. And he took that on board. . . . We sent him somebody who had built some enclosures here at the Bristol Zoo, and this expert built him a lemur enclosure. . . . So he has a couple of lemur species out there, which all came from zoos—most of them from European zoos, some of them from South African zoos—and the [lemurs] are all living there.[77]

Clearly, the movement of endangered lemurs from zoos to the semi-wild enclosures of Moskito Island was not the only translocation in this story; there was also a translocation of knowledge, with captivity experts building the island's enclosures and sharing their expertise. Moskito Island, like Maria and Rotoroa Islands discussed later in this book, is one of a growing number of islands and enclosed areas that are becoming hybrid sites, amalgams of wild and captive.

Conclusion

Along with many other imperiled species, lemurs, hellbenders, and Schaus swallowtail butterflies are attracting much attention from conservationists and generating momentum for the regulation of animal movement in its different manifestations—an effort on the part of conservationists to tighten the controls over the transitional stages between *in situ* and *ex situ*. This chapter has focused on IUCN's guidelines for the movement of animals from and into captivity.

Such attempts to govern *in situ–ex situ* traffic are not confined to IUCN norms, however.[78] In addition to the scientific guidelines, formal national laws also govern the movement of animals, and international treaties regulate such matters when they occur across national borders. The Convention on International Trade in Endangered Species of Wild Fauna and Flora (CITES) is an example of such formal international regulation. This is an important international treaty that aims "to ensure that international trade in specimens of wild animals and plants does not threaten their survival."[79]

The issuance of CITES permits for moving animals across national borders is immensely complicated.[80] Today, CITES accords varying degrees of protection to more than 35,000 species of animals and plants, whether they are traded as live specimens, fur coats, or dried herbs.[81]

Puerto Rican Parrot

The parrots do all the work, in the wild and in the captive population. I think that is the main key of the success of this program.
—Gustavo Olivieri, Coordinator, José Vivaldi Aviary[1]

Paracelsus used to say: "Everything is poison. There is nothing without poison. What stops something from being poison is the dose." In management it's the same. You want to get to the proper dose of management, not too much management or too little, and that's where we work.
—Ricardo Valentin, Coordinator, José Vivaldi Aviary[2]

The Puerto Rican parrots (*Amazona vittata*) stand approximately one foot tall, with bright green feathers, coal black eyes surrounded by white, and red face markings (Figure 20). The only parrots endemic to Puerto Rico, they declined from an estimated one million birds before European colonization to between 200 and 250 birds in the mid-1950s.[3] The major reason for the decline was loss of habitat through deforestation: the parrots rely on old or decaying trees for nest cavities to rear their young, and 90 percent of Puerto Rico had been deforested by the mid-1950s.[4] The remaining parrot population was confined to the Luquillo Mountains of northeastern Puerto Rico.[5]

By 1973, the parrot population amounted to thirteen adult birds, placing them on the brink of extinction by any criterion. At this point, a decision was made to start a breeding population in captivity. "It was a big risk," recalls Jafet Vélez-Valentín, Iguaca Aviary manager for the USFWS at

Figure 20: A Puerto Rican parrot feeds in a flight cage, the last stage before full release, Iguaca Aviary, El Yunque Forest, Puerto Rico. Photo by author, January 14, 2014.

Luquillo.[6] To minimize the risk, rather than pulling out any of the thirteen remaining breeding-age adults, the team selected eleven eggs and chicks and took them into captivity. All captive birds to date are descendants of those eleven founders.[7] The first breeding population was established at the Luquillo (now Iguaca) Aviary near Pico El Yunque in the Caribbean National Forest in 1973. A second breeding population was established in the José Vivaldi Aviary at Río Abajo in 1993.

At first, the captive breeding program produced one to three chicks per year. But by 2000, biologists had become relatively successful at breeding parrots in captivity, and by 2014, the program was producing between seventy-five and one hundred chicks per year.[8] Many of these birds have been released into one of two sites: El Yunque and Río Abajo. Both sites utilize complex strategies that interweave captive and wild management for the recovery of the Puerto Rican parrot. El Yunque, considered the last remaining natural habitat for the parrot, is an island of tropical rainforest in a sea of urban development.[9] In 2000, the first captive-bred parrots were released there.[10] Rather than attempting to establish a new population from scratch, the parrot program in this location has been augmenting the existing wild population. It can therefore be defined, technically, as "population supplementation" rather than as a traditional reintroduction.[11] During the first three years, thirty-four captive-reared birds were released, of which twenty or so died, mostly due to predation by red-tailed hawks (*Buteo jamaicensis*). The first offspring of a released bird was observed in 2004.[12]

The Puerto Rican parrot program has principally relied on experiments with a closely related parrot: the Hispaniolan Amazon (*Amazona ventralis*) of the Dominican Republic. Unlike the Puerto Rican parrot, the Hispaniolan is not listed as endangered and was therefore a convenient surrogate for experimentation.[13] From 1997 to 1999, forty-nine Hispaniolan parrots were released in the Dominican Republic. At first many died, but through experimentation a team of scientists learned that the parrots require both pre- and post-release management to thrive in the wild, including flight training before release, acclimation to release sites, and food supplementation.[14] On the basis of these findings, for their initial releases in El Yunque the Puerto Rican parrots were held for at least four months in large flight cages before being transferred to acclimation cages at the release site. Additionally, one month prior to their release the parrots underwent a three-phase training process to recognize hawks and other threats. Using progressively stronger stimuli—first, a hawk call and a silhouette of a hawk moving in the sky above the cage, then an actual fly-over by a trained hawk, and finally a hawk attacking a tethered (protected) Hispaniolan for the caged parrots to witness—the researchers sensitized the parrots to the sights and sounds of hawks. After this experimentation, 84 percent of the parrots showed increased vigilance that would, the experts hoped, help them survive in the wild.[15] The same general procedure, with some site-specific modifications, has been used in the Río Abajo releases.

Another release strategy was deployed in El Yunque, this time to ensure that the captive-bred parrots would join the existing wild flock upon their release. This strategy, developed by Thomas White, captive release coordinator at El Yunque, is called "precision release." According to White, the time of release is calculated precisely so that it falls within the brief window when the wild flock is still stationary, yet their territorial instincts have receded. The injection of captive birds into the wild population thus takes advantage of the behavioral cycles of the wild parrots.[16] Since researchers started using this technique, the survival rate of El Yunque's released birds has risen to an average of 67 percent, well beyond the previous rates.[17] Despite these successes, however, parrot survival is still highly dependent on human management: biologists estimate that the El Yunque flock is likely to become extinct within two decades if intensive human management comes to an end.[18]

Río Abajo and El Yunque are very different. "Whole different habitats, whole different factors, they are a whole different ball game," White tells me.[19] Rather than supplementing an existing parrot population, as is done at El Yunque, the scientists at Río Abajo have established a new population of parrots in their former habitat. In Río Abajo, the parrots are released into a large complex immediately adjacent to the captive birds' cages that is essentially part of the aviary.[20] Indeed, when I visited this site in 2014 I found it hard to discern where the cages ended and the wild began (Figure 21). The Río Abajo aviary is thus itself emblematic of the blurring of captive and wild.

Ricardo Valentin of the Puerto Rican Department of Natural and Environmental Resources Parrot Project and Gustavo Olivieri, a field biologist, are the coordinators of the Puerto Rican parrot release program at the Río Abajo aviary. Valentin tells me that this site was "more like a desperate rescue operation" when it became clear in the 1980s that breeding at the Luquillo (now Iguaca) Aviary was not proceeding as rapidly as they hoped.[21]

Figure 21: Ricardo Valentin, aviculturist with the Puerto Rican Parrot Reintroduction Program at the José L. Vivaldi Aviary, stands beside the Puerto Rican parrots' training cages at Río Abajo, Puerto Rico. Photo by author, January 22, 2013.

The relevant agencies thought that Río Abajo, a former Peace Corps camp located in a dry forest, would be a more suitable habitat for the parrot than El Yunque, and thus chose this location for the new reintroductions.[22] The Río Abajo reintroductions started in 2006 with the initial release of twenty-four parrots.[23] These reintroductions have followed a model of intensive and continuous monitoring, supplementation, and management.[24]

Generally, parrot management has entailed managing the fluidity between populations of wild-born, semi-feral, and captive-bred parrots. White describes the parrots' existing populations as "semi-feral," but believes that they are transitioning toward independence, as evidenced by the first generation of wild-born offspring of released birds having recently reached reproductive age. He adds, "When you're releasing parrots from captivity into the wild . . . you can't expect them just to become wild birds. . . . There's a transition time."[25] People want the birds to "Go! Be free! Be wild!" White tells me. But "it doesn't work that way. One of the reasons that the Río Abajo stuff has really been so successful is because there was lots of post-release support."[26]

Another important parrot conservation strategy performed in this case has been the construction of nests. To overcome the lack of mature trees with natural cavities, parrot experts in both Río Abajo and El Yunque have crafted artificial nests out of PVC that are then attached to trees.[27] In addition to providing nesting opportunities for the parrots, the PVC nests contain special niches for cameras that enable intensive monitoring of the birds, both in the wild and in captivity.[28] The camera room in the El Yunque facility is a sophisticated surveillance operation, containing dozens of screens that show more than forty-five nest locations with eggs or chicks. According to Valentin, the cameras have enabled the staff both to constantly monitor the health of the eggs and chicks and to take eggs from nests and trade them with others, in line with the program's requirements. For example, "we think that four chicks are too much—[because] the last one will probably die—so most of the time we leave [wild] parrots with three chicks."[29]

Diet supplementation with feeders is another conservation strategy practiced in this context.[30] Both artificial nest cavities and supplemental feeding encourage birds to flock around the release site near the aviary rather than disperse into the forest. This is critical for their recovery. When in larger groups, the parrots alert one another to the presence of predators. This is called the "Trafalgar effect," and it significantly increases the rate of parrot survival. Another reason scientists created an integrated captive-wild habitat was their finding that if parrot numbers fall below a certain threshold, the individuals stop forming pairs and breeding—a phenomenon called the "Allee effect." Reintroducing the parrots near the cages that hold their captive counterparts increases their sense of an occupied habitat. The released birds stay together as a flock near the release site, where they are also more easily monitored and protected.[31] Captive and wild parrots are therefore perceived by the experts, and possibly also by the parrots themselves, as one flock.[32] Valentin notes, accordingly, that most of the released birds have remained near the aviary.[33] His hope is that over time, the Río Abajo birds will diffuse from the aviary and begin to use natural cavities. White explains: "That's the next big step. That's the whole goal. And it's working."[34] Indeed, in 2013 Valentin's team recorded the first case of parrots using natural rather than artificial cavities for nesting.

The parrots are managed as one flock not only among wild and captive populations in each aviary, but also between the two aviaries, effectively constituting one metapopulation. Olivieri explains: "We move chicks and eggs from one population to another."[35] For example, infertile wild birds are given captive eggs to foster.[36] Additionally, on-site Hispaniolans sit on eggs pulled out of the nests of Puerto Rican parrots who have recently laid eggs. This impels the endangered parrots to lay another clutch, thereby doubling their chances of successful reproduction for the year.[37] Such efforts require close collaboration across agencies and between experts. For this purpose, the USFWS, USDA's Forest Service in El Yunque, and the Department of Natural and Environmental Resources have created an interagency recovery team that routinely meets at three levels—administrative, operational, and technical—to negotiate the details of parrot management based on the availability of birds, funding, and expertise.[38]

Treating the four populations[39] as one integrated metapopulation requires careful monitoring and computer modeling. To achieve this, meticulous databases for both wild and captive individual parrots are maintained. In 2007, scientists from Lincoln Park Zoo traveled to Puerto Rico to assist with entering hundreds of records into PopLink, a zoo-developed software program that enables managers to analyze trends in parrot populations.[40] "We are the envy of the zoo community," Vélez-Valentín tells me proudly.[41] The key to this success is computer modeling, he explains. In addition to knowing, tracking, and documenting the birds in minute detail, studbooks track genetic similarities between parrot pairs to keep inbreeding below a certain level, and a computer program recommends their pairing.[42]

In 2014, there were three hundred Puerto Rican parrots in Puerto Rico, fifty-eight to eighty of them living in the wild.[43] This success story, as my interviewees have repeatedly pointed out, can be attributed to the various strategies that effectively blur both the *in situ–ex situ* and the captive-wild divides on the individual, population, and habitat scales. Nonetheless, these divides persist in myriad legal norms that maintain and reinforce them.

In 2004, parts of El Yunque were designated as "wilderness areas" under the U.S. Wilderness Act of 1964.[44] As it turns out, this Act prohibits some of the actions deemed necessary for the continued survival of the endangered parrot, such as constructing roads to access and monitor the release sites and using chain saws to create nesting cavities. In the words of Edwin Muñiz, the field supervisor for USFWS's Caribbean ES Field Office, and Marisel López-Flores, the project leader of the USFWS Puerto Rican Parrot Recovery Program: "Every intervention required by the ESA to save a species contradicted what the Wilderness Act required to save the habitat."[45] They continue: "We had to reinvent ourselves in terms of what we did within the 'wilderness'—and that took some getting used to."[46] In order to perform actions that were deemed necessary for parrot recovery, the USFWS ended up undertaking a long permit process under the Wilderness Act.[47]

Another regulatory conflict that developed in this context is between the ESA and the Migratory Bird Treaty Act. An estimated 225 hawks live within the El Yunque forest, giving it the highest hawk population density in the Western Hemisphere—and creating a persistent threat to the released parrots. The red-tailed hawks are legally protected under the Migratory Bird Treaty Act. To negotiate this conflict, a permit was granted through the Migratory Bird Treaty Act that allows the USFWS to "take" (in this case, kill) up to twenty-four hawks a year to protect vulnerable parrots. In the words of López-Flores: "[We] carefully monitor fledglings at nest sites when they are most vulnerable and shoot hawks that seem to be about to prey on them. . . . The [adults] have survived for many years, so they know how to evade the red-tailed hawk, but the babies—they don't."[48] "We only take it [the hawk] when one of those animals [is] going to take a parrot," Muñiz clarifies.[49]

The story of Puerto Rican parrot conservation thus aptly demonstrates the fluidity between captive and wild. It also shows that a flexible interpretation of this divide allows for more creativity in administering certain species and individuals. Additionally, this story highlights the complex and overlapping legal regimes imposed on endangered life, a topic that I will discuss at length in the next chapter. Finally, the parrot story demonstrates the differential treatment between lives that matter more (endangered parrots, and fledglings in particular) and those that matter less (the Hispaniolans and the red-tailed hawks). While centered on affirmative "make live" projects, species conservation is thus undeniably also a story of violence and death.

CHAPTER 5

Regulatory Life

For many, the term "law" inspires images of majestic courtyards, solemn judges, and massive, dusty, statutory books. My use of this term is slightly different. By "law," I mean everything from federal statutes and case law to departmental regulations, city ordinances, and industry standards, as well as routines and practices that are not codified into written rules and standards. Threatened species lists, professional guidelines, and recovery plans are all part of what I consider law.[1] In other words, I see law as an "ensemble formed by institutions, procedures, analyses and reflections, calculations, and tactics"—what Michel Foucault calls "governmentality."[2] This book argues that the application of such regulatory ensembles to the life of populations—and to the life of nonhuman species in particular—constitutes a biopolitical regime. This chapter will explore how conservation laws' biopolitical regime both reinforces the *in situ–ex situ* dichotomy and also negotiates and resists it.

The chapter will focus on one regulatory context in particular: the U.S. Endangered Species Act (ESA) of 1973. This focus serves my broader goal of exploring both the powers and the limits of legal technologies for regulating conservation practices, and their specific implications for the *in situ–ex situ* divide. Discussing four legal strategies in which the captive is distinguished from the wild—the "take" clause and its exceptions, the designation of non-essential experimental populations, hybridization policies, and split-listing practices—I will show how the *in situ–ex situ* divide still very much informs the work of administrators who assess, count, or discount animal bodies for listing and recovery.

The Endangered Species Act

Unlike the CBD's explicit definition of *ex situ* as executed "predominantly for the purpose of complementing in-situ measures" (Chapter 1),[3] the ESA makes no explicit mention of the *in situ–ex situ* distinction. "As a matter of law, there is no regulation that speaks to this issue," Kierán Suckling of the Center for Biological Diversity tells me in the context of U.S. federal law. "In fact, this is probably not a codified official policy," he says, referring to the preference of *in situ* over *ex situ* conservation. "Just look at how the ESA has evolved to deal with the problem, without it being explicitly in the statute," notes legal scholar Dale Goble along the same lines. "It's exponentially *more* interesting!"[4]

Despite the differences between them on the textual level, the ESA and the CBD both privilege *in situ* over *ex situ* in practice. USFWS director Dan Ashe tells me flatly that "the context of the [ESA] is entirely oriented toward conserving species *in the wild*. We don't count species that are in captivity for recovery purposes."[5] Goble explains the historical context of ESA's preferential treatment of *in situ* over *ex situ*: "You have to remember that this was 1973—essentially the dark ages when it comes to the science of extinction. If you take a step back and look at the Act, it's essentially a fish and game management statute. . . . Things have changed a whole lot since then. . . . But I do think that the basic presumption of the Act is *in situ* conservation."[6] Finally, Suckling suggests that "while the ESA does not explicitly discuss the status or role of *ex situ* populations, it has many statements and provisions making it indirectly clear to all that the primary purpose [of the law] is to establish self-sustaining populations in the wild. The lack of express statement is because no one believes recovery can be accomplished within captivity alone. It didn't need to be stated."[7]

While *ex situ* conservation is not addressed explicitly in the Act, the term "captivity" is defined in the *Federal Register*, which is the formal compilation of guidelines and policies by U.S. governmental agencies. According to the *Federal Register*:

> As compared to populations that exist in the wild, "captivity" is defined as "living wildlife" held in a controlled environment that is intensively manipulated by man for the purpose of producing wildlife of the selected species, and that has boundaries designed to prevent animal [*sic*], eggs or gametes of the selected species from entering or leaving the controlled environment. General characteristics of captivity may include but are not limited to artificial housing, waste removal, health care, protection from predators, and artificially supplied food.[8]

The policy's choice of the terms "controlled," "boundaries," "producing," "artificial," and "intensively manipulated" creates a certain image of the captive environment that is then contrasted with "populations that exist in the wild," which, it is implied by this text, are quite different.

Nonetheless, various court decisions emphasize the benefits of *ex situ* conservation. Captive breeding can benefit wild populations by "increasing the likelihood that captive breeding populations will be established as a source of known genetic stock to bolster or reestablish populations in the wild; . . . reducing the need to take stock from the wild for scientific or other purposes; and . . . providing opportunities for research that can lead to improved management of wild populations."[9] Despite the complexity of current conservation regimes and the blurring of the *in situ* and *ex situ* divide in practice, the traditional dichotomy between wild and captive still clearly informs the rhetoric of legal norms and administrative standards regarding conservation.

What connects *in situ* to *ex situ* conservation, it is assumed in the legal norms and by many conservationists, is the wildness of the animals in both locations. Protecting a domesticated donkey or a dog is typically not considered conservation, precisely because it has nothing to do with wild species. Such wildness is often understood as the animals' perceived capacity to survive in a similar environment as their ancestors did or their conspecifics still do. The assumed wildness of a particular species is thus what ties both *in situ* and *ex situ* actions to conservation and to each other. This connection is also what renders the animal at the zoo or in a frozen genebank valuable for conservation. A shared understanding of the wildness of life, in other words, is the glue that binds *in situ* and *ex situ* conservation together.[10]

Yet as many have acknowledged, the boundaries between wildness and domestication are never stable: the threat of domesticity accompanies the condition of captivity, and so the dichotomy between nature and culture is always in danger of spilling into the interrelated dichotomy between wild and domesticated life. The following statement is from a footnote in one of the decisions by the USFWS—the central agency overseeing the implementation of the ESA:

> The analysis in this document addresses only situations where it is not disputed that the specimens are members of a wildlife species. This analysis does not address situations where members of a species have been held in captivity for a sufficiently long period that they have developed into a separate domesticated form of the species, including where the domesticated form is sufficiently distinct to be considered a separate taxonomic species or subspecies (e.g., domesticated donkey vs. the African wild ass).[11]

J. Michael Scott, professor of fish and wildlife resources at the University of Idaho and leader of the Idaho Cooperative Fish and Wildlife Research Unit, explains that "once you bring a species into captivity, you change the evolutionary trajectory of that species; it starts becoming a different organism—because the selective forces in captivity are much different than the selective forces in the wild." For example, he adds, "salmon raised in hatcheries start to change . . . and the longer you keep them in captivity, the greater [the] variation from what you originally had."[12] Captivity thus emerges as the intermediate site between wild and domesticated.

Listing Life

The ESA protects only species listed as endangered or threatened. A species may be listed in one of two ways: the USFWS or the National Marine Fisheries Service (NMFS: the federal agency responsible for managing the recovery of protected marine species and for all federal fisheries) can directly list a species it determines to be imperiled (i.e., either threatened or endangered), or an individual or organization may petition the USFWS or the NMFS to list such a species. To be considered for listing, species must meet one of five criteria: (1) that there is current or threatened destruction, modification, or curtailment of their habitat or range; (2) that their habitat is over-utilized for commercial, recreational, scientific, or educational purposes; (3) that they are declining due to disease or predation; (4) that regulatory mechanisms are inadequate; or (5) that other natural or man-made factors exist that affect the species' continued existence.[13] Notably, the USFWS lacks a written policy regarding the conditions under which it recommends transferring wild animals into captivity. Instead, the decision is made on a case-by-case basis by the parties of the relevant recovery plan.

Of an estimated 45,816 nonhuman species in the United States,[14] approximately 1,400 appear on ESA's domestic endangered and threatened list, and another 900 appear on its foreign list.[15] The number of species awaiting their turn to be included on both domestic and foreign lists is constantly on the rise. Indeed, researchers have estimated that the actual number of species threatened with extinction is at least ten times greater than the number of species protected under the ESA.[16]

The exploding number of imperiled species vying for the government's limited resources has resulted in the need to prioritize: the USFWS must continually assess which species to protect and, simultaneously, which do not merit legal protection. "Whether or not we're ultimately going to be successful with the California condor remains to be seen," J. Michael Scott tells me. "But if we *hadn't* done it, they'd be extinct. And on the other hand, we didn't bring in the palila [bird] to captively rear it, . . . nor the Molokaī thrush, nor the Hawaiian thrush. We had the opportunity—but we didn't do it. And, forty years later, what's the consequence of that? They're extinct."[17] The power to list, de-list, down-list and up-list, as well as the power to *not* list, is an executive power to "make live or let die"—the prerogative of the biopolitical regime. At its most literal, this is the power of the state to provide or withdraw support for the lives within its purview, thereby rendering them either grievable or killable.

Even when such protections are designated, however, they may not apply in all circumstances and to every population or individual of the imperiled species. Through numerous exceptions and loopholes, even endangered species in the wild are sometimes made killable. Of the various instances of reduced legal protections, the ones that interest me most in this context are those based on the captive state of the imperiled species. As this book shows, captive populations are often marginalized in relation to their wild conspecifics. This chapter will demonstrate this marginalization in the regulatory context, which both enables and reinforces it, effectively normalizing the split between *in situ* and *ex situ*.

Take and Captivity

Once a species is listed as endangered, the general rule is that no one can "take" any member of this species without a permit. Among the take prohibitions are the importation and exportation of endangered and threatened species, which require a permit under the ESA.[18] Of course, every rule has its exceptions, and in the case of endangered species there are many—some of which I will discuss here. As the central concept in the ESA, the "take" will serve as my starting point for exploring the construction of conservation's heightened regulatory regime.

The ESA broadly defines "take" as "to harass, harm, pursue, hunt, shoot, wound, kill, trap, capture or collect,"[19] and the USFWS has broadened the definition even further by interpreting "take" as including "significant habitat modification or degradation."[20] Timothy (Tim) Male, formerly of Defenders of Wildlife, explains the historical trajectory of the ESA:

> The ESA was created thirty or forty years ago, when scientists really viewed the world as moving towards a set of climax ecosystems—where if people just left every place alone it would all slowly transform into some sort of idyllic alternate state that would then be stable. It was built around the idea that if you just took people out of the picture, things would move in the right way. So the ESA is very much built to make human action hard. That's a good thing when you're fighting a dam project, but it also makes interventions very hard if you're trying to help a species [when] it needs intensive management.[21]

According to Male, while the ESA originally revolved around the idea of protecting nature through keeping humans out, current enforcement practices negotiate the possibilities of more intensive human management. In the last several decades, then, conservation has shifted from "letting be" to "making be," in Foucauldian terms, which can also be characterized as a shift from wilderness-based conservation to a biopolitical conservation regime.[22]

The ESA expressly prohibits the take of "*any* endangered species of fish or wildlife,"[23] and the USFWS has stated on multiple occasions that both captive and wild endangered species are protected by the take provision. In practice, however, the USFWS has not applied the same standards for the take of wild and captive members of the same species. One example of USFWS's different standards is the normal husbandry exception. USFWS Director Dan Ashe explains that "the exemption for normal husbandry is that people—especially zoos and aquariums who often hold those specimens for the benefit of the species—have to be allowed to handle the [animals]. They have to do invasive things: they have to treat them when they're ill, they have to feed them, they have to move them. Those things would normally otherwise be a 'take.' But in order to allow people to maintain those populations, we have enacted the exemption for normal husbandry."[24]

The exception for normal husbandry does not apply in the wild, where the very same actions constitute a take and, as such, require a Section 10 permit.[25] Ashe explains: "If you're going to trap and collar a grizzly bear—you need a permit. If you had an endangered pronghorn, and you had a disease that was running through the population and you needed to go in and vaccinate the wild animals—then you would do that under a permit."[26] According to Mike Carpenter, senior biologist at the USFWS, the rationale behind what he refers to as the "captivity exception" is that the captive animal "doesn't come from the wild in the first place. All [the] animals in zoos were born in zoos, [so] it doesn't make a difference."[27] An act is defined as a take only when it disrupts the animal's normal behavior, he further explains, which is "of course different in captivity and in the wild."[28] Suckling of the Center for Biological Diversity supports this distinction, portraying the attempt to define normal behavior for captive animals as a meaningless exercise. In his words:

> What would it mean to disrupt the normal feeding behavior of an animal whose food is delivered to it in a tray each day by a zoo keeper? How should one disrupt the breeding behavior of a female animal that has no access to a male animal unless a handler puts them in the same cage? I think the USFWS is fundamentally correct to say that captive animals, much like prisoners in a jail, are fundamentally outside the frame of normal behavior. . . . To apply the same concepts to wild and captive animals is incompatible with the conditions of captivity.[29]

In addition to the different application of the take clause for captive and wild members of the same endangered species, the USFWS's 1979 Captive-Bred Wildlife (CBW) regulations grant blanket permission to engage in activities otherwise prohibited by Section 9 with respect to non-native endangered or threatened animals that are bred in captivity, but only if "the purpose of such activity is to enhance the propagation or survival of the affected species."[30] The USFWS explains that "a wide range of activities involved in maintenance and propagation of captive wildlife should readily be permitted when wild populations are sufficiently protected from unauthorized taking, and when it can be shown that such activities would not be detrimental to the survival of the wild or captive populations of the species."[31] Those activities include, according to the USFWS, "normal practices of animal husbandry needed to maintain captive populations that are self-sustaining and that possess as much genetic vitality as possible." Under the CBW regulations, zoo facilities that engage in legitimate captive breeding programs may avail themselves of the general permit by registering with the USFWS, keeping records about their activities, and submitting annual reports.[32] Katherine Meyer, a leading animal rights attorney, explains that the blanket permit makes it easier for captive breeders, mainly zoos, to continue operating without having to go through the notice, comment, and "findings" process required for each permit issued per Section 10(c) of the ESA.[33]

As with so many other instances that I explore in this book, regulatory norms—here, the definition of a take—are also bifurcated between captive and wild. The assumption in this case is that while management and husbandry are the exception in wild settings, they are the norm in captivity. Given the intensifying levels of husbandry and management performed in the wild, however, one can expect to see an erosion of the legal distinctions between zoo husbandry and wildlife management. Currently, most U.S. states do in fact have what are called Section 6 Agreements with the USFWS that grant them blanket authority to perform such actions in the wild.[34]

Clearly, then, alongside ESA's robust protections for endangered and threatened species, the Act also establishes mechanisms for carving out exceptions. In addition to the take exceptions, the USFWS may request an exemption from the Endangered Species Committee, which exercises the biopolitical power of deciding which species will live and who will die and, for this reason, is often referred to as "the God Squad."[35] A range of additional exceptions to the legal protection of endangered species include exceptions for "incidental take,"[36] "safe harbor,"[37] and the "No Surprises rule."[38] Also, invertebrates and plants are granted a lower level of protection across the board: plants are protected only when on federal lands, and invertebrates can be listed only at the species or subspecies level, and not as distinct population segments (DPSs), the smallest taxonomic units of protection under the ESA.[39] Finally, designating endangered species as non-essential experimental populations is another strategy for decreasing the level of legal protection assigned to endangered species.[40]

Non-Essential Experimental Populations

When species are fully protected by the ESA, it is purposely difficult and onerous to make risky management decisions for their conservation. For this reason, a regulatory exception was inserted into the law that grants the USFWS the discretionary power to define populations of endangered or threatened species that are part of a reintroduction effort (typically captive animals, but sometimes wild animals from other *in situ* locations) as non-essential experimental populations.[41] Assigning this status enables the USFWS to separately determine each population's level of protection and management.[42] Depending on the circumstances, experimental populations may be downlisted from the category "endangered" to the lower-protection category of "threatened," or even to the Act's category of "a species proposed to be listed."[43] Suckling explains that

> technically, a non-essential [experimental] population designation is not a downlisting. It retains the formal listing status of its parent population, either threatened or endangered, but is managed with a lesser degree of protection. This lesser degree is similar in some ways to those applying to threatened species, but is similar in other ways to those applying to proposed species, and most importantly, [it] differs from all of these in being managed according to a unique plan crafted for each species.[44]

When listed as experimental, the hybrid captive-wild body is removed from ESA's strict legal protections of endangered bodies, hence rendering this body more killable than its wild conspecific. But even this construction does not fully account for the fluidity of the killable status. Suckling argues that to better understand this killability, one must attend to the distinction between purposeful and unpurposeful killing. In his words:

> Note that fully protected species are also killable and killed all the time. Federal agencies are allowed to kill them via a Section 7's "take" statement, non-federal and private parties are allowed to kill them via a Section 10 permit.

So the difference is not exactly in killability. [Instead,] the difference is about purposeful killing. Fully protected species may be killed only incidentally. For experimental species, however, execution is allowed. The animal can be purposefully targeted and killed, or rounded up, according to the specific rules established by the experimental designation.[45]

Suckling's contentious characterization of USFWS's experimental designation illuminates how easily the "letting die" that is so central to biopolitical conservation spills into the "making die" of sovereign power. The fluidity between these two forms of killing, and the importance of killability in the biopolitical scheme, resonate with Donna Haraway's remark that "it is not killing that gets us into extermination, but making things killable."[46]

Although he is fully aware of the criticisms directed toward the non-essential experimental designation, USFWS Assistant Director Gary Frazer is a strong believer in the importance of this re-designation strategy for successful reintroductions of captive animals. In his words: "Which landowner is going to willingly constrain their future options by allowing a listed species to be reintroduced on their property? The concept of experimental population was designed to allow the Service to . . . craft regulations that would reduce the prohibitions that come with a fully protected species when we're doing a reintroduction."[47]

A couple of examples will illustrate how the USFWS has been using this designation. I will start with the American burying beetles (*Nicrophorus americanus*): bright red, orange, and black beetles once found in thirty-five U.S. states and in three Canadian provinces.[48] The beetles were listed as endangered in 1989, at which point they were found only in Rhode Island.[49] Bob Merz is director of the Center for American Burying Beetle Conservation at the Saint Louis Zoo's WildCare Institute.[50] Between 2005 and 2014, Merz oversaw the breeding of more than 8,000 captive beetles. In 2012, 236 captive-bred individuals from the captive population were first reintroduced into southwest Missouri. Merz tells me that this was the direct result of the collaboration between the Saint Louis Zoo, the USFWS, the Missouri Department of Conservation, and The Nature Conservancy.[51] As of 2014, 1,000 beetles have been reintroduced into Missouri, each carefully identified, documented, and tagged.[52] The reintroduction site in Wah'Kon-Tah prairie is a 4,040-acre area jointly owned and managed by the Missouri Department of Conservation and The Nature Conservancy.[53]

Merz strongly believes that the beetles' reintroductions would not have

been possible, let alone successful, without the designation of the reintroduced beetle as an experimental population. "I don't think that local landowners [from adjacent sites] would have let it go through," he tells me,
explaining the landowners' concern that their ability to cultivate their land
might be compromised if the endangered reintroduced beetles were found
there.[54] In preparation for their reintroduction, the beetles are paired and
marked by notching their elytra (their hard wing covers). The notch distin-
guishes captive-bred beetles from wild beetles, thereby inscribing the *in situ–
ex situ* divide, along with the distinct levels of legal protection afforded to
each population, into the beetles' physical bodies.[55]

Thomas Emmel also speaks to the importance of the experimental designation, this time in the context of the Schaus swallowtail butterfly (discussed in Chapter 4). In his words: "One of the mosquito control districts
in the Keys, Monroe County Control District, filed suit against [my] university and the Florida Game and Freshwater Fish Commission to stop
the captive propagation of the Schaus swallowtail. And why did they do
that? They were afraid we were going to release them in areas in the Keys
where they were spraying, and then they would be responsible for any
deaths."[56] The parties finally agreed to designate the reintroduced populations as non-essential experimental. "Otherwise, we would have shut down
the program," Emmel tells me. Under this designation, mosquito spraying
was permitted, but only under certain circumstances, such as spraying at
night when the butterflies are less active. The same agreement stipulated
that when reintroduced into state park lands, captive-bred butterfly populations would remain fully protected. In these sites, "no one could do anything but photograph them," Emmel says.[57]

Even when a species is designated as non-essential, a few restrictions and
protections still apply. For instance, experimental populations can be (re)
introduced only to areas that are outside the current range of their wild
conspecifics, but still within the species' historic range.[58] "We can't treat a
population as experimental if it's in an area that already has a population of
the listed species," USFWS's Gary Frazer explains. By maintaining the geographical distinction between the wild and the reintroduced populations,
members of the wild endangered species can continue enjoying stricter protections than their captive-born kin. In other words, even when captive-born
species are released to the wild, both their legal designation as experimental
and their geographical segregation set them apart from the "truly" wild.

Such legal and physical distinctions are drawn so as to avoid contaminating the wild bodies or undermining their legal protection.

One of the contested questions regarding USFWS's legal and physical segregation policies is what counts as a population. This question became particularly important in the case of the reintroduction of gray wolves (*Canis lupus*) into the Yellowstone ecosystem.[59] Frazer says: "There was a legal challenge saying that there were wolves already in the Yellowstone ecosystem," and hence that the experimental wolves cannot be released there. "We acknowledged that there were scattered individual wolves dispersing from northwest Montana," he explains, "but [argued] that [they were not] a population—namely, that [they] did not have breeding pairs that had established and produced young over a successive period of time." "This all comes down to biological decisions," Frazer emphasizes.[60]

But the distinction between individuals and populations is neither clear-cut nor exclusively biological, Suckling tells me. He further complicates the picture: "In some cases where the species is highly mobile, like wolves, the fully protected and the experimental populations have mixed together, spawning lawsuits over the proper level of protection afforded the mixed populations."[61] In such cases, the courts have ruled that when wild animals enter the formally established zone of the experimental population of their own accord, they lose their fully protected status and may be managed according to the rules governing the experimental population.[62]

The motivation behind the experimental practice, Suckling argues, is political rather than biological. He asks derisively: "How can we create new populations of [imperiled] species, where we have maximum discretion to kill them, where we are shielded from litigation to protect them, and where we have very few to no commitments about the long-term management of these populations? For most non-essential experimental populations, there's no experiment going on. There are no guys with white coats testing anything. They've just introduced the animal somewhere, and the animal lives there."[63] The government's use of the term "experimental" in this context is therefore not incidental, Suckling suggests; rather, it assumes a laboratory-like form of human control, extending this control into the wild through the transfer of captive animals into these spaces. The killability of these animals thus travels with them from captivity into what then becomes the non-essential wild.

Philosopher Judith Butler's contemplations on killability and grievability are relevant here. Butler suggests that those who have been made killable "cannot be mourned because they are always already lost or, rather, never 'were.'"[64] In other words, to be killable precludes mourning over death, because life never "counted" in the first place and is therefore not grievable. Moreover, making something killable—making it a "thing"—disposes that thing more readily to its death. Suckling argues along these lines that the legal designation of imperiled populations as non-essential has in fact resulted in the actual death of animals from these populations. "Take the Mexican gray wolves as an example," he tells me. "Once they go outside the arbitrary zone of the non-essential experimental population then [the USFWS] will go and kill them, or capture them and put them back into captivity."[65] The wolf's designation as non-essential has "resulted in hundreds of dead wolves," Suckling exclaims.[66]

Listing Hybrids

Both ESA's threat categories and its designation of non-essential experimental populations rely on the species as the central unit of classification. The strong orientation of the ESA toward species has sparked ongoing debates, including on the meaning of hybridity and its consequences. While the ESA does not explicitly address hybrids, the USFWS enacted a policy on this topic in 1977. This policy regards hybrids as a threat to the purity of endangered species because of their capacity to interbreed with each other, thereby diluting or eliminating the "original" gene pool.[67] Since the goal of the ESA is to protect endangered species, so the policy's logic goes, it must condemn hybrids. Nonetheless, federal agencies have also recognized that a strict implementation of this policy would be detrimental to conservation goals, because under certain conditions hybridization is in fact crucial for the continued survival of endangered species. As a result, USFWS's hybrid policy is enforced selectively and with careful discretion.

One of the first instances in which the USFWS confronted the question of hybrids and their management under the ESA was the case of the dusky seaside sparrow (*Ammodramus maritimus nigrescens*). As I have mentioned in the book's introduction, in the 1970s the dusky experienced a sharp decline. In response to this decline, in 1978 the USFWS initiated an *ex situ* operation: it purposely hybridized the last known dusky seaside sparrows with the closely related Scott's seaside sparrows. The plan was to breed the female hybrids with the dusky males to produce near-pure duskies within six generations, a process referred to by conservationists as "back-breeding." However, in 1980, a few months after Ronald Reagan was elected U.S. president, the new administration shut down the dusky hybridization program, arguing that the hybrids were not pure duskies and could therefore not be part of the listed species used for recovery.[68] The dusky seaside sparrow became extinct in 1987.[69]

This dramatic episode triggered intense scrutiny of the federal treatment of hybrids. Acclaimed biologists Ernst Mayr and Stephen O'Brien pointed out, for example, that hybridization between subspecies is a natural process and suggested that it should not result in the lifting of legal protections. In their words: "While discouraging hybridization between species was appropriate in most cases with severely threatened species, hybridization might be necessary to preserve the organism's genetic heritage."[70] The hybrid policy of 1977 still exists on the books; however, the USFWS currently implements a complex practice that "discourages hybridization of endangered species generally, prevents it aggressively where it presents a known threat, and conserves or even promotes hybridization in those infrequent cases where it serves a conservation purpose."[71]

The case of the Columbia Basin pygmy rabbit provides another hybridization example. The Columbia Basin pygmy rabbit is a distinct population segment of the pygmy rabbit (*Brachylagus idahoensis*) and the smallest rabbit in North America. The last known wild subpopulation of pygmy rabbits was extirpated in the wild (or Extinct in the Wild, in IUCN's terminology) in 2004. Three years earlier, the Washington Department of Fish and Wildlife (WDFW) placed sixteen rabbits in a captive breeding program managed collaboratively by the WDFW, the Oregon Zoo, Washington State University, Northwest Trek Wildlife Park in Washington, and the USFWS. Soon, severe inbreeding resulted in depression in the purebred captive animals. To facilitate the Columbia Basin pygmy rabbits' genetic restoration, the USFWS conducted "carefully controlled matings between the founding purebred Columbia Basin animals and pygmy rabbits of the same taxonomic classification from a discrete population in Idaho."[72] In 2007, twenty captive-bred hybrid pygmy rabbits were reintroduced into their historical range. None survived. Reintroduction was again attempted in 2011, this time successfully. The WDFW then developed techniques for breeding captive-bred pygmy rabbits in protected enclosures on wildlife refuges. In 2012, captive breeding operations were discontinued in light of the pygmy rabbit's recovery,[73] and in 2013, the Oregon Zoo and Northwest Trek received the AZA's North American Conservation Award for their collaboration on this project.[74] This conservation success was likely only possible because the Columbia Basin pygmy rabbits are defined primarily by their geographic isolation, not so much by their genome. Had this rabbit been a genetic species or subspecies, hybridization on this scale probably would not have been allowed.

Finally, the two most famous examples of the debate about the merits of deliberate hybridization for conservation are the Florida panther (*Puma concolor coryi*) and the peregrine falcon (*Falco peregrinus*). The Florida panther was listed as endangered in 1967.[75] As state and federal wildlife authorities intensified their captive breeding efforts, the panther was showing strong signs of inbreeding depression, including a curled tail and high mortality rates. To increase the Florida panthers' genetic diversity, scientists spent several years studying their genetic makeup and discovered that historically, certain members of this species interbred with Florida cougars. This was no longer possible since the panther's range had shrunk due to habitat loss.[76] The experts thus deemed the hybridization of the Florida panther with the Florida cougar to be a natural occurrence and, as a result, the USFWS granted permission to deliberately hybridize the two species. Defenders of Wildlife's Tim Male points out that "at the time, this was an incredibly controversial decision. But people quickly decided that a creature that looks like a Florida panther is a Florida panther."[77] Similarly, the peregrine falcon underwent deliberate hybridization in captivity and subsequent reintroductions into the wild. The reintroduced crossbred falcons fared so well that they were later delisted from the ESA.[78]

It is worth noting in this context how certain officials at the USFWS characterize these events. USFWS Assistant Director Bryan Arroyo tells me that his agency never hybridized the Florida panthers but, instead, that they deliberately interbred them with cougars, as would have happened naturally in the wild had human-caused fragmentation not occurred.[79] Similarly, Arroyo explains that the peregrine falcons hybridized naturally in the wild. "In nature, there are hybrids," he says. And so he sees this as one of those instances "where the law can't keep up with what happens [and] we need to practice some discretion."[80] Whether a taxon is defined as a species, as a subspecies, or as neither, and whether a hybridization event is framed as natural or as a human manipulation therefore determine either the survival or the extinction of the becoming-hybrid animal. The precariousness of the hybrid animal in the context of *inter situ* management will further be explored in my next story about the red wolf.

Clearly, hybrids and the policies that regulate them are highly contested categories in the regulation and management of wildlife species. Hybrids have not been embraced by zoos, either. In Germany's Magdeburg Zoo, genetic analysis performed by American researchers indicated that the sire of three tiger cubs was not a pure Amur tiger (*Panthera tigris altaica*), but in fact was crossbred. The zoo, owner of both sire and cubs, euthanized the tiger cubs in 2008, triggering a highly visible court case that ended with the suspension of the zoo's director and three of its employees.[81] Sarah Christie of the Zoological Society of London coordinated the Amur tiger's captive breeding program at the time. She recalls receiving the initial genetic report from the American researchers, reflecting that "nobody wants a hybrid tiger. . . . Some zoos just bite the bullet and say, 'Okay, we'll keep these until they die.' But Magdeburg bravely decided that they would do a very righteous thing."[82]

Why wouldn't zoos want a hybrid tiger? I suggest that hybridity has been such a focal concern for the captive Amur tiger program (and for many other zoo programs) precisely because of the perceived interdependency of *in situ* and *ex situ*. To serve as insurance to Amur tiger populations in the wild, the zoo's population must sustain its genetic purity within the scientific classification system that governs both worlds. Deemed worthless from a genetic perspective, the hybrid tiger cubs must be culled (killed) so that the limited captive space is made available for "purer," more valuable genes. It is precisely such interplays between valued and valueless life that sustain the *in situ–ex situ* relationship and make it into such a powerful biopolitical regime.

Split-Listing

The take exceptions and the experimental designations distinguish wild from captive populations without changing their formal listing status. But could captive populations of a species be "split-listed," or listed separately, from their wild counterparts so that one is listed under one category, and the other under another? This question has been at the core of several legal battles. In what follows, I will trace the legal split-listing controversies over three antelope species, chimpanzees, one killer whale named Lolita, and salmon and steelhead fish.

THREE ENDANGERED ANTELOPES

Until fairly recently, one could still spot the scimitar-horned oryx (*Oryx dammah*), the dama gazelle (*Nanger dama*), and the addax (*Addax nasomaculatus*) as they grazed through the sub-Saharan range of northern Africa.[83] In 2005, however, the IUCN Red List of Threatened Species listed the oryx as Extinct in the Wild and the addax and dama gazelle as Critically Endangered, with fewer than 300 and 500 individuals documented for each species, respectively.[84]

While diminishing in the wild, these populations have thrived in captivity: more than 5,000 scimitar-horned oryx, 1,500 addax, and 750 dama gazelle live in captivity worldwide,[85] both in special breeding facilities and on private game farms and ranches in the Middle East and in the United States.[86] As part of future plans to reintroduce them into their historic range, captive-bred individuals of the three antelope species have recently been released into fenced areas in Tunisia, Morocco, and Senegal.[87]

Although the ESA generally prohibits the take of endangered species, in 2005 the USFWS issued a special rule that permitted the hunting of excess males of the three antelope species on game ranches. The rule stated: "For U.S. captive-bred live wildlife, including embryos and gametes, and sport-hunted trophies of the three species, this rule authorizes otherwise prohibited activities that enhance the propagation or survival of the species."[88] The USFWS explained the rationale of this rule in that "hunting of U.S. captive-bred specimens of these species reduces the threat of the species' extinction," noting that in Texas the number of ranched oryx grew from 32 specimens in 1978 to 2,149 in 1996.[89] In other words, the USFWS depicted what it referred to as the "selective culling" of the antelope species to be beneficial for their overall survival as a species.

After a long legal battle, however, a 2012 USFWS rule revoked the above policy, declaring that "captive-held animals [will not] be assigned separate legal status from their wild conspecifics on the basis of their captive state."[90] Under this new interpretation of the ESA, the USFWS currently prohibits the split-listing of captive and wild members of the same species, subspecies, or distinct population segments. Despite these legal changes, however, the hunting of the three antelope species continues through special permits granted by the USFWS.[91]

Soon, other species were standing "before the law," their legal spokespersons demanding a similar application of the new "no-split" rule. One such species was the chimpanzee.[92] The long battle over the status of captive chimpanzees took a dramatic turn when the USFWS announced in 2013: "We, the U.S. Fish and Wildlife Service, propose to list all chimpanzees (*Pan troglodytes*) as endangered."[93] This proposal, if accepted, would extend ESA's protections to captive chimpanzee populations in the United States— populations previously designated as threatened, in contrast to their wild counterparts, who were listed as endangered. Under this proposal, all activities that constitute a take under the ESA—mostly invasive research for biomedical testing (since, as I have noted, normal husbandry is excepted)—will newly require a permit from the USFWS. Such a permit may be issued only to enhance the propagation or survival of chimpanzees, interpreted as providing conservation benefits to chimpanzees in the wild.[94]

While many conservationists celebrated this decision, others remained skeptical about the real effects of such formal changes in the law. Steve Ross, Chimpanzee SSP coordinator, says along these lines: "Even if they do get an endangered status, the breeders will continue to breed and sell and [then] someone will still need to identify the problem and enforce the law." Nonetheless, even Ross commends the new interpretation, stating that "at least now the law is in place, and [someone] might be able to take action."[95] Concurrent with the USFWS decision, in 2013 the National Institutes of Health declared the retirement of approximately 300 of 360 chimps from its facilities to nongovernmental sanctuaries.[96]

Captive orca "Lolita" is another example for the powers of split-listing. In 2013, People for the Ethical Treatment of Animals (PETA), the Animal Legal Defense Fund, and the Orca Network filed a petition to include Lolita as a member of the southern resident killer whale (*Orcinus orca*) population under the ESA.[97] Since she was taken from this population in 1970, Lolita has been held at the Miami Seaquarium in Florida, where she has been performing twice daily. Today, Lolita is the only captive member of the southern resident killer whales in the world. In 2005, the NMFS listed the southern resident killer whales as endangered under the ESA. However, in its final rule for this listing, the agency stated that the endangered listing "does not include killer whales . . . placed in captivity prior to listing, nor does it include their captive born progeny."[98] Since the thirty-five other captive southern resident killer whales died decades before the listing decision, Lolita was the sole subject of this provision. PETA's 2013 petition sought to apply the endangered status of her conspecifics in the wild to Lolita, requesting her transfer to non-harmful living conditions in a sea pen and, eventually, into the wild.[99] The petition stated: "The differential treatment of members of a species under the ESA, sometimes referred to as split listing, is extremely rare."[100]

Relying heavily on the 2013 reassessment of captive chimpanzees, the petition argued that the ESA protects all members of endangered and threatened species, both captive and wild.[101] They based their argument on the assumption discussed earlier in this book that captive and wild animals are the same and thus should not be treated differently, an assumption that rests primarily on the animals' genetic makeup.[102] Indeed, the petitioners argued that "Lolita is *biologically* a member of a listed species."[103] Lolita's undisputed genetic heritage was thus perceived as providing sufficient support for her equal listing with her conspecifics in the wild. This again goes to highlight both the importance of the species category and its strong genetic orientation for the legal regimes that govern endangerment. On January 24, 2014, the NMFS found that the petitioners' argument was warranted.[104]

SPLIT-LISTING SALMON AND STEELHEAD

Endangered fish have also been the focus of split-listing practices. The vast majority of species protected by the NMFS are salmon (the common name for species in the genus *Salmo* and *Oncorhynchus*). The salmon's genetic pattern can differ from stream to stream. Additionally, wild salmon who interbreed with hatchery salmon change their genetic identity much more rapidly than many other species. The NMFS employs the term "evolutionary significant unit" (ESU) to assess fish species on a smaller scale than that of species or subspecies, thereby enabling the consideration of distinct evolutionary groups of fish as independent assessment units.[105]

In 1993, the NMFS decided that only "natural fish" can be listed under the ESA. In 2001, this policy was challenged successfully by the Alsea Valley Alliance. The district court found that the NMFS "may consider listing only an entire species, subspecies, or distinct population segment."[106] In other words, because they belong to the same biological species and subspecies, the NMFS could list *both* or *neither* hatchery and natural salmon as endangered, but not only the natural population.[107]

In the case of another fish, the Upper Columbia River steelhead (*Oncorhynchus mykiss*), the NMFS assessed the hatchery steelhead in the context of "their contributions to conserving natural self-sustaining populations."[108] The result was a modified ESU composed of natural steelhead as well as six hatchery stocks. On the basis of the integration of both *in situ* and *ex situ* fish into one legal unit, in 2004 the NMFS downlisted the Upper Columbia River steelhead from endangered to threatened.[109] This decision was soon challenged in court. The district court found for the environmental petitioners, holding that the ESA should primarily be concerned with preserving *natural* populations and that listing determinations must be based exclusively on the status of the *natural* components of the ESU.[110] The court ruled, in other words, that only the wild fish counted for recovery purposes, discounting the hatchery fish from the assessment.

The government appealed. In 2009, the case reached the U.S. Court of Appeals for the Ninth Circuit, the highest federal judiciary authority in the region, just below the Supreme Court. The court was required to decide "whether the National Marine Fisheries Service may distinguish between natural and hatchery-spawned salmon and steelhead when determining the level of protection the fish should be afforded under the Endangered Species Act."[111] Although it agreed with the lower district court that ESA's primary goal is to preserve the ability of natural populations to survive in the wild, the Ninth Circuit reversed the decision, holding that the plaintiff "casts the policy in an overly simplistic light [when in fact] it mandates a more complex evaluation process that considers both the positive and the negative effects of hatchery fish on the viability of natural populations."[112] The court explained that a good hatchery program could positively contribute to the productivity of the natural population by serving to repopulate unoccupied habitat and by conserving genetic resources of depressed natural populations. As a result, the appeals court upheld the NMFS policy that hatchery fish may, under certain conditions, count for the listing assessment. The court emphasized, however, that the inclusion of the *ex situ* population can occur only when this population effectively contributes to the wild population, emphasizing that a hatchery program managed without adequate consideration of its conservation effects could also negatively impact the determination of conservation status. The NMFS, with the court's backing, decided to assess this case on its own merit.

In upholding the NMFS policy on hatcheries, the court carved out a nuanced legal space in which natural and captive portions of certain populations are neither totally separable nor absolutely inseparable. This story demonstrates that both the government and the judiciary are increasingly taking part in an integrative interpretation of conservation that involves more and more complex and nuanced co-productions of *in situ* and *ex situ*. Whether this is good or bad depends on one's ideological position.

Kierán Suckling argues, for example, that the debates over split-listing in general, and the instances of split-listing salmon and steelhead in particular, have been determined by narrow economic interests rather than by conservation agendas. In his words: "Dam building, logging, mining, livestock, agribusiness, energy, and development interests oppose split-listings because they believe that by combining the very large number of hatchery fish with the small number of wild born fish, they will reduce the need to protect wild born fish and more quickly reach recovery goals, all of which will mean less habitat protections, more take permits, and more profits."[113] Suckling highlights that unlike the commercialized *ex situ* populations of the antelope and orca cases, commercial hatcheries present a threat to the existence of the fish species because they mix the very bodies of captive and wild individuals, resulting in considerable genetic changes in the individuals themselves.[114]

Counting for Conservation

Two major legal decisions determine whether and how captive populations should count in conservation assessments: first, whether captive members should count for the initial listing of a taxon as imperiled, and second, whether they should count when re-assessing the threat status of their taxon as part of a recovery plan. While the split-listing discussion above attended to the first question, this section will deal with assessments for recovery.

As I have mentioned earlier, USFWS Director Dan Ashe holds that wild animals are "not counted for recovery purposes when they're in captivity."[115] Suckling explains this approach: "All recovery measures are based on wild populations; it doesn't matter how many are in captivity. They're going to treat the million in captivity not as a population in themselves, but just as a potential reservoir to hopefully augment the wild population."[116] In other words, wild populations count for conservation, captive populations are excluded from this calculus.[117] Ashe provides an example: "If we have a Mexican wolf that is being held in a pen at Sevilleta National Wildlife Refuge, the wolf is not counted for purposes of recovery. But if that wolf is impregnated and then released into the wild, and she has six pups, and they survive, then we add six wolves to our tally of wolves in the wild."[118] Even if she lives the bulk of her life in the wild, then, the captive-born mother will never count as wild. Once captive, always (discounted as) captive, implies the current policy.

To evaluate the conservation status of a species the USFWS must therefore constantly negotiate the boundaries between captive and wild. As I have already stressed in Chapter 3, this is not an easy task. "Is a large refuge surrounded by a fence captive or wild?" I ask Ashe, and he responds: "If you have a large park that has a fence—a military installation, for instance—but the animals are free-roaming, and they're reproducing in the wild, and they're feeding naturally—they're wild. Just because there's a fence doesn't mean they're not wild."[119] According to Ashe, the fence has lost its power as a defining feature of captivity. He further reflects: "If you are a desert tortoise . . . does the fence mean anything to you? It doesn't."[120] Taken to its extreme, defining captivity based on the perspective of the animal will end up depicting the *Partula* snails of the London Zoo, the eastern hellbenders of the Buffalo Zoo, and the American burying beetles of the Saint Louis Zoo as non-captive animals, even though they live within the zoo's confines. Such an outcome is counterintuitive for many, again highlighting the challenges in defining captivity's boundaries.

The wild-captive distinction becomes even murkier when considering other factors, such as assisted reproduction and artificial construction of habitats. What if a site includes both a fence and an irrigation system, as in the case of the pronghorns in the Kofa and Cabeza Prieta Refuges? Should the animals who inhabit such semi-wild conditions count when tallying the numbers for the species' risk assessment? And should the reintroduced pronghorns count? Finally, what should be the status of species such as the woundfin minnow, who no longer reproduce in the wild and who thus depend on reintroductions from captivity?[121] Should the captive-dependent minnow count as wild?

The case of the endangered North Atlantic roseate tern (*Sterna dougallii*) also demonstrates how "people's sense of what's acceptable and what counts toward recovery is fairly fluid," in Tim Male's words.[122] This seabird flies around independently through the year, but lands and breeds successfully in human-made nest boxes and in predator-free locations with artificial shelters. "They are farmed to help maximize their reproductive success and then they go off and do their own thing for the rest of the year," Male tells me.[123] Male says that despite their dependence on artificial conditions for survival, the seabirds are in fact counted in USFWS's threat and recovery assessments under the ESA.

The stories I have told about the Mexican wolf, the Sonoran pronghorn, and the roseate tern, as well as so many other stories in this book, establish that the distinction between wild and captive sites is anything but "easy to see," to refer back to the epigraph of Chapter 2. Instead, this distinction is constantly negotiated and reproduced through legal norms and regulatory mechanisms. Thousands of assessments for listing and recovery[124] and numerous court decisions have firmly established the preference of state agencies and other relevant actors toward *in situ* conservation, while at the same time acknowledging the importance of captive management. These myriad decisions represent a move away from the ideal of an absolute wild to a more nuanced and case-by-case disposition toward "as wild as possible," which, as Suckling has remarked, is "sometimes not very wild."

Conclusion: "As Wild as Possible"

While the terms *in situ* and *ex situ* are conspicuously absent from the relevant legal texts in the United States, their long shadows are cast throughout. This chapter has delved into the complexities of the ESA to cast light on some of these shadows. I have explored myriad attempts to legally negotiate the captive-wild relationship and to administer a biopolitical regime that takes this relationship into account. Whereas the official narrative is that captive populations do not count for conservation, this policy is becoming increasingly difficult to apply. Despite the still-dichotomized rhetoric of *in situ* and *ex situ* and the *in situ* orientation of most laws, a flexible and pragmatic interpretation is already under way. Rather than clinging to romantic versions of a pure wild, such efforts by conservationists and other legal actors in fact adopt an open-ended and creative interpretation of conservation laws (broadly defined), striving toward the humbler goal of a life that is "as wild as possible."

Red Wolf

The general public sees hybridity in black and white. But as we see it, hybridity is a matter of scale and, as such, it can be managed.

—David Rabon, Coordinator, Red Wolf Recovery Program, USFWS[1]

"There's a certain time of year when [red wolves] have their puppies," relates William Waddell, coordinator of AZA's Red Wolf Species Survival Plan (SSP), which encompasses forty-four North American zoos and wildlife centers.[2] Like many of my interviews, this interview, too, takes place over the telephone—I am in Buffalo, New York, Waddell is at Point Defiance Zoo & Aquarium in Tacoma, Washington, and the wolves we are talking about are in North Carolina. Waddell tells me: "The female will . . . localize her movements, she won't move around a lot. And that indicates to the field crew [that] there might be a den there. And they'll go out and traipse around, and crawl, until they find the den. And then they'll do a puppy

Figure 22: Female red wolf 1470 was one of a litter of five pups born at Point Defiance Zoo & Aquarium in 2006. Thirteen days later, she and her two siblings were placed in the den of a wild female in Tyrrell County, North Carolina, for foster rearing. Since then, 1470 has raised two litters in the red wolf recovery area. This photo was taken in early 2013, after 1470 was fitted with a new radio collar and released. Photo by B. Bartel/USFWS, Creative Commons Attribution-2.0-Generic license.

count, and—depending on how many, and where it's at—they'll give me a call, and say, 'Hey, are there some wolves that were born in the SSP population that are about this age? And how many are in that litter?'"[3]

The reason for these questions would be obvious to wolf experts: switching pups between wild and zoo litters is a routine management strategy for diversifying the genes of both populations. When a species includes only a few animals, managers need to be creative, I am told. I ask Waddell if the field team replaces the entire litter. "No," he responds. Rather than replacing the whole litter, they will usually supplement the wild wolf's new litter with a few pups from the captive population. Reared by a wild mother, the fostered pups will have a much greater likelihood of surviving in the wild than if they are reintroduced later in life. "Does the mother notice?" I ask. "She probably does," Waddell answers, adding after a pause, "I wonder what they think, or if they can count. But their maternal instincts kind of take over, and it's been successful."[4]

The red wolf (*Canis rufus*) recovery program provides another important example of the complex and dynamic relationship between *in situ* and *ex situ* animals, administrators, and administrations. Once found throughout the south-central and southeastern United States, by the 1960s the red wolves were decimated both by predator-control programs and by habitat loss. In 1967, the ESA listed the red wolves as endangered, and they are currently considered one of the most imperiled canids in the world.[5] In the 1970s, the USFWS attempted to locate and capture as many red wolves as possible for the purpose of establishing a captive breeding program, with the intention of later reintroducing the wolves into a portion of their former range. More than four hundred wolves were captured. Of these, only seventeen were found to be "pure," and then only fourteen were capable of reproducing. This group of fourteen wolves became what conservationists refer to as the "founders" of the entire red wolf population in existence today. By 1980, the red wolves were extirpated from the wild; the few surviving wolves were housed in captive facilities.[6]

In 1987, the first four pairs of red wolves were reintroduced from captivity into North Carolina. The process was not easy: "Some of them had to be returned to their enclosures because they were too visible or tolerant of people, . . . not knowing what they were supposed to do."[7] Such "unwildy" wolves were either replaced or reacclimated. Waddell tells me: "They were recaptured, and then there was some experimenting: what if we put this pair together in an acclimation pen? We'll allow them to breed, and if they have pups, we'll open up the enclosure gates and see if it's going to keep the pair more localized to the area where they were acclimated."

Overall, approximately eighty wolves were reintroduced from the zoo population into North Carolina. "Some of them died, some of them had to be brought back to the zoo population, and some—[we] don't know what happened to them," Waddell tells me. Nonetheless, the wolf population has grown over time, and the recovery area has expanded to include three national wildlife refuges, a bombing range, and state and private lands—encompassing approximately 1.7 million acres.[8] In 2013, the red wolf population amounted to 199 animals in captive institutions across the United States and an estimated 100 to 120 animals in the forests of eastern North Carolina.[9]

In addition to captive rearing in zoos, the red wolf recovery program includes an island propagation site at St. Vincent National Wildlife Refuge in northwestern Florida. Since its approval as a propagation site in 1989, the island has been home to twenty-one adult wolves as well as twenty-five pups, who were born on location. David Rabon, coordinator of the Red Wolf Recovery Program, says: "We release wolves on an island for them to breed and raise pups that we can capture and release in the wild population once they are about eighteen months of age" (Figure 23).[10] Rabon sees this component of the program as "another technique [for] integrating *in situ–ex situ* management."[11] He explains that this technique is "kind of an interme diate step between fostering pups from captivity to the wild and releasing captive-reared adults directly from captivity."[12]

The red wolf recovery program was initiated in the early 1970s and, as such, was one of the earliest recovery programs that included zoo-based breeding and management as a strategy for species recovery—preceding the black-footed ferret program and even that of the Californian condor.[13] For the supplementation of North Carolina's wild wolf populations by captive and semi-wild wolves to succeed, field and captive experts must work together, Waddell tells me. In his words: "If there's any sort of exchange between the zoo population and the wild population, it's based on conversations and discussions between myself [as the zoos' SSP coordinator] and the red wolf recovery biologists at the USFWS."[14] According to Waddell, the SSP collaborates with the USFWS to manage both captive and free-ranging red wolves. Rabon clarifies, however, that although the manage-

Figure 23: Female red wolf 1276 is one of a long-established breeding pair in the captive red wolf recovery program, and the pups in the photo are from her 2008 litter with male 1200. Her future offspring will be released to the island propagation site at St. Vincent National Wildlife Refuge. Photo by Ryan Nordsven, 2009. Courtesy of David Rabon, USFWS.

ment of red wolves is performed by two separate administrative bodies, the USFWS "is still responsible for and has jurisdiction over all red wolves."[15]

Waddell describes the relationship between the *in situ* and *ex situ* populations: "Zoo animals are the safety net. A fine balance must be struck in the zoo population between supporting the wild population and maintaining a genetically diverse and stable captive population."[16] Although the red wolf's reintroductions were discontinued in the early 1990s, constant interactions and exchanges still occur between the wild and captive populations, as well as between their respective human managers. "There's no black and white," Waddell tells me; both *in situ* and *ex situ* red wolf populations are closely monitored, captive and wild red wolves alike are given a studbook number, and blood samples are taken from all wild-born pups for paternity testing.

The red wolf recovery program has faced many challenges over the years. Alongside myriad administrative and scientific challenges, debates over the red wolf's classification as a species and related debates over the wolf's hybridization have threatened this program's existence. The taxonomy of the North American *Canis* has a complicated and controversial history.[17] The red wolf is currently classified as one of three wolf species. However, scientists have long debated whether the red wolf is a species after all, and some have even questioned their definition as a subspecies.[18] Kierán Suckling is skeptical about the scientific merits of this debate. He believes that "in fact, the changes in policy and the inconsistent positions were driven by the fairly simple environmental politics of successive presidential administrations and have nothing to do with [USFWS's] supposed understanding of taxonomy and nature."[19] Instead, Suckling claims, these policy changes had everything to do with the narrow interests of the ranching industry.

A series of delisting petitions filed by members of the ranching industry during the 1990s demonstrate the political manifestations of the taxonomic debate. In 1991, immediately after molecular evolutionists Robert Wayne and Susan M. Jenks published a paper suggesting that the red wolf species might be a hybrid,[20] the American Sheep Industry Association petitioned the USFWS to delist the red wolf on hybridization grounds.[21] In response, the USFWS issued a negative ninety-day finding, citing the lack of conclusive evidence that the species is invalid and asserting that low levels of hybridization do not conflict with ESA's goals.[22] In 1997, the USFWS denied a second hybridization-based delisting petition from the ranching industry, stating that "the petition did not present substantial scientific or commercial information indicating that delisting this species may be warranted."[23] In 1999, Wayne and other scientists again suggested that the red wolves may be of "a recent origin by hybridization" of gray wolves (*Canis lupus*) and coyotes (*Canis latrans*), potentially within the last 2,500 years.[24] Using microsatellite alleles and mitochondrial DNA as well as skull analyses, more recent articles argue that the red wolf is indeed a separate species.[25]

The ongoing debate about the red wolves' identity as a species, as well as about their hybridization with coyotes, looms over the existence of the recovery program and, if history is any guide, over the wolves' survival as well. Rabon tells me: "Some people say that because we can't stop the red wolf from hybridizing with coyote, then the wild red wolf is doomed, which means the end of the program." Certain landowners in the red wolf's range would probably welcome such a result, he adds. "They think that red wolves are really cool—as long as they're in zoos."[26]

Rabon criticizes the hysteria around hybridization. No creature is "pure," he explains, and so hybridity is a matter of scale. The coyote of the eastern United States, too, is a mixture of various genes—dog and wolf in particular. When certain animals are found to retain a certain level of "coyoteness," Rabon says, they are referred to as a fixed entity, for the ease of conservation. "People don't understand that hybridization is a natural process that has little effect on populations when they are healthy and of sufficient size," Rabon tells me. "But when we tell them it's natural, people then don't get why we attempt to manage it." According to Rabon, communicating the complex message to the public that many natural entities can, and indeed must, be managed for their survival is the current challenge of the red wolf program and of conservation in general. In practice, such nuanced management of hybridization in the wolf context has resulted in the sterilization of those individual coyotes who threaten the survival of the red wolf as a species. "We don't need to sterilize every coyote to make this work," Rabon clarifies, as he describes in excruciating detail the precise identity, location, and genetic composition of the coyotes who interact with the wolves in his program.[27]

The red wolf management efforts constitute a complex everyday "conviviality"—namely, a way of living in and among the "diversity of ecological attachments and heterogeneous associations" that make up the modern world.[28] Such conviviality between captive, semi-wild, and wild red wolves, between wolves and coyotes, and between captive and wild experts and databases erodes the physical and administrative boundaries between *in situ* and *ex situ* conservation.

This conviviality has been long in the making. "The joint USFWS/SSP recovery plan for the red wolf was one of the first of its kind," Rabon tells me, "and the culmination of two groups bringing their expertise together to better collaboratively manage *ex situ* and *in situ* populations as one."[29]

According to Rabon, "the red wolf was the early model for this type of management and has been copied in the black-footed ferret and Mexican gray wolf programs, among others." Currently, he tells me, the recovery program is working with Lincoln Park Zoo on a new management approach: "a new PVA addressing the management of the two populations independently (because they have differing management goals) and as one (because we see benefits that each can provide to the other to achieve recovery of the red wolf)."[30]

But the years of effort and commitment by red wolf conservationists may have been in vain. Just before I sent this essay for final typesetting, I was informed that David Rabon had been dismissed from his longtime position as the red wolf program's coordinator and that the USFWS had officially eliminated the position altogether. This elimination is likely part of USFWS's recent review process of the red wolf recovery program, which is intended "to help the Service determine the program's future." "The determination is expected to be finalized in early 2015," states the USFWS website.[31] These events lay bare the precarious state of this uniquely integrative and historical conservation program, as well as the precarious existence of the red wolves themselves, both *in* and *ex situ*.

CHAPTER 6

Integrated Life

Power is situated and exercised at the level of life, the species, the race, and the large-scale phenomena of population. . . . At stake is the biological existence of a population.

—Michel Foucault, *The History of Sexuality*[1]

People say to me, "What do you do for a living?" and I say, "I manage species to extinction," because that's what we do, really.

—"Chris," Conservation Biologist[2]

In April 2013, I attended a three-day workshop on the recovery of the endangered Sonoran pronghorn antelope (*Antilocapra americana sonoriensis*) populations in Arizona and Mexico. The Arizona Game and Fish Department has been monitoring the Sonoran pronghorn for more than twenty years. Although their numbers have fluctuated considerably during this time, they averaged approximately 140 animals on the U.S. side. In 2002, however, the population plummeted to 19 individuals. At that point, the USFWS decided to capture 7 of the remaining pronghorns and place them in a specially constructed, one-square-mile pen at the Cabeza Prieta Refuge, where they were to be supplemented with food and water to mitigate the persistent drought conditions. Since then, the USFWS has been breeding and reintroducing pronghorns from the captive population to optimize the genetic diversity of the wild animals. Because the pronghorn are extremely skittish (they are commonly known as "prairie ghosts"), their captive breeding in zoos has not been an option.

Facilitated by IUCN's Conservation Breeding Specialist Group (CBSG), the workshop's central mission was to apply a One Plan approach—an approach that incorporates the perspectives of all experts and population.s of the managed species—in order to craft a metapopulation plan for the Sonoran pronghorn. The meeting I attended brought together representatives of more than a dozen relevant organizations and agencies; twenty or so of the world's leading experts on this species were seated around the table. Most of the meeting was quite technical, focusing on obtaining the data required for applying the metapopulation model to this case.

The high point of the workshop was undoubtedly when Philip (Phil) Miller, senior officer at CBSG and co-facilitator of the workshop, used a computerized metapopulation model to transform the participants' painstakingly collected data into a series of legible graphs and charts. Miller presented the end results to an entranced audience (Figure 24). Although all the participants knew the data as well, if not better, than Miller, no one, not even Miller, could have predicted what the thousands of mathematical simulations of the metapopulation model would reveal. As it was, the result

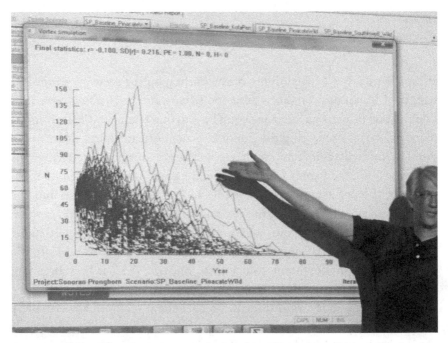

Figure 24: Philip Miller of CBSG presenting the results of the PHVA modeling at the Sonoran pronghorn recovery meeting held in Tucson, Arizona. Photo by author, April 24, 2013.

was quite obvious to everyone present: E = 1.0, which meant that under the current management plans, the pronghorn will become extinct within a few decades. This outcome came as a slap in the face to many in the room who have dedicated their careers to saving the pronghorn, triggering a heated debate about the accuracy of the data and the tipping factors that have led to this simulated extinction. Clearly, something significant had happened during the algorithmic process. But what was it?

This book's final chapter turns to examine the relationship between *in situ* and *ex situ* as it manifests in databases and population management models, examining biopolitical technologies that utilize datasets, computer programs, and algorithms to effect change in the lives of species. The image of Phil Miller dressed nicely and gesturing at a PowerPoint slide displaying an algorithm in an air-conditioned room may seem a far cry from that of Thomas Emmel, clad in heavy anti-mosquito wear, chasing Schaus swallowtails in the heat of the Florida summer, or that of Ricardo Valentin crouched behind a tree for long hours to protect Puerto Rican parrots from red-tailed hawks. Yet the science behind the population models that compile data and translate it through algorithms into recommendations for action is part of the same family of biopolitical technologies that are increasingly deemed necessary for the success of *in situ* and *ex situ* projects alike.

This chapter will depict the rise of the bifurcated database systems and population models for *in situ–ex situ* management as well as how these two systems and models are increasingly bleeding into each other. The science of small population management has provided the language for integrating the two management models, and CBSG's One Plan approach has translated the geographic and genetic fragmentation between *in situ* and *ex situ* populations and the alienation between their managers into a productive relationship. Like previous chapters, this chapter, too, will demonstrate that although the rhetorical distinction between *in situ* and *ex situ* conservation is far from dead, the connections between these two conservation poles are increasingly realized in practice.

Zoo and Wild Database Systems

Initially, *in situ* and *ex situ* experts developed two discrete systems to identify, record, and process data for managing wildlife populations. Jonathan

(Jon) Ballou is a population biologist at the Smithsonian Institution and one of the early masterminds behind the science of small population management. Ballou explains the differences between *ex situ* and *in situ* in terms of data management. He first reflects on *ex situ* management: "In zoos, all animals are monitored. We know the details of individuals in captivity, because they're individually marked and because we know their birth dates and death dates. Data standards and software [have] been developed [with] specifics that deal with those kinds of data."[3] In captivity, then, experts have been able to both identify and obtain the data required for managing non-human animals and populations and to develop appropriate software to process this data.

In *Zooland*, I discussed the various databases at work in zoos.[4] Alongside studbooks, these include the Animal Records Keeping System (ARKS), which situates the animals' identification at their home zoo; MedARKS, a separate medical database for zoo animals; Single Population Analysis and Records Keeping System (SPARKS), the dedicated database for zoo studbook management; and, most recently, the Zoological Information Management System (ZIMS), which incorporates these different databases into one global, standardized system.[5] The zoo's massive database apparatus is facilitated by the International Species Information System (ISIS), which records information on every zoo animal, often on a daily basis.[6] Similar information about *in situ* animals has been harder to come by. Ballou explains that in the wild, "you don't know individuals: you don't see when they're born, you don't see when they die. They just disappear—you don't know if they're dead or if they've left. So it's a much more complicated system to document."[7]

Such major differences between captive and wild settings in terms of the type and amount of data that may be collected have resulted in the configuration of separate and isolated database systems for their management. Population biologist Karin Schwartz describes this isolation—and its consequences. "There never was a direct link between captive and wild data management," she explains.[8] The differences are most apparent, she continues, when a particular animal is transferred from one setting to the other. In Schwartz's words:

> The animal's record stops at ISIS and then separate database systems are used for monitoring the animals in the wild. That's where the disconnect occurs. Right now, [most programs make] no direct link between the records kept on an animal while in captivity and the records kept when monitoring

it after release to the wild. This disconnect limits the effective communication between the people caring for the animal while in a zoological institution and the people monitoring the animal in the wild.[9]

According to Schwartz, when a captive animal is transferred from the captive facility—where it was intensively tracked, documented, and recorded in studbooks and international database systems—into the wild, the monitoring diminishes abruptly. The *ex situ* administration also renders the data more easily translatable into algorithmic formulations and global exchange, she says.

On the other hand, wild animal database management has its own documentation technologies and database configurations.[10] Only a few decades back, individual wild animals were not identified, documented, and managed—at least not intensively. Insufficient data also made it nearly impossible to carry out reliable viability projections of *in situ* populations. This more hands-off approach to *in situ* conservation management was not only a result of the technological limitations of the time, but also ideological: the traditional Western idea of wildlife conservation was of preservation (also referred to, in certain contexts, as "fortress" conservation[11]). Indeed, as I have already suggested in my discussion of conservation laws, until recently wilderness was defined as the site of least human intervention ("untrammeled by man," per the Wilderness Act[12]). Yet over the last several decades, conservation has evolved into an affirmative and proactive biopolitical project. The transition of conservation into the realm of biopolitics has manifested, among other things, in the intensification of *in situ* management. As a result, comprehensive digital databases that were previously used only in captivity are increasingly implemented by *in situ* wildlife managers.

The golden lion tamarin program discussed earlier in this book is a good example of the bleeding of database management strategies from *ex situ* into the wild. The software program SPARKS was developed by zoos as a record-tracking device for studbook keepers. Jon Ballou tells me:

> In the golden lion tamarins example, a subset of the wild population was very carefully followed, and so we actually applied SPARKS to collect data [on wild animals]. . . . We used it to create life tables, to monitor the pedigrees of the [wild] animals and their relationships; we've used it to determine movements of animals between groups; we've used it to monitor the changing size of the population. The information first went into field notes, and then into SPARKS.[13]

Despite these changes, most *in situ* and *ex situ* data administrations still differ in terms of the types of information collected about individual animals and populations, in terms of the database systems into which this information is fed, and in terms of how the respective experts collect data in the first place.

Collecting Data

In *Zooland*, I discussed the ways in which zoo animals are identified, named, recorded, and thereby governed through their naturalization.[14] Here, I would like to discuss how data is collected and recorded on what has been configured as the "other" side of the divide: in the wild.

In situ experts (or field scientists) often use Global Positioning System (GPS) and very high frequency (VHF) collar technologies to document the movement of the otherwise untrackable animals across large territories. Conversely, in captive settings, where the animals are confined and thus can be, and sometimes are, surveilled 24/7, no GPS or sophisticated technology is necessary, except perhaps a camera.[15] Whereas the uses of radio and satellite telemetry technologies reveal more information about animal movement in the wild than previous technologies did, they are nonetheless limited: collars fall off or stop transmitting signals after six months, and their signals are often delayed so that by the time the surveyors reach a location, the animals have already moved on.[16] Such radio collar devices are also limited in that they operate on batteries, with weight restrictions that dictate the size of the animal that can be tracked.[17] External tags—for example, ear and leg bands, dart tags, painted marks, and scale clippings—have also facilitated animal tracking. While these are relatively cost-effective, their external location on the animal's body increases their susceptibility to being damaged; also, they are often illegible upon recapture. These and other issues have posed significant obstacles to *in situ* data collection.

Increasingly, however, new technologies are being developed and implemented for optimizing knowledge about *in situ* animals with less and less disruption to their behavior. For example, the Passive Integrated Transponder (PIT) tags, tiny bar codes inserted into animals, enable managers to track them through their lifetime. When activated, the PIT tag projects an alphanumeric code back to the reader, who can then use it to track the animal.[18] Internal PIT tags were used by scientists in the 1980s for tracking the movement of fish. Increasingly, they have enabled the monitoring of other taxa, both in the wild and in zoos.[19] Because PIT tags turn on only when they are activated by a low-frequency radio signal, they require very little battery power.[20]

"Capture-recapture" is yet another strategy—albeit statistical rather than physical—developed by wildlife managers to overcome the problem of unknown data, this time for estimating population size. This method deduces the known from the unknown populations based on the ratios of marked to unmarked individuals. As a scientific and administrative tool, statistics is particularly well suited to the government of populations, and is emblematic of what Foucault described as the "new art of government."[21] The most famous early application of capture-recapture was Pierre-Simon Laplace's estimate of the size of France's human population in 1802.[22] Since then, statistical analysis has expanded from a tool for governing human populations to a tool for governing nonhuman populations.

Recently, the capture-recapture assessment has provided demographic assessments of polar bears worldwide. "Now, it's not quite that simple," says Steven Amstrup, director of Polar Bear International, who has been promoting the use of this method for polar bear research. But here is the idea, he explains:

> Calculating the proportion of marked animals to an unmarked sample, and then to the unmarked animals in a second sample, gives you information about the ratio of marked animals to the total population. [For example,] if in one year you capture and mark one hundred bears, and in the following year you capture another one hundred bears in the same area, and ten of them are marked—you might conclude that one in ten bears in the population was marked. Because the total sample size was one hundred bears, the total population size could be estimated as N = 1,000.[23]

Through this process, the unknown, too, is harnessed toward calculating the known.

In North America, much of the data collected by scientists on *in situ* species is standardized by database managers and incorporated into one system: NatureServe.[24] NatureServe's dataset on at-risk *in situ* populations includes more than 900,000 location records from a network of "biological inventories" in the United States and some in Canada. From NatureServe's materials: "For nearly four decades, this network has collected and managed detailed local information on plants and animals of conservation concern and has become a leading source for information about North America's endangered species."[25] Leslie Honey, vice president of conservation services at NatureServe, tells me: "We have over 60,000 species that we try to keep our finger on the pulse of. All of our programs have data managers, [who] work together with the scientists to populate the databases."[26] When "populated" into databases by scientists through standardization, the data about an animal population comes to stand for the physical bodies of animals in this population.

For Honey, "standardization" is the magic word. "Standards," she tells me, "are the only way that we're able to aggregate the data and use [it] across jurisdictions. Otherwise, you're comparing apples and oranges, and that's not very helpful. It's tasty, but not helpful!"[27] An abstracting process thus translates local knowledge into units that can be read and compared by experts removed from the particular sites. I ask Honey how information about captive or semi-captive populations is incorporated into NatureServe's databases. After a slight pause, she replies: "We have so much work to do with tens of thousands of species in the wild that we don't do this stuff."[28] This, then, is yet another example for how certain databases are still both determined and constrained by the traditional *in situ–ex situ* divide.

In other instances, however, the administrators of *in situ* and *ex situ* programs are gradually bridging the long-standing divide between wild and captive databases. Schwartz suggests that creating such a link between the previously disconnected databases will significantly impact the management of both sites, since "the issue is that the history of an animal while in captivity and the methodologies used for rearing, care, and release are important in determining the success and future for that animal in the wild." To achieve this, she says, "the records should be linked to cover the entire life of the animal."[29] It is no coincidence, arguably, that the most recent version of the new zoo database system—ZIMS version 3—is currently being developed to record data not only on zoo animals but also on animals in the wild. This technological expansion is part of a broader transition toward integrating *in situ* and *ex situ* information into one global database system. With ZIMS 3, animal databases that constitute "working archives" are currently shifting toward "planetary management."[30] "ZIMS will put everything in *one place*," Schwartz says.[31] This "one place" is in a sense placeless, since it translates bodies and events into abstractions far removed from their local context, as I will discuss shortly.

Population Management Models: Ex Situ

Alongside the new database systems and the related software models for integrating *in situ* and *ex situ* population databases, hybrid computer models for population management are also proliferating. Here, too, the starting point has been the bifurcation of and isolation between wild and captive population management systems, with the practices increasingly shifting toward their integration.

Good data is not enough, population biologists often explain; this data also needs to be aggregated and then translated into an operational scheme. To generate such a scheme, zoo experts have designed computerized data assessment tools. The major computer programs used by North American zoos are ZooRisk and PMx. Developed by Lincoln Park Zoo, ZooRisk provides a quantitative assessment of a captive population's sustainability based on demographic and genetic calculations.[32] ZooRisk starts off with a studbook database containing each animal's genealogy, age, breeding history, and restrictions. Using this data, the program then projects the future of the population at year-by-year intervals based on probabilities of death and reproduction for each individual, up to hundreds of years into the future. ZooRisk users can simulate a variety of breeding management options: they can minimize inbreeding, prohibit genetically detrimental pairs, reach a target population size, and allow imports or exports to and from the population. Management decisions are then generated by running hundreds of random simulations and observing the range of likely possibilities. Thus, a sophisticated mathematical analysis transforms the data on individual zoo animals into knowledge about the sustainability of their population.

As solid as these projections may seem to the untrained eye, a closer look at the language of these programs reveals the fragility of their assessments. For example, ZooRisk's manual highlights the importance of data quality: "For populations that are small and/or have historically been small, it is possible that demographic rates cannot be accurately determined, and you should seriously consider the appropriateness of running analyses with poor quality data," reads the user's manual.[33] For this reason, the AZA dedicates significant effort to data quality, advising regional studbook keepers on their data preparation for population modeling. At the end of the day, all *ex situ* population models are predicated upon the assumption that by applying algorithmic abstractions on standardized data one can derive knowledge about the sustainability of the relevant population.

Extinction and Viability

Whereas the focus of zoo management has been on sustainability, that of *in situ* management has been on extinction and viability. Until quite recently, extinction was the exclusive focus of conservation biology, which has emerged to combat it.[34] "Current rates of extinction are about 1,000 times the likely background rate of extinction," write Stuart Pimm et al. in a 2014 *Science* article that presents rates of extinction, distribution, and protection of "the most vulnerable species."[35] "Extinction is a different kind of death; it's bigger," says de-extinction expert Stewart Brand,[36] while Michael Soulé remarks: "It's not death I mind. It's the end of life that bothers me."[37]

Soulé's statement illustrates the fluid boundaries between life and death in conservation. In a different context, sociologists have introduced the notion of "social death" to illustrate that death is not a brief event but rather extends temporally both forward and backward. Michael Mulkay observes: "The causes of human death, the social distribution of death and the social organisation of dying have all changed dramatically during the last century in the industrialized societies. . . . For the majority of people, death approaches slowly over years of gradual decline and its final advent is supervised by qualified personnel in systematically organised settings where technical facilities for prolonging life are to hand."[38] Such insights about the rational and temporal reorganization of human death may also be applied in the context of nonhuman species on the brink of extinction, whose lives, too, are managed systematically and prolonged over time. Through hyper-documentation, catastrophe narratives, and mourning, endangered lives extend beyond the moment of their corporeal death, both physically and figuratively.

But the conservation context also provides a substantially different angle on death than that of the literature on social (human) death. Extinction is death of a particular kind: unlike the typical understanding of death as occurring on the scale of the individual, extinction occurs on the scale of the species. For conservationists, the species is indeed the foundational unit for knowing and calculating life.[39] Lacy explains that "population modeling in the past twenty-five years has been species-focused: you plug in all the biology of that species and you determine how well that species is doing."[40] As a result, questions of classification are of acute importance in conservation's biopolitical regime. Geographers Christine Biermann and Becky Mansfield reflect on the perspective of conservation experts: "Managing individual nonhuman lives is meaningless in responding to the crisis of biodiversity loss; individual lives acquire meaning only when they advance the long-term well being of the broader population or are essential to sustaining key biological processes, especially evolution."[41] In this way of thinking, the death of a nonhuman individual can be evaluated only on the basis of the extinction risk of her or his species.

Recently, however, certain conservation biologists have come to advocate a move away from the discipline's initial focus on extinction. For example, Eric Sanderson, senior conservation ecologist at the WCS, has argued that a focus on viability, rather than on extinction, is necessary to move conservation beyond the problematically limited management of populations for the goal of reducing extinction rates.[42] Caroline Lees, population biologist for CBSG, explains Sanderson's approach through a human analogy: "Do you think about life as continuing to breathe on a life support machine, or as being able to get up and *choose* what you do during the day?"[43] Considering the definition of a life worth saving, Lees remarks: "At what point do we draw the line? If wolves went extinct in the wild tomorrow, would we consider that we had saved the species because we've got a domestic dog? It's interesting to see on a scale what we mean by 'life,' or what we mean by 'viability' when we're talking about an entire species, and not just a cluster of individuals."[44] Lees' statements call for a broader understanding of life, one that not only extends beyond the corporeal "cluster of individuals" but that also takes the whole of the species into account. This understanding of life also extends beyond statistics and numerical thresholds, adding quality considerations to those of quantity (I will come back to this shortly).

The relationship between the individual and the species is key in conservation's regime. This regime moves beyond the individual focus of disciplinary modalities (anatomo-politics) to govern life on the scale of the species (biopolitics).[45] Yet unlike Foucault's abstract statistical population, the species has a face and a context; it is situated. The project of governing species thus sits somewhere between that of governing individuals and that of governing statistical or generalized populations, and corresponds with both. In this way, thinking and governing through species enables an abstraction—a grid over the Linnaean kingdoms[46]—as well as an embodiment—a materialization of the more abstract notions of ecosystems, habitats, and populations. Because humans understand themselves primarily as a species and therefore both relate to and differentiate themselves from other species, it is important to critically examine this lens and the work that it performs in the world.

As mentioned earlier, another species-centered concept in conservation is "viability." Partly in response to the critique of conservation's pervasive focus on extinction, conservationists are paying increased attention to the notion of viability—namely, life on the scale of the species. But the definition of viability can be tricky. Although Phil Miller calculates it every day, he is acutely aware of this term's convoluted nature. "There are multiple views on viability," he tells me. "Are you talking about numbers of adults? Are you talking about the growth rate of the population being above a certain threshold? Are you talking about the number of adults being observable in the population over a specified period of time?"[47] Despite their differences, these options are all based on numerical thresholds, demonstrating again the dominance of numbers in conservation management, albeit newly harnessed toward measuring viability rather than extinction.

When I ask Jon Ballou whether viability and extinction are two sides of the same coin, he responds in the negative: "It's like asking are you healthy or are you dead—viability's got to do with your health; extinction is death."[48] For Ballou, viability is much broader than low extinction rates. He explains the potential benefits of such calculations: "If you're managing your health, and you do a viability analysis, and it says: 'Hey, you've got a fifty percent chance of dying in five years, and it's because you smoke too much'—then you will go: 'Ah, so my PVA—my evaluation of my health—tells me I can change my probability of extinction by stopping smoking.'"[49] Here Ballou switches between the scales of the individual and the species—again demonstrating the importance of the relationship between these scales in conservation discourse.

Viability Models: Comparing In Situ *and* Ex Situ

Around the mid-1980s, two viability measures—one for *in situ* and the other for *ex situ*—emerged. On the *ex situ* pole, zoo experts have been calculating the viability of their captive populations—which translates in this context into sustainability—based on a goal of 90 percent genetic diversity in one hundred years. On the *in situ* pole, wildlife managers have been using population viability analysis (PVA) models and demographic criteria to measure the viability of small *in situ* populations.[50] Lees explains: "There is no single definition of viability. You have to decide what you mean by it."[51] She remarks with regard to wild population models that "we usually decide it in terms of an extinction probability over a defined period of time, because that's what we can measure."[52] Still in the context of wild populations, Lees tells me:

> Even though we know that species will all go extinct, what we're aiming for, eventually, is perpetual life. *What we are aiming for is immortality, really*—or at least the trajectory of life that the species might have had if people had not stood in the way. . . . In PVA models we look at how many times this population dies, or disappears below zero, or disappears below a number where we feel that it's going to start to lose its character as a species.[53]

By contrast, viability calculations for captive populations typically cover a shorter time span. Lees explains:

> Often, the tools that we use for [captive management] don't have a stochastic element. They're a *calculation* rather than a *simulation*. The PVA was traditionally coined for a probabilistic analysis of extinction risk. With captive populations, we don't think of extinction risk because there are very few captive populations where there isn't also a wild population. So we don't tend to use the word "extinction," we just use words like "unsustainable."[54]

Notably, with the increase of captive-for-life situations, the term extinction is becoming more and more applicable also for *ex situ* populations (as discussed in Chapter 2).

The task of conserving captive populations carries its own risks and challenges, for which specific institutional methods have been developed. As I have already mentioned in the separate section on *ex situ* management, experts in zoo animal programs identify and recommend reproductive choices for their animals—namely, which pair of animals from which institution will be mated and when—to optimize gene diversity. Breeding recommendations for zoo animals are generated through programs like ZooRisk and PMx.[55]

Until recently, zoos have been relying on the measure of 90 percent genetic diversity over a hundred years to rank the sustainability of their animal populations.[56] Although this criterion is "clearly arbitrary," as acknowledged by Soulé and colleagues who first proposed it in 1986, it nonetheless represents "the zone between a potentially damaging and a tolerable loss of heterozygosity."[57] To maintain this level of genetic variability, the founding population of the captive breeding program must contain as many unrelated individuals as possible. The minimum number of individuals, as well as the future genetic health of the population, is determined through computerized population models.

Viability has manifested differently in the *in situ* context. Until recently, genetic information has largely been unobtainable for wild populations; hence, their risks of extinction were calculated without configuring the genetic component. "Some of the PVA models don't even have a way to incorporate genetics," Jon Ballou tells me. He explains:

> You could go back to a wildlife manager textbook in the 1980s and even in the 1990s, and there would be no mention of genetic management at all. But that's changed. Now, we know that wild populations can become small, can become inbred, can have problems—and there are plenty of examples of that. Still, there is a bit of an attitude in the wildlife community that genetics aren't as important in wild populations. The majority of conservation biologists would certainly disagree with that.[58]

Still in the context of *in situ* management, the PVA analysis evaluates extinction processes that operate on small and often fragmented populations by predicting the probable consequences of various management decisions on their viability. Lees explains: "When we think about population viability, we think about all the threats to a population—all the things that might reduce it in numbers towards zero, which is extinction." "What we're interested in," she explains, "is how *big* the population needs to be to keep going."[59] Unlike the zoo, which focuses on the genetic sustainability of their population, *in situ* management focuses on the demography of the population.

Indeed, wildlife managers attach great importance to population size, to the point of "manifest demographic or numerical minimalism," in the words of Michael Soulé and colleagues.[60] Kent Redford and his colleagues explain that "this trend is still evident in the fact that successful conservation is defined by many conservation biologists with reference to minimum population sizes, minimum areas, and minimally sufficient sets of sites."[61] The IUCN Red List of Threatened Species—the world's most important classificatory system for imperiled nonhuman species—uses minimum population sizes as a primary criterion for estimating the conservation status of species.[62] This criterion refers to a set numerical threshold of mature individuals in a population below which a species is considered to be in increased danger of extinction.[63] David Reed and colleagues further suggest applying a specific threshold across the board: "In order to ensure long-term persistence of vertebrate populations," they claim, "sufficient habitat must be conserved to allow for approximately 7,000 breeding age adults."[64] Other conservationists present other numerical thresholds, and still others question the supposition that one can effectively use a single threshold of population size to indicate the level of threat for all nonhuman species, arguing instead for species-by-species thresholds.[65]

While many conservationists would likely agree that no single figure can represent the viable population size for all species, many would also agree that for a population to be viable it must be "as numerate and as quantitative as possible."[66] Again, such an emphasis on numbers has become, for many conservationists, the ultimate measure of viability. Science historian Theodore Porter reflects upon the deep trust in numbers among scientists in general. "Quantification is a way of making decisions without seeming to decide," he writes. "Objectivity lends authority to officials who have very little of their own."[67]

Eric Sanderson of the WCS challenges conservationists' overwhelming trust in numbers from a different perspective. "Setting Population Target Levels (PTLs)—the numbers of organisms we want to save—is a bugaboo of conservation," he observes.[68] Instead, he argues that demographic sustainability should only be a threshold requirement. "Having animals acting like animals, not just persisting, seems the standard that conservationists should seek."[69] In addition to demographic calculations, Sanderson and others believe that conservation analysis should include interactions, ecological functions, and social dynamics (recall Lees' earlier statement).[70]

Despite the difference in nuance, both *in situ* and *ex situ* are governed through an affirmative focus on viability calculated by statistical norms that rank the demography, genetic diversity, threat level, and risk of extinction of nonhuman populations. In this sense, too, conservation management is distinctly biopolitical. Foucault defines biopower as "a power that exerts a positive influence on life, that endeavors to administer, optimize, and multiply it, subjecting it to precise controls and comprehensive regulations."[71] At stake, for Foucault, "is the biological existence of the population."[72] In no place is this affirmative biopolitical focus stronger than in conservation. The conservation management of nonhuman populations is, as Foucault has suggested in the human context, "situated and exercised at the level of life, the species, the race, and the large-scale phenomena of populations."[73] Such management is increasingly planned and executed through algorithms.

Algorithmic Life

Viability—the measure of a species' or a population's life, as distinct from the life of the individual—translates in conservation into a series of complex algorithms that quantify various characteristics of a population with the goal of projecting its risk of extinction (E = 1.0) within a particular time frame. This section will draw extensively on my conversations with population biologist Robert (Bob) Lacy of CBSG.

In the broadest sense, algorithms are "encoded procedures for transforming input data into a desired output, based on specified calculations."[74] In Lacy's definition: "I would typically use the word 'algorithm' to describe a mathematical process of estimating some outcome from a chained series of equations (or steps in the algorithm), . . . [which are] pieces that go into an overall algorithm for projecting rates of overall reproductive success."[75] Equations such as $((A = 1)*5)+((A > = 2)*95)$ for breeding analysis[76] and $(0.2)*1 + (0.8)*2$ for offspring distribution[77] are the stock-in-trade of viability calculations in conservation biology.[78] Lacy explains that "such equations describe the details of how some demographic rates (e.g., percentage of breeding females) can depend on other factors (e.g., age, population density, or measures of environmental quality)." The algorithm harnesses such equations into a generalized statement. As an example, Lacy presents a simplified algorithm for calculating the number of surviving progeny produced in a year (Figure 25), along with the key to this algorithm's notation (Figure 26). Lacy further clarifies that many of the rates configured in these equations and algorithms "would actually themselves be determined by other algorithms, because they might be different in different years, or when the population is at different levels of crowding, or in different habitat patches, et cetera. Also, pieces of the above algorithm, such as 'kinship' and 'RAND,' would each need to be calculated by yet other algorithms."[79] "Often," Lacy continues, "doing this reveals that we didn't have a clear idea of what the problem is, or we find that different people had different ideas about what is the situation and [what is] the problem!"[80]

nBF = nAF * prBreeder
nBroods = nBF*(prBrood1 + prBrood2 + ... + prBroodN)
nBirths = nBroods*(prLitterSize1 + 2*prLitterSize2 + ... + n*prLitterSizeN)

For each newborn:
IC = kinship(Dam, Sire)
Survival = S0 * exp(-LE*IC)
IF (Survival > RAND) then nRecruits = nRecruits + 1

nAF = number of adult females
nBF = number of breeding females
prBreeder = probability that an adult female breeds that year
prBrood1 = probability that a breeding female produces one brood (or litter or clutch) that year
nBirths = number of births that year
prLittersize1 = probability that a brood (or litter or clutch) has 1 offspring
IC = inbreeding coefficient
S0 = survival rate for non-inbred newborns
LE = "lethal equivalents," a measure of the damage done by inbreeding
RAND = a random number from 0 to 1
nRecruits = number of surviving newborns that year

Figures 25 & 26: Algorithms for surviving progeny produced per year (top) and notation (bottom). Both figures by Robert (Bob) Lacy. Used with permission.

When performed at the scale of the population, algorithmic calculations generate rates of viability and extinction. Such an intense focus on probabilities and risk—and on mathematical calculations in general—has not gone unnoticed by mid-twentieth-century philosophers. In 1944, Max Horkheimer and Theodor Adorno contemplated what they called "the mathematization of the world." In their words,

> When in mathematics the unknown becomes the unknown quantity in an equation, it is made into something long familiar before any value has been assigned. Nature, before and after quantum theory, is what can be registered mathematically; even what cannot be assimilated, the insoluble and irrational, is fenced in by mathematical theorems. In the preemptive identification of the thoroughly mathematized world with truth, enlightenment believes itself safe from the return of the mythical.[81]

While I agree with their general point about the translation of different phenomena (which they problematically refer to as "nature") into a series of mathematical registers, I take issue with Horkheimer and Adorno's argument that the mathematization process is also exclusively one of demystification. My fieldwork has demonstrated, to the contrary, that the transformation of data into predictions through algorithmic configurations is a highly specialized enterprise known by a few and viewed by the vast majority of conservation experts with awe, almost as if it were alchemy.

The mystical quality of algorithms has also been explored by communications scholar Tarleton Gillespie, who insists that algorithms operate upon data, and that they do so by "selecting" the most relevant data. "Algorithms are inert, meaningless machines until paired with databases upon which to function," writes Gillespie.[82] The data is prepared for the algorithm, he argues, "cleaned up" so that the algorithms can then act upon it, seemingly automatically. The ostensibly automatic work of the algorithm is both an intentional and a crucial part of its function, as "algorithms are also stabilizers of trust, practical and symbolic assurances that their evaluations are fair and accurate, free from subjectivity, error, or attempted influence."[83] The criteria and code of algorithms are generally obscured and their procedures hidden, Gillespie argues. There is something "impenetrable about algorithms. . . . They are deliberately obfuscated, and they work with information on a scale that is hard to comprehend"[84] (as demonstrated by Figures 25 & 26). The algorithm is thus what Bruno Latour refers to as a blackboxing technology, a form of scientific knowledge whose "work is made invisible by its own success," becoming obscure through its own complexity.[85]

At the Sonoran pronghorn workshop, only one population expert knew how to work the algorithms. Still, the other experts in the room questioned neither the validity of the algorithmic process nor the values embedded in it; their concerns were at the level of data accuracy and over figuring out the parameters that contributed most to the undesirable result. Regardless of the desirability of the results, the growing dependency of conservation management on algorithms is undeniable.[86]

Metapopulations and the One Plan Approach

Many conservationists have come to acknowledge that managing different populations of an imperiled species in isolation is no longer effective, promoting instead what they call "metapopulation" management. They explain that the viability of small and fragmented populations increases when managed interactively. "Any small, isolated population is at high risk of extinction. In a system of such small populations, the same factors of extinction still operate but not at the same time or in the same way. Hence, the overall system, the metapopulation, has a higher probability of survival."[87] To achieve viability, a metapopulation strategy recommends the number, size, and distribution of what are newly defined as "subpopulations," as well as the level of interchange among them.[88] I will argue here that the metapopulation model, and its manifestation in the One Plan approach in particular, bridges between the *in situ* and *ex situ* worlds.

The metapopulation concept was developed by Finnish ecologist Ilkka Hanski in the 1970s during his field observations of butterflies. Hanski realized that fragmented butterfly patches do not operate in isolation; instead, the corridors between these patches enable the creation of a metapopulation that ensures that if one patch goes extinct, another patch recovers quickly.[89] Heribert Hofer, director of the Leibniz Institute for Zoo and Wildlife Research, explains the novelty of the metapopulation model: "The naive picture is that there is one population that is set up in a patch and another population in another patch and they're fragmented and they don't really talk to each other. This comes from the fairly static view of thinking about how speciation occurred in the first place."[90] However, "the fact is that populations actually talk to each other, that animals move between two corridors, and that there are quick extinction successions of local populations and a quick rebirth of the population."[91] The understanding that seemingly disparate populations are in fact interrelated micro-species units in a larger macro-species system has recently been imported from field science into conservation management more broadly. Increasingly, human management purports to do for the fragmented nonhuman populations what these populations had previously done for themselves: connect.

To encourage and institutionalize the communications between *in situ* and *ex situ* conservation experts, in 1979 Ulysses Seal formed the Conservation Breeding Specialist Group (CBSG). As I mentioned earlier, CBSG is one of more than 130 committees, specialist groups, and task forces in the IUCN Species Survival Commission (SSC), a network of volunteer experts that provides "information to IUCN on biodiversity conservation, the inherent value of species, their role in ecosystem health and functioning, the provision of ecosystem services, and their support to human livelihoods."[92] Since its establishment, CBSG has been developing, testing, and applying an array of scientific tools and processes to assist species management. One of the tools it has employed is the use of neutral facilitators to moderate small working group sessions called Population and Habitat Viability Assessments (PHVA) (not to be confused with PVAs). By 2014, CBSG had assisted in developing conservation plans for more than 240 species through over 500 PHVA workshops held in 67 countries.[93] CBSG scientists have offered that "the success of the workshop is based on the cooperative process of dialogue, group meetings, and detailed modeling of alternative species and habitat management scenarios."[94]

In 2010, CBSG Chairperson Onnie Byers coined the term "One Plan" to describe the organization's goal of integrating *in situ* and *ex situ* conservation practices under one framework. Byers defines the One Plan approach as "an integrated species conservation planning that considers all populations of the species, both inside and outside their natural range, under all conditions of management, involving all responsible parties, and engaging all available resources."[95] Christoph Schwitzer of Bristol Zoo Gardens explains that "the One Plan approach essentially regard[s] the entire population of a species, no matter whether that is in the wild, in captivity, in a zoo, in a reserve, in a semi-reserve, or whatever." He continues: "Obviously, the wild population (however you want to define wild) is the one that we want to ultimately conserve in that 'wild' state. But the lines become very blurry, and we want to acknowledge that, [we want to] not just look at the *wild* population—whatever that is—but look at all the animals from a given species or a group of species *in any population*."[96] Schwitzer's statement reflects the erosion, in certain scientific quarters at least, of the wild-captive divide in the interest of a more effective management of species and populations across the board. At the same time, this statement also demonstrates the continued relevance of the "wild" to conservation practices. Wildness is configured as both the wedge between captive and wild populations and the tie that binds them together.

The One Plan is not only about synchronizing animal populations of a given species through integrated metapopulation management; it is also about synchronizing the behavior of their respective human experts. Schwitzer explains that "it means bringing together all the experts that manage these populations." In addition to the biologists who work with these animals in the field, he says, "we should also have people around the table who manage populations of that species in zoos as well as government officials." The purpose: "that all these people will be sitting at one table and can all bring their expertise together, rather than having separate conservation planning initiatives."[97] From the human point of view, the One Plan is literally a *one table* approach.

As part of the transition toward integrative One Plan management, population biologists are currently tweaking computer models so that they can be applied to animal populations across the captive-wild continuum. For example, population simulation models initially developed for *in situ* use—Vortex in particular—are being modified to include modules for captive populations. "There's nothing to stop anybody from doing PVAs on captive populations," Ballou tells me. "In fact, the people at the Lincoln Park Zoo have a grant to pursue doing PVAs for all of the AZA-sponsored populations."[98] Lisa Faust of Lincoln Park Zoo coordinates this pilot program, which has been applying the PVA model to a select number of animal programs in zoos. As of December 2014, her team had already analyzed fifty zoo animal programs, with another nineteen in progress.[99] Ballou explains that such viability models are "more comprehensive than just using the 90 percent over a hundred years criterion," which, as noted, has been the central model for calculating the sustainability of zoo populations thus far.[100] Many of the interviewees have pointed to the black-footed ferret and the golden lion tamarin programs as "the closest examples of true metapopulation management," where "you are trying to maintain the genetic variability of these populations by moving animals between them—and moving them between captivity and the wild and then back from the wild into captivity, too."[101]

Despite its successes, the metapopulation model has nonetheless been controversial. "It comes back to the 'pure science' versus 'applied science' division," Lacy offers. "The Vortex modeling that I do is absolutely abhorred by some theoretical ecologists, who say it's getting down to the very specific and not revealing the grand scheme of ecology." Rather than ecology's "Einstein-like grand equations that explain the universe," he explains, the kind of applied science promoted by the One Plan metapopulation approach "gets down to a whole lot of nitty-gritty natural history."[102]

A broader critique of the One Plan approach is that it is never truly inclusive. In such complex operations, certain actors are bound to be left out—and the One Plan paradigm makes this exclusion that much more pronounced. One such instance occurred in the Puerto Rican crested toad program mentioned earlier. There, local conservationists who opposed shipping the toads to captive facilities outside of Puerto Rico and who preferred not to focus on the sites identified by the federal agency were not invited to sit around the "one table."[103]

Along with the critiques of the applied science approach and the exclusion of certain parties, a third and related critique of the One Plan approach sees some of its strengths as potential problems: whereas the One Plan's capacity to deal with global issues and connect a variety of resources and actors that would otherwise be working separately is one of the core strengths of this approach, it also potentially undermines the role of local actors and cultures. Along the same lines, the One Plan's reliance on the use of algorithms to reveal otherwise hidden problems might at the same time be abstracting particular nonhuman bodies, as well as human expertise, from their lived materialities.

The next and final story I will tell in this book is about the Tasmanian devil program. The quest to save the Tasmanian devils demonstrates both the benefits of and the frustrations with the One Plan approach, as experienced by the Australian conservationists who have been adapting this approach to the local context. Evidently, conservation strategies can never be a "One Plan fits all."

From Metapopulation to Meta-Models

While the metapopulation model enables a One Plan approach where there is more than one population of the same species or subspecies, meta-modeling travels further down this managerial path. Miller explains the difference between them: "A metapopulation model would use one single modeling tool, like Vortex, and would model within it multiple populations that interact demographically. A meta-model, on the other hand, links different models together."[104]

The year 2013 saw the launching of the MetaModel Manager software program. This program is designed to link population demographics of multiple interacting species with other processes such as emerging diseases, habitat and climate change, landscape dynamics, and animal movement patterns (Figure 27). Lacy explains the significance of the meta-model approach and how it relates to metapopulation analysis. "The problem is that species do not exist in vacuums," he tells me, explaining that:

> The tools that were developed for doing very specific population modeling always made the implicit assumption that the rest of the world was static [and] that everything outside of the population could be treated as a constant. What we are moving toward is an approach of modeling where you cannot ignore the fact that what is outside the species is changing. So when you model a ferret you have to model a prairie dog and you have to model climate change—because conservation problems arise from the interactions between those threats. So we are enacting an approach called "meta-model," where we are doing a fifty-year projection on the systems model.[105]

The species-focused system of the metapopulation model thus serves as the foundation for the meta-model system.[106] The goal of this exercise, as stated in the MetaModel manual, is as follows: "The program runs iteratively and its results are generated in the form of means or probabilities, within the linked-program platforms. Analysis and interpretation of results can be used in the establishment of conservation goals and to direct or prioritize conservation action."[107]

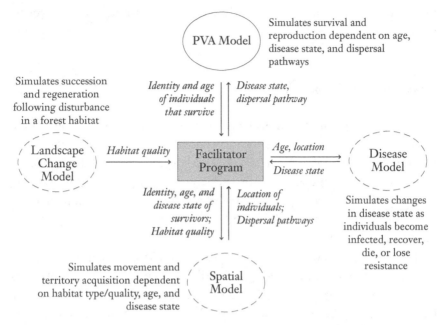

Figure 27: A graphic depiction of a meta-model that integrates demography, landscape change, dispersal, and disease status. Lacy and his colleagues write: "A PVA program acts as the system model to simulate individual survival and reproduction based on individual and population state variables (shown in italics) passed from other models. Modifier models (dashed outlines) simulate habitat dynamics, individual movements, and individual transitions in disease status. A central facilitator program passes state variables between the system and modifier models at appropriate time steps. The ultimate results are measures of population dynamics and extinction risk for a species impacted by habitat change and disease" (Lacy et al. 2013, 3). Used with permission.

A hypothetical situation presented by Lacy and his colleagues in an article from 2013 demonstrates the advantages of the meta-model system.[108] In this situation, an infectious disease is introduced to a metapopulation of one species that consists of ten subpopulations with a total population of N = 250. In the meta-model, population viability is predicted within the PVA software Vortex, while disease processes are simulated within the epidemiological model Outbreak. These two model processes are then linked through MetaModel Manager. Lacy and his colleagues show how using the two models separately leads to contradictory results, whereas integrating them takes into account the dual effects of synchronicity and disease. In their words: "Stochastic processes threaten small, isolated populations and are countered by dispersal while infectious disease transmission threatens interconnected populations and is blocked by isolation. Both processes impact many real populations, but the balance between these forces would be difficult to predict from the application of standard PVA methodology for population modeling, from standard epidemiological models of disease, or even from the examination of both models independently."[109]

And yet much is still unaccounted for in these models. Ballou sketches what he believes are the future steps toward an even more comprehensive integration of *in situ* and *ex situ* management models. The next step after meta-modeling, according to Ballou, is to move beyond the individual as the basic unit for the management of species and to calibrate metapopulation management models for herds, flocks, and groups of species. In his words,

> We have really good tools to manage individuals, where we know their pedigrees. But we don't have good concepts or tools yet to manage groups. [For example,] if you have fifty fish tanks, and you have fifty fish in each tank, or you have flocks of birds, or you have herds of animals, where you don't necessarily know the individuals and you can't necessarily manage matings within the group. . . . Those tools will then be very useful for managing wild populations, especially where you may have fragmented populations.[110]

The management of groups that are not configured as clusters of individuals, he concludes, "is definitely going to be a place where the concepts for management are going to be very similar between small wild and captive populations."[111] Such a shift in scale will finally enable a governance of populations that surpasses the need to know individuals, thereby ushering in a new era in the biopolitical governance of nonhuman, and perhaps even human, populations.

Conclusion

This chapter has traced the genealogy of the split between *in situ* and *ex situ* databases and population models in conservation as well as their gradual and ongoing integration. I have pointed out that historically, wild and captive animals were managed separately, using software programs such as ZooRisk in controlled *ex situ* settings and Vortex and PVA models for *in situ* settings.

I have also noted a few additional differences between *in situ* and *ex situ* population management, including the focus of *in situ* on demography and simulation and the focus of *ex situ* on genetics and calculation. The population biologists I have interviewed in this context explained that whereas captive populations typically confront such threats as inbreeding and genetic drift, small populations in the wild are more vulnerable to stochastic (random) events. Finally, while the management of species in the wild has generally been conceived of in terms of survival and extinction, the management of captive populations in zoos has been performed in terms of sustainability and diversity. These myriad differences between *in situ* and *ex situ* conservation have resulted in segregated systems of management, which have in turn reinforced the systemic differences between them.

Alongside my explorations of their distinctiveness, this chapter has also depicted the gradual merging of *in situ* and *ex situ* databases and population models. Integrated databases such as ZIMS 3, as well as metapopulation and meta-models, are emerging in myriad constellations across the divide, promoting the cooperative management of small animal populations. The particular focus of this chapter has been on one such integrative model: the One Plan approach. The One Plan, as its name denotes, is a unifying scheme. One of the strategies for achieving this unification, especially between different animal populations along the divide, is the use of algorithmic abstractions. Attending the One Plan PHVA meeting for the Sonoran pronghorn in Arizona, I witnessed the mystifying power of algorithms firsthand. Drawing on that experience, this chapter has discussed the growing importance of algorithms in the conservation management of both *in situ* and *ex situ* populations.

A large component of using computer models to evaluate threats to species and to generate options for conservation actions has been the translation of data into mathematical algorithms. I have shown how population models translate individual bodies and socio-material phenomena into condensed algorithmic properties that then enable calculated projections of extinction risks. The modelers of these new regimes are population biologists motivated by the aim of increasing viability and preventing extinction. When expressed as algorithms, material relations between corporeal bodies—in this case, the bodies of nonhuman animals—are objectified and abstracted, alienating science from the social world.[112] Algorithmic configurations also alienate many conservation experts, who are often not versed in this language and are thus marginalized as mere suppliers of data. Drawing on the particular genealogy of the *in situ–ex situ* relationship in conservation, this chapter has only just begun to unravel the algorithmic properties of biopolitics so as to "anti-program" them back into society[113]—namely, to show how inescapably social and rooted in particular epistemological practices they are.

Tasmanian Devil

Rather than us saying, "We're saving the species," it should be: "We are one part of saving this species; we're doing our part well, but there's a far greater need for more to be done."
—Tim Faulkner, General Manager, Devil Ark[1]

We've all had a bit of a giggle over the One Plan approach that's been put out by CBSG—because in Australia and New Zealand we're like, "Oh, we've been doing that for years! Nothing new, people!" Yes, we know very well that if you don't all cooperate and get along you're not going to get anywhere.
—"Chris," Conservation Biologist[2]

On November 14, 2012, on a small island three miles off the east coast of Tasmania, members of the Save the Tasmanian Devil Program held their breath as fifteen young devils stepped out of specially designed Mooney devil containers[3] and into the cool spring morning (Figure 28). These fifteen Tasmanian devils (*Sarcophilus harrisii*) became the first of their species ever to populate Maria Island. Once numerous in the Australian island state of Tasmania,[4] in the 1990s the devils suddenly started mysteriously dying. In 1996, biologists discovered that they were developing carcinogenic facial tumors, transmitted through biting during mating periods. The tumors, known as the devil facial tumor disease (DFTD), kill the devils within a few months.

Under these urgent circumstances, the Tasmanian government—in collaboration with universities, scientists, conservation organizations, and zoos around the world—declared an ambitious rescue plan. "We needed

Figure 28: A one-year-old male Tasmanian devil from a Tasmanian Free Range Enclosure walks away from the Mooney devil container used to transport him to Maria Island, November 2012. Courtesy of Save the Tasmanian Devil Program.

to plan for the possibility that, at some point, the captive population would be all that was left of the species," Caroline Lees, the IUCN partner in this collaboration, tells me. She continues: "As there are no natural barriers to movement of the disease across [Tasmania], extinction remains a possibility. Should the disease succeed in wiping devils from the landscape, the insurance population could be used to re-establish the species in [the] vacated habitat."[5] The disease is currently neither curable nor preventable in the wild, leaving biologists no option but to monitor its progress across the island. As Lees tells me, the best hope for the species lies in the continued growth of a biosecure insurance population. Within a fifty-year period, the experts hope, the disease attacking the Tasmanian devils will have run its course.[6] The species might become extinct in the wild, says Tim Faulkner, general manager of Devil Ark. "And then we can [renew it] . . . with the retention of the existing genetic diversity that we've captured."[7]

For this purpose, the government devised a rescue plan that consists of building and maintaining four interconnected management sites: (1) an intensively managed captive population in zoos, where "we track the movements of every individual and control which of them are paired for breeding"; (2) free-ranging facilities, where groups of devils are housed in large pens and "pretty much no one sees them from dawn until dusk, they're fed, and then three times a year they're censused"; (3) large but closely monitored Managed Environmental Enclosures (MEEs); and (4) biosecure "island" sites, which range from actual islands to large areas on the mainland that are fenced to keep out diseased devils.[8] By managing the devils in these four sites, the program's partners hope to isolate the healthy Tasmanian devils and build up their numbers in order to sustain the species' genetic diversity, while strengthening the devils' resilience to future challenges.

In 2013, the program had 660 DFTD-free Tasmanian devils, divided between the four types of enclosure. According to Carolyn Hogg, Tasmanian devil species coordinator and manager of science and policy at Australasia's Zoo and Aquarium Association (ZAA), these devils represent 161 founder lines and 99 percent of wild-sourced gene diversity. However, "maintaining this number of animals in an intensive situation is not economically and operationally viable for us," she tells me, "and so we are moving to a more semi-wild (fenced peninsulas, and offshore island) based population, whilst still maintaining a core population in zoos as an insurance against something happening to the fenced sites."[9]

Maria Island has been selected in the hopes of developing a breeding population in isolation from the mainland. The Tasmanian devils released on the island were first quarantined to ensure that they contain no traces of the disease that has killed so many of their kind. The purpose of this semi-wild management is to maintain a portion of the metapopulation under wild conditions, thereby safeguarding the larger insurance population against becoming too adapted to captive conditions, which could in turn hinder their successful return to the wild. The goal of safeguarding wild behaviors is often referred to by biologists as maintaining "behavioral integrity," and the Save the Tasmanian Devil Program mentions it in the same breath as "genetic diversity."[10] Since roadkill and human predation account for a large number of non-disease-related Tasmanian devil deaths every year, the released devils undergo behavioral testing to ensure that they will know to avoid humans when in the wild.[11]

Because the devils have never lived on Maria Island, their impact on the local ecology, and especially on shorebirds, is being carefully monitored. Conservationists also track the impact of other resident carnivores, such as feral cats, on the devils. The Tasmanian environment minister referred to the coexistence of the notoriously crabby devils with the local ecology as "a balancing act."[12] "We learned a lot from Maria Island because we'd never introduced captive-bred devils to a site where devils have not historically resided before," notes "Chris," a conservation expert who asked to remain anonymous.[13] Although the devils roam freely across the island, Chris does not consider them as wild. "It's an island; it's fenced in by water," she explains. "If you're putting them into a finite space, where they will hit capacity and you will need to move animals out of there and supplement animals back in there—then it's not truly wild."[14] So far, the Tasmanian devils of Maria Island seem to be thriving, and the population has more than doubled in size.[15] This is a mixed blessing, I am told; such rapid reproduction means that the population will reach carrying capacity quickly, and alternative management strategies will need to be implemented.[16]

In addition to the isolated island population, another significant management site for Tasmanian devil recovery is the Devil Ark. A project of the Australian Reptile Park, in 2014 the Devil Ark managed 109 devils, approximately one-third of the total managed population. Tim Faulkner, who manages both the Reptile Park and the Devil Ark, read through a draft of this story, and was disappointed that I chose to begin with Maria Island. In his words: "You've probably fallen into the trap of how romantic it is to have devils on islands." In Faulkner's view, this romance hides a lot of less romantic realities. The island sites "come with *huge* cost inefficiencies; they come with a lack of ability to genetically manage; they come with a consequence of infant or juvenile mortality upon weaning; they come at a huge cost, comparatively speaking, to what others can manage devils for. But islands are good at grabbing the attention, and that's a real success."[17]

Faulkner believes that unlike the island sites, the Devil Ark provides a cost-efficient and straightforward way to breed devils. He is especially excited about the successful use of Managed Environmental Enclosures (MEEs). Under an intensive captive breeding model (Figure 29, left), one male is introduced to one female. This costs the program between $5,000 and $20,000 per devil and is often ineffective because the females can be aggressive and refuse to breed.[18] In the much larger MEEs (Figure 29, right), which measure three hectares each (almost the size of six American football fields), four males and four females are enclosed together and allowed to

Figure 29: Intensive enclosures, on left, are the traditional enclosures used for the captive breeding of devils; they measure approximately 100 square meters. On right, a fence marks an adjacent MEE enclosure, which measures three hectares, or 30,000 square meters. Courtesy of Tim Faulkner, 2011.

choose their mates. Devils for each enclosure are selected on the basis of careful genetic modeling that calculates all possible breeding combinations. "We've enjoyed between 60 and 75 percent success rate of reproduction," Faulkner tells me proudly.[19]

But successful breeding is only the first step toward full recovery; the ultimate goal, the experts agree, is the reintroduction of devils into their historic range. "If you're going to take them out and not put them back," Chris says, "then these devils become living taxidermy. It's like being a museum."[20] "The thing that a lot of people in the zoo world need to realize," she emphasizes, "is that you cannot take these animals out of the wild and put them in captivity without some expectation that they need to go back at some point."

To get to that point, however, conservationists will need to strike a fine balance between the different management sites and strategies. Chris views the four types of enclosure as different sites on a continuum of management intensity, from "intensive captive" (zoos), through "less-intensive captive" (MEEs), then "semi-wild" (Maria Island), and finally the "wild" (Tasmania).[21] Although they may never interact directly with one another, she tells me, each isolated population of Tasmanian devils is a component of the larger metapopulation. "These animals are being held in isolated populations in a range of facilities throughout Australia but are managed as one metapopulation," Sarah Graham of the Save the Tasmanian Devil Program explains along these lines.[22] Every healthy devil—wild, captive, or reintroduced—is an essential part of the program.

In 2008, the CBSG facilitated a PHVA workshop to develop an overall plan for the Tasmanian devil program. After a long data intake process, the CBSG asserted that the total insurance metapopulation—namely, the captive, free-ranging, and disease-free wild components—will need to number between 1,500 and 5,000 devils to maintain the species' genetic diversity through an extinction event of an unknown length. This number is three to five times the current number of insurance devils. "The model indicated that we need an N_e [effective population size[23]] of 500," Chris explains. "But the thing is that at the moment we've [only] got an N_e of about 100." The program is already costing $1.2 million a year for 500 devils, which is unsustainable for the long term, she tells me. But Chris raises concerns about focusing solely on numbers and population modeling while disregarding operational and fiscal realities. "Conservation dollars are finite," she explains, and "the reality is [that] we would prefer to build a fence line and put animals back in the wild than to reconvene a large workshop to do further modeling." The algorithmic modeling has a time and place, she concedes, "but it very quickly outlives its own utility if it is not revised on an ongoing basis. Much of the modeling they did for the PHVA in 2008 is [now] obsolete."[24]

Instead of the PHVA model of the One Plan approach, Chris prefers to work with what she calls an "adaptive management" approach, which enables high flexibility and ultra-quick management responses. She explains that "in our situation in our region, we sometimes need to make decisions very quickly. We don't have the luxury of talking about it all the time. If we sat around and waited twelve months to have a chat—everything would be dead. Because they're dying now!" Chris explains that she is referring to the rampant threat by a variety of feral pests on Australia's native species.[25]

In addition to coordinating the Tasmanian Devil SSP, Carolyn Hogg of the ZAA has been working with forty-four species programs throughout Australia. It is from this comparative perspective that she offers her overall take on the Tasmanian devil program:

> The Tassie devil program is becoming one of the benchmark programs globally for conservation. It is built on the back of those programs that have come before [it], the black-footed ferret and the golden lion tamarin, which developed new methods for analysis and management. We are breaking new ground on new management strategies for managing multiple fenced sites for the long-term survival of a species, which will [then] go on to assist those programs that come after us.[26]

Hogg also comments on the relevance of the *in situ–ex situ* distinction for the devils' program. In her words, "Terms such as *in situ* and *ex situ* are meaningless for us, as it is difficult to determine where *ex situ* ends and *in situ* begins."[27] The divide is blurred in countless ways and situations, she tells me. For example, "we know that we are able to source orphans from diseased mothers in the wild to assist with the long-term maintenance of gene diversity and sustainability [in captivity]."[28] Hogg adds:

> [While] a fenced peninsula is essentially *in situ*, the devils will reach a carrying capacity within the area and will need to be moved and supplemented to be sustainable. Is it then *ex situ* because we are managing it, or [is it] semi-*in situ* or managed, or *in situ* because they are in their native environment? The

take-home message is that *ex situ* and *in situ* are terms that were coined years ago when we were in a different place.[29]

Instead of *in situ* and *ex situ*, Hogg prefers the terms "intensive," "less intensive," and "wild." "It is a very fluid continuum where we need to be able to provide adaptive management," she tells me. "This program has shown us that things change. That nothing is set in stone."[30]

Wild Life

In 2012, the Rotoroa Trust and Auckland Zoo in New Zealand announced a unique partnership. Their aim: to create a wildlife sanctuary on Rotoroa Island for some of New Zealand's most endangered species. For nearly one hundred years, this eighty-acre island on the Hauraki Gulf was owned and managed by the Salvation Army as a rehabilitation center for humans with drug and alcohol addictions. In 2013, the trust announced: "This ground-breaking project with Auckland Zoo will ensure that the island's legacy of recovery, salvation and renewal, will continue into its future by eventually becoming a sanctuary for a range of endangered New Zealand species."[1] Auckland Zoo Director Jonathan Wilcken was recorded saying that this project "will see us extending the zoo beyond our grounds in a way that's never been done before in New Zealand."[2]

The goals of the Rotoroa project are twofold, Wilcken tells me. The first is to conserve New Zealand's diverse flora and fauna, which have become threatened largely due to the recent arrival of invasive mammalian "pests." Wilcken explains: "Although we're not trying to re-create a formal ecosystem, [which would be] totally artificial, we do care about the diversity of what's unique to New Zealand, [and so] we should not introduce species that arrived here in the last handful of hundred years."[3] In other words, New Zealand species are welcome; newcomers are not. To re-establish a viable and diverse habitat, all mammalian pests and predators have been "removed"—the biopolitically correct term for killed—from the island. The mice were the last to be removed in 2013, under a license from New Zealand's Department of Conservation. "I'm not worried about mice and rats," Wilcken tells me. "I would be if they were threatened with extinction, but I'm not because they're not." Quite the contrary, he elaborates, "in New Zealand they themselves threaten some unique elements of the world's biodiversity."[4] This statement invites a broader question: is it a species' state of endangerment that makes the species valuable, or does near extinction become noteworthy only for those species who are valuable in the first place?[5]

Like Rotoroa, five or six other island restoration projects in the Hauraki Gulf are also managed with a focus on recovering New Zealand's species. The Rotoroa project is unique, however, in its privileging of intense human management over self-sustainability. "We are looking for species that allow us to demonstrate interventionist techniques," Wilcken tells me. "Species that will be reliant on management in [an] ongoing way or [that] will be brought to the island by artificial techniques." "I would like to be able to see the idea of conserving wildlife in the future as being one that involves people," he says, "rather than one that has as its ultimate aim to establish an ecosystem that has nothing to do with us—it's over here, and we're over there, and it's self-sustaining and doesn't need us."[6] Wilcken therefore advocates "deliberately setting up ecosystems that *do* need our help." Otherwise, he cautions, we will all become alienated from nature, because "we're living in an increasingly urbanized world." "If the ultimate aim of conservation is to establish self-sustaining ecosystems where humans do not play a role, then all you are doing is saying 'get involved with wildlife, but then step out of the picture!'" As part of his species management philosophy, Wilcken argues that conservationists need to "make sure that everything we do involves as many people as we can . . . and maybe gives [people] a chance to get their hands dirty."[7]

Wilcken's approach is somewhat of an outlier in the conservation community. Kierán Suckling voices his concern about this approach, and others like it, identifying this project as yet another manifestation of the dangerous agenda promoted by proponents of the Anthropocene. "Welcome to the bourgeois planet," he says about Rotoroa. "This new nature is to be available by commercial tour only on designated trails with four-star cabins, where endangered species are promoted as visitor attractions along with music festivals and gift shops." "It's not nature anymore, it's capitalism," Suckling exclaims. "How awesome is that?"[8]

The Rotoroa restoration team has already selected twenty species for translocation to the island during the first four years of the project.[9] Wilcken points out that this process is very rapid in ecological restoration terms and can only be justified in that "we were able to say 'intervention is a good thing, and providing artificial support for the populations once they get on the island is a good thing—it's part of what we're aiming to do.' And that means that we can bring forward some species that would otherwise have to sit back and wait until the trees grew bigger." Part of the species selection process has involved screening a priority list through questions such as: "Are these species going to be manageable side by side? Are we going to be able to [obtain] them in the next little while?"[10]

While recognizing the need to choose certain species who provide food for others, species have also been prioritized according to their level of conservation reliance—namely, species who are *not* self sustaining are privileged over others who are so that they may establish avenues for human care and stewardship. Wilcken refers to this type of intense human management as *kaitiakitanga*, a Maori term that implies holistic, proactive, and interventionist stewardship in environmental management. He explains, "Essentially, *kaitiakitanga* is this idea of stewardship—but it's slightly more than stewardship: it's stewardship that imagines your care for, and management of, an environment also having to do with the environment nurturing you. So it's a mutual theme."[11]

Rotoroa's conservation plan is part of a broader metapopulation strategy for the management of key species across different islands in the Hauraki Gulf as well as in the mainland's Auckland Zoo, itself configured as an island in the metapopulation model because of its isolated physical geography. In the interim, new rules have been enacted to ensure the biosecurity of the island: "Check bags for rodents, insects (especially ants) and other pests prior to boarding the ferry," read the visitor instructions.[12]

Wild Life

How do Rotoroa and *kaitiakitanga* contribute to our understanding of the place of wild nature in contemporary conservation discourses? What do they reveal about the recent changes in *in situ* and *ex situ* conservation models and, as a corollary, what is the difference between conservation on the mainland, on the island, and at the zoo? Does the fact that Rotoroa's species will depend on human management in perpetuity matter for how we should understand their endangerment? Will such species be assessed and counted as part of threatened lists and recovery plans despite the intensively managed settings in which they will occur?

Bob Lacy reflects on this project. For Wilcken, he explains, "there's no conservation except through management."[13] Although he may very well agree with Wilcken that this is the current state of conservation, Lacy none-theless insists that the long-term goal of conservation should be to restore and protect functioning ecosystems that require less, rather than more, human management. And while Lacy concurs that populations on the is-lands will have "lots of natural interactions among species, predator-prey cycles, nutrient cycling, and balances between flora and fauna—rather than being a barn with a bunch of animals in a stall," he nonetheless insists that the island is "*not natural*—in the sense that it [doesn't] represent perfectly what was present there before human settlement." Instead of seeing this unnaturalness in a positive light as an incentive to conservation work, Lacy sees it as the central problem that conservation must overcome. "This can only be a station on the way to getting to where these species don't disap-pear," he says. "They know that they are going to have to constantly be moving animals back and forth to other populations because the popula-tions will be too small to be healthy on their own; they know they're going to have to manage disease on the island in very interventionist ways—so it's basically a zoo. It's an open zoo, but still a zoo."[14]

Clearly, a zoo is not what Lacy has in mind when he considers the ulti-mate mission of nature conservation. "Species only in zoos are like words only in dictionaries," he tells me. "If wildlife species [are] maintained solely within artificial settings that have no relationship to the context in which they evolved, further evolution [will] only [become] more and more depen-dent on the few human constructed environments that we decide to provide for them."[15] Similarly, many conservation practitioners I have interviewed for this book would not regard species as "conserved" even when they consist of millions of members, if those survive only outside their "natural" environment. For these conservationists, once nonhuman animals are divorced from a particular spatial and temporal context, their wildness is irreparably damaged.

Posed side by side, these narratives by Wilcken and Lacy, two prominent conservation biologists at CBSG, convey some of the tensions in contemporary species conservation as well as the vitality and complexity of this field. They also convey that this is very much a time of transition for species conservation. Whereas Wilcken's narrative takes us into the exciting yet daunting possibilities of a post-natural world, or at least a world that does not view human intervention as exclusively negative, Lacy insists on careful management with an eye to historical processes, framed by the romantic notion of "before human settlement." The goal, according to Lacy, is for a species to be *self*-sustaining; humans must stay out of the picture as much as possible.

Earlier, I wondered what would happen to conservation if idealized notions of nature and captivity—as well as their multiple placeholders—were erased from the conservation lexicon. I proposed that the rationale for distinguishing *in situ* from *ex situ* conservation would then cease to exist. With no nature "out there" versus a human world "in here," conservation would need to find more nuanced and dynamic foundations; each recovery effort would be case-specific, as each particular story would depend on myriad interspecies networks and on an open and transparent discussion of what humans are trying to conserve. After more than 120 interviews as well as multiple observations, I can say with some certainty that this type of dynamic and relational conservation is already happening.

It is happening not only in Rotoroa Island but also in the multiple exchanges of Tasmanian devils among Australia's Maria Island and its Devil Ark, as well as between multiple zoos around the globe; it is happening in the cultivation of forest corridors for golden lion tamarins in Brazil and their management across seventeen fragmented populations and within zoos; it is happening with artificially inseminated and immunized captive black-footed ferrets that have been reintroduced into the North American prairies under extensive legal arrangements, and with the closely monitored reproduction of Sumatran rhinos at the Cincinnati Zoo and their release in Indonesian reserves; it is happening in helicopters loaded with Gila trout that fly between the river and the hatchery every season, and with the careful construction of *in situ* artificial pools for zoo-bred Puerto Rican crested toads; it is happening with the hybridization (or whatever term one wants to use) of the northern with the southern white rhino and of the northern with the southern Puerto Rican crested toad. It is happening, finally, all over the globe, in myriad contexts and variants. No example is exactly like another. Not only is every nonhuman and human participant different from all the others, but each social, technological, and spatiotemporal constellation paves a distinct path for conservation. While these stories illustrate the dizzying array of wild life, each and every one is unique and therefore prescribes its own unique path for conservation.

And yet, while all this is already happening on the ground, mainstream conservation discourses lag far behind. Indeed, many of the conservationists I have spoken with act with nuance but then fail or decline to articulate this complexity in their personal and professional narratives. This dissonance between rhetoric and practice may indicate their political sensitivity to the Anthropocene-era predicaments that mushroom by the day, which conceivably threaten the planet's survival. But alongside the political explanations, there are likely emotional and personal ones: the current generation of conservation practitioners grapples with both the attachment to, and the need to let go of, the ideal of human versus nature.

Biopolitics in Conservation

Alongside the empirical and ethnographic material excavated throughout this book, I have also drawn extensively on a long lineage of scholarship about nature and wildness, as well as on Foucault's writings on biopower. The biopolitical framework has been especially helpful to me in thinking through and narrating the rhetoric and practices of contemporary Western species conservation.

While in the not-so-distant past, conservation generally focused on enforcing strict boundaries between human and wilderness spaces and protecting one from the other, contemporary realities have shuffled the cards. Now, as conservation practitioners from around the globe have told me, conservation and hands-on management cannot be separated. To frame this in Foucauldian terms: whereas many practices from the first century of modern conservation were restricted to the domain of "let live and make die"—Foucault's depiction of sovereign power—nature conservation is gradually shifting into the domain of "make live and let die"—namely, a focus on "foster[ing] life or disallow[ing] it to the point of death."[16] As ecologist Thomas Foose and his colleagues have argued, while "conservation has traditionally concentrated on ecosystems and on protection, . . . [it] must [now] be increasingly based on management and on populations."[17] Conservation's contemporary biopolitical characteristics include both its foundational goal of affirmatively saving life and its operations on the macro-scale of the species.

Wild Life illuminates not only how the biopolitical framework may explain contemporary practices of species conservation, but also how the rhetoric and practices of conservation can shed new light on certain aspects of biopolitics. In what follows, I will describe six interrelated biopolitical aspects that have permeated this book.

The first biopolitical aspect is the shift of conservation practices from wilderness to wildness. Instead of conservation's prior focus on wilderness and its geographical zones of separation between wild and urban spaces, the central idea of contemporary conservation has been wildness. Several of my interviewees have pointed out accordingly that Henry David Thoreau has been misquoted for many years. What Thoreau actually wrote in his 1850s essay "Walking" was this: "In Wildness [rather than the common misquotation "in Wilderness"] is the preservation of the world."[18] Both the prevailing misquotation and the recent insistence by conservationists on preservation's origins in wildness are not incidental: after decades of wilderness, wildness has now become the guiding principle of conservation.[19] The shift in conservation from wilderness to wildness can be understood, I argue, as a transition from sovereign power to biopolitics.

This realignment of conservation around wildness has enabled a more dynamic and relational *modus vivendi*: it is no longer necessary to understand conservation in extreme terms; a species can be "wilder" and a site can be "semi-wild" or "as wild as possible," with neither being "wilderness" per se. In other words, the wild has come to be perceived as a multidimensional matrix of possibilities. The matrix upon which wildness has been traced in this book is nevertheless regularly spoken of as a set of nodes between the polarities of *in situ* and *ex situ*. I have argued in response that the recasting of wildness along a continuum does not ultimately replace the deep bifurcation embodied in the wilderness concept, or the kindred split between *in situ* and *ex situ*, but rather reinforces that bifurcation. By contrast, this book illuminates that practices of wildness are nonlinear and dynamic, messy even, and that they are not necessarily attached to distinct bodies or geographies. In wildness, the *situ* is no longer configured as either "in" or "out," but rather as flowing from and through myriad *situ*ations. Conservation practices based in wildness are often softer and sophisticated; they are relational and contextual. Conservationists of wildness value life when it is lived in its context, which is understood as constantly evolving.

The second biopolitical aspect explored in this book is the configuration of the species as the central unit of government. Foucault's general focus on species and populations as the primary subjects of regulatory control highlights the important interplay between individuals, species, and populations as performances of nuanced biopolitical dynamics. In conservation discourses, the foundational assumption is that it is life on the level of the (imperiled) species that must be saved, inevitably leaving other forms of life—non-species, or non-pure species—to contend with less livable conditions.

To render species' lives more comprehensible and calculable to humans, conservationists have ordered them into myriad classifications. Lately, population biologists have come up with algorithmic models and meta-models to account for and to manage complex interspecies relationships, translating conservation into a sophisticated mathematical apparatus. The biopolitical project of "making live" thus manifests as a detailed calculation of how wild the life of this species is: the more wild, the more the species is valued in the scheme of conservation. As this book has shown, *ex situ* has traditionally been viewed as less wild than *in situ*, thereby splitting the species into individual members whose value is determined by the perceived wildness of their conservation site.

The third biopolitical aspect illuminated by this book regards the interplay between political and biological life, and the biopolitical technologies that emerge from the management of both. According to Foucault, only (certain) humans are privileged with political life. Animals and plants, along with all that is considered natural or wild, have long been confined to the realm of biological life—namely, that which is killable. Conversely, *Wild Life* has shown the efficacy of applying the distinction between biological and political life to the nonhuman context. When they receive the designation "endangered," *in situ* members of certain species are granted political life, while others—most notably, *ex situ* members of the same species—often remain biological, or mere, life. As with *in situ–ex situ*, political–biological is a fluid construction that takes on diverse forms in practice.

I have described various biopolitical technologies that separate the savable from the killable, the political from the biological, and the viable from those bred to extinction. Threatened species lists in particular present a primary affirmative biopolitical technology of conservation. Through documentation, classification, quantification, and ranking, threatened species lists elevate the listed nonhuman species from the realm of mere, or biological, life to that of a political life worth saving. The political nonhuman species is valued numerically according to its place in the list's threat scheme. Even among those species who are deemed threatened, then, categories and criteria prioritize the ones who are perceived to be *the most threatened of all*: those whose lives are even more, and finally most, worth saving. Eventually, the last individuals of a near extinct species who die, or who are in the elongated process of dying despite the efforts, are deeply grieved. The threatened species list is thus the biopolitical technology *par excellence*, the ultimate expression of conservation's battle for "making live."

The fourth aspect of biopolitics I have explored in this book is the subtle integration of regulatory norms and protections—both on the books and in practice—into the affirmative "making life" project. Law, in its myriad forms and variations, plays a central role here. Whereas many have criticized Foucault for his restrictive use of law as pertaining only to sovereign or juridical power (law with a capital "L"),[20] this book introduces a more nuanced account of the variety of legalities at work in conservation—from traditional national and international laws and regulations, through standards and guidelines of various sorts, to the less obvious legalities of threatened species lists, risk assessments, and recovery plans. Taxonomic classifications, breeding recommendations, non-essential experimental designations, hybridization policies, split-listing strategies, reintroduction guidelines, and culling standards are but a few legal strategies that both facilitate the wild-captive divide and are simultaneously used to resist it.

However, when it comes to law's operation, what is in plain view is not always what is most important. And in this context, despite the egalitarian appearance of threatened species lists, their enactment and enforcement inevitably result in preferential treatment. "Not all threatened species are created equal," Mike Hoffmann of the IUCN tells me.[21] While IUCN's

Red List of Threatened Species is "applied to grasshoppers as well as blue whales," some listed species end up being more equal than others. "Even if you list a whole lot of dragonflies on the Red List, they're not going to suddenly get as much attention as a panda," another Red List expert tells me.[22] Additionally, members of a threatened species are not all and not always protected in the same way. This book has explored various ways in which the legal protections assigned to individuals, populations, and species are applied and constantly negotiated between *in situ* and *ex situ*.

This brings me to the fifth biopolitical aspect demonstrated in this book: death. Conservation focuses on "making live." Less apparent, perhaps, is that within this imperative, conservationists must also determine which life shall be privileged over another, that is then let to die. Powerful examples of such deaths in the name of life have permeated the book. My interviewees have entrusted me with stories about individual golden lion tamarins, sacrificed for their species in the early reintroduction days so that experts might learn how to "do it right" with the next batch; I have been told of rainbow trout and other "non-native" fish routinely electro-shocked in streams to ensure the purity of "native" fish like the Gila trout; I have documented legal strategies that differentiate experimental from wild populations and that split captive from wild members of a species, thereby negotiating lesser protections to the few (individuals, populations) in the name of the survival of the whole (species). As Emmel told me: "So what if a golfer hits a line drive through a [Schaus swallowtail] butterfly and it falls down on four wings. That's one butterfly sacrificed for years of successful reproduction."[23]

While sick Tasmanian devils are "let to die," healthy devils are "made to live" in biosecure zones; red-tailed hawks are legally shot down when they threaten fledglings of endangered Puerto Rican parrots; and "pest" rats and mice are "removed" from Rotoroa Island to clear the way for endangered New Zealand species. Finally, zoo giraffes and tigers are culled by their institutions in the name of the viability and purity of their *in situ* counterparts, and hybrids are deemed unprotected in zoo and wild settings alike. All of these stories and so many others justify the deaths of individuals and populations—both *in situ* and *ex situ*—in the name of the survival of the species. These terminal choices made in the name of life are the other, lesser-told consequences of conservation's affirmative biopolitics.

Still in death's domain, this book has also illustrated how in modern conservation, the death of an individual acquires meaning according to the level of endangerment of his or her species. Once on the brink of extinction, the individual becomes larger than a singular life, and her death is therefore more than a singular death: it is the death of a form of life, the end of nature. And so mourning this animal moves beyond the loss of her life into the loss of life conceived more broadly. Importantly, as more and more extinctions become known and documented, the death of species is simultaneously prolonged. Efforts such as captive propagation stretch species' death in time until the physical death of their very last individuals, followed by extensive acts of mourning that extend the death of species even further into the future.

Wild Life has also illuminated a sixth and final biopolitical aspect: the value and significance of multispecies dynamics, and of the interrelations between humans and nonhumans in particular. In such a relational scheme, human-nonhuman dynamics tend to serve as mirrors of each other. To counteract animal fragmentation (such as the fragmentation of forest habitats in Brazil and Puerto Rico), humans must overcome their own fragmentation and—as Christoph Schwitzer relayed—sit together around one table, implementing a metapopulation approach that may bring their respective fragmented nonhuman populations together. By dying out, individual nonhumans enlist humans to care and take action on their species' behalf. At the same time, as the northern white rhino story has so clearly shown, when humans fail to cooperate in saving them, species in decline will go extinct. Furthermore, human collaboration is not always enough for successful conservation: more often than not, human and nonhuman species, as well as nonliving entities and technologies, must cooperate for a species to recover.

Charisma is another realm where the individual lives of humans and nonhumans intersect in ways that affect the lives of multiple species.[24] Some species, such as rhinos, golden lion tamarins, Schaus swallowtails, and lemurs, are saved for their charisma; others, like the Puerto Rican crested toads, the hellbenders, and the American burying beetles—are saved precisely because they are less charismatic in human eyes. Charisma, or the lack thereof, can thus inform and explain the intimate bond between particular human and nonhuman animals across the *in situ–ex situ* divide. Terri Roth and Sumatran rhinos, Miguel Canals and Puerto Rican crested toads, David Rabon and red wolves, Adelmar Coimbra-Filho and golden lion tamarins, Thomas Emmel and Schaus swallowtails, Bob Merz and American burying beetles—these are but a few examples from this book of how intimate multispecies bonds can ignite enough care and passion to pave a meaningful path for the conservation of entire species. And there are many others.

*   *   *

In their 2013 article, "The Long Overdue Death of the *Ex Situ* and *In Situ* Dichotomy in Species Conservation," Kent Redford, Deborah Jensen, and James Breheny argue that "both the world and the understanding that gave rise to the easy dichotomy of *in situ* and *ex situ* have disappeared. We need a new understanding, new science and new ways of communicating the imperatives of species conservation in this new world. Let us declare the death and burial of the false dichotomy between *in situ* and *ex situ* conservation!"

As tempting as it may be, it is nonetheless insufficient to simply declare the death of the *in situ–ex situ* dichotomy. To truly give it up—to move on to a "new understanding" in a "new world"—we must carefully unpack how deeply enmeshed this dichotomy is within the rhetoric and practices of species conservation, both past and present. Only then can we emerge out of the rigid bifurcations of "in" and "out" of nature into the messy and productive entanglements of wild life.

Notes

INTRODUCTION: NATURAL LIFE

1. William Cronon, "The Trouble with Wilderness," in *Uncommon Ground: Rethinking the Human Place in Nature*, ed. William Cronon (New York: W. W. Norton, 1995), 89.

2. Stephen Jay Gould, "Unenchanted Evening," *Natural History* 100, no. 9 (1991): 4.

3. The IUCN Red List of Threatened Species contains 4 Critically Endangered, 11 Extinct in the Wild, and 48 Extinct *Partula* species in French Polynesia alone. See search results for *Partula*, French Polynesia, *The IUCN Red List of Threatened Species, Version 2013.2*, http://www.iucnredlist.org.

4. Paul Pearce-Kelly (senior curator of invertebrates and lower vertebrates, Zoological Society of London), interview by author, on-site, London, UK, March 14, 2013.

5. Bob Merz, "*Partula* Snails: Are You a Glass Half Empty or Glass Half Full Person?" *Connect* (2014): 17.

6. Erin Sullivan, "The Latest Buzz: Updates from the Terrestrial Invertebrate Taxon Advisory Group," *Connect* (2014): 11.

7. "Conservation Breeding," Bristol Zoo Gardens, http://www.bristolzoo.org .uk/conservation-breeding.

8. Bryan Arroyo (assistant director for international affairs, USFWS), interview by author, telephone, July 25, 2013.

9. David A. Burney and Lida Burney, "Inter Situ Conservation: Opening a 'Third Front' in the Battle to Save Rare Hawaiian Plants," *BGjournal* 6, no. 1 (2010): 16.

10. Sheila Jasanoff writes: "Co-production is shorthand for the proposition that the ways in which we know and represent the world (both nature and society) are inseparable from the ways in which we choose to live in it. Knowledge and its material embodiments are at once products of social work and constitutive of forms of social life; society cannot function without knowledge any more than knowledge can exist without appropriate social supports." Sheila Jasanoff, "The Idiom of Co-Production," in *States of Knowledge: The Co-Production of Science and the Social Order*, ed. Sheila Jasanoff (London: Routledge, 2004), 2–3.

11. Diane Barber (curator of ectotherms, Fort Worth Zoo; SSP coordinator and population manager, Puerto Rican crested toad), e-mail communication, April 24, 2014.

12. Robert Lacy, "Re-thinking *ex situ* vs. *in situ* Species Conservation," in *Proceedings of 65th WAZA Annual Conference* (Cologne, Germany, October 2010), 27.

13. Kimberly Ward (head aquarist, ABQ BioPark), interview by author, telephone, July 19, 2013.

14. Ward explains: "The Moore egg collector is essentially a box with a window screen placed at an angle within it. It filters river water, and 'catches' the eggs, which are too large to go through the screen. RGSM [Rio Grande silvery minnow] eggs are semi buoyant and float into the collectors at the water line and are carefully removed from the screen, using a spoon." Ward, e-mail communication, May 9, 2014. According to Tom Sinclair, Project Leader of USFWS's New Mexico Fish & Wildlife Conservation Office: "We normally collect between 30,000 and 150,000 RGSM eggs in the spring. . . . [The number] ranges depending on how 'big' the river is that year: good spring flows mean very few eggs collected (but lots of fish/good recruitment in the fall) and poor spring flows increase the sampling efficiency (so more eggs collected)." Tom Sinclair (project leader, New Mexico Fish & Wildlife Conservation Office, USFWS), e-mail communication, December 22, 2014.

15. Ward, e-mail communication.

16. Mike Oetker (deputy regional director, Southeast Region, USFWS), interview by author, telephone, August 2, 2013.

17. Ibid.

18. Ward expressed concern about my use of the spoon illustration in this context. She writes me: "I apologize if I placed too much emphasis on the 'spoon.' It is simply a tool in removing the eggs from the egg collector. Yes, a lot of effort goes into conservation of the Rio Grande silvery minnow, but 'chasing after it with spoons' and 'no spoons required' is inaccurate and the image it might evoke in readers' minds is comical and trivializes the efforts." Ward, e-mail communication.

19. My use of "who" rather than "that" throughout the book is intentional, as it makes a statement about the animal-as-subject rather than object. This statement is integral to the overall argument and project of this book and its repositioning of human-animal relations.

20. The information in this paragraph is from Kierán Suckling (director, Center for Biological Diversity), e-mail communication, July 26, 2013, as well as from "New CU-Boulder Study Clarifies Diversity, Distribution of Cutthroat Trout in Colorado," http://www.colorado.edu/news/releases/2012/09/24/new-cu-boulder-study-clari fies-diversity-distribution-cutthroat-trout#sthash.pDz2RCLs.dpuf.

21. Mark Jerome Walters, *A Shadow and a Song: The Struggle to Save an Endangered Species* (White River Junction, VT: Chelsea Green, 2007).

22. Peter B. Gallagher, "Dusky Seaside Sparrow Extinction Is Certain with Four Males Left," *Schenectady Gazette*, April 7, 1984, http://news.google.com/newspapers?nid=1917&dat=%2019840407&id=xAwhAAAAIBAJ&sjid=S3MFAAAA IBAJ&pg=2492,1570063.

23. Suckling, e-mail communication, July 26, 2013.

24. Jennifer Mickelberg (curator of primates, Zoo Atlanta; coordinator and studbook keeper, Golden Lion Tamarin SSP), interview by author, telephone, May 13, 2013.

25. Ibid.

26. Caroline Lees (convener, CBSG-Australasia), interview by author, telephone, May 20, 2013.

27. "Natureculture" is a term used to emphasize the non-binary and hybrid connection between "nature" and "culture" and to demonstrate that the two are never separate. Donna Haraway, *The Companion Species Manifesto: Dogs, People, and Significant Otherness* (Chicago: Prickly Paradigm Press, 2003), 1–10.

28. Sarah Whatmore and Lorraine Thorne, "Wild(er)ness: Reconfiguring the Geographics of Wildlife," *Transactions of the Institute of British Geographers* 23, no. 4 (1998): 451.

29. Timothy Morton, *Ecology without Nature: Rethinking Environmental Aesthetics* (Cambridge, MA: Harvard University Press, 2007), 1.

30. Ibid., 5.

31. Ibid., 1.

32. Ibid., 5. See also Timothy Morton, *The Ecological Thought* (Cambridge, MA: Harvard University Press, 2010).

33. Cronon, "The Trouble with Wilderness," 80.

34. Ibid., 89. Kierán Suckling criticizes Cronon's writing, stating that "Cronon is utterly comical in his ability to write 10,000 words about wilderness without mentioning that plants and animals live there or that most wildernesses and parks were created precisely to ensure the plants and animals have a place to live." E-mail communication, May 11, 2014.

35. See, for example, Paul Wapner, *Living Through the End of Nature: The Future of American Environmentalism* (Cambridge: MIT Press, 2010); Nigel Dudley, *Authenticity in Nature: Making Choices about the Naturalness of Ecosystems* (London: Routledge, 2011); Dan Brockington, Rosaleen Duffy, and James Igoe, *Nature Unbound: Conservation, Capitalism, and the Future of Protected Areas* (London: Routledge, 2008).

36. Carrie Friese, *Cloning Wild Life: Zoos, Captivity, and the Future of Endangered Animals* (New York: New York University Press, 2013), 11.

37. Bruno Latour, *Politics of Nature: How to Bring the Sciences into Democracy* (Cambridge, MA: Harvard University Press, 2004), 9–52.

38. Cited in Friese, *Cloning Wild Life,* 11.

39. Carrie Friese similarly notes in her work on cloning endangered species in zoos that "these institutions continue to be highly invested in and organized around older ideas of nature as something that is separate from and prior to human culture." Ibid., 11.

40. James P. Evans, as paraphrased in Jamie Lorimer and Clemens Driessen,

"Wild Experiments at the Oostvaardersplassen: Rethinking Environmentalism in the Anthropocene," *Transactions of the Institute of British Geographers* 39, no. 2 (2014): 177.

41. See, for example, James P. Evans, "Resilience, Ecology, and Adaptation in the Experimental City," *Transactions of the Institute of British Geographers* 36 (2011): 223–37.

42. Michel Foucault, *The History of Sexuality, Vol. 1: An Introduction* (New York: Vintage, 1990), 135–36.

43. Ibid., 138 (emphasis in original). An expansive literature has evolved that is concerned with the "disallow it to the point of death" (or "let die") aspect of Foucault's equation, with scholars coining terms such as "thanatopolitics," "necropolitics," and "politics of death" to express their divergence from Foucault's biopower. This literature includes Giorgio Agamben, *Homo Sacer: Sovereign Power and Bare Life* (Stanford: Stanford University Press, 1998); Achille Mbembe, "Necropolitics," *Public Culture* 15, no. 1 (2003): 11–40; Tania Murray Li, "To Make Live or Let Die? Rural Dispossession and the Protection of Surplus Populations," *Antipode* 41, no. 1 (2009): 66–93; and Roberto Esposito, *Bíos: Biopolitics and Philosophy*, trans. Timothy Campbell (Minneapolis: University of Minnesota Press, 2008). For the purposes of this book, I prefer to restrict myself to Foucault's biopower, because it corresponds to the affirmative aspects of conservation practices, thereby providing a productive theoretical framework for conservation's focus on both the survival and the extinction of species. Australian animal studies scholar Matthew Chrulew states similarly that "the task remains to examine the biopolitics of endangered species preservation as a form of power/knowledge devoted to making animals live, but nonetheless perilously bound up in the production of impairment and death." Matthew Chrulew, "Managing Love and Death at the Zoo: The Biopolitics of Endangered Species Preservation," in "Unloved Others: Death of the Disregarded in a Time of Extinction," ed. Deborah Bird Rose and Thom van Dooren, special issue, *Australian Humanities Review* 50: 141.

44. Foucault, *The History of Sexuality*, 143. Foucault's (extensive) use of the term "power" is different from the common usage of this term and thus merits some explanation. Alan Hunt and Gary Wickham offer this distillation of Foucault's account of power:

> Perhaps the best way to explore his account of power is to focus on the view of power that he is trying to escape. He wants to get away from the simple equation of power with repression. He sees this as particularly characteristic of the Marxist tradition. However, one can make his point even more strongly by drawing attention to the pervasiveness of the negative, normative view that "power is bad." It is of the greatest importance to stress that he does not try to reverse this commonsense view in order to say "power is good." Rather he encourages us to focus on a more analytical and even descriptive approach . . . . Indeed he is concerned to reject the very idea that power is something that is possessed, that some sorts of agents "hold" power and that others lack it. We should view power as present in all forms of social relations, as something that is "at work" in every situation; for Foucault, power is everywhere.

Alan Hunt and Gary Wickham, *Foucault and Law: Towards a Sociology of Law as Governance* (London: Pluto Press, 1994), 14–15. For Foucault, then, "power" is neither good nor bad; it is, rather, at work in every social situation. Foucault, *The History of Sexuality*, 143.

45. Foucault, *The History of Sexuality*, 139 (emphasis in original). In other words, biopolitics is a certain aspect of biopower. Paul Rabinow and Nikolas Rose further explain the differences between these two terms: "And, whilst Foucault is imprecise in his use of the terms, it might be helpful to suggest that, within the field of biopower, we can call 'biopolitics' the specific strategies and contestations over problematizations of collective human vitality, morbidity and mortality [and] over the forms of knowledge, regimes of authority, and practices of intervention that are desirable, legitimate and efficacious." Paul Rabinow and Nikolas Rose, "Biopower Today," *BioSocieties* 1 (2006): 199.

46. Foucault, *The History of Sexuality*, 139–40.

47. Cited in Friese, *Cloning Wild Life*, 13.

48. Ibid., 13–14. Judith Butler asks along similar lines, "Whose lives count as lives? And finally, what *makes for a grievable life?*" "From where," she continues, "might a principle of violence emerge by which we vow to protect others from the kinds of violence we have suffered, if not from an apprehension of a common *human* vulnerability?" Judith Butler, *Precarious Life: The Powers of Mourning and Violence* (London: Verso, 2004), 26, 27 (my emphasis). Wolfe agrees with Butler on all but one word. "Why shouldn't nonhuman lives count as 'grievable'?" he asks. Cary Wolfe, *Before the Law: Humans and Other Animals in a Biopolitical Frame* (Chicago: University of Chicago Press, 2013), 18. Also consider: "So when Butler calls for 'a politics that seeks to recognize the sanctity of life, of all lives,' I believe she needs to expand her call across species lines, to declare the human/animal distinction irrelevant, strictly speaking, to such a call." Wolfe, ibid., 21.

49. A few comments are in order about my use of the term "government" in this book. Here, again, I draw heavily on Foucault. Hubert Dreyfus and Paul Rabinow explain Foucault's approach in this context:

> This word ["government"] must be allowed the very broad meaning which it had in the sixteenth century. "Government" did not refer only to political structures or the management of states; rather it designates the way in which the conduct of individuals or states might be directed: the government of children, of souls, of communities, of families, of the sick. It did not cover only the legitimately constituted forms of political or economic subjection, but also modes of action, more or less considered, which were designed to act upon the possibilities of action of other people. To govern, in this sense, is to structure the possible field of action of others.

Hubert Dreyfus and Paul Rabinow, "The Subject and Power," in *Michel Foucault: Beyond Structuralism and Hermeneutics* (Chicago: University of Chicago Press, 1982), 221.

50. I am especially inspired by science and technology studies and feminist scholar Donna Haraway's argument that imposing human boundaries upon practices of biopower is yet another form of human exceptionalism. Donna Haraway, *When Species Meet* (Minneapolis: University of Minnesota Press, 2008), 53. Along-

side her rejection of the notion that nonhuman animals cannot be subjects, Haraway argues that animals, humans, and technologies are intimately entangled in scientific practices in ways that expose the traffic of knowledge across the permeable human-nonhuman species divide. Friese explains that it is precisely the translatability of knowledge between human and nonhuman species that has rendered the calculative work of biopower a relevant enterprise for zoo animals in the first place. Friese writes: "Endangered species have been cloned in part because biotechnology companies wanted to find out if they could use interspecies nuclear transfer as part of human embryonic stem cell research." Friese, *Cloning Wild Life*, 14. For another application of biopower to animal life that draws more strongly on Agamben, see Nicole Shukin, *Animal Capital: Rendering Life in Biopolitical Times* (Minneapolis: University of Minnesota Press, 2009).

51. Foucault, *The History of Sexuality*, 138–42. I will draw on Foucault's concept of power/knowledge in this book to highlight the mutually constitutive development of biopolitical regimes and scientific knowledge. Foucault writes:

> We should admit . . . that power produces knowledge (and not simply by encouraging it because it serves power or by applying it because it is useful); that power and knowledge directly imply one another; that there is no power relation without the correlative constitution of a field of knowledge, nor any knowledge that does not presuppose and constitute at the same time power relations. . . . The subject who knows, the objects to be known and the modalities of knowledge must be regarded as so many effects of these fundamental implications of power/knowledge and their historical transformations.

Michel Foucault, *Discipline and Punish: The Birth of the Prison*, trans. Alan Sheridan (New York: Vintage Books, 1995), 27–28, 184. See also Michel Foucault, *Power/Knowledge: Selected Interviews and Other Writings, 1972–1977*, ed. Colin Gordon, trans. Colin Gordon, Leo Marshall, John Mepham, and Kate Soper (New York: Pantheon, 1980).

52. See also Mick Smith, *Against Ecological Sovereignty: Ethics, Biopolitics, and Saving the Natural World* (Minneapolis: University of Minnesota Press, 2011), xv; Bruce Braun, "Towards a New Earth and a New Humanity: Nature, Ontology, Politics," in *David Harvey: A Critical Reader*, ed. Noel Castree and Derek Gregory (Oxford: Blackwell, 2006), 191–222; Jamie Lorimer, "Multinatural Geographies for the Anthropocene," *Progress in Human Geography* 36, no. 5 (2012): 593–612.

53. Suckling, e-mail communication, May 11, 2014.

54. Geography scholar Nigel Clark coined the term "wild life" with a different focus in mind: to consider new ideas of nature that are made possible by both digital and biological technologies, highlighting not only the destructive elements in human-created biologies but also their constitutive and surprising qualities. Nigel Clark, "Wild Life: Ferality and the Frontier with Chaos," in *Quicksands: Foundational Histories in Australia and Aotearoa New Zealand*, ed. Klaus Neumann, Nicholas Thomas, and Hilary Ericksen (Sydney: University of New South Wales Press, 1999). Drawing on Clark's articulation of wild life, sociologist Carrie Friese asks: "Can we still use the term 'wildlife' to denote animals that may not be tamed, but have nonetheless been remade from the inside out by humans in order to fit the planet as it

exists today?" Friese, *Cloning Wild Life*, 91. I continue this line of inquiry by illumi-
nating the biopolitical properties inherent in the contemporary conservation project
of managing nature.

55. Mary Beth Mader, "Foucault and Social Measure," *Journal of French Philosophy* 17, no. 1 (2007): 4.

56. Irus Braverman, *Zooland: The Institution of Captivity* (Stanford: Stanford University Press, 2012). For an in-depth reflection on my methodology in *Zooland* that
can also shed light on my methodology here, see Irus Braverman, "Who's Afraid of
Methodology? Advocating a Reflective Turn in Legal Geography," in *The Expanding Spaces of Law: A Timely Legal Geography*, ed. Irus Braverman, Nicholas Blomley,
David Delaney, and Alexandre (Sandy) Kedar (Stanford: Stanford University Press,
2014), 120–41. See also S. Eben Kirksey and Stefan Helmreich, "The Emergence of
Multispecies Ethnography," *Cultural Anthropology* 25, no. 4 (2010): 545–76.

57. Luke Eric Lassiter, *The Chicago Guide to Collaborative Ethnography* (Chicago:
University of Chicago Press, 2005), 16.

58. Christoph Schwitzer (head of research, Bristol Zoo Gardens; vice president of
captive care and breeding, International Primatological Society; adviser, Primate Specialist Group, IUCN), interview by author, telephone, April 5 and 11, May 13, 2013.

59. At the same time, the selection of species programs highlighted in the inter-
chapter stories is not meant to be pluralistic, as it reflects the preferences of the
conservation community. That four of the seven stories presented in the inter-chapter sections of this book are about mammals and that there are no so-called lower
life forms, for example, possibly reflects the tendency of conservation experts and
funders to direct efforts and attention toward what they refer to as keystone and
charismatic species and toward those species that tend to be more-like-humans. In
dedicating such enormous efforts to saving certain species, others are inevitably left
out. These stories are thus not only testimonies to valued life forms, but also testimonies to those that are not.

PUERTO RICAN CRESTED TOAD

1. Miguel Canals (forest ranger, Guánica State Park), interview by author, on-site,
Guánica, PR, January 16, 2014.

2. WAZA, "Puerto Rican Crested Toad," http://www.waza.org/en/zoo/choose
-a-species/amphibians/frogs-and-toads/peltophryne-lemur.

3. Robert (Bob) Johnson (curator of amphibians and reptiles, Toronto Zoo), interview by author, telephone, July 24, 2013.

4. CBSG, "Population and Habitat Viability Analysis for the Puerto Rican
Crested Toad," 45, http://www.cbsg.org/sites/cbsg.org/files/documents/PRToad
.FINAL_.pdf.

5. Johnson, interview.

6. Ibid.

7. Ibid.

8. Braverman, *Zooland*, 164–67.

9. Barber, e-mail communication; Ariadne Angulo, "*Peltophryne Lemur* (Puerto Rican Crested Toad)," *The IUCN Red List of Threatened Species, Version 2013.2*, http://www.iucnredlist.org/details/full/54345/0. A technical note: this book follows the common citation format for the species' threat designation. Accordingly, I capitalized the threat designation when assigned by the IUCN Red List of Threatened Species (e.g., Endangered), but I did not capitalize the ESA designations (e.g., endangered), as the USFWS typically does not use capitalization in its materials.

10. Johnson, interview.

11. Ibid. According to Diane Barber, the ponds are now constructed differently. Barber, e-mail communication.

12. Johnson, interview.

13. Barber, e-mail communication.

14. Carlos Pacheco, "The Puerto Rican Crested Toad: Once Thought Extinct, Now Recovering," USFWS, http://www.fws.gov/endangered/map/ESA_success_stories/PR/PR_story2/index .html; Barber, e-mail communication.

15. Barber, e-mail communication.

16. Ibid.

17. "Puerto Rican Crested Toad," Toronto Zoo, http://www.torontozoo.com/AdoptAPond/pdfs/Puerto%20Rico%20crested%20toads.pdf.

18. Barber, e-mail communication.

19. Johnson, interview.

20. Ibid.

21. Ibid.

22. Canals, interview.

23. Johnson, interview.

24. Canals, interview.

25. Barber, e-mail communication. See also Lacy, "Re-Thinking *Ex Situ* vs. *In Situ* Species Conservation," 27.

26. Barber, e-mail communication.

27. Robert (Bob) Lacy (senior conservation scientist, Chicago Zoological Society (Brookfield Zoo); member, CBSG), interview by author, telephone, October 22, 2013.

28. Johnson, interview.

29. Lacy, interview. See also Frank S. González García (Puerto Rican conservationist), interview by author, telephone, September 19, 2013. Chapter 6 returns to this example in the context of the One Plan approach, formalized in 2010 to indicate integrative management facilitated by CBSG using extensive population modeling. According to Lacy, the holistic approach applied in the crested toad program is an early version of the One Plan approach.

30. Lacy, interview.

31. Marisel López-Flores (project leader, Puerto Rican Parrot Recovery Program, USFWS) and Edwin E. Muñiz, Esq. (field supervisor, Caribbean ES Field Office, USFWS), joint interview by author, on-site, Iguaca Aviary, PR, January 14, 2014.

32. Canals, interview.

33. "Marine Toad," Toronto Zoo, http://www.torontozoo.com/explorethezoo/animaldetails.asp?pg=639.

34. Canals, interview.

35. Pacheco, "The Puerto Rican Crested Toad: Once Thought Extinct, Now Recovering."

36. See Chapter 6.

37. Barber, e-mail communication; Gloria C. Lee, "Recovery Plan for the Puerto Rican Crested Toad (*Peltophryne lemur*)," U.S. Department of the Interior, Fish and Wildlife Service, Southeast Region, August 7, 1992, http://www.fws.gov/caribbean/PDF/Recovery_Plans/Peltophryne_lemur.pdf, 11.

38. According to Canals, four of the twelve toads equipped with transmitters were eaten, which he believes was because they were too heavy to escape. For this reason, although he is one of the only two biologists trained to fit the transmitters on the toads in Puerto Rico, he is no longer willing to monitor toads in this way. In any case, he tells me, "new techniques using transponders are being used now." Canals, interview, and e-mail communication, April 24, 2014.

39. Barber, e-mail communication. For a detailed description of the reproductive goals of SSPs in North American zoos, see Braverman, *Zooland*, 104–9, 172–73.

40. Canals, e-mail communication.

41. Johnson, interview.

42. Ibid.

43. Ibid.

44. Lacy, interview.

45. Canals, interview.

46. Barber, e-mail communication. For a discussion of conservation translocations, see Chapter 4.

47. Johnson, interview.

48. Barber, e-mail communication.

49. Ibid.

50. Johnson, interview.

51. Ibid.

52. Barber, e-mail communication.

CHAPTER I: BIFURCATED LIFE

1. Quoted in Jonathan D. Ballou, Michael Gilpin, and Thomas J. Foose, *Population Management for Survival and Recovery: Analytical Methods and Strategies in Small Population Conservation* (New York: Columbia University Press, 1995), xix.

2. Kent H. Redford, Deborah B. Jensen, and James J. Breheny, "The Long Overdue Death of the *Ex Situ* and *In Situ* Dichotomy in Species Conservation," *WAZA Magazine* 14 (2013): 20.

3. Ibid., 20–21. See also Kent H. Redford, Deborah B. Jensen, and James J.

Breheny, "Integrating the Captive and the Wild," *Science* 338, no. 6111 (2012): 1157–58.

4. Wikipedia, "*In Situ*," http://en.wikipedia.org/wiki/In_situ.

5. George Abungu (former director general, National Museums of Kenya; cultural heritage expert), interview by author, telephone, February 13, 2013.

6. Kenneth Hamma (executive director for technology strategy, Getty Museum; cultural heritage consultant), interview by author, telephone, February 5, 2013.

7. Abungu, interview.

8. Redford et al., "The Long Overdue."

9. Gian Tommaso Scarascia-Mugnozza and P. Perrino, "The History of *Ex Situ* Conservation and Use of Plant Genetic Resources," in *Managing Plant Genetic Diversity*, ed. Johannes M. M. Engels et al. (Oxford: CABI Publishing, 2002), 5. See also Edward O. Guerrant, Kayri Havens, and Michael Maunder, eds., *Ex Situ Plant Conservation: Supporting Species in the Wild* (Washington, DC: Island Press, 2004). For an updated discussion of plant conservation, see Sergei Volis and Michael Blecher, "Quasi *In Situ*: A Bridge Between *Ex Situ* and *In Situ* Conservation of Plants," *Biodiversity and Conservation* 10, no. 9 (2010): 2441–54.

10. Instead of "captivity," many zoo professionals prefer the term "in human care." Jesse Donahue and Erik Trump, *The Politics of Zoos: Exotic Animals and Their Protectors* (Dekalb: Northern Illinois University Press, 2006). For a critique of zoo practices from an animal rights perspective, see Dale Jamieson, "Against Zoos," in *In Defense of Animals*, ed. Peter Singer (New York: Basil Blackwell, 1985), 108–17; from a welfare perspective, see Marc Bekoff, "Why 'Good Welfare' Isn't 'Good Enough': Minding Animals and Increasing Our Compassionate Footprint," *Annual Review of Biomedical Sciences* 10 (2008): T1–T13.

11. Evan Blumer (former director, The Wilds; board member, CBSG), interview by author, telephone, February 18, 2013.

12. John E. Fa, Stuart Harrop, Sara Oldfield, and Diana Pritchard, "The Need to Balance *Ex Situ* and *In Situ* Conservation," *WAZA Magazine* 14 (2013): 15.

13. United Nations, "Article 2: Use of Terms," *Convention on Biological Diversity*, Rio de Janeiro, Brazil, June 5, 1992, http://www.cbd.int/convention/articles/default. shtml?a=cbd-02 (my emphasis).

14. Ibid.

15. United Nations, Article 9, "Ex-situ Conservation," *Convention on Biological Diversity*, Rio de Janeiro, Brazil, June 5, 1992, http://www.cbd.int/convention/articles /default.shtml?a=cbd-09.

16. Ibid.

17. For a discussion of conservation's drive for what is "natural," see Marc Bekoff, "Redecorating Nature: Reflections on Science, Holism, Community, Reconciliation, Spirit, Compassion, and Love," *Human Ecology Review* 7, no. 1 (2000): 59–67.

18. Fa et al., "The Need to Balance," 15.

19. IUCN, "IUCN Technical Guidelines on the Management of *Ex Situ* Populations for Conservation" (paper presented at the 14th Meeting of the Programme

Committee of Council, Gland, Switzerland, December 10, 2002), https://portals
.iucn.org/library/efiles/documents/Rep-2002-017.pdf.

20. Ibid. (my emphasis).

21. WAZA, *Building a Future for Wildlife: The World Zoo and Aquarium Conservation Strategy* (Berne, Switzerland: WAZA Executive Office, 2005), http://www
.waza.org/files/webcontent/1.public_site/5.conservation/conservation_strategies/
building_a_future_for_wildlife/wzacs-en.pdf (my emphasis).

22. IUCN, *The IUCN Red List of Threatened Species, Version 2012.2,* iucnredlist.org.

23. Onnie Byers (chairperson, CBSG), interview by author, telephone, August 1,
2012.

24. Schwitzer, interview, April 5, 2013.

25. Fa et al., "The Need to Balance," 16.

26. Pierre Comizzoli (reproductive physiologist, Smithsonian Institution), interview by author, on-site, Washington, DC, June 11, 2013.

27. Alex Travis (faculty director, environment, Atkinson Center for a Sustainable Future; associate professor of reproductive biology, Baker Institute for Animal
Health, Cornell Center for Wildlife Conservation), interview by author, on-site,
Cornell University, Ithaca, NY, March 6, 2014.

28. Ibid.

29. Ibid.

30. Ibid.

31. For example, Susie Ellis, executive director of the International Rhino
Foundation—a global nonprofit umbrella organization dedicated to the survival of
the world's rhino species—insists in our interview that there are in fact no tensions
between *in situ* and *ex situ*; interview by author, telephone, September 10, 2013.
Similarly, Sarah Christie of the Zoological Society of London explains that whereas
in the past, insufficient welfare standards in zoos were the cause of much tension
with field biologists, this is no longer the case. Now, she says, "there's massive cooperation." "Zoos are the third biggest funder of field conservation worldwide, after
the World Wildlife Fund and The Nature Conservancy." Sarah Christie (head of
regional programmes, Field Conservation Office, Zoological Society of London),
interview by author, on-site, London, UK, March 14, 2013. This, again, was the
minority opinion among my interviewees; others pointed to the continued tensions
between *in situ* and *ex situ*.

32. Schwitzer, interview.

33. Ibid.

34. Kathy Traylor-Holzer (senior program officer, CBSG), interview by author,
telephone, May 2, 2013.

35. Schwitzer, interview. Onnie Byers of IUCN's CBSG explains, similarly, that
"there are still tensions between [the] captive and wild [conservation] communities."
Byers, interview.

36. Tara Stoinski (manager of conservation partnerships and director of primate
research, Zoo Atlanta; Pat and Forrest McGrath Chair of Research and Conserva-

tion, Dian Fossey Gorilla Fund International), interview by author, telephone, January 7, 2013.

37. Arroyo, interview.

38. Ibid.

39. Center for Biological Diversity, "About the Center," http://www.biological-diversity.org/about/index.html.

40. Suckling, interview by author, telephone, July 5 and 12, 2013.

41. Suckling, e-mail communication, May 11, 2014.

42. CBSG, *Intensively Managed Populations for Conservation Workshop*, San Diego, CA, 6–9 December 2010, http://www.cbsg.org/sites/cbsg.org/files/documents/IMP%20Workshop%20Final%20Report.pdf.

43. Ibid.

44. John Robinson (vice president and director of international conservation, WCS), interview by author, telephone, July 19, 2013.

45. Ibid.

46. Ibid. Suckling criticizes Robinson's perspective, stating: "To imagine that because the managers are thinking about sociology that they must not be thinking about demography and ecology is just silly. On the other side, . . . if Robinson thinks that elephant zoo keepers live in a scientific bubble outside of sociologic interests he's completely ignorant of the history of zoos and elephants." E-mail communication, May 11, 2014.

47. Irus Braverman, "Conservation without Nature: The Trouble with *In Situ* versus *Ex Situ* Conservation," *Geoforum* 51 (2014): 47–57.

48. On the fluidity of the precise moment of the human entry into nature, see Dolly Jorgensen, *Drawing Lines in Time* (blog), June 15, 2014, http://dolly.jorgensenweb.net/nordicnature/?p=1717. Jorgensen argues that the Red List is formed by subjective decisions, because different countries draw different temporal lines around what constitutes "belonging" for the threatened species.

49. William Conway (former director, Bronx Zoo; president, WCS, 1992–99), interview by author, telephone, January 28, 2013. Kierán Suckling offers a different perspective that moves away from the debate about historicity: "You need to try to keep or restore the [original] habitat, . . . but that's not because you have some abstract belief in pristine nature, or nature separated from humans. It's just a practical matter: this animal cannot live unless the canopy cover in the forest is between 60 and 80 percent, because that's what it evolved into for the last million years." Suckling, interview, July 12, 2013. This perspective represents a shift from a species-focused conservation to a more holistic conservation that understands organisms as inseparable from their ecosystems. However, in many instances leaving nature to its own devices does not reestablish viability. Suckling acknowledges that sometimes "the species or its habitat have been so damaged that they no longer possess the power to restore themselves (or at least not in a sufficiently fast manner) if humans simply stop oppressing them." Such restoration work is difficult and prone to failure, he explains, mostly "because the work is fundamentally a nature-replication task,

[and] reproducing ecosystems (or, more accurately, key aspects of them) is harder work than desisting from interfering with them." Suckling, e-mail communication, July 26, 2013. For a discussion of restoration ecology, see, for example, Michael L. Rosenzweig, *Win-Win Ecology: How the Earth's Species Can Survive in the Midst of Human Enterprise* (Oxford: Oxford University Press, 2003).

50. Cronon, "The Trouble with Wilderness," 86.

51. Mark David Spence, *Dispossessing the Wilderness: Indian Removal and the Making of the National Parks* (Oxford: Oxford University Press, 1999), 5.

52. Ibid. See also J. Baird Callicott and Michael P. Nelson, eds., *The Great New Wilderness Debate* (Athens: University of Georgia Press, 1998).

53. Cronon, "The Trouble with Wilderness," 81.

54. Caroline Fraser, *Rewilding the World: Dispatches from the Conservation Revolution* (New York: Picador, 2009), 3. In contrast to Morton and Cronon, who call for the death of Nature (as they define it), Bill McKibben's *The End of Nature* mourns this death. In his words: "By changing the weather, we make every spot on earth man-made and artificial. . . . We have ended the thing that has, at least in modern times, defined nature for us—its separation from human society." Bill McKibben, *The End of Nature* (New York: Anchor, 1989), 58, 64.

55. Ursula K. Heise, "Martian Ecologies and the Future of Nature," *Twentieth-Century Literature* 57, no. 3 (2011): 447–71. See also Ursula K. Heise, *Sense of Place and Sense of Planet: The Environmental Imagination of the Global* (Oxford: Oxford University Press, 2008).

56. Heise, "Martian Ecologies," 448.

57. Ibid., 451.

58. Ibid.

59. Friese, *Cloning Wild Life*, 10.

60. Latour, *Politics of Nature*, 9.

61. Ibid., 33.

62. Many have critiqued the neologism "natureculture," which was adopted by Donna Haraway in *When Species Meet*, suggesting that it produces the same problem as the previous bifurcated entities, now newly cramped in one word. For instance, Morton refers to this concept as a "jerry-built idea" (*Ecology without Nature*, 21), and Heise argues that it is "clumsy." Heise, "Martian Ecologies," 449.

63. Latour, *Politics of Nature*, 21.

64. Whatmore and Thorne, "Wild(er)ness"; Lorimer, "Multinatural Geographies for the Anthropocene"; Steve Hinchliffe, "Reconstituting Nature Conservation: Towards a Careful Political Ecology," *Geoforum* 39, no. 1 (2008): 88–97.

65. Whatmore and Thorne, "Wild(er)ness," 452.

66. Hinchliffe, "Reconstituting Nature Conservation."

67. Steve Hinchliffe, *Geographies of Nature* (London: Sage, 2007), 145. Hinchliffe makes a similar argument together with geographer Nick Bingham that the process of composing a common world necessitates a sense of natures as *active* outcomes rather than as pre-given starting points, as they are not "reducible to their condi-

tions for they will go on to do more work in their own right." For Bingham and Hinchliffe, it is because natures are "neither made-up nor pre-existing, both formed and forming, [that they] mark the lures that mobilise an indeterminate world." Nick Bingham and Steve Hinchliffe, "Reconstituting Natures: Articulating Other Modes of Living Together," *Geoforum* 39, no. 1 (2008): 85.

68. Lorimer and Driessen, "Wild Experiments," 170 (quoting from Gieryn and Kohler).

69. Ibid., 171.

70. Ibid., 170.

71. Ibid., 171 (quoting Michel Callon).

72. Ibid., 170.

73. For further discussions of the Anthropocene, see Bronislaw Szerszynski, "The End of the End of Nature: The Anthropocene and the Fate of the Human," *Oxford Literary Review* 34 (2012): 165–84; Will Steffen, Paul J. Crutzen, and John R. McNeill, "The Anthropocene: Are Humans Now Overwhelming the Great Forces of Nature?" *Ambio* 38 (2007): 614–621; Will Steffen et al., "The Anthropocene: Conceptual and Historical Perspectives," *Philosophical Transactions of the Royal Society A* 369 (2011): 842–67.

74. Peter Kareiva, Michelle Marvier, and Robert Lalasz, "Conservation in the Anthropocene: Beyond Solitude and Fragility," *The Breakthrough Institute*, February 1, 2012, http://thebreakthrough.org/index.php/journal/past-issues/issue-2/conservation-in-the-anthropocene.

75. Kierán Suckling, "Conservation for the Real World," *The Breakthrough Institute*, April 2012, http://thebreakthrough.org/index.php/journal/debates/conservation-in-the-anthropocene-a-breakthrough-debate/conservation-for-the-real-world.

76. Peter Kareiva and Michelle Marvier, "What Is Conservation Science?" *BioScience* 62, no. 11 (2012): 965. See also Reed Noss et al., "Humanity's Domination of Nature Is Part of the Problem: A Response to Kareiva and Marvier," *BioScience* 63, no. 4 (2013): 241–42. In *Rambunctious Garden*, science writer Emma Marris uses a travelogue style to explore conservation sites across the globe, arguing for a new form of conservation in the Anthropocene epoch that explicitly involves humans and human management. Embracing non-native plants, rewilding landscapes with predators, assisted migration, and engineering ecosystems for human goals, Marris uses the lens of ecosystem conservation to question existing definitions of nature. She suggests that significant parts of the modern world are, or will become, "rambunctious gardens"—unruly entanglements of weedy species. Marris concludes that because nature is dynamic, rambunctious gardens are as natural as any other manifestations of nature. Emma Marris, *Rambunctious Garden: Saving Nature in a Post-Wild World* (New York: Bloomsbury, 2011).

77. Kareiva, Marvier, and Lalasz, "Conservation in the Anthropocene."

78. Daniel F. Doak et al., "What Is the Future of Conservation?" *Trends in Ecology and Evolution* 29, no. 2 (2014): 77–81.

79. Michael Soulé (conservation biologist; professor emeritus, environmental

studies, University of California, Santa Cruz), interview by author, telephone, February 6, 2013.

80. Kareiva, Marvier, and Lalasz, "Conservation in the Anthropocene."

81. Doak et al., "What Is the Future of Conservation?" 80.

82. For example, "the Gordon and Betty Moore Foundation, the Long Now Foundation, TNC's Board of Directors, and social justice advocates Ted Nordhaus and Michael Shellenberger of The Breakthrough Institute." Michael Soulé, "The Faith-Based, Trickle-Down Model of Conservation 4.0," *Tompkins Conservation*, April 22, 2013, http://www.tompkinsconservation.org/read/category/biodiversity-conservation.

83. Despite their importance, this book mentions only in passing the political ties between conservation, scientification, and neoliberalism. A growing body of scholarship offers a critique of neoliberal natures. See, e.g., Karen Bakker, "The Limits of 'Neoliberal Natures': Debating Green Neoliberalism," *Progress in Human Geography* 34 (2010): 715-32; Noel Castree, "Neoliberal Ecologies," in *Neoliberal Environments: False Promises and Unnatural Consequences*, ed. Nik Heynen et al. (London: Routledge, 2008), 281–86; Noel Castree, "Neoliberalizing Nature: The Logics of Deregulation and Reregulation," *Environment and Planning A* 40, no. 1 (2008): 131–52; Nik Heynen and Paul Robbins, "The Neoliberalization of Nature: Governance, Privatization, Enclosure, and Valuation," *Capitalism Nature Socialism* 16, no. 1 (2005): 5–8; Neil Smith, *Uneven Development: Nature, Capital, and the Production of Space* (New York: Blackwell, 1984). But whereas much attention has been devoted to neoliberal *nature*, considerably less attention has been devoted to neoliberal *conservation*. Martin O'Connor argued already in 1994 that "environmental crisis has given liberal capitalist society a new lease on life. Now, through purporting to take in hand the saving of the environment, capitalism invents a new legitimation for itself: the *sustainable and rational use of nature*." Martin O'Connor, "On the Misadventure of Capitalist Nature," in *Is Capitalism Sustainable? Political Economy and the Politics of Ecology*, ed. Martin O'Connor (New York: Guilford Press, 1994), 125. In a more recent articulation by Dutch geographer Bram Büscher and colleagues, "Neoliberal conservation's core axiom is that in order for natures to be 'saved,' acts of 'nature saving' must be imbued with profit potential or else there is little incentive for rational actors to pursue it." Conservation, they argue, "becomes the basis for further economic growth." Bram Büscher et al., "Towards a Synthesized Critique of Neoliberal Biodiversity Conservation," *Capitalism Nature Socialism* 2, no. 23 (2012): 13-14. Critics of green neoliberalism offer, furthermore, that it is characterized by acceleration and proliferation of economic activity, enhanced discourses of disaster capitalism, emerging re-regulation processes, a global conservation apparatus with universal standards, and new commodities that perform spectacles of nature. Brockington, Duffy, and Igoe, *Nature Unbound*, 150, 155, 190–93.

84. Suckling, e-mail communication, June 8, 2014.

85. Jason W. Moore, "The Capitalocene: Part I: On the Nature and Origins

of Our Ecological Crisis," May 13, 2013, http://www.jasonwmoore.com/uploads/ The_Capitalocene__Part_I__for _website__30_March__2014_.pdf.

86. Suckling, e-mail communication.

87. Ibid.

88. Suckling, e-mail communication, July 26, 2013.

89. Elizabeth Corry (senior birdkeeper, Durrell Wildlife Conservation Trust), interview by Eleanor Gold (research assistant), on-site, Jersey, UK, July 28, 2013.

90. Ibid.

NORTHERN WHITE AND SUMATRAN RHINOS

1. Kes Smith objects: "What millions and millions of dollars?! For much of the 22 years we were working . . . to conserve Garamba and the rhinos, our field budget was in the region of $200,000 per year for the whole park, not just the rhinos. In 1990, for example, while Natal in South Africa had a budget equivalent to $4,350 per kilometer, Garamba's was $2 per kilometer. Yet with that we achieved a huge amount, with rhinos and elephants doubling their numbers in the first half of the project. *This proved that if they can be protected in their natural habitat, this is by far the best place for them.*" Kes Hillman Smith (conservation biologist), e-mail communication, October 25, 2013 (my emphasis).

2. John Lukas (general director, White Oak Plantation and White Oak Conservation Center; president, International Rhino Foundation), interview by author, telephone, September 17, 2013.

3. Ellis, interview, September 10, 2013. Kes Smith provides her perspective on the differences between the taxa: "They do look different. Northerns look somewhat like a cross between black rhinos and Southern Whites." The difference is especially striking, she explains, "when you see Northerns and Southerns together at Ol Pejeta. However, it's true that in isolation, the layperson would probably not see a difference." Smith, e-mail communication.

4. In fact, George Rabb, a prominent zoo and conservation expert, declined to discuss the northern white rhino with me, asking that we focus instead on the positive stories of integrated *in situ–ex situ* conservation. George Rabb (president emeritus, Chicago Zoological Society; director, Brookfield Zoo, 1976–2003), interview by author, telephone, August 28, 2013. Similarly, Kes Smith commented after reading a draft of this story: "I hope you will now include a few positive and somewhat more optimistic comments as well as negative." Smith, e-mail communication.

5. Lawrence Anthony and Graham Spence, *The Last Rhinos: My Battle to Save One of the World's Greatest Creatures* (New York: St. Martin's Press, 2012), 2.

6. Ibid., 5.

7. John Lukas, interview.

8. Smith, e-mail communication.

9. Ibid.

10. Richard Emslie and Martin Brooks, "African Rhino Status Survey and Con-

servation Action Plan," 1999, https://portals.iucn.org/library/efiles/edocs/1999-049
.pdf, vii.

11. John Lukas, interview.

12. Smith continues: "The zoo directors did actually agree between themselves
for some exchange and consolidation of animals, which led to Najin being mated
and Fatu being born in 2000. Both of them are now part of the group in Ol Pejeta."
Smith, e-mail communication.

13. John Lukas, interview.

14. Ibid.

15. Lacy, interview, in person, Disney, Orlando, FL, October 11, 2013.

16. John Lukas, interview.

17. Ibid.

18. Richard Emslie, "*Ceratotherium simum ssp. cottoni*," *The IUCN Red List of
Threatened Species, Version 2014.2*, http://www.iucnredlist.org/details/4183/0; John
Lukas, interview. Kes Smith tells me that "when the problems first started, several
[rhinos were] moved out into the wooded reserves and one was reported seen in
December 2012." Smith, e-mail communication.

19. Ellis, interview; Emslie, "*Ceratotherium simum ssp. cottoni*."

20. Smith, e-mail communication.

21. Elizabeth Kolbert, "Building the Ark," *National Geographic*, October 2013,
http://ngm.nationalgeographic.com/2013/10/zoos/kolbert-text.

22. Ibid.

23. Ellis, interview.

24. Emslie, "*Ceratotherium simum ssp. cottoni*."

25. Ibid.

26. In 2010, three scientists published a paper reassessing the two subspecies
in light of research over the past three decades. They argued that the northern
and southern subspecies should be reclassified, on the basis of morphology and
genetics, as two distinct species, *Ceratotherium simum* and *Ceratotherium cottoni*,
rather than as two subspecies. They also acknowledged that "the recognition of the
northern form as a distinct species has profound implications for its conservation."
Colin Groves, Prithiviraj Fernando, and Jan Robovsky, "The Sixth Rhino: A Taxonomic Re-Assessment of the Critically Endangered Northern White Rhinoceros,"
PLoS One 5, no. 2 (2010): e9703. The IUCN expressed skepticism about this paper
and made note of a forthcoming rebuttal by a rhino geneticist. This skepticism
was highly pragmatic: "It has also been argued that given conservation objectives
the issue of whether or not Northern White Rhino should be treated as a species
or subspecies is for practical purposes somewhat academic," given that the four
remaining rhinos were very closely related and unlikely to form a viable, long-term
population. The IUCN also states: "Conservation biologists Bob Lacy and Kathy
Traylor-Holzer have advised that given the above situation and overall conservation objective, a stage has been reached where one doesn't really have any choice of
achieving medium to longer term conservation goals without trying inter-crossing

NWR [northern white rhinos] with Southern White Rhino." Emslie, *"Ceratotherium simum ssp. cottoni."*

27. Kolbert, "Building the Ark."

28. Ellis, interview.

29. Ibid.

30. Ibid. Kes Smith says in response: "Conservation and negotiations were not done in the wrong ways, but they were undermined for political power and other non-conservation reasons. Such things are much more difficult to deal with than straightforward conservation and poaching." Smith, e-mail communication.

31. Widodo Ramono (executive director, Yayasan Badak Indonesia (YABI), Rhino Foundation of Indonesia), interview by author, telephone, September 12, 2013.

32. Terri Roth (vice president, Conservation and Science; director, Center for Conservation and Research of Endangered Wildlife, Cincinnati Zoo & Botanical Garden), interview by author, telephone, September 16, 2013; Ramono, interview.

33. Ramono, interview.

34. Roth, interview.

35. Ibid.

36. Ibid.

37. Ramono, interview.

38. Roth, interview.

39. Ramono, interview.

40. Roth, interview.

41. Cincinnati Zoo & Botanical Garden, "Sumatran Rhino," http://cincinnatizoo.org/conservation/crew/rhino-signature-project/sumatran-rhino/.

42. Cincinnati Zoo & Botanical Garden, "Emi, In Loving Memory," 2009, http://cincinnatizoo.org/conservation/crew/rhino-signature-project/sumatran-rhino/.

43. Roth, interview.

44. Ibid.

45. Ibid.

46. Ibid.

47. Karen Dixon (SOS Rhino), interview by author, in person, CBSG Annual Meeting, Disney, Orlando, FL, October 11, 2013.

48. Lacy, interview, in person, October 11, 2013.

CHAPTER 2: CAPTIVE LIFE

1. Dan Ashe (director, USFWS), interview by author, telephone, July 18, 2013. Ashe couldn't have chosen a more controversial definition upon which to rest his case. This statement (actually by Justice Potter Stewart) was expressed in a 1964 decision that yielded four different opinions from the majority—with none garnering the support of more than two justices—as well as two dissenting opinions. In *Jacobellis v. Ohio*, 378 U.S. 184 (1964), Justice Potter Stewart concurred with the majority opinion, creating the legal standard that speech, except "hard-core" pornogra-

phy, should be protected, and he went on to say, "I shall not today attempt to define the kinds of material I understand to be embraced within that shorthand description. . . . But I know it when I see it."

2. Liz Tyson, "Why Arguments for Killing of Giraffe Marius Don't Stand Up to Scrutiny," February 10, 2014, http://www.cnn.com/2014/02/10/opinion/giraffe-culling-against/. Tyson also cited a 2003 study that suggested that "at least 7,500 individual animals in European zoos are 'surplus' at any one time." See Captive Animals' Protection Society, "Sad Eyes and Empty Lives," http://www.captiveanimals.org/wp-content/uploads/2011/02/Sad-Eyes-Empty-Lives.pdf, 1.

3. Tyson, "Why Arguments for Killing of Giraffe Marius Don't Stand Up to Scrutiny."

4. EAZA, "EAZA Antelope and Giraffe TAG," http://www.eaza.net/activities/cp/yearbook20072008/41_Antelope_Giraffe_TAG.pdf, 4.

5. Copenhagen Zoo, "Why Does Copenhagen Zoo Euthanize a Giraffe?" http://zoo.dk/BesogZoo/Nyhedsarkiv/2014/Februar/Why%20Copenhagen%20Zoo%20euthanized%20a%20ogiraffe.aspx.

6. Braverman, *Zooland*, 174–80.

7. In addition to the above, those include: Lars Eriksen, "Marius the Giraffe Killed at Copenhagen Zoo Despite Worldwide Protests," *The Guardian*, February 9, 2014, http://www.theguardian.com/world/2014/feb/09/marius-giraffe-killed-copenhagen-zoo-protests; Cahal Milmo, "The Killing of Marius the Giraffe Opens an Important Debate about Genetics, Animal Rights, and Zoo Inbreeding," *The Independent*, February 10, 2014, http://www.independent.co.uk/news/world/europe/the-killing-of-marius-the-giraffe-opens-an-important-debate-about-genetics-animal-rights-and-zoo-inbreeding-9120219.html; "Why Did Copenhagen Zoo Kill Its Giraffe?" BBC, http://www.bbc.com/news/science-environment-26118748.

8. Braverman, *Zooland*.

9. Ibid.; Eric Baratay and Elisabeth Hardouin-Fugier, *Zoo: A History of Zoological Gardens in the West* (London: Reaktion Books, 2004).

10. Braverman, *Zooland*.

11. David Berry, "Tradescant Collection," Ashmolean Museum of Art and Archaeology, University of Oxford, www.ashmolean.org/ash/amulets/tradescant/tradescanto4.html.

12. Ibid.

13. Ibid.

14. Paula Findlen, *Possessing Nature: Museums, Collecting, and Scientific Culture in Early Modern Italy* (Berkeley: University of California Press, 1994), 4. For a discussion on the changing views of museums in the twentieth and twenty-first centuries, see Gail Anderson, ed., *Reinventing the Museum: Historical and Contemporary Perspectives on the Paradigm Shift* (Lanham, MD: AltaMira Press, 2004).

15. Ibid., 2–3.

16. Ibid., 5.

17. Braverman, *Zooland*, 26–28.

18. Ibid., 111–26.

19. On the importance of registrars in contemporary zoo administration, see ibid.

20. Judith Block (registrar emeritus, Smithsonian Institution, National Zoological Park), interview by author, telephone, September 4, 2009, quoted in Braverman, *Zooland*, 125.

21. Conway, interview.

22. Some argue that human domination is still central to the operations of the modern zoo. See, for example, Kay Anderson, "Culture and Nature at the Adelaide Zoo: At the Frontiers of Human Geography," *Transactions of the Institute of British Geographers* 20 (1995): 275–94.

23. Braverman, *Zooland*, 73–75.

24. Laura Penn, Markus Gusset, and Gerald Dick, *77 Years: The History and Evolution of the World Association of Zoos and Aquariums 1935–2012* (WAZA, 2012).

25. Braverman, *Zooland*.

26. Ibid., 33–38.

27. Irus Braverman, "Zootopia: Utopia and Dystopia in the Zoological Garden," in *Earth Perfect? Nature, Utopia, and the Garden*, ed. Annette Giesecke and Naomi Jacobs (London: Black Dog Publishing, 2012), 242–57.

28. Braverman, *Zooland*, 30–49.

29. Ibid., 28–30. Contemporary zoo design attempts to create an oasis of "wild nature" in the midst of the urban landscape, recasting the line between city and wild.

30. Ibid., 159–85.

31. Andrew Balmford, Georgina M. Mace, and Joshua R. Ginsberg, *Conservation in a Changing World* (Cambridge: Cambridge University Press, 1998).

32. WAZA, "WAZA Code of Ethics and Animal Welfare," adopted at the 58th Annual Conference of the World Association of Zoos and Aquariums, San José, CR, 19 November 2003, http://www.waza.org/files/webcontent/1.public_site/5 .conservation/code_of_ethics_and_animal_welfare/Code%20of%20Ethics_EN.pdf.

33. Chris West and Lesley A. Dickie, "Introduction: Is There a Conservation Role for Zoos in a Natural World under Fire?" in *Zoos in the 21st Century: Catalysts for Conservation?*, ed. Alexandra Zimmermann et al. (Cambridge: Cambridge University Press, 2007), 5. See also Bengt Holst and Lesley A. Dickie, "How Do National and International Regulations and Policies Influence the Role of Zoos and Aquariums in Conservation?" in *Zoos in the 21st Century: Catalysts for Conservation?*, ed. Zimmermann et al. (Cambridge: Cambridge University Press, 2007), 22–36.

34. Andrew Moss, Eric Jensen, and Markus Gusset, "Zoo Visits Boost Biodiversity Literacy," *Nature* 508 (2014): 186.

35. EAZA, "About EAZA," http://www.eaza.net/about/Pages/Introduction.aspx.

36. Moss, Jensen, and Gusset, "Zoo Visits."

37. AZA, "Association of Zoos and Aquariums 5-Year Strategic Plan," adopted at the 2010 AZA Annual Conference, Houston TX, September 12–16, 2010, https:// www.aza.org/StrategicPlan/.

38. EAZA, "About EAZA."

39. JAZA, "Chairman's Address," http://www.jaza.jp/english.html.

40. ALPZA, "Mission," http://www.alpza.com/eng/mision.php.

41. African Association of Zoos and Aquariums (PAAZAB), "Our Values," http://www.zoosafrica.com/about/our-values.html; Zoo and Aquarium Association (ZAA), "Who We Are," http://www.zooaquarium.org.au/index.php/who-we-are/.

42. Lesley A. Dickie, Jeffrey P. Bonner, and Chris West, "In Situ and Ex Situ Conservation: Blurring the Boundaries Between Zoos and the Wild," in *Zoos in the 21st Century: Catalysts for Conservation?*, ed. Zimmermann et al. (Cambridge: Cambridge University Press, 2007), 220–35.

43. Moss, Jensen, and Gussett, "Zoo Visits," 186.

44. Ibid.

45. Michael Soulé et al., "The Millennium Ark: How Long a Voyage, How Many Staterooms, How Many Passengers?" *Zoo Biology* 5, no. 2 (1986): 101–13.

46. As of 1995, more than three thousand vertebrate species were being bred in zoos and other captive breeding facilities, some for reintroductions. Dickie, Bonner, and West, "In Situ and Ex Situ Conservation," 224.

47. Fred Koontz, "Wild Animal Acquisition Ethics for Zoo Biologists," in *Ethics on the Ark: Zoos, Animal Welfare, and Wildlife Conservation*, ed. Bryan G. Norton et al. (Washington, DC: Smithsonian Institution Press, 1995), 132. See also Braverman, *Zooland*, 159–85. However, I was unable to obtain more recent and comprehensive statistics on zoo animal reintroductions. In 2011, zoos held 424 vertebrate species as part of reintroduction programs. Also in 2011, 15 percent of threatened terrestrial vertebrate species (one in seven) were held in zoos. Dalia A. Conde et al., "An Emerging Role of Zoos to Conserve Biodiversity," *Science* 331, no. 6023 (2011): 1390. See also Philip J. Seddon, Pritpal S. Soorae, and Frédéric Launay, "Taxonomic Bias in Reintroduction Projects," *Animal Conservation* 8 (2005): 53.

48. Ballou, Gilpin, and Foose, *Population Management for Survival and Recovery*.

49. Lacy, interview, telephone, July 31, 2012.

50. Gerald Durrell, *Beasts in My Belfry* (West Sussex County, UK: Summersdale Press, 1973), 203.

51. Schwitzer, interview, April 5, 2013.

52. Pearce-Kelly, interview.

53. Joshua Ginsberg (senior vice president, WCS), interview by author, telephone, September 28, 2012.

54. Ibid.

55. Lacy, interview.

56. IUCN/SSC, "About the Species Survival Commission," http://www.iucn.org/about/work/programmes/species/who_we_are/about_the_species_survival_commission_/.

57. Simon Stuart (chair, SSC, IUCN), interview by author, telephone, July 13, 2013.

58. Braverman, *Zooland*, 162.

59. Debborah Luke (senior vice president, Conservation & Science, AZA), e-mail communication, January 1, 2015.

60. Gerald Dick (executive director, WAZA), interview by author, telephone, July 16, 2013.

61. "Minnesota Zoo: Home of the Tiger SSP," http://www.mnzoo.com/conservation/conservation_atZootigerSSP.asp.

62. ISIS, "About ISIS," http://www2.isis.org/AboutISIS/Pages/About-ISIS.aspx.

63. Fa et al., "The Need to Balance *Ex Situ* and *In Situ* Conservation," 15.

64. Thomas J. Foose, "Riders of the Last Ark: The Role of Captive Breeding in Conservation Strategies," in *The Last Extinction*, ed. Lee Kaufman and Kenneth Mallory (Cambridge: MIT Press, 1986), 149–78.

65. Richard R. Reading and Brian J. Miller, "Captive Breeding Ethics," in *Encyclopedia of Animal Rights and Animal Welfare*, ed. Marc Bekoff, 2nd ed. (Santa Barbara: Greenwood, 2010), 101–5.

66. Kent Redford et al., "What Does It Mean to Successfully Conserve a (Vertebrate) Species?" *BioScience* 61, no. 1 (2010): 39. See also Dickie, Bonner, and West, "In Situ and Ex Situ Conservation," 224; Soulé et al., "The Millennium Ark."

67. Michael Hutchins, Brandie Smith, and Ruth Allard, "In Defense of Zoos and Aquariums: The Ethical Basis for Keeping Wild Animals in Captivity," in "Animal Welfare Forum: The Welfare of Zoo Animals," special issue, *Journal of the American Veterinary Medical Association* 223, no. 7 (2003): 960. See also Noel F. R. Snyder et al., "Limitations of Captive Breeding in Endangered Species Recovery," *Conservation Biology* 10, no. 2 (1996): 338–48.

68. Soulé et al., "The Millennium Ark."

69. Paul Boyle (senior vice president, Conservation and Education, AZA), interview by author, telephone, November 24, 2010, quoted in Braverman, *Zooland*, 174.

70. Braverman, *Zooland*, 180–81.

71. Ibid., 183.

72. Robert Lacy, "Achieving True Sustainability of Zoo Populations," *Zoo Biology* 32, no. 1 (2013): 20.

73. See Chapter 5 of this book for a discussion of the role of recovery plans in conservation by the USFWS under the ESA.

74. Trevor Sandwith (director, Global Protected Areas Programme, IUCN), interview by author, telephone, May 22, 2013.

75. Kevin Zippel (program director, Amphibian Ark), interview by author, telephone, August 3, 2012.

76. The Amphibian Ark, http://www.amphibianark.org/ (emphasis removed).

77. Zippel, interview.

78. The Amphibian Ark was formed to address the captive (*ex situ*) components of the Amphibian Conservation Action Plan. IUCN/SSC Amphibian Action Conservation Plan, Amphibian Summit 2005, http://www.amphibianark.org/pdf/ACAP.pdf.

79. Peter Dollinger (former director, WAZA; director, Alpine Zoo Secretariat, Zoo Office Berne), interview by author, telephone, January 9, 2013.

80. Heini Hediger, *Wild Animals in Captivity* (New York: Dover Publications, 1964), paraphrased in Chrulew, "Managing Love and Death at the Zoo."

81. Dick, interview.

82. Monika Fiby (zoo designer and director, Zoolex), interviews by author, telephone, September 24, 2012, and November 20, 2012; see also Marc Bekoff, *Ignoring Nature No More: The Case for Compassionate Conservation* (Chicago: University of Chicago Press, 2013).

83. Morten Tønnessen, "Is a Wolf Wild as Long as It Does Not *Know* That It Is Being Thoroughly Managed?" *Humanimalia* 2, no. 1 (2010): 1.

84. Redford, Jensen, and Breheny, "Integrating the Captive and the Wild," 1157.

85. See also Irus Braverman, "Captive for Life: Conserving Extinct Species through *Ex Situ* Breeding," in *The Ethics of Captivity*, ed. Lori Gruen (Oxford: Oxford University Press, 2014), 193–212.

86. IUCN, "Red List Overview," *The IUCN Red List of Threatened Species, Version 2012.2*, http://www.iucnredlist.org/about/red-list-overview.

87. IUCN Standards and Petitions Subcommittee, "Guidelines for Using the IUCN Red List Categories and Criteria," Version 11 (February 2014), http://jr.iucnredlist.org/documents/RedListGuidelines.pdf.

88. Ibid. One example of this is the "threat calculator," initially developed by the IUCN and then adapted by NatureServe, as well as by other agencies such as the Committee on the Status of Endangered Wildlife in Canada (COSEWIC). See, e.g., http://www.natureserve.org/conservation-tools/data-maps-tools/conservation-rank-calculator.

89. IUCN Standards and Petitions Subcommittee, "Guidelines for Using the IUCN Red List Categories and Criteria," 11.

90. Schwitzer, interview.

91. IUCN, *The IUCN Red List of Threatened Species, Version 2013.2*, search under "Animalia" and "Extinct in the Wild," http://www.iucnredlist.org/search.

92. Pearce-Kelly, interview.

93. Jiang Zhigang and R.B., "*Elapharus davidianus*," *The IUCN Red List of Threatened Species, Version 2012.2*, www.iucnredlist.org.

94. Zippel, interview.

95. Robert Loftin, "Captive Breeding of Endangered Species," in *Ethics on the Ark: Zoos, Animal Welfare, and Wildlife Conservation*, ed. Bryan Norton et al. (Washington, DC: Smithsonian Institution Press, 1995), 164–80.

96. Dickie, Bonner, and West, "In Situ and Ex Situ Conservation," 224.

97. Zippel, interview.

98. Conway, interview.

99. Rich Stallcup, "Farewell Skymaster," quoted in Burr Heneman, "The Condor Recovery Debate, 30 Years Later," *Golden Gate Birder*, http://www.goldengate audubon.org/blog-posts/the-condor-recovery-debate-30–years-later/).

100. Tom Regan, *The Case for Animal Rights* (Berkeley: University of California Press, 1983), 363.

101. Ibid., 359.

102. Ibid., 362.

103. Loftin, "Captive Breeding of Endangered Species," 169.

104. Ibid., 178 (citing from David Brower).

105. *National Audubon Society v. Fish & Wildlife Service*, 801 F.2d 405 (1986), at 408. See also John Nielson, *Condor: To the Brink and Back: The Life and Times of One Giant Bird* (New York: HarperCollins, 2006).

106. Conway, interview. The information in Figure 7's caption is from Jane Braxton Little, "The Plight of the Condors," *Scientific American*, 5 January 2011, http://www.scientificamerican.com/article/plight-of-the-condors/.

107. Ashe, interview.

108. Ibid.

109. Ibid.

110. Suckling, interview, July 15, 2013.

111. Ibid.

112. USFWS, Whooping Crane Recovery Plan, 1994, https://www.fws.gov/south-west/es/arizona/Documents/RecoveryPlans/WhoopingCrane.pdf.

113. USGS, "Whooping Crane: Return from the Brink of Extinction," February 2012, https://www.pwrc.usgs.gov/whoopers/publications/CraneInfoSheet_4pp.pdf; International Crane Foundation, "Whooping Crane Conservation," https://www.savingcranes.org/whooping-crane-conservation.html.

114. USFWS, "Whooping Crane (*Grus americana*)," May 1, 2013, http://www.fws.gov/northflorida/WhoopingCrane/whoopingcrane-fact-2001.htm.

115. Whooping Crane Eastern Partnership, "Project Update, August 18 to September 30, 2014," http://www.bringbackthecranes.org/technicaldatabase/projectupdates/2014/18AugTo30Sept2014.html.

116. Hutchins, Smith, and Allard, "In Defense of Zoos and Aquariums," 964.

117. Bryan Norton, "Caring for Nature: A Broader Look at Animal Stewardship," in *Ethics on the Ark: Zoos, Animal Welfare, and Wildlife Conservation*, ed. Bryan Norton et al. (Washington, DC: Smithsonian Institution Press, 1995), 375–95.

118. Ibid.

119. But see Josephine Donoway, "Animal Rights and Feminist Theory," in *Beyond Animal Rights: A Feminist Caring Ethic for the Treatment of Animals*, ed. Josephine Donoway and Carol Adams (New York: Continuum, 1996), 34–59. Donoway reconstructs animal ethics not through an animal rights lens but through care.

120. Liz Tyson (director, Captive Animals' Protection Society), interview by author, telephone, April 29, 2013.

121. University of Technology Sydney, "Compassionate Conservation," http://www.uts.edu.au/about/faculty-science/what-we-do/uts-science-focus/environment/compassionate-conservation. See also Bekoff, *Ignoring Nature No More*.

122. Compassionate Conservation, "Compassionate Conservation Guiding Principles," http://compassionateconservation.net/about/principles/.

123. Quoted in Michael Charles Tobias, "Compassionate Conservation: A Dis-

cussion from the Frontlines with Dr. Marc Bekoff," *Forbes*, May 9, 2013, http://www
.forbes.com/sites/michaeltobias/2013/05/09/compassionate-conservation-a-discus
sion-from-the-frontlines-with-dr-marc-bekoff/2/.

124. Draper, interview.

125. Ibid.

126. Koen Margodt, "Zoos as Welfare Arks? Reflections on an Ethical Course
for Zoos," in *Metamorphoses of the Zoo: Animal Encounter after Noah*, ed. Ralph R.
Acampora (Plymouth, MA: Lexington Books, 2010), 30.

127. Stuart Pimm (conservation biologist), interview by author, in person, Sudbury, Canada, November 15 and 16, 2013.

128. Loftin, "Captive Breeding of Endangered Species," 177.

129. Schwitzer, interview.

130. Loftin, "Captive Breeding of Endangered Species," 165.

131. Ibid.

132. Ashe, interview.

133. Butler, *Precarious Life*, 26.

134. Ashe, interview.

135. Ibid.

136. Arroyo, interview.

137. Oetker, interview.

138. Ibid.

139. Ballou, Gilpin, and Foose, *Population Management for Survival and Recovery*,
283.

140. "Progressive Zoo Houses Animals in Natural Destroyed Habitat," *The
Onion*, April 11, 2014, http://www.theonion.com/articles/progressive-zoo-houses
-animals-in-natural-destroye,35760/.

141. Ibid.

142. Anonymous zoo designer, personal e-mail communication, April 16, 2014.

143. According to Baudrillard: "Today abstraction is no longer that of the map,
the double, the mirror, or the concept. Simulation is no longer that of a territory, a
referential being, or a substance. It is the generation by models of a real without origin or reality: a hyperreal." Jean Baudrillard, *Simulacra and Simulation* (Ann Arbor:
University of Michigan Press, 1997), 1.

144. Geographers Rob Bartram and Sarah Shobrook suggest that while the zoo
is increasingly presenting itself as a representation—a simulacrum even—of nature,
nature is increasingly becoming a simulacrum of the zoo. Rob Bartram and Sarah
Shobrook, "Endless/End-Less Natures: Environmental Futures at the Fin de Millennium," *Annals of the Association of American Geographers* 90, no. 2 (2004): 370–80.
Similarly, Carrie Friese draws on Gregg Mitman's argument, that the immersion
exhibit in zoos has enabled conservationists to see wildlife in new ways, to point out
that the zoo can be perceived as a particular kind of nature, and that in fact nature is
being remade in the image of the zoo. In Friese's words: "While the 'unnaturalness'
of the zoo has in a sense always been one of its defining features, this is now increas-

ingly understood as continuous with . . . the 'unnatural histories' of most habitats and ecological niches that make up the planet." Friese, *Cloning Wild Life*, 180. See also Gregg Mitman, *The State of Nature: Ecology, Community, and American Social Thought, 1900–1950* (Chicago: University of Chicago Press, 1992).

GOLDEN LION TAMARIN

1. Pimm, interview.

2. Adrian Barnett, "*Lion Tamarins: Biology and Conservation* by Devra Kleiman and Anthony Rylands," *New Scientist*, December 14, 2002, 54, http://www.newsci entist.com/article/mg17623736.000-lion-tamarins-biology-and-conservation-by -devra-kleiman-and-anthony-rylands.html.

3. Adelmar F. Coimbra-Filho and Russel A. Mittermeier, "Distribution and Ecology of the Genus *Leontopithecus* Lesson, 1840 in Brazil," *Primates* 14 (1973): 53.

4. Barnett, "*Lion Tamarins*," 54.

5. Mickelberg, interview.

6. Jon Ballou, Devra Kleiman, J. J. C. Mallinson, et al., "History of the Golden Lion Tamarin Captive Breeding Program," National Zoo, http://nationalzoo.si.edu/ scbi/EndangeredSpecies/GLTProgram/ZooLife/History.cfm.

7. Bengt Holst (director of research and conservation, Copenhagen Zoo), interview by author, in person, Disney, Orlando, FL, October 11, 2013. See also Braverman, *Zooland*, 137–39.

8. Associação Mico-Leão-Dourado (AMLD), "Introduction to Conservation of Golden Lion Tamarins," 2013, http://www.micoleao.org.br/. There are a few major threats to achieving viable populations of tamarins. The most significant ones are forest fragmentation due to logging (for timber and charcoal burning) and agriculture and urban expansion (especially of Rio de Janeiro, located only approximately 100 kilometers from the species range). In addition, the golden lion tamarins are threatened by increased predation, contamination from offshore petroleum drilling, and potential inbreeding. See AMLD, "Introduction," http://www.micoleao .org. br/; James Dietz (founding director, Save the Golden Lion Tamarin), e-mail communication, April 17, 2014.

9. Mickelberg, interview.

10. Mickelberg, e-mail communication, October 21, 2013.

11. AMLD, "Protected areas," http://www.micoleao.org.br/template.php?pagina =/ing/como_trabalhamos/manejando/unidades_conservacao.php&link=29.

12. Ibid.

13. Dietz, e-mail communication; see also Save the Golden Lion Tamarin, "Save the Golden Lion Tamarin—About Us," http://www.savetheliontamarin.org/who -we-are/; Save the Golden Lion Tamarin, "Our Partner: AMLD in the Field," http:// www.savetheliontamarin.org/our-partner-amld/.

14. Benjamin Beck, *Thirteen Gold Monkeys* (Parker, CO: Outskirts Press, 2013).

15. Tara Stoinski et al., "A Behavioral Comparison of Captive-Born, Reintro-

duced Golden Lion Tamarins and Their Wild-Born Offspring," *Behavior* 140, no. 2 (February 2003): 137–60.

16. Benjamin Beck et al., "Losses and Reproduction in Reintroduced Golden Lion Tamarins *Leontopithecus rosalia*," *The Dodo: Journal of the Jersey Wildlife Preservation Trust* 27 (1991): 50–61.

17. Mickelberg, interview.

18. Beck et al., "Losses and Reproduction," 60; see also Stoinski et al., "A Behavioral Comparison," 156.

19. Mickelberg, interview.

20. Ibid. See also Maria Cecilia M. Kierulff et al., "Reintroduction and Translocation as Conservation Tools for Golden Lion Tamarins," in *Lion Tamarins: Biology and Conservation*, ed. Devra Kleiman and Anthony Rylands (Washington, DC: Smithsonian Institution Scholarly Press, 2002), 277–82.

21. Dietz, e-mail communication.

22. Beck, *Thirteen Gold Monkeys*, cover matter.

23. Maria Cecilia M. Kierulff et al., "Meso and South America: Re Introduction and Translocation as Conservation Tools for Golden Lion Tamarins in Brazil," *Reintroduction News* no. 21 (2002): 8, http://www.iucnsscrsg.org/STORAGE/RSG%20 CD/14th/PDFs/RNews21.pdf. See also Kierulff et al., "Reintroduction and Translocation," 271.

24. Kierulff et al., "Reintroduction and Translocation," 271.

25. Ibid., 277.

26. It took three years for the number of tamarins in the translocated populations to exceed the number initially reintroduced, compared to the twelve years it took the reintroduced populations to achieve the same. Ibid., 273.

27. Mickelberg, interview.

28. Beck, *Thirteen Gold Monkeys*.

29. Mickelberg, interview.

30. Ulysses S. Seal, Jonathan D. Ballou, and C. V. Padua, eds., "Leontopithecus: Population Viability Analysis Workshop Report," CBSG/Species Survival Commission/IUCN, 1990, http://www.cbsg.org/sites/cbsg.org/files/documents/Lion%20 Tamarin%20PVA%201990%20reduced.pdf; Escola de Administracão Fazendária (ESAF), "Lion Tamarin PHVA Workshop Final Report," CBSG, 2006, http://www .cbsg.org/sites/cbsg.org/files/documents/Lion%20Tamarin%20PHVA%203.pdf; Save the Golden Lion Tamarin/AMLD, "You Can Help Save Golden Lion Tamarins from Extinction," 2014, http://www.micoleao.org.br/template.php?pagina=/ing/as sociacao/historico.php.

31. Jonathan (Jon) Ballou (research scientist, Smithsonian Institution; former studbook keeper, Golden Lion Tamarin), interview by author, telephone, June 6, 2013.

32. Ibid.

33. AMLD, "Highlights of Our Results from 2013," http://www.savetheliontama rin.org/storage/progress-reports/AMLD%20Annual%20Report%202013%20sum mary2.pdf.

34. For an extensive discussion of the One Plan approach, see Chapter 6.

35. Ballou, interview.

36. Ibid.

37. Mickelberg, interview.

38. Ibid.

39. Maria Cecilia M. Kierulff, Anthony Rylands, and Paula Procopio de Oliveira, "*Leontopithecus rosalia*," *The IUCN Red List of Threatened Species, Version 2013.1*, http://www.iucnredlist.org/details/11506/0.

40. "AMLD, "Highlights of Our Results from 2013," 2. Another AMLD document estimated the number as over 1,700. See AMLD, "Introduction to Conservation of Golden Lion Tamarins," http://www.micoleao.org.br/. And the IUCN estimates from 2008 are for "over 1,000." Kierulff, Rylands, and de Oliveira, "*Leontopithecus rosalia*."

41. Kierulff et al., "Reintroduction and Translocation," 274; Save the Golden Lion Tamarin, "Save the Golden Lion Tamarin," http://www.savetheliontamarin.org/.

42. Mickelberg, interview.

43. Dietz, e-mail communication.

44. Holst, interview.

45. Ibid.

46. Kierulff, Rylands, and Oliveira, "*Leontopithecus rosalia*"; Save the Golden Lion Tamarin/AMLD, "You Can Help Save Golden Lion Tamarins from Extinction."

47. Mickelberg, interview.

48. Jane Goodall, Gail Hudson, and Thane Maynard, *Hope for Animals and Their World: How Endangered Species Are Being Rescued from the Brink* (New York: Grand Central Publishing, 2009), 70.

49. "Save the Golden Lion Tamarin: Our Partner: AMLD in the Field," http://www.savetheliontamarin.org/our-partner-amld/.

50. Holst, interview.

CHAPTER 3: CONTINUOUS LIFE

1. Suckling, e-mail communication, July 26, 2013.

2. The term *inter situ* was coined by David and Lida Burney in "Inter Situ Conservation: Opening a 'Third Front' in the Battle to Save Rare Hawaiian Plants." They suggest that the *inter situ* model emerged "to conserve rare species by reintroducing them to sites where they once grew, but have been eliminated in recent decades or centuries by human agencies." My use of the term is broader and denotes hybrid configurations along or beyond the *in situ–ex situ* divide.

3. Some of the myriad *inter situ* nodes that I will *not* explore here are: sanctuaries, hunting reserves, military zones, restoration sites, land trusts, agricultural areas, rewilding zones, and (sub)urban spaces. It is not that these nodes are not important, but my argument can be made without exhausting the examples, which are inevitably inexhaustible.

4. Redford, Jensen, and Breheny, "The Long Overdue Death."

5. Ibid., 19.

6. Lee Ehmke (director and CEO, Minnesota Zoo; president, WAZA), interview by author, telephone, July 12, 2012.

7. Suckling, interview.

8. Stoinski, interview.

9. Soulé, interview.

10. Blumer, interview.

11. Ibid.

12. IUCN/SSC CBSG, "Intensively Managed Populations for Conservation (IMP) Workshop: Final Workshop Report," San Diego, CA, December 6–9, 2010, http://www.cbsg.org/sites/cbsg.org/files/documents/IMP%20Workshop%20Final%20Report.pdf.

13. David Wildt (senior scientist and head, C2S2, Smithsonian Conservation Biology Institute, National Zoological Park), interview by author, telephone, May 3, 2013.

14. CBSG Pronghorn Antelope Workshop, participatory observation, Tucson, AZ, April 21–23, 2013.

15. Conway, interview.

16. Kathy Traylor-Holzer, "Identifying Gaps and Opportunities for Interregional *Ex-situ* Conservation." *WAZA Magazine* 12 (2011): 30, 31. See also Traylor-Holzer, interview.

17. Traylor-Holzer, interview.

18. See Pierre Comizzoli and Nucharin Songasen, "A Historical Overview of Embryo and Oocyte Preservation in the World of Mammalian in Vitro Fertilization and Biotechnology," in *Preservation of Human Oocytes: From Cryobiology Science to Clinical Application*, ed. Andrea Borini and Giovanni Coticchio (London: Informa Healthcare, 2009), 1–11; Comizzoli, interview.

19. Comizzoli, e-mail communication, August 15, 2013.

20. National Zoo, *Genome Resource Banking for Global Conservation*, http://nationalzoo.si.edu/SCBI/ReproductiveScience/GenomeResTech/default.cfm; for details about this program, see the Black-footed Ferret section, next in this volume.

21. Ibid.

22. Ibid.

23. Friese, *Cloning Wild Life*, 176.

24. Comizzoli, interview and e-mail communication. Friese quotes an interviewee who suggests, similarly, that "conservation biologists are not lab-based. . . . I think it scares them." Friese, *Cloning Wild Life*, 169.

25. Comizzoli, interview.

26. William Conway, "Keynote Address: Why Are Zoos Doing *In Situ* Conservation? Adapting to a New Reality," in *Proceedings of the 68th WAZA Annual Conference*, ed. Gerald Dick (Orlando, FL: WAZA, 2013), 5–7.

27. C2S2, "Conservation Centers for Species Survival," http://www.conservationcenters.org/what-is-c2s2/.

28. Paul Marinari (senior curator, C2S2, Smithsonian Conservation Biology Institute, National Zoological Park), interview by author, on-site, Front Royal, VA, June 11, 2013.

29. Blumer, interview. On the legal status of AZA's recommendations, see Braverman, *Zooland*, 127–58.

30. C2S2, "Conservation Centers for Species Survival"; Boyle, interview.

31. A holding area is the non-exhibit space removed from public view where, typically, the more intensive management of zoo animals occurs. Braverman, *Zooland*, 72.

32. Marinari, interview.

33. Extractive reserves present another, albeit mostly theoretical, management model along the *in situ–ex situ* continuum. Envisioned by William Conway in the late 1990s, extractive reserves are large nature reserves situated in the species' "natural range" that receive financial and other support from zoos and that are managed for animal reproduction. Animals are moved between the reserve and the zoo to improve the genetic diversity of both populations. Dickie, Bonner, and West, "In Situ and Ex Situ Conservation," 228. In theory, zoos would benefit from these reserves through monitored animal harvesting for zoo displays. While used successfully in aquariums, this model has not gained much popularity in zoos. William Conway, "The Changing Role of Zoos in the 21st Century" (paper presented at the Annual Conference of the World Zoo Organization, Pretoria, South Africa, October 18, 1999).

34. Justina Ray (executive director and scientist, WCS Canada; co-chair of Terrestrial Mammals Subcommittee, COSEWIC), interview by author, on-site, COSEWIC meeting, Halifax, Canada, April 28, 2014.

35. Marty Leonard (chair, COSEWIC; professor of biology, Dalhousie University), e-mail communication, May 30, 2014.

36. COSEWIC, "COSEWIC Guidelines on Manipulated Populations," April 2010, http://www.cosewic.gc.ca/eng/sct2/sct2_8_e.cfm.

37. Ibid.

38. For a discussion of similar distinctions in the U.S. context, see Chapter 5.

39. The concept "wild by nature" is central to the Canadian Species at Risk Act (2002) and is of interest here because of its crucial role in determining which form of life will and which will not be protected. Section 2 of the Act defines wildlife species as "a species, subspecies, variety or geographically or genetically distinct population of animal, plant or other organism, other than a bacterium or virus, that is wild by nature and (*a*) is native to Canada; or (*b*) has extended its range into Canada without human intervention and has been present in Canada for at least 50 years." Species at Risk Act, S.C. 2002, c. 29. Assented to 2002-12-12.

40. Leonard, e-mail communication.

41. Ibid.

42. Eric Taylor (professor of zoology, University of British Columbia; member, COSEWIC), interview by author, on-site, Halifax, Canada, April 28, 2014.

43. COSEWIC, participatory observation, Halifax, April 27–May 2, 2014.

44. Ray, interview.

45. Ibid.

46. COSEWIC, "COSEWIC Assessment and Status Report on the Plains Bison *Bison bison bison* and the Wood Bison *Bison bison athabascae* in Canada" (Ottawa: Committee on the Status of Endangered Wildlife in Canada, 2013), http://www.registre lep-sararegistry.gc.ca/virtual_sara/files/cosewic/sr_Plains%20Bison%20and%20 Wood%20Bison_2013_e.pdf.

47. Anonymous COSEWIC member, interview by author, in person, Halifax, Canada, April 27, 2014. But according to Justina Ray, "it's usually clear-cut. . . . They're generally separated from one another. [M]ost ranchers don't want them mixing because there's disease concerns and they don't tend to be right up against each other, so you can distinguish that by geography better than you can genetically. You can't distinguish them genetically." Ray, interview.

48. Leonard, e-mail communication.

49. COSEWIC, "COSEWIC Assessment."

50. Dollinger, interview.

51. Ibid.

52. WWF, "WWF Position Statement," 13th Meeting of the Conference of the Parties to CITES, Bangkok, Thailand, October 2–14, 2004, assets.panda.org/down loads/ecop13insituexsitupositionpaper.pdf.

53. Ibid.

54. Gary Frazer (assistant director for endangered species, USFWS), interview by author, telephone, July 26, 2013.

55. Oetker, interview.

56. Ibid.

57. Jeff Powell (project leader, Mora National Fish Hatchery, USFWS), interview by author, telephone, July 22, 2013.

58. Frazer, interview.

59. Powell, interview and e-mail communication, May 9, 2014.

60. Powell, interview.

61. Ibid.

62. Ibid.

63. Ibid.

64. Powell, e-mail communication.

65. Ibid.

66. "Pallid Sturgeon—*Scaphirhynchus albus*," Montana Fish, Wildlife & Parks, http://fwp.mt.gov/fishAndWildlife/species/endangered/pallidSturgeon/default .html.

67. Ibid.

68. Center for Biological Diversity, "Study: 90 Percent of Endangered Species Recovering on Time," http://www.biologicaldiversity.org/news/press_releases/2012/ esa-success-california-05-17-2012.html.

69. The California Department of Fish and Wildlife's recommendations for future projects for the tui chub include: "placement of additional 24-hour water meters [at] the Lark Seep System; continuation of tamarisk removal; a complete dissolved oxygen study of the North Channel habitat; a complete topographical study of channel depths; and implementation of a bullfrog eradication program." California Department of Fish and Wildlife, Mohave Tui Chub (*Siphateles bicolor mohavensis*), http://www.dfg .ca.gov/regions/6/Conservation/Desert_Fish/Mohave_Tui_Chub.html.

70. Suckling, interview, July 12, 2013.

71. IUCN, "Hope for a Protected Planet with Protected Areas," http://www.iucn.org/about/work/programmes/gpap_home/pas_gpap.

72. Sandwith, interview.

73. Ibid. For the study of management effectiveness see Fiona Leverington et al., "A Global Analysis of Protected Area Management Effectiveness," *Environmental Magazine* 46, no. 5 (2010): 685–698. http://cmsdata.iucn.org/downloads/globalanalysismgmteffectiveness.pdf.

74. Ibid.

75. Ibid.

76. Ibid.

77. The Green List is currently being applied also to the assessment of species management. Elizabeth Bennett (vice president for species conservation, WCS), interview by author, in person, New York City, NY, December 20, 2013.

78. See, respectively, Barney Long (director, Species Protection and Asian Species Conservation, WWF), interview by author, telephone, January 9, 2014; Bennett, interview.

79. USFWS, "Short History of the Refuge System," http://www.fws.gov/refuges/history/over/over_hist-a_fs.html.

80. Ibid.

81. Defenders of Wildlife, "Sonoran Pronghorn, Fact Sheet," http://www.defenders.org/sonoran-pronghorn/basic-facts. See Chapter 6 for a detailed analysis of the population management aspect of this program.

82. James Atkinson (Sonoran pronghorn recovery coordinator, USFWS), interview by author, in person, Tucson, AZ, April 25, 2013.

83. CBSG Pronghorn Antelope Workshop, participatory observation.

84. Dollinger, interview.

85. Ballou, Gilpin, and Foose, *Population Management for Survival and Recovery*, xv.

86. Cited in Ballou, Gilpin, and Foose, *Population Management for Survival and Recovery*, xvi.

87. Andrew Norton, "Experiencing Nature: The Reproduction of Environmental Discourse through Safari Tourism in East Africa," *Geoforum* 27, no. 3 (1996): 369.

88. Stoinski, interview.

89. Ibid.

90. Kristen Lukas (curator of conservation and science, Cleveland Metroparks Zoo), interview by author, telephone, January 7, 2013; Stoinski, interview.

91. Kristen Lukas, interview.

92. Braverman, *Zooland*, 180–84. Also see discussion in Chapter 2.

93. Kristen Lukas, interview.

94. One such instance was described by Damian Aspinall, chairman of the Aspinall Foundation, which released fifty-one western lowland gorillas, mostly born in captivity, from the United Kingdom into Gabon. In 2013, ten gorillas were released into Gabon, only one of them wild-born and the rest born in captivity. "This was a historic moment in conservation," Aspinall was quoted saying. From the foundation's blog: "Djala has been coming to the feeding part of the island doing the Silverback Strut although the group are proving to be remarkably independent and prefer the wild plants to the goodies we brought from Kent! The gorillas have tried some native fruit called Gambeya Lacoutiana (Latin) and have even been climbing the trees like wild born gorillas." Aspinall Foundation, http://www.aspinallfoundation. org/backtothewild/blog/update-gorilla-island-damian-aspinalls-blog.

95. Craig Packer et al., "Conserving Large Carnivores: Dollars and Fence," *Ecology Letters* 16, no. 5 (2013): 635–41. See also Glen Martin, *Game Changers: Animal Rights and the Fate of Africa's Wildlife* (Berkeley: University of California Press, 2012).

96. "Carrying capacity: the average population density or population size of a species below which its numbers tend to increase and above which its numbers tend to decrease because of shortages of resources. The carrying capacity is different for each species in a habitat because of that species' particular food, shelter, and social requirements." *Encyclopaedia Britannica*, "Carrying Capacity," http://www.britannica .com.gate.lib.buffalo.edu/EBchecked/topic/97118/carrying-capacity.

97. Hamish Curric (director, Back to Africa), interview by author, telephone, January 10, 2013.

98. Ibid.

99. James Cuno, *Who Owns Antiquity: Museums and the Battle over Our Ancient Heritage* (Princeton: Princeton University Press, 2008); James A. R. Nafziger and Ann M. Nicgorski, *Cultural Heritage Issues: The Legacy of Conquest, Colonization, and Commerce* (Danvers, MA: Martinus Nijhoff Publishers, 2009).

100. Hugh Eakin, "The Great Giveback," *New York Times*, January 26, 2013.

101. Karin Schwartz (PhD candidate in population biology, George Mason University), interview by author, telephone, April 1, 2013.

102. Hinchliffe, "Reconstituting Nature Conservation," 89.

103. Ibid.

BLACK-FOOTED FERRET

1. Colorado Independent CattleGrowers, "Bull by the Horns: A Black-Footed Problem," *Cattle Call* 8, no. 1 (2013): 2; see also Candice Kreb, "Ferret's Link to Prairie Dogs Underlies Opposition," *BCDemocrat Online*, July 26, 2013, http://www.bcdemocratonline.com/article/20130726/NEWS/130729959/-1/ Entertainment%20%20%20Life.

2. Kreb, "Ferret's Link to Prairie Dogs Underlies Opposition." Here, from the e-mail announcement sent by Ross Melinchuk, deputy executive director of natural resources at the Texas Parks and Wildlife Department, on November 5, 2013:

> The principal intent of this SHA is to provide for the reintroduction of BFFs [black-footed ferrets] on private land without adversely affecting either a cooperating landowner or his/ her neighbors. . . . Participation in the BFF SHA is strictly voluntary and withdrawal may occur at any time. Neighbors and non-participating interests are protected for any incidental BFF "take" related to any legal activity. Take coverage remains for both those enrolled and for neighbors and non-participating interests if withdrawal occurs. Based on many years of recovery experience, the BFF Recovery Team anticipates that only a few hundred landowners across the 12 state historical range of the species will need to be enrolled in this SHA over the next decade in order for the species to be delisted pursuant to the Endangered Species Act.

Filed with author.

3. "Animal Profile," Black-Footed Ferret Recovery Program, http://www.black footedferret.org/animal-profile. On the basis of a 1902 survey, many believe that a single population of around 250 prairie dogs can consume an equal amount of grass as a single cow. Yet subsequent studies have called these numbers into question. Constantine N. Slobodchikoff, Bianca S. Perla, and Jennifer L. Verdolin, *Prairie Dogs: Communication and Community in an Animal Society* (Cambridge, MA: Harvard University Press, 2009), 4.

4. "Black Tailed Prairie Dog (*Cynomys ludovicianus*)," Prairie Dog Coalition, http://www.prairiedogcoalition.org/pd-black-tailed-prairie-dog.php.

5. "History of the Black-Footed Ferret," Black-Footed Ferret Recovery Program, http://www.blackfootedferret.org/history.

6. Susan G. Clark (former director, Biota Research and Consulting, Jackson, WY; professor, Yale University School of the Environment), interview by author, telephone, November 1, 2013; "History of the Black-Footed Ferret," Black-Footed Ferret Recovery Program, http://www.blackfootedferret.org/history.

7. David Wildt, quoted in Hannah Foster, "Nearly Extinct Ferret Population Restored," *Global Animal*, October 4, 2011, http://globalanimal.org/2011/10/04/ nearly-extinct-ferret-population-restored/52555/.

8. Marinari, interview.

9. Ibid.

10. "Captive Breeding," Black-Footed Ferret Recovery Program, http://www .blackfootedferret.org/captive-breeding.

11. Marinari, interview.

12. Ibid.

13. Ibid.

14. Onnie Byers et al., "The One Plan Approach: The Philosophy and Implementation of CBSG's Approach to Integrated Species Conservation Planning," *WAZA Magazine* 14 (2013): 4.

15. Marinari, interview.

16. "Captive Breeding," Black-Footed Ferret Recovery Program.

17. Marinari, interview.

18. Ibid.

19. Ibid.

20. Ibid.

21. "Preconditioning," Black-Footed Ferret Recovery Program, http://www.black footedferret.org/preconditioning.

22. Lacy, interview, October 11, 2013.

23. Ibid.

24. Ibid.

25. Ibid.

26. Melinchuk, e-mail announcement (note 2 above).

CHAPTER 4: DYNAMIC LIFE

1. Philip Miller (senior program officer, CBSG), interview by author, in person, Tucson, AZ, April 22–24, 2013; telephone, May 6, 2013.

2. For a discussion of "soft law" in the context of animal regulation, see *Zooland*, 127–29, 148–56.

3. The Xerces Society for Invertebrate Conservation, "Swallowtails: Schaus Swallowtail (*Heraclides aristodemus ponceanus*)," http://www.xerces.org/schaus-swallowtail/.

4. United States Golf Association, "Turfgrass and Environmental Research Online," June 1, 2004, http://usgatero.msu.edu/v03/n11.pdf.

5. Craig Pittman, "Endangered Schaus Swallowtail Butterfly May Be All but Gone," *Tampa Bay Times*, August 30, 2012. http://www.tampabay.com/news/environment/wildlife/endangered-schaus-swallowtail-butterfly-may-be-all-but-gone/1248986.

6. United States Golf Association, "Turfgrass and Environmental Research Online."

7. Suckling, e-mail communication, May 11, 2014.

8. Schaus Swallowtail Butterfly (*Heraclides aristodemus ponceanus*), Multi-Species Recovery Plan for South Florida, http://www.xerces.org/wp-content/uploads/2008/09/schaus_swallowtail_recovery_plan_1999_revised.pdf.

9. Thomas C. Emmel (founding director, McGuire Center for Lepidoptera and Biodiversity, Florida Museum of Natural History), interview by author, telephone, June 5, 2014.

10. Ibid.

11. Ibid.

12. Ibid.

13. Pittman, "Endangered Schaus Swallowtail."

14. Emmel, interview.

15. Ibid.

16. Pittman, "Endangered Schaus Swallowtail."

17. National Park Service, "Schaus Swallowtail Emergency Response, Biscayne

N.P.," http://www.nps.gov/resources/2016.htm?id=5D38495B-155D-451-3E155 CCE C04E3F73.

18. Ken Warren, Elsa Alvear, and Jeffrey Olson, "National Park Service Release," June 13, 2012, http://home.nps.gov/news/release.htm?id=1346.

19. Pittman, "Endangered Schaus Swallowtail."

20. Ibid.

21. Emmel, interview.

22. Suckling, e-mail communication.

23. Ibid.

24. Biscayne National Park, "Schaus Swallowtail Sighting Alert," Facebook post, August 16, 2013, https://www.facebook.com/photo.php?fbid=609437239078519&1=36.

25. Jenny Staletovich, "Rare Butterflies Fight for Survival in South Florida," *Miami Herald*, May 20, 2014, http://www.miamiherald.com/2014/05/20/4127917/rare-butterflies-fight-for-survival.html.

26. IUCN/SSC, "IUCN Guidelines for Reintroductions and Other Conservation Translocations," Version 1.0., Gland, Switzerland (2013), https://portals.iucn.org/library/sites/library/files/documents/2013-009.pdf.

27. Ibid.

28. Pritpal S. Soorae, ed., *Global Re-Introduction Perspectives: 2011. More Case Studies from around the Globe* (Gland, Switzerland: IUCN/SSC Re-Introduction Specialist Group, 2011). See also Pritpal S. Soorae, ed., *Global Re-Introduction Perspectives: 2013. Further Case Studies from around the Globe* (Gland, Switzerland: IUCN/SSC Re-Introduction Specialist Group, 2013). IUCN's Reintroduction Specialist Group designates the cases as "highly successful," "successful," "partially successful," or "failure." In 2011, of 41 programs, only one was a failure and 22 were partially successful. In 2013, mammal species made up more than half of the case studies.

29. Benjamin Beck, "Reintroduction, Zoos, Conservation, and Animal Welfare," in *Ethics on the Ark: Zoos, Animal Welfare, and Wildlife Conservation*, ed. Bryan G. Norton et al. (Washington, DC: Smithsonian Institution Press, 1995), 156.

30. Ibid., 155.

31. Ibid.

32. Brad Griffith, et al., "Translocation as a Species Conservation Tool: Status and Strategy," *Science* 245, no. 4917 (1989): 478.

33. Suckling, e-mail communication, July 24, 2013.

34. Mark Stanley Price (former director, Jersey Zoo; senior research fellow, Wildlife Conservation Research Unit (WildCRU); board member, CBSG; chair, IUCN's Task Force of the Reintroduction and Invasive Species Specialist Groups), interview by author, in person, Oxford, UK, March 12, 2013.

35. Friese, *Cloning Wild Life*, 175.

36. Ibid.

37. Stanley Price, interview.

38. The eastern hellbender is one of two hellbender subspecies. The other, the Ozark hellbender (*Cryptobranchus alleganiensis bishopi*), was listed as endangered under the ESA in 2011. Jane J. Lee, "U.S. Giant Salamanders Slipping Away: Inside the Fight to Save the Hellbender," *National Geographic*, December 19, 2013, http://news.nationalgeographic.com/news/2013/12/13122-hellbender-salamander-conservation-endangered-animals-science/.

39. Virginia Department of Game and Inland Fisheries (DGIF), "Eastern Hellbender," http://www.dgif.virginia.gov/hellbender/. According to the Virginia DGIF, human interventions in waterways are highly damaging to the species:

> Dams eliminate free-flowing sections of rivers and produce low oxygen conditions on the river bottom. Untreated sewage, sedimentation, and chemical runoff from lawns, fields, and parking lots all contribute to a reduction in their populations. Because their respiration is through the skin, any toxic substance in the water can have significant adverse health effects on the hellbenders. Removal of streamside vegetation and soil disturbance can also increase sedimentation. Sedimentation affects hellbender survival by suffocating eggs, filling in hiding places of the young and killing invertebrates, such as the crayfish they feed on.

40. Ibid.

41. Ibid.

42. The Center for Biological Diversity, "Lawsuit Seeks to Save North America's Largest Amphibian," June 27, 2013, http://www.biologicaldiversity.org/news/press_releases/2013/hellbender-06-27-2013.html.

43. See Irus Braverman, "En-Listing Life: Red Is the Color of Threatened Species Lists," in *Critical Animal Geographies*, ed. Rosemarie Collard and Kathryn Gillespie (London: Routledge/Earthscan, 2015), 184–202.

44. Department of Environmental Conservation, "Partnership Creates New Habitat for Species of Special Concern: Collaborative Efforts Focus on Habitat Restoration and Breeding of State's Largest Salamander," April 24, 2012, http://www.dec.ny.gov/press/81854.html.

45. Ibid.

46. Hellbenders reach sexual maturity at the age of five to eight years and may live as long as thirty years in the wild and fifty in captivity. Jill Utrup and Kim Mitchell, "The Ozark Hellbender: Out from Under a Rock," USFWS, April 4, 2013, http://www.fws.gov/midwest/news/tipsheet/hellbender.htm.

47. Will James, "Bronx Zoo Team Helps Hellbender Salamanders Go Home," *Wall Street Journal*, August 20, 2013, http://online.wsj.com/news/articles/SB10001424127887324108204579024753735118762.

48. For more about the PIT tag, see Chapter 6. On naming, tracing, identifying, and documenting zoo animals, see Braverman, *Zooland*, 92–126.

49. Penny Felski (herpetology manager, Buffalo Zoo), interview by author, on-site, Buffalo, NY, June 7, 2013.

50. Ibid.

51. Ibid.

52. Kenneth Roblee (wildlife biologist, Region 9, DEC), interview by author, on-site, Allegheny River, WNY, Hellbender reintroduction, August 1, 2013.

53. Felski, interview and Roblee, interview, respectively.

54. Felski, e-mail communication, May 30, 2014.

55. IUCN/SSC, "IUCN Policy Statement on Captive Breeding," Gland, Switzerland (1987), http://cmsdata.iucn.org/downloads/1987_iucn_policy_statement___captive_breeding.pdf.

56. Byers, interview.

57. Soulé et al., "The Millennium Ark."

58. Ballou, Gilpin, and Foose, *Population Management for Survival and Recovery*, 284. In 2013, there were approximately 450 captive breeding programs in North America's AZA alone.

59. Lee Durrell and Jeremy Mallinson, "Reintroduction as a Political and Education Tool for Conservation," *The Dodo: Journal of the Jersey Wildlife Preservation Trust* 24 (1987): 6–19.

60. IUCN/SSC, "IUCN Guidelines for Reintroductions," viii (emphasis in original).

61. Ibid.

62. Ibid.

63. Stanley Price, interview.

64. Byers, interview.

65. Stanley Price, interview.

66. IUCN, "IUCN Technical Guidelines on the Management of *Ex Situ* Populations for Conservation" (paper presented at the 14th Meeting of the Programme Committee of Council, Gland, Switzerland, December 10, 2002), https://portals.iucn.org/library/efiles/documents/Rep-2002-017.pdf.

67. Traylor-Holzer, interview.

68. Ibid.

69. IUCN/SSC, "IUCN Guidelines for Reintroductions," viii.

70. Ibid., 1.

71. Ibid., 19–23.

72. Schwitzer, interview, April 11, 2013.

73. Richard Black, "Richard Branson's Lemur Plan Raises Alarm," *BBC News*, April 16, 2011, http://www.bbc.co.uk/news/science-environment-13095307.

74. Ibid.

75. Rory Carroll, "Richard Branson to Create Sanctuary for Lemurs—8,000 Miles from Their Home," *The Guardian*, April 18, 2011, http://www.theguardian.com/environment/2011/apr/18/richard-branson-lemur-moskito. See also Schwitzer, interview.

76. Schwitzer, interview, April 5, 2013.

77. Schwitzer, interview, April 11, 2013.

78. But see Braverman, "En-Listing Life."

79. CITES, "What Is CITES?" http://www.cites.org/eng/disc/what.php.

80. At the USFWS, policy advisor Frank Kohn's job is to ensure that wildlife

transport, both of CITES-listed and of non-CITES-listed species, is executed "humanely," in his words. Kohn explains that every transport of CITES-listed species must specify the legal origin of the species and must not be detrimental to the wild population. CITES has adopted the International Air Transport Association (IATA) Guidelines, which prescribe an exact format for each animal movement by air. Kohn tells me, for example, that he recently came across a case with a seahorse importer who wanted to get his animals released. He recounts the incident: "The inspector claimed that our regulations say that the animals must have something to anchor themselves to, and the importer was claiming that they were anchoring themselves to each other." As a result of this case, Kohn says, the USFWS spelled out that "animals must anchor themselves to a material, and then we added that 'anchoring to another animal is unacceptable.'" Frank Kohn (CITES policy specialist, live animal transport; coordinator, Plant Rescue Center, Wildlife Trade and Conservation Branch, Division of Management Authority, USFWS), interview by author, telephone, June 25, 2013.

81. CITES, "What Is CITES?" Polar bears are an apt example for the heightened role of regulation in conservation. The polar bear is a CITES Appendix II species. As such, it may be imported internationally without a CITES import permit. In the United States, the polar bear is regulated by *both* the ESA and the Marine Mammal Protection Act (MMPA). Lisa Lierheimer (supervisory policy specialist, Division of Management Authority, USFWS), interview by author, telephone, July 16, 2013. Because polar bears are classified as threatened under the ESA, they automatically classify as depleted under the MMPA. These classifications, Steve Amstrup of Polar Bear International and Kierán Suckling tell me, have a variety of consequences, including tight restrictions on their importation. Steve Amstrup (director, Polar Bears International), interview by author, telephone, June 26, 2013; Suckling, e-mail communication, June 14, 2014.

PUERTO RICAN PARROT

1. Gustavo Olivieri (coordinator, José Vivaldi Aviary, Puerto Rican Parrot Reintroduction Program), interview by author, on-site, Río Abajo State Forest, PR, January 22, 2014. Joint interview with Ricardo Valentin.

2. Ricardo Valentin (coordinator, José Vivaldi Aviary, Puerto Rican Parrot Reintroduction Program), interview by author, on-site, Río Abajo State Forest, PR, January 22, 2014. Joint interview with Gustavo Olivieri.

3. Jafet Vélez-Valentín (wildlife biologist, Iguaca Aviary, USFWS), interview by author, on-site, Iguaca Aviary, PR, January 14, 2014.

4. Thomas H. White, Jr. et al., *Niche Restriction and Conservatism in a Neotropical Psittacine: The Case of the Puerto Rican Parrot* (Hauppauge, NY: Nova Science Publishers, 2014), 14.

5. Ibid., 2, 9.

6. Vélez-Valentín, interview.

7. Ibid.

8. Ibid.

9. "El Yunque National Forest: About the Forest," USDA Forest Service, http://www.fs.usda.gov/main/elyunque/about-forest; see also Vélez-Valentín, interview; Thomas H. White Jr., Jaime A. Collazo, and Francisco J. Vilella, "Survival of Captive-Reared Puerto Rican Parrots Released in the Caribbean National Forest," *The Condor* 107 (2005): 425.

10. White et al., "Survival of Captive-Reared Puerto Rican Parrots," 424.

11. Thomas H. White, Jr. (wildlife biologist, Puerto Rican Parrot Recovery Program, USFWS), interview by author, on-site, Iguaca Aviary, PR, January 14, 2014.

12. White et al., "Survival of Captive-Reared Puerto Rican Parrots," 424.

13. White, interview.

14. Jaime A. Collazo et al., "Survival of Captive-Reared Hispaniolan Parrots Released in Parque Nacional del Este, Dominican Republic," *The Condor* 105 (2003): 198–207; White et al., "Survival of Captive-Reared Puerto Rican Parrots," 425.

15. White et al., "Survival of Captive-Reared Puerto Rican Parrots," 424–26; White et al., *Niche Restriction and Conservatism*, 112.

16. White, interview.

17. White et al., *Niche Restriction and Conservatism*, 17.

18. Ibid., 6, 52.

19. White, interview.

20. Ibid.

21. Olivieri and Valentin, joint interview.

22. Collazo et al., "Survival of Captive-Reared Hispaniolan Parrots"; Douglas H. White, Jr. et al., "Psittacine Reintroductions: Common Denominators of Success," *Biological Conservation* 148 (2012): 106–15.

23. Olivieri and Valentin, joint interview.

24. White, interview.

25. Ibid.

26. Ibid.

27. Olivieri and Valentin, joint interview.

28. Ibid.

29. Ibid.

30. White, interview; White et al., "Psittacine Reintroductions," 112.

31. White, interview.

32. White et al., *Niche Restriction and Conservatism*, 51.

33. Olivieri and Valentin, joint interview.

34. White, interview.

35. Olivieri and Valentin, joint interview.

36. Ibid.

37. Vélez-Valentín, interview.

38. Olivieri and Valentin, joint interview; White et al., *Niche Restriction and Conservatism*.

39. Or even five, if one counts the Mayaguez Zoo, which has two Puerto Rican parrots.

40. Lincoln Park Zoo, "Protecting the Puerto Rican Parrot," http://www.lpzoo .org/conservation-science/projects/protecting-puerto-rican-parrot. See also James Seidler, "Census in the Caribbean," *Lincoln Park Zoo Magazine*, Spring 2008, http:// www.lpzoo.org/magazine/articles/census-carribean.

41. Vélez-Valentín, interview.

42. Ibid.

43. Lilibeth Serrano, "Federal and State Agencies Reaffirm Their Commitment to the Recovery of the Endangered Puerto Rican Parrot," USFWS, August 6, 2012, http://www.fws.gov/caribbean/ParrotMoU2012.html.

44. The Wilderness Act, 16 U.S.C. 1131–1136; Pub. L. 88–577 (1964). In 2005, a 10,000–acre area of El Yunque National Forest/Luquillo Experimental Forest was designated as El Toro Wilderness. USDA Forest Service, "Fact Sheet—El Toro Wilderness," January 19, 2006, http://www.fs.fed.us/news/2006/releases/01/cnf-el-toro-fact-sheet.pdf.

45. López-Flores and Muniz, joint interview.

46. Ibid.

47. Ibid.

48. Ibid.

49. Ibid.

CHAPTER 5: REGULATORY LIFE

1. See also in Braverman, *Zooland*, 11, 54–55, 133–35.

2. Michel Foucault, *Security, Territory, Population: Lectures at the Collège de France, 1977–1978*, ed. Michel Senellart, trans. Graham Burchell (New York: Picador, 2007), 108. See also Nikolas Rose, Pat O'Malley, and Mariana Valverde, "Governmentality," *Annual Review of Law and Social Science* 2 (2009): 83–104; Majia Holmer Nadesan, *Governmentality, Biopower, and Everyday Life* (New York: Routledge, 2008).

3. United Nations, Article 9, "Ex-situ Conservation."

4. Dale Goble (distinguished professor of law, University of Idaho; convener, ESA at 30), interview by author, telephone, July 1, 2013.

5. Ashe, interview (my emphasis). USFWS senior biologist Mike Carpenter explains similarly: "Generally speaking, captive animals don't have a lot to do with the wild population, but they might lend themselves to support the wildlife population." Mike Carpenter (senior biologist, Division of Management Authority, USFWS), interview by author, telephone, July 16, 2013.

6. Goble, interview.

7. Suckling, e-mail communication, June 11, 2014.

8. Endangered and Threatened Wildlife and Plants: Listing All Chimpanzees as Endangered, 50 C.F.R. §17.3. Quoted in USFWS, 78 Fed. Reg. 33792 (June 5, 2013).

9. *Babbitt v. Sweet Home*, 515 U.S. 687 (1995); 44 Fed. Reg. 30044–45 (May 23,

1979); *see also* 58 Fed. Reg. 32632 (June 11, 1993) (explaining that "the Service will continue to enforce the stringent prohibitions of the Act as they relate to captive individuals of a species that is endangered in the wild [because] captive individuals provide gene pools that deserve continued preservation and such individuals make it possible to re-establish or rejuvenate wild populations"; 63 Fed. Reg. 48634, 48636 (September 11, 1998) (explaining that "take" was defined by Congress to apply to endangered or threatened wildlife *"whether wild or captive"*) (my emphasis). I am grateful to Katherine A. Meyer of Meyer Glitzenstein & Crystal for providing the information upon which this, the following footnote, and their related texts are based. Katherine A. Meyer (founding partner, Meyer Glitzenstein & Crystal law firm), e-mail communications, October 3, 2013, and June 4, 2014.

10. See Braverman, *Zooland*, 66–68.

11. Endangered and Threatened Wildlife and Plants: Listing All Chimpanzees as Endangered, 50 C.F.R. §17, note 2 (2013), www.regulations. gov/#!documentDetail;D=FWS-R9–ES-2010–0086–12977.

12. J. Michael Scott (leader, California Condor Research Center, 1984–86; leader, Idaho Cooperative Fish and Wildlife Research Unit; professor of fish and wildlife resources, University of Idaho), interview by author, telephone, June 26, 2013.

13. ESA, 16 U.S.C. §1531, *et seq.* (4)(a)(1) (1973).

14. NatureServe, "Data Coverage" (2014), http://explorer.natureserve.org/sum mary.htm.

15. Ashe, interview.

16. David S. Wilcove and Lawrence L. Master, "How Many Endangered Species Are There in the United States?" *Frontiers in Ecology and the Environment* 3, no. 8 (2005): 419.

17. Scott, interview.

18. ESA, 16 U.S.C. §1531, *et seq.* (9)(a)(1973); ESA, 16 U.S.C. §1531, *et seq.* (10) (e)(1973); Carpenter, interview.

19. ESA, 16 U.S.C. §1532, *et seq.* (19)(1973).

20. *Babbitt v. Sweet Home*, 515 U.S. 687 (1995).

21. Timothy Male (former vice president of conservation policy, Defenders of Wildlife), interview by author, telephone, July 1, 2013.

22. Still, not everyone agrees with Male's description. For example, Kierán Suckling states: "What made the ESA so interesting and pathbreaking was its radical departure from the 'take' model. In calling for a new ESA, [President] Nixon expressly pointed out that the old laws were not sweeping enough and not based on modern conservation science. Thus the ESA goes far beyond the take regulation to include habitat protection, recovery plans, funding of state and private conservation initiatives, captive breeding, et cetera." According to Suckling, Male's critique of the ESA is thus relevant only to the earlier ESA versions of 1967 and 1969. Suckling, e-mail communication, June 11, 2014.

23. "Fish or wildlife" is defined as *"any* member of the animal kingdom." 16 U.S.C. § 1532(8) (my emphasis); see also *Dep't of Hous. & Urban Dev. v. Rucker*, 535 U.S. 125,

131 (2002) ("the word 'any' has an expansive meaning, that is, 'one or some indiscriminately of whatever kind'") (citation omitted).

24. Ashe, interview. For a more detailed description of the exceptions to the take provision, see Sam Kalen and Adam Pan, "Chapter 9: Exceptions to the Take Prohibition," in *Endangered Species Act: Law, Policy, and Perspectives*, ed. Donald C. Baur and William Robert Irvin, 2nd ed. (American Bar Association, 2010), 192–205.

25. Section 10(a)(1) of the ESA requires that whenever a "person"—defined to include a corporation, 16 U.S.C. § 1532(13)—seeks to engage in an activity that is otherwise prohibited by Section 9, it must first obtain a permit from the USFWS authorizing that activity. 16 U.S.C. § 1539(a)(1). To apply for a permit, the applicant must provide and verify specific information, including: a description of the facilities where the animals are being used, displayed, and maintained; the experience of the animal handlers; the take that will occur; and the reasons such a take is justified—i.e., a demonstration that it will "enhance the propagation or survival" of the species. 50 C.F.R. §§ 17.22(v)–(vii); 16 U.S.C. § 1539(a)(1)(A). To grant such a permit, the USFWS must find (and publish this finding in the *Federal Register*) that the permit (1) was "applied for in good faith, (2) if granted and exercised will not operate to the disadvantage of such endangered species, and (3) will be consistent with the purposes and policy" of the Act. 16 U.S.C. § 1539(d). The USFWS would also have to find that the animals are being maintained under "humane and healthful conditions." 50 C.F.R. § 13.41. Meyer, e-mail communication, June 4, 2014.

26. Ashe, interview. These divergent practices are based on two distinct definitions of the term "harass" (one of the behaviors that constitutes a prohibited take) for captive and wild animals in the federal regulations. 50 CFR §17.3 (2004) defines "harass" as "an intentional or negligent act or omission which creates the likelihood of injury to wildlife by annoying it to such an extent as to significantly disrupt normal behavioral patterns which include, but are not limited to, breeding, feeding, or sheltering." The Federal Regulations then explain that:

This definition, when applied to captive wildlife, does not include generally accepted:

(1) Animal husbandry practices that meet or exceed the minimum standards for facilities and care under the Animal Welfare Act,

(2) Breeding procedures, or

(3) Provisions of veterinary care for confining, tranquilizing, or anesthetizing, when such practices, procedures, or provisions are not likely to result in injury to the wildlife.

50 C.F.R. § 17.3. See also Meyer, e-mail communication.

27. Meyer disagrees: "Many listed species that are held in captivity were originally taken from the wild. The best example of this is Asian elephants used in circuses and zoos. Many were originally taken from the wild before they were listed in 1976 and are still alive because they live to be over sixty." Meyer, e-mail communication.

28. Carpenter, interview.

29. Suckling, interview.

30. 44 Fed. Reg. 54002, 54007 (September 17, 1979); 50 C.F.R. § 17.21(g).

31. 44 Fed. Reg. at 54002; 50 C.F.R. § 17.3.

32. On December 27, 1993, the USFWS further amended the definition of "enhance the propagation or survival" to eliminate "education through exhibition" as the sole justification for relying on the CBW registration, thereby clarifying that the CBW program is available "only [to] those persons who engage in beneficial captive breeding." 58 Fed. Reg. 68323, 68325 (December 27, 1993). The USFWS also noted its "sincere doubts about the relative conservation benefits that are provided to non-native species in the wild from the public exhibition of living wildlife." 58 Fed. Reg. 68324.

33. Meyer, e-mail communication, October 3, 2013.

34. Such agreements are authorized by Section 10's take permits. ESA, 16 U.S.C. §1539 (1973).

35. The "God Squad" was formed by Congress in 1979 and given the power to exempt certain projects from the ESA. The God Squad has met three times: once to determine "whether the snail darter should be protected, . . . once over a dam project in Nebraska that threatened whooping cranes and again concerning the spotted owl in the Northwest." Sarah Matsumoto et al., "Citizens Guide to the Endangered Species Act" (EarthJustice 2003), 39, http://earthjustice.org/sites/default/files/library/reports/Citizens_Guide_ESA.pdf. See also Cornell University Law School Legal Information Institute, "Endangered Species Act (ESA)," http://www.law.cornell.edu/wex/endangered_species_act_esa.

36. An incidental take is "a take that results from, but is not the purpose of, carrying out an otherwise lawful activity." USFWS, "Glossary," http://www.fws.gov/midwest/endangered/glossary/index.html. Incidental take provisions allow agencies to "take" an animal (a) if it is a marine mammal, under the Marine Mammal Protection Act of 1972, or (b) the Secretary of Interior (whose authority, for practical purposes, is vested in the USFWS) determined that there has been appropriate consultation across departments. ESA, 16 U.S.C. § 1531, *et seq.* (7)(b)(4) (1973).

37. "Under the 'enhancement of survival' provision of Section § 10(a)(1)(A), a land owner and FWS may enter into a voluntary agreement where the landowner agrees to alter the property to benefit or even attract a listed or proposed species in exchange for assurances that the [USFWS] will permit future 'takes' above a predetermined level. This may be done in addition to an incidental take permit." Cornell University Law School Legal Information Institute, "Endangered Species Act (ESA)."

38. The "No Surprises" rule is meant "to give the landowner certainty and protection against 'unforeseen circumstances.' Should the landowner's efforts to prevent or mitigate harm to the species fall short, the government will maintain the incidental take permit, and will pay for any new habitat or actions needed." Ibid.

39. Suckling, e-mail communication, July 24, 2013. The ESA uses the term "DPS" without defining it. The criteria for designation as a DPS, as articulated in a joint USFWS-NMFS policy (61 FR 4722: February 7, 1996), are: the discreteness of the population segment in relation to the remainder of the species to which it belongs; the significance of the population segment to the species to which it belongs;

and the population segment's conservation status in relation to the Act's standards for listing (i.e., is the population segment, when treated as if it were a species, endangered or threatened?).

40. Suckling, interview, July 5, 2013.

41. Under Subsection J of the ESA, an experimental population is defined as a population that has been designated as releasable when "wholly separate geographically from nonexperimental populations of the same species." This release is authorized only when the specific population is non-essential to the continued existence of the endangered species, and when the population's release will benefit that species' survival. ESA, 16 U.S.C. §1531, *et seq.* (10)(j)(1973).

42. Suckling, e-mail communication, June 11, 2014.

43. ESA, 16 U.S.C. §1531, *et seq.* (10)(j)(1973).

44. Suckling, e-mail communication.

45. Ibid.

46. Although Haraway's justification of "killing well" was met with criticism, her comments on the act of "making killable" remain relevant here. Haraway, *When Species Meet*, 80.

47. Frazer, interview.

48. The American burying beetles acquired their name from their unique manner of reproduction. The beetles bury dead animals six to eight inches underground, embalm the carrion with a naturally secreted fluid, and lay their eggs in the embalmed carcass. Within four days, the eggs hatch into larvae. Both parents care for the young by regurgitating dead flesh from the carcass into the young's mouth. "Saint Louis Zoo's American Burying Beetles," YouTube video, http://www.youtube .com/watch?v=tgCrcRLZAhc.

49. Erin Muths and Michelle Pellissier Scott, "American Burying Beetle," in *Endangered Animals: A Reference Guide to Conflict Issues*, ed. Richard P. Reading and Brian Miller (Westport, CT: Greenwood Press, 2001), 10; "Saint Louis Zoo's American Burying Beetles." For the beetle's designation as endangered, see USFWS, 54 Fed. Reg. 133, 29652–55. Habitat loss and fragmentation are one possible cause; another is that the beetle needs carrion of a very specific size for breeding (100–250 grams), and that animals of that size (such as the passenger pigeon) have either gone extinct or have become scarcer. "Surveying for the American Burying Beetle," You-Tube video, http://www.youtube.com/watch?v=H75rJGLaSNk&feature=youtu.be.

50. Saint Louis Zoo, "Center for American Burying Beetle Conservation," http:// www.stlzoo.org/conservation/wildcare-institute/americanburyingbeetleconse/.

51. Bob Merz (director, Center for American Burying Beetle Conservation, Saint Louis Zoo), interview by author, telephone, June 20, 2013.

52. Saint Louis Zoo Press Release, "Endangered American Burying Beetles from Saint Louis Zoo Set to Be Reintroduced in Southwest Missouri on June 4," May 30, 2014, http://www.stlzoo.org/about/contact/pressroom/pressreleases/ american-burying-beetles-be-reintroduced-southwest-missouri/.

53. Merz, interview. See also "Saint Louis Zoo's American Burying Beetles."

54. Merz, interview.

55. Beetles are also notched according to release locations. See Saint Louis Zoo Press Release, "Endangered American Burying Beetles from Saint Louis Zoo Set to Be Reintroduced in Southwest Missouri on June 4."

56. Emmel, interview.

57. Ibid.

58. Frazer, interview.

59. Ibid.

60. Ibid.

61. Suckling, e-mail communication.

62. Ibid.

63. Suckling, interview.

64. Butler, *Precarious Life*, 33.

65. Suckling, interview.

66. Ibid.

67. Memorandum from Assistant Solicitor, USFWS, to Deputy Associate Director, Federal Assistance, USFWS (Aug. 2, 1977), quoted in Kevin D. Hill, "The Endangered Species Act: What Do We Mean by Species?" *Boston College Environmental Affairs Law Review* 20, no. 2 (1993): 244, note 43.

68. Memorandum from Assistant Solicitor, USFWS, to Associate Director, Federal Assistance, USFWS (May 6, 1981).

69. Ibid.

70. Quoted in Hill, "The Endangered Species Act," 262.

71. Suckling, interview.

72. USFWS, "Recovery Plan for the Columbia Basin Distinct Population Segment of the Pygmy Rabbit (Brachylagus idahoensis)," 78 Fed. Reg. 4865–4866 (Jan. 1, 2013), http://www.gpo.gov/fdsys/pkg/FR-2013-01-23/pdf/FR-2013-01-23.pdf, 4866.

73. Oregon Zoo, "Columbia Basin Pygmy Rabbits," http://www.oregonzoo.org/conserve/species-recovery-and-conservation/columbia-basin-pygmy-rabbits.

74. Ibid.

75. Hill, "The Endangered Species Act," 242.

76. Suckling, e-mail communication, July 24, 2013.

77. Male, interview.

78. The Arctic peregrine falcon was delisted in 1994, and the American peregrine falcon was delisted in 1999. See also J. Michael Scott et al., "Conservation-Reliant Species and the Future of Conservation," *Conservation Letters* 3 (2010): 91.

79. Arroyo, interview.

80. Ibid.

81. Braverman, *Zooland*, 176–77.

82. Christie, interview.

83. USFWS, 70 Fed. Reg. 52,319 (Sept. 2, 2005).

84. IUCN/SSC Antelope Specialist Group, "*Oryx dammah*," *The IUCN Red List of Threatened Species, Version 2012.2,* http://www.iucnredlist.org/details/15568/0;

J. Newby and T. Wacher, *"Addax nasomaculatus," The IUCN Red List of Threatened Species, Version 2012.2,* http://www.iucnredlist.org/details/512/0; J. Newby et al., *"Nanger dama," The IUCN Red List of Threatened Species, Version 2012.2,* http://www .iucnredlist.org/details/8968/0. Additionally, the addax, oryx, and dama gazelle are protected by both local and international laws. CITES Appendix I lists all popula-tions of these species as endangered, and the ESA lists them as endangered in their entire range. 50 C.F.R. § 17.11(h) (2012). See also the "species information" section in USFWS, 78 Fed. Reg. 33,791 (June 5, 2013).

85. USFWS, 70 Fed. Reg. 52,319 (Sept. 2, 2005).

86. IUCN/SSC Antelope Specialist Group, *"Oryx dammah"*; Newby and Wacher, *"Addax nasomaculatus"*; Newby et al., *"Nanger dama"*; USFWS 70 Fed. Reg. 52,310 (Sept. 2, 2005).

87. USFWS, 70 Fed. Reg. 52,319 (Sept. 2, 2005).

88. USFWS, 70 Fed. Reg. 52,310 (Sept. 2, 2005).

89. USFWS, 70 Fed. Reg. 52,315 (Sept. 2, 2005).

90. USFWS 77 Fed. Reg. 431 (Jan. 5, 2012). This rule was the end result of a long battle, which reached its high point in 2009 with a decision by the U.S. District Court for the District of Columbia. The court held that the USFWS 2005 rule that excluded game ranches was illegal. As a result, the USFWS enacted a new rule in 2012, which was upheld by the district court in *Safari Club International v. Salazar,* 852 F. Supp. 2d 102 (D.D.C. 2012). In 2013, the USFWS found unwarranted a peti-tion to delist captive-bred populations. USFWS, 78 Fed. Reg. 33,790 (June 5, 2013).

91. Kierán Suckling provides his perspective on the unfolding of these events: "They allowed the hunting, lying that it serves a conservation purpose [when] the Agency knows very well that there is no conservation purpose to the hunting. It pro-duces lots of money for rich, politically powerful people. These people twisted the arms of the DC bureaucrats and forced them to do so." E-mail communication, July 24, 2013. Also according to Suckling: "It is likely that such hunting permits, being commercially valuable, will continue to be issued for antelopes." Suckling, interview, July 12, 2013.

92. Anna Frostic (attorney, Humane Society of the United States), interview by author, telephone, July 12, 2013.

93. USFWS, 78 Fed. Reg. 35,201 (June 12, 2013).

94. USFWS, "USFWS Proposes Protection for All Chimpanzees—Captive and Wild—as Endangered," http://www.fws.gov/home/newsroom/serviceproposeschim panzeesNR06112013.html. Mike Carpenter of the USFWS states along these lines: "Any kind of invasive research would be prohibited and would require permits; any kind of behavioral research that modifies the natural behavior of the animal." Car-penter, interview.

95. Steve Ross (coordinator, Chimpanzee SSP; director, Lester E. Fisher Center for the Study and Conservation of Apes, Lincoln Park Zoo), interview by author, telephone, July 15, 2013.

96. National Institutes of Health, "NIH to Reduce Significantly the Use of

Chimpanzees in Research," June 26, 2013, http://www.nih.gov/news/health/jun2013/od-26.htm.

97. PETA et al., Petition to Include the Orcinus Orca Known as Lolita in the Endangered Species Act Listing of the Southern Resident Killer Whales (January 23, 2013). http://www.nmfs.noaa.gov/pr/pdfs/petitions/killerwhale_lolita.pdf.

98. USFWS, 70 Fed. Reg. 69,054 (Nov. 18, 2005).

99. PETA et al., Petition to Include the Orcinus Orca Known as Lolita in the Endangered Species Act Listing of the Southern Resident Killer Whales, 21.

100. Ibid.

101. USFWS, 44 Fed. Reg. 30,044–45 (May 23, 1979); USFWS, 63 Fed. Reg. 48,634, 48,636 (Sept. 11, 1998). The petitioners claimed that the USFWS has made clear in public comments that the "take" and other provisions of the ESA apply to captive members of listed species as well as to those in the wild. They also pointed out that in its response to public comments, the USFWS clarified that the take clause applies to endangered or threatened wildlife, "whether wild or captive."

102. This assumption also relies on the widely accepted definition of "species" proposed in the early 1940s by Ernst Mayr. Mayr defined a species as "a reproductive community of populations (reproductively isolated from others) that occupies a specific niche in nature." Ernst Mayr, *Systematics and the Origin of Species* (New York: Columbia University Press, 1942), 4–8, quoted in Hill, "The Endangered Species Act: What Do We Mean by Species?" 250. The central concept in this definition is reproductive isolation: the existence of an isolating mechanism renders the organism a member of a distinct category. In other words, a species is a protected gene pool. From the ESA: "The term 'species' includes any subspecies of fish or wildlife or plants, and any distinct population segments of any species of vertebrate fish or wildlife *which interbreeds when mature*." ESA, 16 U.S.C. §1531, *et seq.* (3)(16) (1973) (my emphasis). Applying this definition, Lolita was classified as belonging to the same species as the wild killer whales. Suckling, interview, July 15, 2013.

103. PETA et al., Petition to Include the Orcinus Orca Known as Lolita in the Endangered Species Act Listing of the Southern Resident Killer Whales, 10.

104. "Listing Endangered or Threatened Species: Proposed Amendment to the Endangered Species Act Listing of the Southern Resident Killer Whale Distinct Population Segment," 50 CFR § 224 (2014).

105. The USFWS and the NMFS each define and apply the term "ESU" differently, taking into account the particular nature of their species along with the scientific tendencies of their experts.

106. *Alsea Valley Alliance v. Evans*, 161 F. Supp. 2d 1154, 1163 (D. Or. 2001), *appeal dismissed*, 358 F.3d 1181 (9th Cir. 2004).

107. Hill writes: "The rule of thumb in determining a subspecies is: if you can distinguish 75 percent of the organisms of a given population from those of another there is a subspecies." Hill, "The Endangered Species Act: What Do We Mean by Species?" 252. He adds that subspecies vary from one another only by geographic distribution. Since all subspecies belong to a single species, their members must be

able to reproduce with one another. On a smaller scale than that of species and subspecies, the ESA also recognizes the distinct population segment (DPS) as a designatable unit.

108. *Trout Unlimited v. Lohn* 559 F. 3d 953 (2009).

109. Ibid.

110. *Trout Unlimited v. Lohn* 645 F. Supp. 2d 929 (2007).

111. *Trout Unlimited v. Lohn* 559 F. 3d 947–48 (2009).

112. Ibid.

113. Suckling, e-mail communication, June 11, 2014.

114. Ibid.

115. Ashe, interview.

116. Suckling, interview, July 12, 2013.

117. Ashe, interview.

118. Ibid.

119. Ibid.

120. Ibid.

121. Jim Deacon (retired fisheries professor, University of Nevada, Las Vegas; author of original recommendations for native fish recovery), interview by author, telephone, July 13, 2013.

122. Male, interview.

123. Ibid.

124. Inspired by our numerous interviews and conversations for this book, Kierán Suckling traced the formal delisting criteria, obtained from the official USFWS recovery plans, of sixty-three threatened and endangered species that have been subject to captive breeding. He was curious to learn how captive breeding is accounted for in the official delisting goals. This informal study led him to the general observation that "USFWS's evaluation of recovery is strongly biased toward *in situ* conditions." More specifically, Suckling noticed that all species with a recovery goal require an "in the wild" population status and that none define recovery simply in terms of the establishment of a sustainable captive breeding population. In other words, the USFWS never views a captive breeding population as achieving recovery on its own merit. Second, Suckling noticed that most federal recovery plans do not include the continuation of a captive breeding program in their goals, despite the existence of captive breeding in those instances; those few recovery plans that do include captive breeding are for species whose conditions in the wild are never likely to be secure. In the latter cases, the recovery plan notes that the species will need a backup captive program in perpetuity in case the wild population is extirpated. Lastly, Suckling noticed that those rare recovery plans that do include captive breeding goals either have no recovery goals, because those could not be determined, or the USFWS states point-blank that recovery is impossible. Implied is the USFWS's perspective that although the population can reliably be sustained in captivity, it should not be assessed as recovered because it is not self-sustaining in the wild. To reiterate: even when the USFWS believes that the establishment of

wild, secure, self-sustaining populations is impossible or unlikely, it still does not see the fulfillment of the captive breeding criterion as sufficient for recovery. Instead, it announces that recovery is impossible. I am grateful to Kierán Suckling for engaging with me in this exchange. Suckling, e-mail communication, July 26, 2013.

RED WOLF

1. David Rabon (coordinator, Red Wolf Recovery Program, USFWS), interview by author, telephone, June 20, 2014.

2. William Waddell (coordinator, Red Wolf SSP; biologist, Point Defiance Zoo & Aquarium), interview by author, telephone, June 6, 2013.

3. Ibid.

4. Ibid.

5. USFWS, Red Wolf Recovery Program, 2013, http://www.fws.gov/redwolf.

6. Waddell, interview.

7. Ibid.

8. USFWS, Red Wolf Recovery Program.

9. Waddell, interview.

10. Rabon, e-mail communication, June 23, 2014.

11. Ibid.

12. Ibid.

13. Waddell, interview.

14. Ibid.

15. Rabon, interview.

16. Waddell, interview.

17. The controversies are largely due to the variation in their morphological features, their tendency to interbreed, and their extirpation after the arrival of Europeans. Steven M. Chambers et al., "An Account of the Taxonomy of North American Wolves from Morphological and Genetic Analyses," *North American Fauna* 77 (2012): 2.

18. Hill, "The Endangered Species Act: What Do We Mean by Species?" 262.

19. Suckling, e-mail communication, July 15, 2013. See also Memorandum from Assistant Solicitor, USFWS, to Director, USFWS (December 14, 1990).

20. Robert K. Wayne and Susan M. Jenks, "Mitochondrial DNA Analysis Implying Extensive Hybridization of the Endangered Red Wolf *Canis rufus*," *Nature* 351 (1991): 565–68; see also Robert K. Wayne et al., "Molecular and Biochemical Evolution of the Carnivora," in *Carnivore Behavior, Ecology, and Evolution*, ed. John L. Gittleman (London: Chapman and Hall, 1989), 465–94.

21. USFWS, "Recovery Timeline," http://www.fws.gov/redwolf/timeline.html.

22. USFWS, 57 Fed. Reg. 1246–1250.

23. USFWS, 62 Fed. Reg. 64799–64800 (Dec. 9, 1997); see also Kevin J. Madonna, "The Wolf in North America: Defining International Ecosystems vs. Defining International Boundaries," *Journal of Land Use and Environmental Law* 10, no. 2 (1995): 305–42. For a discussion of other hybridization debates, see Chapter 5.

24. David E. Reich, Robert K. Wayne, and David B. Goldstein, "Genetic Evidence for a Recent Origin by Hybridization of Red Wolves," *Molecular Ecology* 8 (1999): 139–44.

25. See Paul J. Wilson et al., "DNA Profiles of the Eastern Canadian Wolf and the Red Wolf Provide Evidence for a Common Evolutionary History Independent of the Gray Wolf," *Canadian Journal of Zoology* 78, no. 12 (2000): 2156–66; Ronald M. Nowak, "The Original Status of Wolves in Eastern North America," *Southeastern Naturalist* 1, no. 2 (2002): 95–130; Chambers et al., "An Account of the Taxonomy of North American Wolves," 1–66.

26. Rabon, interview.

27. Ibid.

28. Steve Hinchliffe and Sarah Whatmore, "Living Cities: Toward a Politics of Conviviality," *Science as Culture* 15, no. 2 (2006): 135.

29. Rabon, e-mail communication.

30. A 2013 red wolf workshop facilitated by Lincoln Park Zoo used integrated modeling (Chapter 6) to discuss "database validation" across the *in situ–ex situ* divide. In 2014, efforts were under way to formalize the population management model that has emerged through that collaborative process. Ibid.

31. USFWS, "Eastern North Carolina Red Wolf Population Under Review," Press Release, August 29, 2014, http://www.fws.gov/news/ShowNews.cfm?ID=21 F9771B-D79B-0B5A-47D45DAAFEB3AC6C.

CHAPTER 6: INTEGRATED LIFE

1. Foucault, *The History of Sexuality*, 137.

2. Anonymous conservation biologist (hereinafter "Chris"), interview by author, telephone, May 14, 2014.

3. Ballou, interview.

4. Braverman, *Zooland*, 104–9.

5. Ibid.

6. Ibid., 192–94. There, I examined this form of management in the case of Timmy the gorilla.

7. Ballou, interview.

8. Schwartz, interview.

9. Schwartz, e-mail communication, May 20, 2014.

10. The Excel spreadsheet is a central documentation technology of *in situ* management. Based on her experience working with the tapir (*Tapirus*) in Brazil, Schwartz has observed that field conservationists often "have several different Excel spreadsheets for different aspects [of the animal]: one is for blood values, one is for capture events, one is for reproduction events, [et cetera]. So you can't look at an animal [in one database] and find out everything that's happened to it. You have to find the animal in this spreadsheet and then to find it in that spreadsheet." Schwartz, interview. By contrast, *ex situ* managers have replaced the single Excel spreadsheets

with databases that correlate all the various inputs: a centralized administration that takes data management to more sophisticated and abstract levels. Ibid.

11. Dan D. Brockington, *Fortress Conservation: The Preservation of the Mkomazi Game Reserve* (Bloomington: Indiana University Press, 2002). In this book, Brockington critiques Western conservation models' exclusion of both the local populations and the regional economy of the Mkomazi Game Reserve, explicating the tensions between what he sees as the two problematic models of "fortress conservation," on the one hand, and "community conservation," on the other.

12. Wilderness Act of 1964, 16 U.S.C. 1131–1136; Pub. L. 88–577, § 2(c).

13. Ballou, interview.

14. Braverman, *Zooland*.

15. Ibid.

16. Waddell, interview.

17. Brian Smyth and Silke Nebel, "Passive Integrated Transponder (PIT) Tags in the Study of Animal Movement," *Nature Education Knowledge* 4, no. 3 (2013): 3.

18. Ibid.

19. Ibid.

20. Ibid.

21. Foucault, *Security, Territory, Population*, 312.

22. Polar Bear Specialist Group, "Mark-Recapture," http://pbsg.npolar.no/en/methods/markrecap.html.

23. Amstrup, interview.

24. NatureServe is a North American organization that operates scientific databases for use in conservation work. NatureServe's mission, according to its website, "is to provide the scientific basis for effective conservation action" by collating the information from a "network of natural heritage programs" to support conservation projects. NatureServe, "About Us," http://www.natureserve.org/about-us.

25. NatureServe, "National Species Dataset" (2011), filed with author.

26. Leslie Honey (vice president of conservation services, NatureServe), interview by author, telephone, July 12, 2013.

27. Ibid.

28. Ibid.

29. Schwartz, interview.

30. Geoffrey C. Bowker, "Biodiversity Datadiversity," *Social Studies of Science* 30, no. 5 (2000): 644–45.

31. Schwartz, interview.

32. Lisa Faust and Joanne M. Earnhardt, *ZooRisk: A Risk Assessment Tool*, Version 3.8, User's Manual (Chicago: Lincoln Park Zoo, 2008).

33. Ibid.

34. "Plink, plink, plink, extinctions occur, steadily but without any evident cause. Species disappear. Whole categories of plants and animals vanish," writes science author David Quammen. David Quammen, *The Song of the Dodo: Island Biogeography in an Age of Extinctions* (New York: Scribner, 1996), 12.

35. Stuart Pimm et al., "The Biodiversity of Species and Their Rates of Extinction, Distribution, and Protection," *Science* 344, no. 6187 (2014): 987.

36. Stewart Brand, "The Dawn of De-extinction. Are You Ready?" April 22, 2013, http://longnow.org/revive/de-extinction/2013/stewart-brand-the-dawn-of -de-extinction-are-you-ready/.

37. Quoted in Fraser, *Rewilding the World*, 3.

38. Michael Mulkay, "Social Death in Britain," *Sociological Review* 40, no. S1 (1992): 31.

39. Braverman, "En-Listing Life." See also Ronald L. Sandler, *The Ethics of Species: An Introduction* (Cambridge: Cambridge University Press, 2012).

40. Lacy, interview, telephone, July 31, 2012.

41. Christine Biermann and Becky Mansfield, "Biodiversity, Purity, and Death: Conservation Biology as Biopolitics," *Environment and Planning D: Society and Space* 32, no. 2 (2014): 264.

42. Eric W. Sanderson, "How Many Animals Do We Want to Save? The Many Ways of Setting Population Target Levels for Conservation," *BioScience* 56, no. 11 (2006): 911–22.

43. Lees, interview. Lees' question is clearly influenced by the human rights perspective that applies the liberal modality of choice and its interrelated idea of freedom to animals. Elsewhere, I offered a critique of this approach. See Irus Braverman, "More-than-Human Legalities," in *The Wiley Handbook of Law and Society*, ed. Patricia Ewick and Austin Sarat (Hoboken: Wiley Press, forthcoming).

44. Lees, interview.

45. Foucault, *The History of Sexuality*, 141.

46. Carl Linnaeus's system for the classification of living things splits the highest rank of classification (known as "kingdoms") into Monera, Protista, Fungi, Plantae, and Animalia. The kingdoms are followed by four ranks, in descending order of specificity: class, order, genus, and species. *Encyclopædia Britannica Online*, s.v. "Taxonomy," http://www.britannica.com/EBchecked/topic/584695/taxonomy/48693/ The-Linnaean-system. See also Michel Foucault, *The Order of Things: An Archaeology of the Human Sciences* (New York: Vintage, 1970).

47. Miller, interview.

48. Ballou, interview.

49. Ibid.

50. Ibid.

51. Lees, interview.

52. Ibid.

53. Ibid. (my emphasis).

54. Ibid.

55. Ballou, interview.

56. Ibid.

57. Soulé et al., "The Millenium Ark," 107.

58. Ballou, interview.

59. Lees, interview.

60. Michael Soulé et al., "Ecological Effectiveness: Conservation Goals for Interactive Species," *Conservation Biology* 17, no. 5 (2003): 1247.

61. Redford et al., "What Does It Mean to Successfully Conserve a (Vertebrate) Species?" 40.

62. Alexander H. Harcourt, "Empirical Estimates of Minimum Viable Population Sizes for Primates: Tens to Tens of Thousands?" *Animal Conservation* 5, no. 3 (2006): 237.

63. IUCN, "2001 Categories & Criteria," http://www.iucnredlist.org/static/cat egories_criteria_3_1. By contrast, the term "minimum viable population," or MVP, refers more specifically to a threshold population size that is large enough to ensure a 99 percent probability of persistence for 40 generations. Harcourt, "Empirical Estimates," 237; David H. Reed et al., "Estimates of Minimum Viable Population Sizes for Vertebrates and Factors Influencing Those Estimates," *Biological Conservation* 113, no. 1 (2003): 23.

64. Reed et al., "Estimates of Minimum Viable Population Sizes," 30.

65. Harcourt, "Empirical Estimates," 241; see also Luis F. Pacheco, "Large Estimates of Minimum Viable Population Sizes," *Conservation Biology* 18, no. 5 (2004): 1178–79.

66. Ballou, Gilpin, and Foose, *Population Management for Survival and Recovery*, 277.

67. Theodore M. Porter, *Trust in Numbers: The Pursuit of Objectivity in Science and Public Life* (Princeton, NJ: Princeton University Press, 1995), ix, 8. The growth of a dependence on and trust in numbers, Porter argues in his book, is part of the growth of democratization and the bureaucratization of society.

68. Sanderson, "How Many Animals?" 911 (citations omitted).

69. Ibid., 918.

70. Ibid.

71. Foucault, *The History of Sexuality*, 137.

72. Ibid.

73. Ibid.

74. Tarleton Gillespie, "The Relevance of Algorithms," in *Media Technologies*, ed. Tarleton Gillespie, Pablo Boczkowski, and Kirsten Foot (Cambridge, MA: MIT Press, 2014), 167–93.

75. Lacy, e-mail communication, May 13, 2014.

76. Bob Lacy explains this equation: "[This is] a function that we would often use to describe how young females often have much lower breeding rates than do older females. That specific formula, for example, was probably used to specify that only 5 percent of one-year-old females produce young, while 95 percent of older females do each year." Ibid.

77. Lacy explains: "[This is] an example of calculating the mean litter size from the various possible numbers of young that can be produced (just one or two in this case)." Ibid.

78. CBSG Sonoran Pronghorn Antelope PHVA Workshop, participatory observation.

79. Lacy, e-mail communication.

80. Ibid.

81. Max Horkheimer and Theodor Adorno, *Dialectic of Enlightenment*, trans. Edmund Jephcott (Stanford: Stanford University Press, [1944] 2002), 18.

82. Gillespie, "The Relevance of Algorithms," 169.

83. Ibid., 179

84. Ibid., 192

85. Latour continues: "When a machine runs efficiently, when a matter of fact is settled, one need focus only on its inputs and outputs and not on its internal complexity. Thus, paradoxically, the more science and technology succeed, the more opaque and obscure they become." Latour, *Pandora's Hope*, 304.

86. I would like, in conclusion, to share Bob Lacy's response to this section:

> For me (and, I suspect, for people like Phil Miller and Jon Ballou), all the algorithms and computer simulations really are demystifying, because they make clear how the relationships among the data and processes that drive the system can lead to outcomes that would not be easily intuited or described otherwise. And the algorithms make explicit how we think the processes work, rather than leaving the judgments to be based on undocumented conceptual frameworks and arguments by biologists to just "trust me, I am the expert." Yet I can also see that for many others, who don't know what those computer programs are doing, the sense of trust versus demystification goes the other way—they might be willing (or maybe not) to trust that we know what we are doing with the calculations and simulations, but for them the analyses are not at all transparent.

Lacy, e-mail communication, June 24, 2014.

87. Ballou, Gilpin, and Foose, *Population Management for Survival and Recovery*, 280.

88. Ibid.

89. See, e.g., Ilkka Hanski, "Metapopulation Dynamics," *Nature* 396, no. 6706 (1998): 41. This concept was explained to me by Hofer. Heribert Hofer (director, Leibniz Institute for Zoo and Wildlife Research), interview by author, in person, Disney, Orlando, FL, October 11, 2013.

90. Hofer, interview.

91. Ibid.

92. IUCN, "About the Species Survival Commission," http://www.iucn.org/about/work/programmes/species/who_we_are/about_the_species_survival_commission_/.

93. CBSG, "CBSG History" (2013), http://www.cbsg.org/about-cbsg/history.

94. IUCN/SSC, Orangutan PHVA Final Report, January 15–18, 2004.

95. Byers, interview.

96. Schwitzer, interview, April 5, 2013 (emphasis in original).

97. Ibid.

98. Ballou, interview.

99. Lisa Faust (vice president of conservation and science, Lincoln Park Zoo),

interview by author, telephone, June 20, 2013; e-mail communication, December 29, 2014.

100. Ballou, interview.

101. Michael Hutchins (former director, animal programs, AZA; director of conservation and science, Safari Professionals), interview by author, telephone, January 18, 2013; in person, Washington, DC, June 10, 2013.

102. Lacy, interview, in person, October 11, 2013.

103. González García, interview.

104. Miller, interview.

105. Lacy, interview, telephone, October 22, 2013.

106. Meta-models now allow for the linking of "small-scale, individual-based models (e.g., *Vortex*) and population-based models (e.g., *RAMAS Metapop*) in order to extend local analyses to the landscape scale or to understand interactions of species best modeled at the level of a single population with species best modeled at a broader, metapopulation scale." Becky E. Raboy and Robert C. Lacy, *MetaModel Manager User's Manual* (Brookfield, IL: Chicago Zoological Society, 2013), 13.

107. Ibid., 2.

108. Robert Lacy et al., "Metamodels for Transdisciplinary Analysis of Wildlife Population Dynamics," *PLoS One* 8, no. 12 (2013): 1–13.

109. Ibid., 7.

110. Ballou, interview.

111. Ibid.

112. Mader, "Foucault and Social Measure," 20.

113. Latour, *Pandora's Hope*, 166.

TASMANIAN DEVIL

1. Tim Faulkner (general manager, Devil Ark), interview by author, telephone, May 1, 2014.

2. Chris, interview.

3. The containers were named Mooney devil containers after their inventor, Nick Mooney, a Tasmanian wildlife biologist who worked for the program when it was first established by the Australian government. Sarah Graham (senior communications consultant, Save the Tasmanian Devil Program), e-mail communication, May 22, 2014.

4. The devils were the focus of extensive eradication efforts in the nineteenth century, and were listed as "wholly unprotected" in the 1928 Australian Animals and Birds Protection Act. In 1941, the devils were re-listed as "wholly protected" under the Act, due to their disappearance from their original habitat. The devils' population peaked in the early 1990s, after which their numbers started plummeting due to DFDT. Rachel Hibberd, "Tasmanian Devil," *The Companion to Tasmanian History*, 2006, http://www .utas.edu.au/library/companion_to_tasmanian_history/T/Tas%20 devil.htm.

5. Lees, interview.

6. Lees, e-mail communication. See also "Save the Tasmanian Devil: Insurance Population," January 18, 2013. http://www.tassiedevil.com.au/tasdevil.nsf/Insurance-population/208FDBC98145099FCA2576C7001651E1.

7. Faulkner, interview.

8. All quotes from Lees, Faulkner, and Chris, interviews.

9. Carolyn Hogg (manager, science and policy, ZAA; Tasmanian Devil species coordinator), e-mail communication, May 28, 2014.

10. Save the Tasmanian Devil, "Insurance Population."

11. Save the Tasmanian Devil, "The First Translocation of Devils on Maria Island," November 23, 2012, http://www.tassiedevil.com.au/tasdevil.nsf/TheProgram/CF6415771B6874CECA257ABF000AC8A3; C. E. Hawkins et al., "*Sarcophilus harrisii,*" *The IUCN Red List of Threatened Species, Version 2014.2*, http://www.iucnredlist.org/details/40540/0.

12. Fiona Blackwood, "Endangered Devils Breeding on Maria Island," *ABC News*, April 21, 2013, http://www.abc.net.au/news/2013-04-19/island-devils-breeding/4640592.

13. Chris, interview.

14. Ibid.

15. Carl Zimmer, "Raising Devils in Seclusion," *New York Times*, January 13, 2013, http://www.nytimes.com/2013/01/22/science/saving-tasmanian-devils-from-extinction.html?_r=0.

16. Chris, interview.

17. Faulkner, e-mail communication, June 12, 2014 (emphasis in original).

18. Ibid.

19. Ibid.

20. Chris, interview.

21. Ibid.

22. Graham, e-mail communication.

23. Effective population size is "the size of an 'ideal population' of organisms (ideal refers to a hypothetical population . . . with a constant population size, equal sex ratio, and no immigration, emigration, mutation, or selection) that would experience the effects of drift or inbreeding to the same degree as the [actual] population." Luke J. Harmon and Stanton Braude, "Conservation of Small Populations: Effective Population Size, Inbreeding, and the 50/500 Rule," in *An Introduction to Methods and Models in Ecology and Conservation Biology*, ed. Stanton Braude and Bobbi S. Low (Princeton, NJ: Princeton University Press, 2010), 125.

24. Another upcoming PHVA meeting will revisit the modeling numbers. While revisiting the PHVA model is fine, Chris cautions, "it should not be the only thing that drives you." Chris, interview.

25. Ibid.

26. Hogg, e-mail communication.

27. Ibid.

28. Ibid.
29. Ibid.
30. Ibid.

CONCLUSION: WILD LIFE

1. Rotoroa Trust, "Creating a Wildlife Sanctuary on Rotoroa," 2013, http://www.rotoroa.org.nz/conservation.aspx. See also Auckland Zoo, "Rotoroa Wildlife Management and Translocation Plan 2013–2038," Version 1.4, December 18, 2013, http://www.aucklandzoo.co.nz/media/1002159/auckland-zoo-rotoroa-management -plan.pdf; Bernard Orsman, "Rotoroa Island Open to Public after 100 Years," *New Zealand Herald*, February 28, 2011, http://www.nzherald.co.nz/business/news/article .cfm?c_id=3&objectid=10709152; Auckland Zoo, "Rotoroa Island," 2013, http://www.aucklandzoo.co.nz/conservation/rotoroa-island.aspx.

2. Rotoroa Trust, "Creating a Wildlife Sanctuary on Rotoroa."

3. Jonathan Wilcken (director, Auckland Zoo), interview, in person, Disney, Orlando, FL, October 15, 2013.

4. Ibid.

5. "Couldn't ticks be just a little extinct?" asks James Hatley along these lines, and Mick Smith notes that at present, "lists of known extinctions include no microbes," wondering what might constitute a bacterial species or qualify as its equivalent unit. James Hatley, "Blood Intimacies and Biodicy: Keeping Faith with Ticks," in "Unloved Others: Death of the Disregarded in a Time of Extinction," ed. Deborah Bird Rose and Thom van Dooren, special issue, *Australian Humanities Review* 50 (2011): 63 (quoting Tom Horton); Mick Smith, "Dis(appearance): Earth, Ethics and Apparently (In)Significant Others," in "Unloved Others: Death of the Disregarded in a Time of Extinction," ed. Deborah Bird Rose and Thom van Dooren, special issue, *Australian Humanities Review* (2011) 50: 23–24.

6. Wilcken, interview.

7. Ibid.

8. Suckling, e-mail communication, June 8, 2014.

9. The first round of species planned for release in 2014 includes the brown kiwi (*Apteryx mantelli*), Duvaucel's gecko (*Hoplodactylus duvaucelii*), North Island saddleback (*Philesturnus rufusater*), Popokotea whitehead (*Mohoua albicilla*), moko skink (*Oligosoma moco*), shore skink (*Oligosoma smithi*), and South Island takahe (*Pophyrio hochstetteri*). Auckland Zoo, "Rotoroa Wildlife Management and Translocation Plan 2013–2038," 4.

10. Wilcken, interview

11. Ibid. The isolated use of indigenous terms by Western conservationists has been the target of much criticism. Roberts et al. have argued in the Maori context that "major problems with this process are the incommensurability of such attempts whereby the real meaning of a custom or word is frequently debased and divorced from its traditional cultural setting, so that its proper functioning is impaired."

Mere Roberts et al., "Kaitiakitanga: Maori Perspectives on Conservation," *Pacific Conservation Biology* 2, no. 1 (1995): 7. Other scholars have argued that one must consider both the original meaning of *kaitiakitanga* and the rights and responsibilities of those who customarily apply it, and that this concept can be understood only in relation to other principles of Maori society. See, for example, Kawharu Merata, "A Maori Anthropological Perspective of the Maori Socio-Environmental Ethic of Resource Management," *Journal of the Polynesian Society* 109, no. 4 (2000): 349–70.

12. Rotoroa Trust, "Keep Rotoroa Pest Free," 2013, http://www.rotoroa.org.nz/conservation/biosecurity-information.aspx. Certain species are thus configured as a threat, their regulation demonstrating the strong link between wildlife conservation and biosecurity. Who is being threatened, and who threatens, become crucial questions as surveillance expands beyond the human to include multispecies security regimes. On Rotoroa Island, biopolitical regulations become self-disciplining as tourists are tasked with ensuring the purity of the island through practices of spatial hygiene, granting entry only to desirable human and nonhuman visitors. Not much surveillance work has studied biosecurity in a multispecies context. An exception to this is the project "Biosecurity Borderlands," facilitated by Steve Hinchliffe. This interdisciplinary group examines how biosecurity operates within a globalized world in which austerity measures and increasing international movement demand a re-framing of the current discourse across the human-nonhuman divide. "Biosecurity Borderlands," http://www.biosecurity-borderlands.org/. See also Biermann and Mansfield, "Biodiversity, Purity, and Death," 266.

13. Lacy, interview, October 22, 2013.

14. Ibid.

15. Lacy, e-mail communication, October 28, 2013.

16. Foucault, *The History of Sexuality*, 138.

17. Thomas Foose et al., "Conservation Management Strategies Based on Viable Populations," in *Population Management for Survival and Recovery: Analytical Methods and Strategies in Small Population Conservation*, ed. Jonathan D. Ballou, Michael Gilpin, and Thomas J. Foose (New York: Columbia University Press, 1995), 276.

18. The full sentence reads: "The West of which I speak is but another name for the Wild; and what I have been preparing to say is, that in Wildness is the preservation of the world." Henry David Thoreau, "Walking," *The Atlantic*, June 1862, http://www.theatlantic.com/magazine/archive/1862/06/walking/304674/.

19. Some have suggested accordingly that while "wilderness" means "wilderness areas," wildness can be everywhere, even within us. See Gary Snyder, *The Practice of the Wild* (Berkeley: Counterpoint, 1990), 8–19; Paul Shepard, "A Post-Historic Primitivism," in *The Wilderness Condition*, ed. Max Oelschlaeger (Washington, DC: Island Press, 1992), 40–79; Jack Turner, *The Abstract Wild* (Tucson: University of Arizona Press, 1996). Similarly, Sarah Whatmore and Jamie Lorimer have argued for an understanding of wildness that flows through urban or domestic spaces and that makes room for "multispecies others." Whatmore and Thorne, "Wild(er)ness:

Reconfiguring the Geographies of Wildlife"; Lorimer, "Multinatural Geographies for the Anthropocene."

20. Most prominently, Giorgio Agamben criticizes Foucault for his "decisive abandonment" of the juridico-institutional model of power and his subsequent misrepresentation of the politicization of biological life. See Agamben, *Homo Sacer*, 5. By contrast, Ben Golder and Patrick Fitzpatrick argue that "for Foucault, law was never (and nor could it ever be) only a unitary and determinate entity, a monolithic category." Ben Golder and Peter Fitzpatrick, eds., *Foucault's Law* (Surrey and Burlington: Ashgate, 2010), xx; see also Rose, O'Malley, and Valverde, "Governmentality."

21. Michael Hoffmann (senior scientific officer, SSC, IUCN; chair, Red List Committee), interview by author, telephone, January 9, 2014.

22. John Lamoreux (biodiversity analyst, National Fish and Wildlife Foundation), interview by author, telephone, January 7, 2014.

23. Emmel, interview.

24. Jamie Lorimer, "Nonhuman Charisma: Which Species Trigger Our Emotions and Why?" *ECOS* 27, no. 1 (2006): 20–27.

Bibliography

INTERVIEWS AND OBSERVATIONS

Abungu, George. Former director general, National Museums of Kenya; cultural heritage expert. Telephone, February 13, 2013.

Amstrup, Stephen. Director, Polar Bears International. Telephone, June 26, 2013.

Anonymous conservation biologist ("Chris"). Telephone, May 14, 2014.

Anonymous COSEWIC member. In person, Halifax, Canada, April 27, 2014.

Anonymous zoo designer. Personal e-mail communication, April 16, 2014.

Arroyo, Bryan. Assistant director for international affairs, USFWS. Telephone, July 25, 2013.

Ashe, Dan. Director, USFWS. Telephone, July 18, 2013.

Atkinson, James (Jim). Recovery coordinator, Sonoran pronghorn program, USFWS. In person, Tucson, AZ, April 25, 2013.

Ballou, Jonathan (Jon). Research scientist, Smithsonian Institution; former studbook keeper, Golden Lion Tamarin. Telephone, June 6, 2013; e-mail communication, October 24, 2013.

Balmford, Andrew. Professor of conservation biology, University of Cambridge. In person, Oxford, UK, March 12, 2013.

Barber, Diane. Curator of ectotherms, Fort Worth Zoo; SSP coordinator and population manager, Puerto Rican crested toad. E-mail communication, April 24, 2014.

Bennett, Elizabeth. Vice president for species conservation, WCS. In person, New York City, NY, December 20, 2013.

Block, Judith. Registrar emeritus, Smithsonian Institution, National Zoological Park. Telephone, September 4, 2009.

Blumer, Evan. Former director, The Wilds; board member, CBSG. Telephone, February 18, 2013.

Bonner, Jeffrey. President and chief executive officer, Saint Louis Zoo. Telephone, August 1, 2012.

Boyle, Paul. Senior vice president for conservation and education, AZA. Telephone, November 24, 2010.

Byers, Onnie. Chairperson, CBSG. Telephone, August 1, 2012.

Canals, Miguel. Forest ranger, Guánica State Park. On-site, Guánica, PR, January 16, 2014; e-mail communication, April 24, 2014.

Carpenter, Mike. Senior biologist, Division of Management Authority, USFWS. Telephone, July 16, 2013.

CBSG/IUCN Annual Meeting. Participatory observation. Disney, Orlando, FL, October 10–13, 2013.

CBSG Sonoran Pronghorn Antelope Workshop. Participatory observation. Tucson, AZ, April 21–23, 2013.

Christie, Sarah. Head of regional programmes, Field Conservation Office, Zoological Society of London. On-site, London, UK, March 14, 2013.

Clark, Susan G. Former director, Biota Research and Consulting; professor, Yale University School of the Environment. Telephone, November 1, 2013.

Comizzoli, Pierre. Reproductive physiologist, Smithsonian Institution. On-site, Washington, DC, June 11, 2013; e-mail communication, August 15, 2013.

Committee on the Status of Endangered Wildlife in Canada (COSEWIC). Participatory observation. Halifax, Canada, April 27–May 2, 2014.

Conway, William. Former director, Bronx Zoo; president, WCS (1992–99). Telephone, January 28, 2013.

Corry, Elizabeth. Senior birdkeeper, Durrell Wildlife Conservation Trust. Interview by Eleanor Gold (research assistant). On-site, Jersey, UK, July 28, 2013.

Currie, Hamish. Director, Back to Africa. Telephone, January 10 and 18, 2013.

Deacon, Jim. Retired fisheries professor, University of Nevada, Las Vegas; author, original recommendations for native fish recovery. Telephone, July 13, 2013.

Dick, Gerald. Executive director, WAZA. Telephone, July 16, 2013.

Dickie, Lesley. Executive director, EAZA. Telephone, July 30, 2012.

Dietz, James. Founding director, Save the Golden Lion Tamarin. E-mail communication, April 17, 2014.

Dixon, Karen. SOS Rhino. In person, CBSG annual meeting, Disney, Orlando, FL, October 11, 2013.

Dollinger, Peter. Former director, WAZA; director, Alpine Zoo Secretariat, Zoo Office Berne. Telephone, January 9, 2013.

Draper, Chris. Programmes manager, Captive Wild Animals/Science, Born Free Foundation. Telephone, April 2, 2013.

Ehmke, Lee. Director and CEO, Minnesota Zoo; president, WAZA. Telephone, July 12, 2012.

Ellis, Susie. Executive director, International Rhino Foundation. Telephone, August 23, 2012 and September 10, 2013.

Emmel, Thomas C. Founding director, McGuire Center for Lepidoptera and Biodiversity, Florida Museum of Natural History. Telephone, June 5, 2014.

Fascione, Nina. Vice president for development, Defenders of Wildlife. On-site, Washington, DC, June 14, 2013.

Faulkner, Tim. General manager, Devil Ark. Telephone, May 1, 2014; e-mail communication, June 12, 2014.

Faust, Lisa. Vice president of conservation and science, Lincoln Park Zoo. Telephone, June 20, 2013; e-mail communication, December 29, 2014.

Felski, Penny. Herpetology manager, Buffalo Zoo. On-site, Buffalo, NY, June 7, 2013; e-mail communications, May 30 and June 9, 2014.

Fernandez, Erin. Fish and wildlife biologist, Southwest Region, USFWS. In person, Tucson, AZ, March 13, 2013.

Fiby, Monika. Zoo designer and director, Zoolex. Telephone, September 24 and November 20, 2012.

Field, David. Director, London Zoo. On-site, London, UK, March 14, 2013.

Flesness, Nate. Former executive director, ISIS. In person, Disney, Orlando, FL, October 12, 2013.

Frazer, Gary. Assistant director for endangered species, USFWS. Telephone, July 26, 2013.

Frostic, Anna. Attorney, Humane Society of the United States. Telephone, July 12, 2013.

Ginsberg, Joshua. Senior vice president, WCS. Telephone, September 28, 2012.

Gippolitti, Spartaco. IUCN/SSC Primate Specialist Group; curator, Rome Zoo. Telephone, December 20, 2012.

Goble, Dale. Distinguished professor of law, University of Idaho; convener, ESA at 30. Telephone, July 1, 2013.

González García, Frank S. Puerto Rican conservationist. Telephone, September 19, 2013.

Goyenechea, Alejandra. International counsel, Defenders of Wildlife. Telephone, June 27, 2013.

Graham, Sarah. Senior communications consultant, Save the Tasmanian Devil Program. E-mail communication, May 22, 2014.

Greely, Hank. Professor of law, Stanford University; convener, de-extinction workshop. Telephone, June 25, 2013.

Gusset, Markus. Conservation officer and international studbook coordinator, WAZA. Telephone, May 1, 2013.

Hamma, Kenneth. Executive director for technology strategy, Getty Museum; cultural heritage consultant. Telephone, February 5, 2013.

Harrison, Bernard. Principal partner for creativity and design, Bernard Harrison and Friends. Telephone, July 4, 2012.

Hellbender reintroduction, New York State DEC and Buffalo Zoo. Participatory observation. Allegheny River, NY, August 1, 2013.

Hofer, Heribert. Director, Leibniz Institute for Zoo and Wildlife Research. In person, Disney, Orlando, FL, October 11, 2013.

Hoffmann, Michael. Senior scientific officer, SSC, IUCN; chair, Red List Committee. Telephone, January 9, 2014.

Hogg, Carolyn. Manager, science and policy, ZAA; Tasmanian Devil species coordinator. E-mail communication, May 28, 2014.

Holst, Bengt. Director of research and conservation, Copenhagen Zoo. In person, Disney, Orlando, FL, October 11, 2013.

Honey, Leslie. Vice president of conservation services, NatureServe. Telephone, July 12, 2013.

Hutchins, Michael. Former director, animal programs, AZA; director of conservation and science, Safari Professionals. Telephone, January 18, 2013; in person, Washington, DC, June 10, 2013.

Jiménez, Nilda. Biologist, Division of Marine Resources, Department of Natural and Environmental Resources of Puerto Rico. On-site, Boquerón, PR, January 22, 2014.

Johnson, Robert (Bob). Curator of amphibians and reptiles, Toronto Zoo. Telephone, July 24, 2013.

Kohn, Frank. CITES policy specialist, live animal transport; coordinator, Plant Rescue Center, Wildlife Trade and Conservation Branch, Division of Management Authority, USFWS. Telephone, June 25, 2013.

Lacy, Robert (Bob). Senior conservation scientist, Chicago Zoological Society (Brookfield Zoo); member, CBSG. Telephone, July 31, 2012; in person, Disney, Orlando, FL, October 11, 2013; telephone, October 22, 2013; e-mail communications, May 13 and June 24, 2014.

Lamoreux, John. Biodiversity analyst, National Fish and Wildlife Foundation. Telephone, January 7, 2014.

Lees, Caroline. Convener, CBSG-Australasia. Telephone, May 20, 2013; e-mail communication, November 5, 2013.

Leonard, Marty. Chair, COSEWIC; professor of biology, Dalhousie University. E-mail communication, May 30, 2014.

Lierheimer, Lisa. Supervisory policy specialist, Division of Management Authority, USFWS. Telephone, July 16, 2013.

Linehan, John. Director, Zoo New England. Telephone, May 13, 2013.

Long, Barney. Director, Species Protection and Asian Species Conservation, WWF. Telephone, January 9, 2014.

López-Flores, Marisel. Project leader, Puerto Rican Parrot Recovery Program, USFWS. On-site, Iguaca Aviary, PR, January 14, 2014.

Lukas, John. General director, White Oak Plantation and White Oak Conservation Center; president, International Rhino Foundation. Telephone, September 17, 2013.

Lukas, Kristen. Curator of conservation and science, Cleveland Metroparks Zoo. Telephone, January 7, 2013.

Male, Timothy. Former vice president of conservation policy, Defenders of Wildlife. Telephone, July 1, 2013.

Marinari, Paul. Senior curator, C2S2, Smithsonian Conservation Biology Institute, National Zoological Park. On-site, Front Royal, VA, June 11, 2013.

Medici, Patricia. Conservation biologist, Ecological Research Institute, Brazil. Telephone, June 21, 2013.

Merz, Bob. Director, Center for American Burying Beetle Conservation, Saint Louis Zoo. Telephone, June 20, 2013.

Meyer, Katherine A. Founding partner, Meyer Glitzenstein & Crystal law firm. E-mail communications, October 3, 2013 and June 4, 2014.

Mickelberg, Jennifer. Curator of primates, Zoo Atlanta; coordinator and studbook keeper, Golden Lion Tamarin SSP. Telephone, May 13, 2013; e-mail communication, October 21, 2013.

Miller, Philip (Phil). Senior program officer, CBSG. In person, Tucson, AZ, April 22–24, 2013; telephone, May 6, 2013.

Moore, Don. Senior scientist, Living Collection Sustainability, National Zoological Park. On-site, Washington, DC, June 11, 2013.

Muñiz, Edwin E. Field supervisor, Caribbean ES Field Office, USFWS. On-site, Iguaca Aviary, PR, January 14, 2014.

Oetker, Mike. Deputy regional director, Southeast Region, USFWS. Telephone, August 2, 2013.

Olivieri, Gustavo. Coordinator, José Vivaldi Aviary, Puerto Rican Parrot Reintroduction Program. On-site, Río Abajo State Forest, January 22, 2014.

Pacheco, Carlos G. Fish and wildlife biologist, Caribbean Ecological Services Field Office, USFWS. On-site, Guánica, PR, June 16, 2014.

Pearce-Kelly, Paul. Senior curator of invertebrates and lower vertebrates, Zoological Society of London. On-site, London, UK, March 14, 2013.

Pimm, Stuart. Conservation biologist. In person, Sudbury, Canada, November 15–16, 2013.

Plotnik, Joshua. Director, Think Elephants International. Telephone, January 11, 2013.

Powell, Jeff. Project leader, Mora National Fishery, USFWS. Telephone, July 22, 2013; e-mail communications, May 9 and June 9, 2014.

Rabb, George. President emeritus, Chicago Zoological Society; director, Brookfield Zoo (1976–2003). Telephone, August 28, 2013.

Rabon, David. Coordinator, Red Wolf Recovery Program, USFWS. Telephone, June 20, 2014; e-mail communication, June 23, 2014.

Ramono, Widodo. Executive director, Yayasan Badak Indonesia (YABI), Rhino Foundation of Indonesia. Telephone, September 12, 2013.

Ray, Justina. Executive director and scientist, WCS Canada; co-chair, Terrestrial Mammals Subcommittee, COSEWIC. On-site, COSEWIC meeting, Halifax, Canada, April 28, 2014.

Redford, Kent. Conservation biologist. Telephone, June 18, 2013.

Reiss, Diana. Professor of psychology, Hunter College. Telephone, January 3, 2013.

Rivera, Marelisa. Deputy field supervisor, Caribbean Ecological Services Field Office, USFWS. On-site, Cabo Rojo, PR, January 17, 2014.

Robinson, John. Vice president and director of international conservation, WCS. Telephone, July 19, 2013.

Robinson, Michael. Conservation advocate, Center for Biological Diversity. Telephone, July 10, 2013.

Roblee, Kenneth. Wildlife biologist, DEC, Region 9, Buffalo, NY. On-site, Allegheny River, WNY, Hellbender reintroduction, August 1, 2013.

Ross, Steve. Coordinator, Chimpanzee SSP; director, Lester E. Fisher Center for the Study and Conservation of Apes, Lincoln Park Zoo. Telephone, July 15, 2013.

Roth, Terri. Vice president, Conservation and Science; director, Center for Conservation and Research of Endangered Wildlife, Cincinnati Zoo & Botanical Garden. Telephone, September 16, 2013; e-mail communication, October 6, 2013.

Sandwith, Trevor. Director, Global Protected Areas Program, IUCN. Telephone, May 22, 2013.

Sartore, Joel. Photographer, National Geographic. Telephone, July 30, 2013.

Saunders, David. Keeper, Department of Conservation and Scientific Research, British Museum. On-site, London, UK, March 15, 2013.

Schwartz, Karin. PhD candidate in population biology, George Mason University. Telephone, April 1, 2013; e-mail communication, May 20, 2014.

Schwitzer, Christoph. Director of conservation, Bristol Zoo Gardens; vice president of captive care and breeding, International Primatological Society; adviser, Primate Specialist Group, IUCN. Telephone, April 5 and 11, May 13, 2013.

Scott, J. Michael. Leader, California Condor Research Center, 1984–86; leader, Idaho Cooperative Fish and Wildlife Research Unit; professor of fish and wildlife resources, University of Idaho. Telephone, June 26, 2013.

Siminski, Peter. Director of conservation and education, The Living Desert; coordinator, Mexican Wolf SSP. Telephone, June 4, 2013.

Sinclair, Tom. Project leader, New Mexico Fish & Wildlife Conservation Office, USFWS. E-mail communication, December 22, 2014.

Smith, Kes Hillman. Conservation biologist. E-mail communication, October 25, 2013.

Smithsonian Conservation Biology Institute, National Zoological Park. Participatory observation. Front Royal, VA, June 12, 2013.

Soulé, Michael. Conservation biologist; professor emeritus, environmental studies, University of California, Santa Cruz. Telephone, February 6, 2013.

Stanley Price, Mark. Former director, Jersey Zoo; senior research fellow, Wildlife Conservation Research Unit (WildCRU); board member, CBSG; chair, IUCN's Task Force of the Reintroduction and Invasive Species Specialist Groups. In person, Oxford, UK, March 12, 2013.

Stevenson, Miranda. Former executive director, BIAZA. Telephone, March 27, 2013.

Stoinski, Tara. Manager of conservation partnerships and director of primate research, Zoo Atlanta; Pat and Forrest McGrath Chair of Research and Conservation, Dian Fossey Gorilla Fund International. Telephone, January 7, 2013.

Stuart, Simon. Chair, SSC, IUCN. Telephone, July 13, 2013.

Suckling, Kierán. Director, Center for Biological Diversity. Telephone, July 5, 12, and 15, 2013; E-mail communications, July 24 and 26, 2013; May 11, June 8, 11, and 14, 2014.

Taylor, Eric. Professor of zoology, University of British Columbia; member, COSEWIC. On-site, Halifax, Canada, April 28, 2014.

Thomas, Sarah. Head of discovery and learning, Zoological Society of London. On-site, London, UK, March 14, 2013.

Tlusty, Michael. Head of research, New England Aquarium. On-site, Boston, MA, May 31, 2013.

Travis, Alex. Faculty director (environment), Atkinson Center for a Sustainable Future; associate professor of reproductive biology, Baker Institute for Animal Health, Cornell Center for Wildlife Conservation. On-site, Cornell University, Ithaca, NY, March 6, 2014.

Traylor-Holzer, Kathy. Senior program officer, CBSG. Telephone, May 2, 2013.

Tyson, Liz. Director, Captive Animals' Protection Society. Telephone, April 29, 2013.

Valentin, Ricardo. Coordinator, José Vivaldi Aviary, Puerto Rican Parrot Reintroduction Program. On-site, Río Abajo State Forest, PR, January 22, 2014.

Vélez-Valentín, Jafet. Wildlife biologist, Iguaca Aviary, USFWS. On-site, Iguaca Aviary, PR, January 14, 2014.

Waddell, William. Coordinator, Red Wolf SSP; biologist, Point Defiance Zoo & Aquarium. Telephone, June 6, 2013.

Ward, Kimberly. Head aquarist, ABQ BioPark. Telephone, July 19, 2013; e-mail communication, May 9, 2014.

White, Jr., Thomas H. Wildlife biologist, Puerto Rican Parrot Recovery Program, USFWS. On-site, Iguaca Aviary, PR, January 14, 2014.

Wiese, Robert. Chair, Task Force on the Sustainability of Zoo-Based Populations; chief life sciences officer, San Diego Zoo Global. Telephone, November 9, 2010.

Wilcken, Jonathan. Director, Auckland Zoo, New Zealand. In person, Disney, Orlando, FL, October 12, 2013.

Wildt, David. Senior scientist and head, C2S2, Smithsonian Conservation Biology Institute, National Zoological Park. Telephone, May 3, 2013.

Zippel, Kevin. Program director, Amphibian Ark. Telephone, August 3, 2012.

BOOKS AND ARTICLES

Agamben, Giorgio. *Homo Sacer: Sovereign Power and Bare Life*. Stanford: Stanford University Press, 1998.

Anderson, Gail, ed. *Reinventing the Museum: Historical and Contemporary Perspectives on the Paradigm Shift*. Lanham, MD: AltaMira Press, 2004.

Anderson, Kay. "Culture and Nature at the Adelaide Zoo: At the Frontiers of Human Geography." *Transactions of the Institute of British Geographers* 20 (1995): 275–94.

Anthony, Lawrence, and Graham Spence. *The Last Rhinos: My Battle to Save One of the World's Greatest Creatures*. New York: St. Martin's Press, 2012.

Bakker, Karen. "The Limits of 'Neoliberal Natures': Debating Green Neoliberalism." *Progress in Human Geography* 34 (2010): 715–35.

Ballou, Jonathan D., Michael Gilpin, and Thomas J. Foose. *Population Management for Survival and Recovery: Analytical Methods and Strategies in Small Population Conservation*. New York: Columbia University Press, 1995.

Balmford, Andrew, Georgina M. Mace, and Joshua R. Ginsberg. *Conservation in a Changing World*. Cambridge: Cambridge University Press, 1998.

Baratay, Eric, and Elisabeth Hardouin-Fugier. *Zoo: A History of Zoological Gardens in the West*. London: Reaktion Books, 2004.

Bartram, Rob, and Sarah Shobrook. "Endless/End-Less Natures: Environmental Futures at the Fin de Millennium." *Annals of the Association of American Geographers* 90, no. 2 (2004): 370–80.

Baudrillard, Jean. *Simulacra and Simulation*. Ann Arbor: University of Michigan Press, 1997.

Beck, Benjamin. "Reintroduction, Zoos, Conservation, and Animal Welfare." In *Ethics on the Ark: Zoos, Animal Welfare, and Wildlife Conservation*, edited by Bryan G. Norton, Michael Hutchins, Elizabeth F. Stevens, and Terry L. Maple, 155–63. Washington, DC: Smithsonian Institution Press, 1995.

———. *Thirteen Gold Monkeys*. Parker, CO: Outskirts Press, 2013.

Beck, Benjamin, Devra Kleiman, James Dietz, Ines Castro, Cibele Carvalho, Andreia Marins, and Beate Rettberg-Beck. "Losses and Reproduction in Reintroduced Golden Lion Tamarins *Leontopithecus rosalia*." *The Dodo: Journal of the Jersey Wildlife Preservation Trust* 27 (1991): 50–61.

Bekoff, Marc. *Ignoring Nature No More: The Case for Compassionate Conservation*. Chicago: University of Chicago Press, 2013.

———. "Redecorating Nature: Reflections on Science, Holism, Community, Reconciliation, Spirit, Compassion, and Love." *Human Ecology Review* 7, no. 1 (2000): 59–67.

———. "Why 'Good Welfare' Isn't 'Good Enough': Minding Animals and Increasing Our Compassionate Footprint." *Annual Review of Biomedical Sciences* 10 (2008): T1–T13.

Biermann, Christine, and Becky Mansfield. "Biodiversity, Purity, and Death: Conservation Biology as Biopolitics." *Environment and Planning D: Society and Space* 32 (2014): 257–73.

Bingham, Nick, and Steve Hinchliffe. "Reconstituting Natures: Articulating Other Modes of Living Together." *Geoforum* 39, no. 1 (2008): 83–87.

Bowker, Geoffrey C. "Biodiversity Datadiversity." *Social Studies of Science* 30, no. 5 (2000): 643–83.

Braun, Bruce. "Towards a New Earth and a New Humanity: Nature, Ontology, Politics." In *David Harvey: A Critical Reader*, edited by Noel Castree and Derek Gregory, 191–222. Oxford: Blackwell, 2006.

Braverman, Irus. "More-than-Human Legalities." In *The Wiley Handbook of Law and Society*, edited by Patricia Ewick and Austin Sarat. Hoboken: Wiley Press, forthcoming.

———. "En-Listing Life: Red Is the Color of Threatened Species Lists." In *Critical Animal Geographies*, edited by Rosemarie Collard and Kathryn Gillespie, 184–202. London: Routledge/Earthscan, 2015.

———. "Captive for Life: Conserving Extinct Species through *Ex Situ* Breeding." In *The Ethics of Captivity*, edited by Lori Gruen, 193–212. Oxford: Oxford University Press, 2014.

———. "Conservation without Nature: The Trouble with *In Situ* versus *Ex Situ* Conservation." *Geoforum* 51 (2014): 47–57.

———. "Who's Afraid of Methodology? Advocating a Reflective Turn in Legal Geography." In *The Expanding Spaces of Law: A Timely Legal Geography*, edited by Irus Braverman, Nicholas Blomley, David Delaney, and Alexandre (Sandy) Kedar, 120–41. Stanford: Stanford University Press, 2014.

———. *Zooland: The Institution of Captivity*. Stanford: Stanford University Press, 2012.

———. "Zootopia: Utopia and Dystopia in the Zoological Garden." In *Earth Perfect? Nature, Utopia, and the Garden*, edited by Annette Giesecke and Naomi Jacobs, 242–57. London: Black Dog Publishing, 2012.

Brockington, Dan. *Fortress Conservation: The Preservation of the Mkomazi Game Reserve*. Bloomington: Indiana University Press, 2002.

Brockington, Dan, Rosaleen Duffy, and James Igoe. *Nature Unbound: Conservation, Capitalism, and the Future of Protected Areas*. London: Routledge/Earthscan, 2008.

Burney, David, and Lida Burney. "Inter Situ Conservation: Opening a 'Third Front' in the Battle to Save Rare Hawaiian Plants." *BGjournal* 6, no. 1 (2009): 16–19.

Büscher, Bram, Sian Sullivan, Katja Neves, Jim Igoe, and Dan Brockington. "Towards a Synthesized Critique of Neoliberal Biodiversity Conservation." *Capitalism Nature Socialism* 2, no. 23 (2012): 4–30.

Butler, Judith. *Precarious Life: The Powers of Mourning and Violence*. London: Verso, 2004.

Byers, Onnie, Caroline Lees, Jonathan Wilcken, and Christoph Schwitzer. "The One Plan Approach: The Philosophy and Implementation of CBSG's Approach to Integrated Species Conservation Planning." *WAZA Magazine* 14 (2013): 2–5.

Callicott, J. Baird, and Michael P. Nelson, eds. *The Great New Wilderness Debate*. Athens: University of Georgia Press, 1998.

Castree, Noel. "Neoliberal Ecologies." In *Neoliberal Environments: False Promises and Unnatural Consequences*, edited by Nik Heynen, Scott Prudham, James McCarthy, and Paul Robbins, 281–86. London: Routledge, 2008.

———. "Neoliberalizing Nature: The Logics of Deregulation and Reregulation." *Environment and Planning A* 40, no. 1 (2008): 131–52.

Chambers, Steven M., Steven R. Fain, Bud Fazio, and Michael Amaral. "An Account of the Taxonomy of North American Wolves from Morphological and Genetic Analyses." *North American Fauna* 77 (2012): 1–67.

Chrulew, Matthew. "Managing Love and Death at the Zoo: The Biopolitics of Endangered Species Preservation." In "Unloved Others: Death of the Disregarded
in a Time of Extinction," edited by Deborah Bird Rose and Thom van Dooren.
Special issue, *Australian Humanities Review* 50 (2011): 137–57.

Clark, Nigel. "Wild Life: Ferality and the Frontier with Chaos." In *Quicksands:
Foundational Histories in Australia and Aotearoa New Zealand*, edited by Klaus
Neumann, Nicholas Thomas, and Hilary Ericksen, 133–52. Sydney: University
of New South Wales Press, 1999.

Coimbra-Filho, Adelmar F., and Russel A. Mittermeier. "Distribution and Ecology
of the Genus *Leontopithecus* Lesson, 1840 in Brazil." *Primates* 14 (1973): 47–66.

Collazo, Jaime A., Thomas H. White, Jr., Francisco J. Vilella, and Simón A. Guer-
rero. "Survival of Captive-Reared Hispaniolan Parrots Released in Parque Nacional del Este, Dominican Republic." *The Condor* 105, no. 2 (2003): 198–207.

Comizzoli, Pierre, and Nucharin Songasen. "A Historical Overview of Embryo and
Oocyte Preservation in the World of Mammalian in Vitro Fertilization and Bio-
technology." In *Preservation of Human Oocytes: From Cryobiology Science to Clinical
Application*, edited by Andrea Borini and Giovanni Coticchio, 1–11. London:
Informa Healthcare, 2009.

Conde, Dalia A., Nate Flesness, Fernando Colchero, Owen R. Jones, and Alexander Scheuerlein. "An Emerging Role of Zoos to Conserve Biodiversity." *Science*
331, no. 6023 (2011): 1390–91.

Conway, William. "The Changing Role of Zoos in the 21st Century." Paper presented at the annual conference of the World Zoo Organization, Pretoria, South
Africa, October 18, 1999.

———. "Keynote Address: Why Are Zoos Doing *In Situ* Conservation? Adapting
to a New Reality." In *Proceedings of the 68th WAZA Annual Conference*, edited by
Gerald Dick, 5–7. Orlando, FL: WAZA, 2013.

Cronon, William, "The Trouble with Wilderness." In *Uncommon Ground: Rethinking the Human Place in Nature*, edited by William Cronon, 69–90. New York: W.
W. Norton, 1995.

Cuno, James. *Who Owns Antiquity: Museums and the Battle over Our Ancient Heritage*. Princeton: Princeton University Press, 2008.

Dickie, Lesley A., Jeffrey P. Bonner, and Chris West. "In Situ and Ex Situ Conser-
vation: Blurring the Boundaries Between Zoos and the Wild." In *Zoos in the 21st
Century: Catalysts for Conservation?*, edited by Alexandra Zimmermann, Matthew
Hatchwell, Lesley A. Dickie, and Chris West, 220–35. Cambridge: Cambridge
University Press, 2007.

Doak, Daniel F., Victoria J. Bakker, Bruce Evan Goldstein, and Benjamin Hale.
"What Is the Future of Conservation?" *Trends in Ecology and Evolution* 29, no. 2
(2014): 77–81.

Donahue, Jesse, and Erik Trump. *The Politics of Zoos: Exotic Animals and Their Protectors*. Dekalb: Northern Illinois University Press, 2006.

Donoway, Josephine. "Animal Rights and Feminist Theory." In *Beyond Animal*

Rights: A Feminist Caring Ethic for the Treatment of Animals, edited by Josephine Donoway and Carol Adams, 34–59. New York: Continuum, 1996.

Dreyfus, Hubert, and Paul Rabinow. "The Subject and Power." In *Michel Foucault: Beyond Structuralism and Hermeneutics*, 208–26. Chicago: University of Chicago Press, 1982.

Dudley, Nigel. *Authenticity in Nature: Making Choices about the Naturalness of Ecosystems*. London: Routledge, 2011.

Durrell, Gerald. *Beasts in My Belfry*. West Sussex County, UK: Summersdale Press, 1973.

Durrell, Lee, and Jeremy Mallinson. "Reintroduction as a Political and Education Tool for Conservation." *The Dodo: Journal of the Jersey Wildlife Preservation Trust* 24 (1987): 6–19.

Esposito, Roberto. *Bíos: Biopolitics and Philosophy*. Translated by Timothy Campbell. Minneapolis: University of Minnesota Press, 2008.

Evans, James P. "Resilience, Ecology, and Adaptation in the Experimental City." *Transactions of the Institute of British Geographers* 36 (2011): 223–37.

Fa, John E., Stuart Harrop, Sara Oldfield, and Diana Pritchard. "The Need to Balance *Ex Situ* and *In Situ* Conservation." *WAZA Magazine* 14 (2013): 15–18.

Findlen, Paula. *Possessing Nature: Museums, Collecting, and Scientific Culture in Early Modern Italy*. Berkeley: University of California Press, 1994.

Foose, Thomas J. "Riders of the Last Ark: The Role of Captive Breeding in Conservation Strategies." In *The Last Extinction*, edited by Lee Kaufman and Kenneth Mallory, 149–78. Cambridge, MA: MIT Press, 1986.

Foose, Thomas J., Leobert de Boer, Ulysses S. Seal, and Russel Lande. "Conservation Management Strategies Based on Viable Populations." In *Population Management for Survival and Recovery: Analytical Methods and Strategies in Small Population Conservation*, edited by Jonathan D. Ballou, Michael Gilpin, and Thomas J. Foose, 273–94. New York: Columbia University Press, 1995.

Foucault, Michel. *Discipline and Punish: The Birth of the Prison*. Translated by Alan Sheridan. New York: Vintage Books, 1995.

———. *The History of Sexuality. Vol. 1: An Introduction*. New York: Vintage, 1990.

———. *The Order of Things: An Archaeology of the Human Sciences*. New York: Vintage, 1970.

———. *Power/Knowledge: Selected Interviews and Other Writings, 1972–1977*. Edited by Colin Gordon. Translated by Colin Gordon, Leo Marshall, John Mepham, and Kate Soper. New York: Pantheon, 1980.

———. *Security, Territory, Population: Lectures at the Collège de France, 1977–1978*. Edited by Michel Senellart. Translated by Graham Burchell. New York: Picador, 2007.

Fraser, Caroline. *Rewilding the World: Dispatches from the Conservation Revolution*. New York: Picador, 2009.

Friese, Carrie. *Cloning Wild Life: Zoos, Captivity, and the Future of Endangered Animals*. New York: New York University Press, 2013.

Gillespie, Tarleton. "The Relevance of Algorithms." In *Media Technologies*, edited by Tarleton Gillespie, Pablo Boczkowski, and Kirsten Foot, 167–93. Cambridge, MA: MIT Press, 2014.

Golder, Ben, and Peter Fitzpatrick, eds. *Foucault's Law*. Surrey and Burlington: Ashgate, 2010.

Goodall, Jane, Gail Hudson, and Thane Maynard. *Hope for Animals and Their World: How Endangered Species Are Being Rescued from the Brink*. New York: Grand Central Publishing, 2009.

Gould, Stephen Jay. "Unenchanted Evening." *Natural History* 100, no. 9 (1991): 4–15.

Griffith, Brad, J. Michael Scott, James W. Carpenter, and Christine Reed. "Translocation as a Species Conservation Tool: Status and Strategy." *Science* 245, no. 4917 (1989): 477–80.

Groves, Colin, Prithiviraj Fernando, and Jan Robovsky. "The Sixth Rhino: A Taxonomic Re-Assessment of the Critically Endangered Northern White Rhinoceros." *PLoS One* 5, no. 2 (2010): e9703.

Guerrant, Edward O., Kayri Havens, and Michael Maunder, eds. *Ex Situ Plant Conservation: Supporting Species in the Wild*. Washington, DC: Island Press, 2004.

Hanski, Ilkka. "Metapopulation Dynamics." *Nature* 396, no. 6706 (1998): 41.

Haraway, Donna. *The Companion Species Manifesto: Dogs, People, and Significant Otherness*. Chicago: Prickly Paradigm Press, 2003.

———. *When Species Meet*. Minneapolis: University of Minnesota Press, 2008.

Harcourt, Alexander H. "Empirical Estimates of Minimum Viable Population Sizes for Primates: Tens to Tens of Thousands?" *Animal Conservation* 5, no. 3 (2006): 237–44.

Harmon, Luke J., and Stanton Braude. "Conservation of Small Populations: Effective Population Size, Inbreeding, and the 50/500 Rule." In *An Introduction to Methods and Models in Ecology and Conservation Biology*, edited by Stanton Braude and Bobbi S. Low, 125–38. Princeton, NJ: Princeton University Press, 2010.

Hatley, James. "Blood Intimacies and Biodicy: Keeping Faith with Ticks." In "Unloved Others: Death of the Disregarded in a Time of Extinction," edited by Deborah Bird Rose and Thom van Dooren. Special issue, *Australian Humanities Review* 50 (2011): 63–75.

Hediger, Heini. *Wild Animals in Captivity*. New York: Dover Publications, 1964.

Heise, Ursula K. "Martian Ecologies and the Future of Nature." *Twentieth-Century Literature* 57, no. 3 (2011): 447–71.

———. *Sense of Place and Sense of Planet: The Environmental Imagination of the Global*. Oxford: Oxford University Press, 2008.

Heynen, Nik, and Paul Robbins. "The Neoliberalization of Nature: Governance, Privatization, Enclosure, and Valuation." *Capitalism Nature Socialism* 16, no. 1 (2005): 5–8.

Hill, Kevin D. "The Endangered Species Act: What Do We Mean by Species?" *Boston College Environmental Affairs Law Review* 20, no. 2 (1993): 239–64.

Hinchliffe, Steve. "Reconstituting Nature Conservation: Towards a Careful Political Ecology." *Geoforum* 39, no. 1 (2008): 88–97.

———. *Geographies of Nature.* London: Sage, 2007.

Hinchliffe, Steve, and Sarah Whatmore. "Living Cities: Toward a Politics of Conviviality." *Science as Culture* 15, no. 2 (2006): 123–38.

Holst, Bengt, and Lesley A. Dickie. "How Do National and International Regulations and Policies Influence the Role of Zoos and Aquariums in Conservation?" In *Zoos in the 21st Century: Catalysts for Conservation?*, edited by Alexandra Zimmermann, Matthew Hatchwell, Lesley A. Dickie, and Chris West, 22–36. Cambridge: Cambridge University Press, 2007.

Horkheimer, Max, and Theodor Adorno. *Dialectic of Enlightenment.* Translated by Edmund Jephcott. Stanford: Stanford University Press, [1944] 2002.

Hunt, Alan, and Gary Wickham. *Foucault and Law: Towards a Sociology of Law as Governance.* London: Pluto Press, 1994.

Hutchins, Michael, Brandie Smith, and Ruth Allard. "In Defense of Zoos and Aquariums: The Ethical Basis for Keeping Wild Animals in Captivity." In "Animal Welfare Forum: The Welfare of Zoo Animals." Special issue, *Journal of the American Veterinary Medical Association* 223, no. 7 (2003): 958–66.

Jamieson, Dale. "Against Zoos." In *In Defense of Animals*, edited by Peter Singer, 108–17. New York: Basil Blackwell, 1985.

Jasanoff, Sheila. "The Idiom of Co-Production." In *States of Knowledge: The Co-Production of Science and the Social Order*, edited by Sheila Jasanoff, 1–12. London: Routledge, 2004.

Kalen, Sam, and Adam Pan. "Chapter 9: Exceptions to the Take Prohibition." In *Endangered Species Act: Law, Policy, and Perspectives*, edited by Donald C. Baur and William Robert Irvin, 192–205. 2nd ed. Chicago: American Bar Association, 2010.

Kareiva, Peter, and Michelle Marvier. "What Is Conservation Science?" *BioScience* 62, no. 11 (2012): 962–69.

Kierulff, Maria Cecilia M., Paula Procopio de Oliveria, Benjamin Beck, and Andreia Martins. "Reintroduction and Translocation as Conservation Tools for Golden Lion Tamarins." In *Lion Tamarins: Biology and Conservation*, edited by Devra Kleiman and Anthony Rylands, 277–82. Washington DC: Smithsonian Institution Press, 2002.

Kirksey, S. Eben, and Stefan Helmreich. "The Emergence of Multispecies Ethnography." *Cultural Anthropology* 25, no. 4 (2010): 545–76.

Koontz, Fred. "Wild Animal Acquisition Ethics for Zoo Biologists." In *Ethics on the Ark: Zoos, Animal Welfare, and Wildlife Conservation*, edited by Bryan G. Norton, Michael Hutchins, Elizabeth F. Stevens, and Terry L. Maple, 127–45. Washington, DC: Smithsonian Institution Press, 1995.

Lacy, Robert C. "Achieving True Sustainability of Zoo Populations." *Zoo Biology* 32, no. 1 (2013): 19–26.

———. "Re-Thinking *Ex Situ* vs. *In Situ* Species Conservation." In *Proceedings of*

65th WAZA Annual Conference, Cologne, Germany, 18–19 October 2010, edited by Gerald Dick, 25–29. Gland, Switzerland: WAZA, 2010.

Lacy, Robert, Philip S. Miller, Philip J. Nyhus, John Pollak, Becky E. Raboy, and Sarea L. Zeigler. "Metamodels for Transdisciplinary Analysis of Wildlife Population Dynamics." *PLoS One* 8, no. 12 (2013): 1–13.

Lassiter, Luke Eric. *The Chicago Guide to Collaborative Ethnography*. Chicago: University of Chicago Press, 2005.

Latour, Bruno. *Politics of Nature: How to Bring the Sciences into Democracy*. Cambridge, MA: Harvard University Press, 2004.

———. *Pandora's Hope: Essays on the Reality of Science Studies*. Cambridge MA: Harvard University Press, 1999.

Li, Tania Murray. "To Make Live or Let Die? Rural Dispossession and the Protection of Surplus Populations." *Antipode* 41, no. 1 (2009): 66–93.

Loftin, Robert. "Captive Breeding of Endangered Species." In *Ethics on the Ark: Zoos, Animal Welfare, and Wildlife Conservation*, edited by Bryan G. Norton, Michael Hutchins, Elizabeth F. Stevens, and Terry L. Maple, 164–80. Washington, DC: Smithsonian Institution Press, 1995.

Lorimer, Jamie. "Multinatural Geographies for the Anthropocene." *Progress in Human Geography* 36, no. 5 (2012): 593–612.

———. "Nonhuman Charisma: Which Species Trigger Our Emotions and Why?" *ECOS* 27, no. 1 (2006): 20–27.

Lorimer, Jamie, and Clemens Driessen. "Wild Experiments at the Oostvaardersplassen: Rethinking Environmentalism in the Anthropocene." *Transactions of the Institute of British Geographers* 39, no. 2 (2014): 169–81.

Mader, Mary Beth. "Foucault and Social Measure." *Journal of French Philosophy* 17, no. 1 (2007): 1–25.

Madonna, Kevin J. "The Wolf in North America: Defining International Ecosystems vs. Defining International Boundaries." *Journal of Land Use and Environmental Law* 10, no. 2 (1995): 305–42.

Margodt, Koen. "Zoos as Welfare Arks? Reflections on an Ethical Course for Zoos." In *Metamorphoses of the Zoo: Animal Encounter after Noah*, edited by Ralph R. Acampora, 11–36. Plymouth, MA: Lexington Books, 2010.

Marris, Emma. *Rambunctious Garden: Saving Nature in a Post-Wild World*. New York: Bloomsbury, 2011.

Martin, Glen. *Game Changer: Animal Rights and the Fate of Africa's Wildlife*. Berkeley: University of California Press, 2012.

Mayr, Ernst. *Systematics and the Origin of Species*. New York: Columbia University Press, 1942.

Mbembe, Achille. "Necropolitics." *Public Culture* 15, no. 1 (2003): 11–40.

McKibben, Bill. *The End of Nature*. New York: Anchor, 1989.

Merata, Kawharu. "A Maori Anthropological Perspective of the Maori Socio-environmental Ethic of Resource Management." *Journal of the Polynesian Society* 109, no. 4 (2000): 349–70.

Merz, Bob. "Partula Snails: Are You a Glass Half Empty or Glass Half Full Person?" *Connect* (April 2014): 16–17.

Mitman, Gregg. *The State of Nature: Ecology, Community, and American Social Thought, 1900–1950*. Chicago: University of Chicago Press, 1992.

Morton, Timothy. *The Ecological Thought*. Cambridge, MA: Harvard University Press, 2010.

———. *Ecology without Nature: Rethinking Environmental Aesthetics*. Cambridge MA: Harvard University Press, 2007.

Moss, Andrew, Eric Jensen, and Markus Gusset. "Zoo Visits Boost Biodiversity Literacy." *Nature* 508 (2014): 186.

Mulkay, Michael. "Social Death in Britain." *Sociological Review* 40, no. S1 (1992): 31–49.

Muths, Erin, and Michelle Pellissier Scott. "American Burying Beetle." In *Endangered Animals: A Reference Guide to Conflict Issues*, edited by Richard P. Reading and Brian Miller, 10–15. Westport, CT: Greenwood Press, 2001.

Nadesan, Majia Holmer. *Governmentality, Biopower, and Everyday Life*. New York: Routledge, 2008.

Nafziger, James A. R., and Ann M. Nicgorski. *Cultural Heritage Issues: The Legacy of Conquest, Colonization, and Commerce*. Danvers, MA: Martinus Nijhoff Publishers, 2009.

Nielson, John. *Condor: To the Brink and Back: The Life and Times of One Giant Bird*. New York: HarperCollins, 2006.

Norton, Andrew. "Experiencing Nature: The Reproduction of Environmental Discourse through Safari Tourism in East Africa." *Geoforum* 27, no. 3 (1996): 355–73.

Norton, Bryan. "Caring for Nature: A Broader Look at Animal Stewardship." In *Ethics on the Ark: Zoos, Animal Welfare, and Wildlife Conservation*, edited by Bryan G. Norton, Michael Hutchins, Elizabeth F. Stevens, and Terry L. Maple, 375–95. Washington, DC: Smithsonian Institution Press, 1995.

Noss, Reed, Roderick Nash, Paul Paquet, and Michael Soulé. "Humanity's Domination of Nature Is Part of the Problem: A Response to Kareiva and Marvier." *BioScience* 63, no. 4 (2013): 241–42.

Nowak, Ronald M. "The Original Status of Wolves in Eastern North America." *Southeastern Naturalist* 1, no. 2 (2002): 95–130.

O'Connor, Martin. "On the Misadventure of Capitalist Nature." In *Is Capitalism Sustainable? Political Economy and the Politics of Ecology*, edited by Martin O'Connor, 125–51. New York: Guilford Press, 1994.

Pacheco, Luis F. "Large Estimates of Minimum Viable Population Sizes." *Conservation Biology* 18, no. 5 (2004): 1178–79.

Packer, Craig, Andrew Loveridge, Susan Canney, Tim Caro, et al., "Conserving Large Carnivores: Dollars and Fence." *Ecology Letters* 16, no. 5 (2013): 635–41.

Penn, Laura, Markus Gusset, and Gerald Dick. *77 Years: The History and Evolution of the World Association of Zoos and Aquariums, 1935–2012*. Gland, Switzerland: WAZA, 2012.

Pimm, Stuart L., Clinton N. Jenkins, Robin Abell, Thomas M. Brooks, John L. Gittleman, Lucas N. Joppa, Peter H. Raven, Callum M. Roberts, and Joseph O. Sexton. "The Biodiversity of Species and Their Rates of Extinction, Distribution, and Protection." *Science* 344, no. 6187 (2014): 987–98.

Porter, Theodore M. *Trust in Numbers: The Pursuit of Objectivity in Science and Public Life*. Princeton, NJ: Princeton University Press, 1995.

Quammen, David. *The Song of the Dodo: Island Biogeography in an Age of Extinctions*. New York: Scribner, 1996.

Rabinow, Paul, and Nikolas Rose. "Biopower Today." *BioSocieties* 1 (2006): 195–217.

Reading, Richard R., and Brian J. Miller. "Captive Breeding Ethics." In *Encyclopedia of Animal Rights and Animal Welfare*, ed. Marc Bekoff, 101–5. 2nd ed. Santa Barbara: Greenwood, 2010.

Redford, Kent H., George Amato, Jonathan Baillie, Pablo Beldomenico, Elizabeth L. Bennett, Nancy Clum, Robert Cook, et al. "What Does It Mean to Successfully Conserve a (Vertebrate) Species?" *BioScience* 61, no. 1 (2010): 39–48.

Redford, Kent H., Deborah B. Jensen, and James J. Breheny. "The Long Overdue Death of the *Ex Situ* and *In Situ* Dichotomy in Species Conservation." *WAZA Magazine* 14 (2013): 19–22.

———. "Integrating the Captive and the Wild." *Science* 338, no. 6111 (2012): 1157–58.

Reed, David H., Julian J. O'Grady, Barry W. Brook, Jonathan D. Ballou, and Richard Frankham. "Estimates of Minimum Viable Population Sizes for Vertebrates and Factors Influencing Those Estimates." *Biological Conservation* 113, no. 1 (2003): 23–34.

Regan, Tom. *The Case for Animal Rights*. Berkeley: University of California Press, 1983.

Reich, David E., Robert K. Wayne, and David B. Goldstein. "Genetic Evidence for a Recent Origin by Hybridization of Red Wolves." *Molecular Ecology* 8 (1999): 139–44.

Roberts, Mere, Waerete Norman, Nganeko Minhinnick, Del Wihongi, and Carmen Kirkwood. "Kaitiakitanga: Maori Perspectives on Conservation." *Pacific Conservation Biology* 2, no. 1 (1995): 7–20.

Rose, Nikolas, Pat O'Malley, and Mariana Valverde. "Governmentality." *Annual Review of Law and Social Science* 2 (2009): 83–104.

Rosenzweig, Michael L. *Win-Win Ecology: How the Earth's Species Can Survive in the Midst of Human Enterprise*. Oxford: Oxford University Press, 2003.

Sanderson, Eric W. "How Many Animals Do We Want to Save? The Many Ways of Setting Population Target Levels for Conservation." *BioScience* 56, no. 11 (2006): 911–22.

Sandler, Ronald L. *The Ethics of Species: An Introduction*. Cambridge: Cambridge University Press, 2012.

Scarascia-Mugnozza, Gian Tommaso, and P. Perrino. "The History of *Ex Situ* Conservation and Use of Plant Genetic Resources." In *Managing Plant Genetic Diversity*, edited by Johannes M. M. Engels, V. R. Rao, Anthony H. D. Brown, and Michael T. Jackson, 1–22. Oxford: CABI Publishing, 2002.

Scott, J. Michael, Dale D. Goble, Aaron M. Haines, John A. Wiens, and Maile C. Neel. "Conservation-Reliant Species and the Future of Conservation." *Conservation Letters* 3 (2010): 91–97.

Seddon, Philip J., Pritpal S. Soorae, and Frédéric Launay. "Taxonomic Bias in Reintroduction Projects." *Animal Conservation* 8 (2005): 51–58.

Shepard, Paul. "A Post-Historic Primitivism." In *The Wilderness Condition*, edited by Max Oelschlaeger, 40–79. Washington, DC: Island Press, 1992.

Shukin, Nicole. *Animal Capital: Rendering Life in Biopolitical Times*. Minneapolis: University of Minnesota Press, 2009.

Slobodchikoff, Constantine N., Bianca S. Perla, and Jennifer L. Verdolin. *Prairie Dogs: Communication and Community in an Animal Society*. Cambridge, MA: Harvard University Press, 2009.

Smith, Mick. *Against Ecological Sovereignty: Ethics, Biopolitics, and Saving the Natural World*. Minneapolis: University of Minnesota Press, 2011.

———. "Dis(appearance): Earth, Ethics, and Apparently (In)Significant Others." In "Unloved Others: Death of the Disregarded in a Time of Extinction," edited by Deborah Bird Rose and Thom van Dooren. Special issue, *Australian Humanities Review* (2011) 50: 23–44.

Smith, Neil. *Uneven Development: Nature, Capital, and the Production of Space*. New York: Blackwell, 1984.

Smyth, Brian, and Silke Nebel. "Passive Integrated Transponder (PIT) Tags in the Study of Animal Movement." *Nature Education Knowledge* 4, no. 3 (2013): 3.

Snyder, Gary. *The Practice of the Wild*. Berkeley: Counterpoint, 1990.

Snyder, Noel F. R., Scott R. Derrickson, Steven R. Beissinger, James W. Wiley, Thomas B. Smith, William D. Toone, and Brian Miller. "Limitations of Captive Breeding in Endangered Species Recovery." *Conservation Biology* 10, no. 2 (1996): 338–48.

Soorae, Pritpal S., ed., *Global Re-Introduction Perspectives: 2013. Further Case Studies from around the Globe*. Gland, Switzerland: IUCN/SSC Re-Introduction Specialist Group, 2013.

———, ed., *Global Re-Introduction Perspectives: 2011. More Case Studies from around the Globe*. Gland, Switzerland: IUCN/SSC Re-Introduction Specialist Group, 2011.

Soulé, Michael, William Conway, Thomas J. Foose, and Michael Gilpin. "The Millennium Ark: How Long a Voyage, How Many Staterooms, How Many Passengers?" *Zoo Biology* 5, no. 2 (1986): 101–13.

Soulé, Michael, James A. Estes, Joel Berger, and Carlos Martinez Del Rio. "Ecological Effectiveness: Conservation Goals for Interactive Species." *Conservation Biology* 17, no. 5 (2003): 1238–50.

Spence, Mark David. *Dispossessing the Wilderness: Indian Removal and the Making of the National Parks*. Oxford: Oxford University Press, 1999.

Steffen, Will, Paul J. Crutzen, and John R. McNeill. "The Anthropocene: Are Humans Now Overwhelming the Great Forces of Nature?" *Ambio* 38 (2007): 614–21.

Steffen, Will, Jacques Grinevald, Paul J. Crutzen, and John R. McNeill. "The Anthropocene: Conceptual and Historical Perspectives." *Philosophical Transactions of the Royal Society A* 369 (2011): 842–67.

Stoinski, Tara, Benjamin Beck, Molly A. Bloomsmith, and Terry L. Maple. "A Behavioral Comparison of Captive-Born, Reintroduced Golden Lion Tamarins and Their Wild-Born Offspring." *Behavior* 140, no. 2 (2003): 137–60.

Sullivan, Erin. "The Latest Buzz: Updates from the Terrestrial Invertebrate Taxon Advisory Group." *Connect* (April 2014): 10–11.

Szerszynski, Bronislaw. "The End of the End of Nature: The Anthropocene and the Fate of the Human." *Oxford Literary Review* 34 (2012): 165–84.

Tønnessen, Morten. "Is a Wolf Wild as Long as It Does Not *Know* That It Is Being Thoroughly Managed?" *Humanimalia* 2, no. 1 (2010): 1–8.

Traylor-Holzer, Kathy. "Identifying Gaps and Opportunities for Inter-Regional Ex-Situ Conservation." *WAZA Magazine* 12 (2011): 30–33.

Turner, Jack. *The Abstract Wild*. Tucson: University of Arizona Press, 1996.

Volis, Sergei, and Michael Blecher. "Quasi In Situ: A Bridge Between Ex Situ and In Situ Conservation of Plants." *Biodiversity and Conservation* 10, no. 9 (2010): 2441–54.

Walters, Mark Jerome. *A Shadow and a Song: The Struggle to Save an Endangered Species*. White River Junction, VT: Chelsea Green, 2007.

Wapner, Paul. *Living Through the End of Nature: The Future of American Environmentalism*. Cambridge: MIT Press, 2010.

Wayne, Robert K., Raoul E. Benveniste, Dianne N. Janczewski, and Stephen J. O'Brien. "Molecular and Biochemical Evolution of the Carnivora." In *Carnivore Behavior, Ecology, and Evolution*, edited by John L. Gittleman, 465–94. London: Chapman and Hall, 1989.

Wayne, Robert K., and Susan M. Jenks. "Mitochondrial DNA Analysis Implying Extensive Hybridization of the Endangered Red Wolf *Canis rufus*." *Nature* 351 (1991): 565–68.

West, Chris, and Lesley A. Dickie. "Introduction: Is There a Conservation Role for Zoos in a Natural World under Fire?" In *Zoos in the 21st Century: Catalysts for Conservation?*, edited by Alexandra Zimmermann, Matthew Hatchwell, Lesley A. Dickie, and Chris West, 3–11. Cambridge: Cambridge University Press, 2007.

Whatmore, Sarah, and Lorraine Thorne. "Wild(er)ness: Reconfiguring the Geographies of Wildlife." *Transactions of the Institute of British Geographers* 23, no. 4 (1998): 435–54.

White, Jr., Douglas H., Nigel J. Collar, Ron J. Moorhouse, Virginia Sanz, Eric D.

Stolen, and Donald J. Brightsmith. "Psittacine Reintroductions: Common Denominators of Success." *Biological Conservation* 148 (2012): 106–15.

White, Jr., Thomas H., Jaime A. Collazo, Stephen J. Dinsmore, and Ivan Llerandi-Román. *Niche Restriction and Conservatism in a Neotropical Psittacine: The Case of the Puerto Rican Parrot*. Hauppauge, NY: Nova Science Publishers, 2014.

White, Jr., Thomas H., Jaime A. Collazo, and Francisco J. Vilella. "Survival of Captive-Reared Puerto Rican Parrots Released in the Caribbean National Forest." *The Condor* 107 (2005): 424–32.

Wilcove, David S., and Lawrence L. Master. "How Many Endangered Species Are There in the United States?" *Frontiers in Ecology and the Environment* 3, no. 8 (2005): 414–20.

Wilson, Paul J., Sonya Grewal, Ian D. Lawford, Jennifer N. M. Heal, Angela G. Granacki, David Pennock, John B. Theberge, et al. "DNA Profiles of the Eastern Canadian Wolf and the Red Wolf Provide Evidence for a Common Evolutionary History Independent of the Gray Wolf." *Canadian Journal of Zoology* 78, no. 12 (2000): 2156–66.

Wolfe, Cary. *Before the Law: Humans and Other Animals in a Biopolitical Frame*. Chicago: University of Chicago Press, 2013.

Index

European Association of Zoos and
Aquariums (EAZA), 59–60, 65
European Endangered species Programmes
(EEPs), 59–60, 63
Evans, Mike, 22
evolutionary significant units (ESUs), 171,
280n105
Excel (software), 283–84n10. *See also* data
management
exotic pet trade, 88, 103
ex situ conservation: captive-for-life species,
17, 61, 81–83, 197; defined, 3; development of zoos as institutions for, 17, 31–33,
35, 38, 40, 41, 61, 63–64, 70, 97–99, 138–
139, 180; and Extinct in the Wild designation (Red List), 35, 48, 54, 71, 73–75, 105;
as last resort, 10, 22, 39, 70–73, 79, 139;
population modeling for, 193–94, 197–98.
See also captive breeding; *in situ–ex situ*
continuum; *in situ–ex situ* dichotomy; *in
situ–ex situ* integration; zoos
Extinct in the Wild designation (Red List),
35, 48, 54, 71, 73–75, 105, 169. *See also*
Red List of Threatened Species (IUCN)
extinction: vs. captivity, 79, 81; and conservation biology, 73; vs. death, 194–95; and
grievability, 230–31; and individual vs.
species, 54, 195–96; of microbes, 290n5;
rates of, 284n34; and species prioritization, 222, 290n5; vs. viability, 194–96
extractive reserves, 262n33

Fa, John, 34, 36
Faulkner, Tim, 213, 214, 215–16, 217
Faust, Lisa, 205
Felski, Penny, 21, 134, 135, 136
ferrets, 118, 119–23, 206, 266n2
Fiby, Monika, 72
Findlen, Paula, 61–62
Fitzpatrick, Patrick, 292n20
Florida panther (*Puma concolor coryi*), 167
Foose, Thomas J., 84, 227
fortress conservation, 189, 284n11
foster rearing, 150, 177–78
Foucault, Michel: on biopower, 12–13, 200,
236n43, 237n45; on death, 12, 83, 227,
236n43; on government, 12–13, 153,
191, 195–96, 228, 237n49; on knowledge, 238n51; on law, 229, 292n20; on
make live–let die, 13, 83, 151, 157, 227,
236n43; on political vs. biological life,
105, 228–29, 292n20; on power, 12, 185,
200, 236–37n44; on sovereign power, 12,
13, 162, 227, 229; and "take" prohibi-
tions/exceptions, 158. *See also* biopolitics

found-made divide, 44
Franklin, Sarah, 11
Fraser, Caroline, 43
Frazer, Gary, 105–6, 162, 164
Friese, Carrie, 11, 131, 235n39, 238–
39nn50,54, 257–58n144, 261n24
funding for conservation: erratic nature
of, 128–29, 239n59; and *in situ–ex situ*
dichotomy, 3, 4, 36–37, 39–40, 126,
243n31; and population modeling, 217–
18; and public education, 65; and zoos,
64, 243n31

game ranches, 103, 169, 279nn90,91
genebanks, 99–101
genes. *See* genetic management
genetic management: black-footed ferret,
121; in conservation hatcheries, 107, 109,
172; and culling, 60, 168; Florida panther,
167; and fostering, 178; and genebanks,
100; and hybridization, 29, 165, 166–67,
168, 182; monitoring for, 90–91, 122; and
One Plan approach, 206; and population
modeling, 198; Puerto Rican crested
toad, 23, 28, 29; red wolf, 181, 182;
Sonoran pronghorn antelope, 185; and
species prioritization, 7; and studbooks,
90, 92, 121, 150, 181, 193; Tasmanian
devil, 214, 217; translocations for, 90, 91;
and viability, 198
Genome Resource Banks (GRBs), 99–101
giant African land snail (*Lissachatina fulica*), 1
Gila trout (*Oncorhynchus gilae*), 39, 106, 107,
108
Gillespie, Tarleton, 202
Gilpin, Michael, 84
Ginsberg, Joshua, 67
Global Positioning System (GPS), 76, 135,
136, 190
Global Protected Areas Programme
(IUCN), 110
global warming. *See* climate change
Goble, Dale, 154
God Squad (Endangered Species
Committee) (United States), 160, 276n35
golden lion tamarin (*Leontopithecus rosalia*),
8, 86, 87–94, 189, 206, 218, 231, 258n8
Golder, Ben, 292n20
gorillas: eastern mountain gorilla, 113–15;
western lowland gorilla, 114–15, 265n94
government: of individuals/populations/
species, 12, 17, 195–96, 200, 228,
230–31; Foucault on, 12–13, 153, 191,
195–96, 228, 237n49. *See also* biopolitics;
governmentality